Football and the Boundaries of History

Brenda Elsey • Stanislao G. Pugliese
Editors

Football and the Boundaries of History

Critical Studies in Soccer

Published under the auspices of Hofstra University

HOFSTRA
UNIVERSITY.

palgrave
macmillan

Editors
Brenda Elsey
Hofstra University
Hempstead, NY, USA

Stanislao G. Pugliese
Hofstra University
Hempstead, NY, USA

ISBN 978-1-349-95005-8   ISBN 978-1-349-95006-5   (eBook)
DOI 10.1057/978-1-349-95006-5

Library of Congress Control Number: 2016961945

Cover illustration: © Popperfoto / Getty images

Printed on acid-free paper

This Palgrave Macmillan imprint is published by Springer Nature
The registered company is Nature America Inc.
The registered company address is: 1 New York Plaza, New York, NY 10004, U.S.A.

Preface

The Ball Is Round

This collection of 17 essays grew out of an unprecedented three-day international conference, "Soccer as the Beautiful Game: Football's Artistry, Identity and Politics," which took place in April 2014 at Hofstra University in anticipation of the World Cup.[1]

The idea for the conference emerged from the teaching and scholarly research of Brenda Elsey and the personal passion of Stanislao Pugliese, a long-suffering Napoli fan.[2] As part of this gathering we presented a Doctorate of Humane Letters, *honoris causa*, to football legend Pelé.

As we prepare to submit this manuscript for publication, the world of football is in turmoil. The international governing body, FIFA (International Federation of Association Football), is wracked by deeply entrenched corruption, most notably the awarding of World Cup bids to Russia (2018) and Qatar (2022). After the arrest of 14 FIFA officials at the Hotel Baur au Lac in Zurich in May 2015, 27 officials from CONCACAF (The Confederation of North, Central America and Caribbean Association Football) and CONMEBOL (the South American Football Confederation) were arrested in late November. Tellingly, it was the US Department of Justice under Attorney General Loretta Lynch that carried out the investigation and arrests. Embattled FIFA president Sepp Blatter eventually resigned, but his presence hangs as an ominous shadow over the game. New FIFA president, Gianni Infantino has promised to bring reform and transparency to the game. He certainly has a monumental task before him. Betting and match fixing—from Italy to Indonesia—continue to plague the sport. Unprecedented sums of money from television deals and foreign billionaires have created top-heavy leagues in England, France, Spain and Italy. In the United States, controversy swirls even as the US Women's National Team won the 2014 World Cup: the team rightfully complained of having to play on harsh artificial turf (which the USMNT doesn't have to do) and unequal pay compared with the Men's National Team. International top scorer Abby Wambach retired (with a critique of USMNT coach Jürgen Klinsmann) and was invited to Zurich to take part in FIFA's belated reform efforts.

Yet we are still inevitably and invariably drawn to the game. Whether we are scholars studying the semiotics of soccer or working-class fans enjoying a pint and banter before a game at our local pub, or tavern, or tapas joint, the game beckons. The Uruguayan journalist Eduardo Galeano captured the yearning of all football fans when he wrote of us, "I go about the world, hand outstretched, and in stadiums I plead: 'A pretty move, for the love of God.'"[3]

German football manager Sepp Herberger is famous for having led the 1954 West German national team to victory over the favored Hungarians in the so-called "Miracle of Bern." When asked by a journalist about the intricacies of the game, he judiciously responded by saying that only two things were incontrovertibly true: "The ball is round. The game lasts 90 minutes. This much is fact. Everything else is theory."[4] This scornful dismissal missed two critical dimensions of football: its situated-ness in the matrix of politics, economics and ideology; and its extraordinary, even subliminal beauty. As David Goldblatt insightfully notes, "Herberger expresses the virtual autistic refusal of the football world to see its own enmeshment with the social institutions and ideas of its day: its resistance to seeing the game explained by anything other than its own internal rules of chance; its meaning and significance restricted to its own protected times and spaces."[5] Galeano too remarked on "An astonishing void: official history ignores football. Contemporary history texts fail to mention it, even in passing, in countries where it has been and continues to be a primordial symbol of collective memory."[6]

This collection of essays, instead, effectively addresses the myriad ways football acts a prism for the modern and contemporary world. At the same time, we can nod with understanding at the insight that "soccer is the athletic equivalent of stream-of-consciousness writing, and its greatest artists practically scribbled *Finnegans Wake* in the sod with their cleats."[7]

In Italy, "la palla è rotunda"—the ball is round—is a common expression, heard not just at the stadium, but also in the streets, at school and at home. But in Italian the phrase means the opposite of what Herberger meant. For Italians, the roundness of the ball is indicative of its wonderful malleability, the almost infinite permutations of the game, and—in a larger philosophical, metaphorical and metaphysical sense—the contingency and precariousness of life itself.

Stanislao G. Pugliese
New York, USA

Fig. P.1 Ancient Greek Episkyros, Attic Lekythos, 4th cent BC, National Archaeological Museum, Athens

NOTES

1. For the full program, see hofstra.edu/community/culctr/culctr_ events_soccer_conf.html. Additional essays were published in a special edition of *Soccer & Society* 18, nos. 2–3, March–May 2017, edited by Dr. David Kilpatrick.
2. See Brenda Elsey, *Citizens and Sportsmen: Fútbol and Politics in Twentieth Century Chile* (Austin: University of Texas, 2011) and Stanislao G. Pugliese, "On Soccer and Suffering," in *Monthly Review*, http://mrzine.monthlyreview.org/2006/pugliese260706. html
3. Eduardo Galeano, *Soccer in Sun and Shadow.* Revised edition (New York: Nation Book, 2013), 1.
4. See the outstanding history of the game by David Goldblatt, *The Ball is Round: A Global History of Soccer* (New York: Riverhead Books, 2008), xiii.
5. Ibid., xvii.
6. Galeano, 243.
7. Reed Johnson, "A smaller world with Cup" *Los Angeles Times* blog, June 27, 2006.

ACKNOWLEDGEMENTS

This is the first volume in a new collaborative effort in which Palgrave Macmillan will publish the proceedings from academic conferences at Hofstra University. As such, we wish to thank Farideh Koohi-Kamali at Palgrave Macmillan for ushering the agreement through to completion.

The conference itself was organized under the auspices of the Hofstra Cultural Center and its outstanding staff of Natalie Datlof, Athelene Collins, Carol Mallison, Jeannine Rinaldi and Amy Trotta. Institutional support came from former Provost Dr. Herman A. Berliner; current

Fig. A.1   Roger Weber/ThinkStock

Provost Dr. Gail Simmons; Dr. Bernard J. Firestone, Dean of HCLAS; and Melissa Connolly, VP of University Relations.

We would like to thank all those who granted permission to use images, especially Dr. Despina Ignatiadou, Archaeologist and Head Curator of the Sculpture Collection of the National Archaeological Museum in Athens, Greece, for one of the earliest known images of a soccer-like game, and Ana Carolina Fernandes of Rio de Janeiro, Brazil, for her photographs that grace the book.

Finally, we thank our generous colleagues who shared their work, our Hofstra University students whose enthusiasm in class inspires us, our fellow faculty members and our long-suffering families, who have to compete with football year-round.

CONTENTS

1 Introduction: Marking the Field   1
  Brenda Elsey

Part I   Art Criticism   11

2 Drawing the Foul: Diving and Visuality in Contemporary
  English Football   13
  Luke Healey

3 From Galáctico to Head Butt: Globalization, Immigration
  and the Politics of Identity in Artistic Reproductions
  of Zidane   31
  Daniel Haxall

Part II   Collective Psychology and Group Identity   55

4 Soccer in the Shadow of Death: Propaganda and Survival
  in the Nazi Ghetto-Camp of Terezín   57
  Kevin E. Simpson

5   In the Shadow of the State: The National Team and
    the Politics of National Identity in Spain   73
    Jim O'Brien

Part III   Political Science and International Relations   99

6   Beyond the Unfulfilled Promise of Soviet International
    Football, 1945–1991   101
    Mauricio Borrero

7   Post-colonial Outcomes: FIFA, Overseas Territory
    and National Identity   119
    Steve Menary

8   The Hermit Kingdom versus the World: North
    Korea in the 2010 World Cup   137
    Aaron D. Horton

Part IV   Race and Ethnic Studies   159

9   Fausto dos Santos: The Wonders and Challenges of
    Blackness in Brazil's "Mulatto Football"   161
    Roger Kittleson

10 Who Counts as a Real American? Dual Citizenship,
    Hybridity, and the U.S. Men's National Team   179
    Jon D. Bohland

Part V   Sexuality and Gender   203

11 Social Climbing, Cultural Experimentation and
    Trailblazing Metrosexual: Franz Beckenbauer in the
    1960s and 1970s   205
    Kay Schiller

12 Standing on Honeyball's Shoulders: A History
of Independent Women's Football Clubs in England   227
Jean Williams

Part VI   The State and Civil Society   247

13 Politics, Power and Soccer in Postwar Italy:
The Case of Naples   249
Rosario Forlenza

14 The Politics of Football in Post-colonial Sierra Leone   267
Tamba E. M'bayo

15 The Competitive Party: The Formation and
Crisis of Organized Fan Groups in Brazil, 1950–1980   295
Bernardo Buarque de Hollanda

Part VII   Philosophy and Critical Theory   313

16 "Another World (Cup) Is Possible!": Twenty Theses
About Modern Football   315
Tim Walters

17 On Virtue, Irony, and Glory: The Pitch and the People   339
Jason Burke Murphy

Index   361

LIST OF CONTRIBUTORS

Jon D. Bohland is Associate Professor of Political Science and International Studies at Hollins University in Roanoke, Virginia. His published work on the intersections between politics and popular forms of culture have appeared in journals such as *Southeastern Geographer, Dialogues in Human Geography,* and *Southwestern Geographer,* and in collected volumes including *Neo-Confederacy: A Critical Introduction* and *Battlestar Galactica and International Relations.*

Mauricio Borrero is Associate Professor of History at St. John's University, where he teaches Russian and World history. Before turning to sport history, his research focused on the politics of food shortages in revolutionary Russia, leading to a book *Hungry Moscow: Scarcity and Urban Society in the Russian Civil War, 1917–1921.* He is currently writing a biography of the legendary Russian goalkeeper, Lev Yashin.

Bernardo Buarque de Hollanda is Associate Professor at the School of Social Sciences of the Fundação Getúlio Vargas in São Paulo and a researcher at the Center for Research and Documentation of Brazilian Contemporary History. His main topics of research are literary history and modernism; social thought and intellectuals in Brazil; the social history of football and organized soccer support groups. He has authored several books, including *O descobrimento do futebol.* He is co-editor of *The Country of Football: Politics, Popular Culture & the Beautiful Game in Brazil.*

Jason Burke Murphy is Assistant Professor of Philosophy at Elms College in Chicopee, Massachusetts. He primarily works on ethics and public policy but also researches new literature on the "meaning of life." He is on the executive committees of US Basic Income Guarantee Network and Basic Income Earth Network. His playing career was short and embarrassing. He blogs sporadically on soccer and philosophy at http://thegameandtheworld.blogspot.com/

Brenda Elsey is Associate Professor of History at Hofstra University. Her research interests surround the history of gender, popular culture, and politics in Latin America. She is the author of *Citizens and Sportsmen: Fútbol and Politics in Twentieth Century Chile*, with the University of Texas Press. Her recent projects include a co-edited issue of *Radical History Review*, "Historicizing the Politics and Pleasure of Sport," with Duke University Press and a co-authored monograph with Joshua Nadel, *Futbolera: Women, Gender, and Sport in Latin America*. She has written articles on masculinity in Argentina, Chilean solidarity movements, and beauty pageants.

Rosario Forlenza is a Research Fellow at the European Institute at Columbia University and a Marie Curie Fellow at the University of Padua. He is a historian of modern Europe and twentieth-century Italy whose main fields of expertise are political anthropology, symbolic and cultural politics, politics and religion, cinema and propaganda, memory studies, democracy and democratization. He has written two books and his articles have appeared in *Modern Italy, Journal of Modern Italian Studies, International Political Anthropology, History & Memory, Contemporary European History*, and the *Journal of Cold War Studies*. He is completing a manuscript on the birth of democracy in Italy after World War II and, with Bjørn Thomassen, a volume titled *Italian Modernities: Competing Narratives of Nationhood*.

Daniel Haxall is Associate Professor of Art History at Kutztown University of Pennsylvania where he teaches courses on contemporary art. A former fellow at the Smithsonian American Art Museum and Institute of Arts and Humanities at the Pennsylvania State University, he has published on a range of topics including Abstract Expressionism, collage, installation art, corporate patronage, and the intersection of art and sports.

Luke Healey is a writer and Ph.D. candidate in Art History and Visual Studies at the University of Manchester, United Kingdom. His doctoral research concerns the relationship between football and visual culture around the end of the twentieth and the beginning of the twenty-first century.

Aaron D. Horton specializes in modern German and East Asian cultural and intellectual history. He is Assistant Professor of History at Alabama State University in Montgomery, Alabama. In January 2014, he published his first monograph, *POWs, Der Ruf, and the Genesis of Group 47: The Political Journey of Alfred Andersch and Hans Werner Richter*, with Fairleigh Dickenson University Press. He is also an enthusiastic soccer fan, especially of Bayern München and the German national team.

Roger Kittleson is Professor of History at Williams College, where he has served as chair of the Latina/o Studies Program. His book, *The Country of Football: Soccer and the Making of Modern Brazil*, published by University of California press, examined soccer as a vital realm of cultural action in which Brazilians have produced and reproduced conflictive, racialized identities for themselves and their nation since the late 1890s. His first book, *The Practice of Politics in Post-Colonial Brazil: Porto Alegre, 1845–1895*, explored elite and popular political cultures under slavery and in the early post-emancipation years. Other publications have taken on gender and abolitionism, popular culture during the Paraguayan War, and German immigrant religious and ethnic identities.

Tamba E. M'Bayo is Assistant Professor of History at West Virginia University, where he teaches courses in African history and World history. He specializes in the colonial and postcolonial history of Francophone West Africa and carries out research in Senegal. He is completing work on his first book titled *Muslim Interpreters and Mediations of Knowledge and Power in Colonial Senegal, 1850–1920*, which explores the paradoxical and often contradictory roles African interpreters played in mediating relations between the French and Africans in colonial Senegal.

Steve Menary is a freelance journalist and author, an associate lecturer at the University of Winchester, and an associate lecturer at Solent University in Southampton. He contributes to World Soccer, Playthegame.org, and the World Football radio show on BBC World Service, and is the author of five books, including *Outcasts! The Lands that FIFA Forgot*, which was shortlisted for the 2008 UK football book of the year award.

Jim O'Brien is Senior Lecturer in Journalism and Sports Journalism at Southampton Solent University, England. He has formerly held teaching and other posts in the Netherlands, Greece, and the United States. He has written extensively on Spanish football, including most recently on football, politics, and ethnicity in the Basque Country. He is currently completing a book entitled *From La Furia to La Roja; Football, Politics and Culture in Spain*.

Stanislao G. Pugliese is Professor of History and the Queensboro Unico Distinguished Professor of Italian and Italian American Studies at Hofstra University. A former research fellow at the Italian Academy for Advanced Studies at Columbia University, the US Holocaust Memorial Museum in Washington, DC, Oxford University, and Harvard University, he is the author, editor, or translator of fifteen books on Italian and Italian American history. *Bitter Spring: A Life of Ignazio Silone*, nominated for National Books Critics Circle Award, won the Fraenkel Prize in London, the Premio Flaiano in Italy, and the Marraro Prize from the American Historical Association. He is working on a new book tentatively titled *Dancing on a Volcano in Naples: Scenes from the Siren City*.

Kay Schiller is Professor of Modern European History at the University of Durham, UK. He has published widely on modern German cultural and sport history, including *WM74: Als der Fußball modern wurde* (2014) and (co-edited with

Stefan Rinke) *The FIFA World Cup 1930–2010: Politics, Commerce, Spectacle and Identities* (2014). He is a winner of the 2010 North American and British prizes for sports history for *The 1972 Munich Olympics and the Making of Modern Germany* (with Christopher Young).

Kevin Simpson is Professor of Psychology at his alma mater, John Brown University. His recent research and writing centers on visualization techniques in sport psychology and pedagogical innovations in the teaching of the psychology of the Holocaust. Twice a research fellow at the US Holocaust Memorial Museum and the Holocaust Education Foundation at Northwestern University, his academic work has also taken him to Austria, the Czech Republic, Germany, Israel, Scotland, and Poland. A former college soccer player with a long-time passion for the Red Devils of Manchester United, he is currently working on a new book on soccer as both a means of oppression and resistance during the National Socialist era tentatively titled *Soccer under the Swastika: Stories of Survival and Resistance during the Holocaust and WWII*.

Tim Walters is Professor and Chair of the Department of English at Okanagan College in British Columbia, Canada. He writes about Slavoj Žižek, film, football, radical politics, and late capitalism from a Marxist perspective. He is the author of a forthcoming book-length study of the ideological function and revolutionary potential of the commanding heights of modern football—the British Premier League, UEFA Champion's League, and FIFA World Cup—from a Žižekian perspective. For his sins, he supports Middlesbrough FC.

Jean Williams is Professor of Sport at Wolverhampton University. Having written extensively on the history of women's football since publishing *A Game for Rough Girls* in 2003, Williams recently published *A Contemporary History of Women's Sport Part One Sporting Women 1850–1960* (2014). Her current project is a collective biography called *Send Her Victorious: British Women Olympians*.

LIST OF FIGURES

Fig. P.1 Ancient Greek Episkyros, Attic Lekythos, 4th cent BC,
National Archeological Museum, Athens vii

Fig. A.1 Roger Weber/ThinkStock ix

Fig. 2.1 *Laocoön and His Sons*, ca 27 BC–AD 68, Vatican Museums,
photo credit Asier Villafranco Velasco/ThinkStock 19

Fig. 2.2 Didier Drogba, Cote d'Ivoire (Photo credit: Dusan Vraniel,
Press Association, UK) 20

Fig. 2.3 Harry Kewell (Photo credit: Neal Simpson) 22

Fig. 3.1 Martin Schoeller, *Zinedine Zidane*, © August Images, LLC 34

Fig. 3.2 Rodrigo de Florencia, *Star Player #1*, 2002 (acrylic on
canvas, 20 × 16 in) Courtesy of the artist 36

Fig. 3.3 Lyle Ashton Harris, *Blowup IV* (Sevilla), 2006
(collage installation) Courtesy of the artist 38

Fig. 3.4 Chris Beas, *No, That Really Is El Cid, He Only
Thinks He's Zizou*, 2007 (bronze, edition of 3 with 2
artist proofs, 5 ¼ × 10 ½ × 5 ¼ in) Courtesy of the artist 44

Fig. 3.5 Adel Abdessemed, *Coup de tête*, 2011–12. Installation at
the Centre Georges Pompidou, Paris (bronze, approx.
210 ¼ × 137 × 85 7/8 in) © 2015 Artists Rights Society
(ARS), New York/ADAGP, Paris 46

Fig. 3.6 Hassan Musa, *Jacob Wrestling with the Angel*, 2008 (ink on
cloth, 207 × 160 cm) © Pascal Polar Gallery, Brussels 48

Fig. 4.1 Souvenir poster of the Liga Terezín ghetto team, "Aeskulap"
(From Herrmann´s Collection of the Terezín Memorial,
Czech Republic, watercolor by W. Thalheimer.
© Zuzana Dvořáková) 64

Fig. 4.2   Final table from the autumn 1943 Liga Terezín football
league in Ghetto Terezín (From Herrmann's Collection
of the Terezín Memorial, Czech Republic. © Zuzana
Dvořáková)   66
Fig. 4.3   Czech goalkeeper Jirka Taussig making a save in the final
match of Liga Terezín (Photo taken from Nazi propaganda
film. © Chronos-Media Germany)   67
Fig. 5.1   La Liga 2015–2016 team emblems; Nation, Locality,
History and Identity ©Jim O'Brien   83
Fig. 6.1   Club composition of USSR World Cup teams, 1958–1990
(http://www.rssf.com/tablesu/ussr-wc.html; accessed
August 14, 2015)   111
Fig. 7.1   2012 Overseas Cup winners Reunion. © Steve Menary   124
Fig. 8.1   North Korean "fans" at the team's group-stage match
against Brazil (Photo credit: Kim Kyung Hoon/Reuters)   149
Fig. 10.1   USMNT friendly versus Colombia, November 14, 2014.
            Back row: Jozy Altidore, Mix Diskerud, Brad Guzan, John
            Brooks, Jermaine Jones. *Bottom*: Rubio Rubin, Fabian Johnson,
            DeAndre Yedlin, Alejandro Bedoya, Kyle Beckerman, Greg
            Garza. Of this group, Diskerud, Altidore, Brooks, Jones,
            Rubin, Johnson, Bedoya, and Garza are all dual nationals
            (Photo credit: Ben Queenborough/ISIPhotos.com)   192
Fig. 11.1   Franz Beckenbauer of New York Cosmos holds the North
            American Soccer League Trophy (Photo credit: Allsport
            UK/Allsport)   218
Fig. 13.1   Achille Lauro enters Napoli's stadium, 1950s (Photo credit:
            Archivio Riccardo Carbone, Naples)   256
Fig. 14.1   Ready for the game to begin in Makeni, Sierra Leone, Craig
            Bellamy Foundation (Photo credit: Laura Cook)   279
Fig. 16.1   FIFA President Sepp Blatter showered with American dollars
            by British comedian Lee Nelson at a press conference in
            Zurich, July 2015 (Photo credit: Arnd Weigmann/Reuters)   324
Fig. 17.1   Virtue and the people. US Attorney General Loretta
            Lynch as "FIFA Slayer" (Credit: Kate Niemczyk/Marvel
            Comics/ESPNw)   354

Black and white photographs that appear on pages 11,
55, 99, 159, 203, 247, and 313 are from "Football Series"
by Ana Carolina Fernandes and used with permission.

CHAPTER 1

Introduction: Marking the Field

Brenda Elsey

Football, or soccer as it is called in the United States, is a global cultural practice. This volume argues that the study of football's history provides a unique opportunity to understand the human condition. Football has so pervaded language and popular anecdotes that it is difficult to write without using a metaphor or euphemism related to the sport. Critical scholarship on football has emerged from a wide variety of fields in the humanities, social sciences, business, law, and sport medicine. Research structured around football, therefore, is at once discrete and broad. Because of this paradox, the study of football provides fertile ground for interdisciplinary initiatives. This volume explores the disciplinary boundaries that are shifting "beneath our feet." Traditional disciplines in the humanities and social sciences have come to embrace diverse research methodologies. The increased scholarly attention to football over the past decade reflects both the startling popularity of the sport and the trends in historical scholarship that have been termed the "cultural," "interpretive," or "linguistic" turns. This volume uses new work on football to create a dialogue between history and other disciplines, including art criticism, philosophy, and political science. It also includes work on gender, sexuality, and ethnicity, which already blurs disciplinary fault lines.

B. Elsey (✉)
Department of History, Hofstra University, Hempstead, NY, USA

© Hofstra University 2017
B. Elsey, S. Pugliese (eds.), *Football and the Boundaries of History*,
DOI 10.1057/978-1-349-95006-5_1

1

The essays included in this volume represent case studies from around the world. The globalization of popular culture presents a challenge for researchers who have been trained to specialize in a national context. Despite an increasing rhetorical commitment to transnationalism, most historical work is tied to national borders. There are practical and intellectual reasons for this, including the centralization of archives, the nationalization of organized sport, and state power. Although most chapters in this volume take up the nation-state as their unit of analysis, they all grapple with the reality of studying a sport that reflects and drives globalization. The standardized nature of football is a controlled variable that enables scholars to create comparisons of local, regional, and national case studies.

The ambivalent reaction of academics to sport scholarship until recently delayed the development of critical literature on football. Scholars have frequently taken their cues from intellectual memoirs of sport or critical biography.[1] These works explored the relationship of race and empire to sport. Scholars have also been inspired by journalists. Given the long tradition of sport coverage in newspapers, it should not be surprising that there is a rich journalistic literature on football. Lynne Truss's writing on gender and sport, for example, influenced the kinds of questions that scholars pose.[2] There are also books that manage to straddle both academic and popular audiences, including Eduardo Galeano's *Soccer in Sun and Shadows* and David Goldblatt's *The Ball is Round: A Global History of Soccer.*[3]

The manner in which football traveled the globe shaped its significance. Football diffused along the channels of the British Empire during the nineteenth century. Europeans brought the sport to Africa, Asia, and Latin America through educational institutions, commerce, and colonial government.[4] Elites in the global South returned from travels in Europe with a passion for football. As quickly as the sport arrived, local athletes and clubs embraced and reshaped it. The language, the food, the celebrations, and aesthetics that surround the game reflect the rich variety of adaptations that football underwent. The structure of governance and the relationship with local politics differed dramatically across the world. The sporting press, central to the growing popularity of football, became a cornerstone of mass media by the 1920s and 1930s. Along with state enterprises—including the military, schools, and prisons—industrialists and managers played an important role in encouraging the growth of football in private institutions.[5]

At the same moment football was traversing the globe, major changes occurred in the universities of Europe and the United States.[6] In the late nineteenth century, academics professionalized their disciplines. Historians shifted from legitimizing royal families to building the narratives of republican nation-states. When universities institutionalized history, they separated it from economics, political science, and sociology. Leopold von Ranke, a leading figure in this process, wanted to create an empirical basis for historical narrative. He emphasized the importance of primary sources and archival research. Ranke's notion of history as a descriptive telling of events as they happened came under fire, even in his lifetime. Karl Marx criticized Ranke's method for ignoring production, the basis of human civilization, and for lacking any method in deciding which evidence to consider.[7] The act of representing, narrating, and interpreting history became a fertile ground for debate throughout the twentieth century.

By the early twentieth century, a chorus of critics charged that historians who had privileged the "great men" of the past denied agency to the masses and neglected to account for the importance of long-term structures. These voices became dominant by mid-century, reflecting the democratization of higher education in the post-World War II period and the influence of feminist, civil rights, and anti-colonial movements. The first football histories emerged from social histories, which sought to understand the continuities and changes in the lives of everyday people. Sociologists like Pierre Bourdieu pointed to the role of culture in reproducing power relations. "Toward a Sociology of Sport," written in 1978, provided a template for the research agendas that could be pursued through critical consideration of sport.[8] The body as a key locus for the performance of domination and resistance was at the center of Bourdieu's concern to deepen our understanding of sport. The subconscious ways in which people internalize, enact, and resist power structures are performed in a public and routine way through sport. Feminist scholars have expanded upon this work to explore the multiple and fluid processes by which gender hierarchies operate within sport.[9]

The broader concern with sport and power weighs heavily on the study of football. Football, and culture more broadly, does not *reflect* history in any general or obvious way. If that were true then the dominance of players from the global South would reflect the power of their homelands in global affairs. Instead, football reflects elements of reality: reconfigured, twisted, and subjective. Much of the time, football has maintained the status quo in regard to perpetuating stereotypes, enriching elites, and in the service of nationalism. However, it has also inspired alternatives to entrenched identities and inequitable civic organization. Indeed, that is a central part of its attraction for fans. Its global popularity has increased football's capacity to serve as a "field of dreams." This has not been lost on the world governing body, the Fédération Internationale de Football Association (FIFA), or multinational corporations who have used the notion of global language to sell products and garner lucrative contracts.

Because cultural historians study literary texts, theatrical performance, music and other creative production, they frequently dialogue with disciplines outside of mainstream history. William Sewell, an important figure in reconciling historical study with sociology and linguistics wrote,

> System and practice are complementary concepts: each presupposes the other. To engage in cultural practice means to utilize existing cultural symbols to accomplish some end. The employment of a symbol can be expected to accomplish a particular goal only because the symbols have more or less determinate meanings—specified by their systematically structured relations to other symbols. Hence practice implies system. But it is equally true that the system has no existence apart from the succession of practices that instantiate, reproduce, or—most interestingly transform it...It's the relationship between system and practice—and at the heart of that is the social relationships, creativity, and agency.[10]

Symbolic meanings of culture cannot entirely determine what things are, as Sewell said, because the physical, the spatial, bodily integrity, all place different constraints and present different opportunities. Key to Sewell's reflections, and historical thinking, is the idea of change, relationships, and transformation. History has always been central to exploding ideas of static and bounded culture. Recent work has de-naturalized categories of gender, race, class, and nation by showing their contingency.

The increased importance of culture as a subject of study in the social sciences reflects its power in the politics, economy, and society of our era. This awareness has prompted exponential growth in sport history and has put historians in conversation with scholars from anthropology, literature, music, and philosophy, among other fields. Tools of research utilized in other disciplines have gained greater traction among historians. As historians took an interest in non-Western cultures, they relied on non-traditional archival research. Ethnography, visual analysis, and discursive analysis have become standard parts of historians' repertoire. Yet, these influences occurred largely without a contemplation of how they change,

and sometimes challenge, more traditional methods. Historians research-
ing sport sought out sources beyond government archives, including personal scrapbooks, club documents, and popular magazines. Moreover,
new modes of communicating historical analysis, including long form
journalism, public exhibitions, video blogs, or social media have become
important ways to disseminate research.[11]

Underneath the popular refrain of football as a global culture lies the
reality that the social significance of the sport is more different than alike
in its locations. Economic and gender inequalities persist within and
between national contexts. Football and footballers travel throughout the
world, but as often as football is a mode of communication, it is a mode of
miscommunication. The authors included in this anthology wrote original pieces that are sensitive to local case studies. In a variety of ways, they
explore the relationship between history and art criticism, psychology,
philosophy, political science, racial/ethnic studies, gender studies, sociology, and journalism. The pieces are grouped together in order to create a dialogue between case studies. The essays included in this volume
bridge at least two disciplines, and often more. They frame their questions
historically. Yet, many of their intellectual influences and methodological
tools are grounded in traditions of other disciplines. They are grouped
around the questions they seek to answer, including: How are identities
built? What changes the relationship between state and civil society? What
can the history of soccer tell us about equality in societies? Is there a visual
language of football that shapes its social importance? What ways have
subaltern groups found to contest the efforts to control them through
popular culture? If it has served authoritarian governments and institutions, how might we restructure football to serve the ends of equality and
inclusion?

The first chapters explore ways in which soccer crosses linguistic boundaries and has created a common visual vocabulary. This section analyzes
how particular visual stories unfold through two different performances,
the "dive" and the "head butt." Historians rely heavily on textual evidence,
but this section suggests ways to rethink the significance of the visual representation of identity. Although neither, "Drawing the Foul," nor "From
Galáctico to Head Butt," is bounded by a nation, they primarily focus
on England and France, respectively. Luke Healy examines the mechan-
ics whereby photographs of dives contribute to visual culture beyond the
pitch. He also suggests why the dive as a gesture takes on such importance
in English popular culture. The article by Daniel Haxall, "From Galáctico

to Head Butt: Representing Zidane in Contemporary Art," suggests ways of understanding one of football's most iconic moments, when Zinedine Zidane head-butted an Italian defender in the waning minutes of his career. It would be impossible to understand the significance of Zidane's head butt without taking into consideration his historic importance in representing the "good" North African immigrant. At the same time, it would be a partial analysis that did not account for the visual language of the gesture in that moment.

Recognizing the constitutive and oppressive categorizations of identity, scholars have analyzed how identities are constructed over time. Mining the past for change, historians have contributed to repudiating the notion of "natural" identities and their limits. The sections on gender, sexuality, race, and ethnicity demonstrate the ways in which soccer provides a unique lens on the experience of identities. Gender is a primary category of identity and one that structures power relations. Football serves as an important site for the production of different gender models. As an organized sport, football is fiercely segregated by gender. Kay Schiller's essay analyzes one of the most prominent stars of the game, Franz Beckenbauer, in order to understand the redefinition of masculinity in post-World War II Germany, which shifted toward a more fluid sexual identity and away from military archetypes of masculine control. Schiller argues that Beckenbauer, as a global celebrity, contributed to the sport's emergence as a commodified culture industry. Changes in masculinity occurred, not coincidentally, alongside feminist organization. When Jean Williams's essay refutes the contemporary idea that women's soccer began in the 1960s, she sheds light on the ways in which history is misappropriated to cultivate disinterest in women's clubs. Williams provides a rich and nuanced picture of female athletes and the significance of soccer to their lives. As history can be used to confer legitimacy upon its subjects, Williams's historical work is of pressing importance to challenging current media discourses.

Racism has been a problem for global football since its inception, whether because of formal or informal discrimination toward people of color. Football has been an important site for the construction, circulation, and contestation of racial ideologies. Through cartoons and match descriptions, the popular sport press played an important role in shaping racial discourse throughout the twentieth century. Roger Kittleson's research on Brazil focuses on the life of famed footballer, Fausto dos Santos. At the moment when an important group of Brazilian intellectuals promoted Brazilian racial democracy through a positive reevaluation of the mulatto, Fausto dos Santos burst onto the scene as a gifted

Black footballer. Fausto challenged racial segregation in Brazil, but like other Black athletes, the struggle took a tremendous personal toll. Soccer in the United States, which has yet to attract the academic attention of other sports such as basketball and baseball, poses a very interesting case. Like Brazil, the United States is a post-slave society shaped by ongoing immigration. Jon Bohland's research focuses on the history of citizenship, immigration, and race on the US Men's National Soccer Team. He argues that dual national players face unfair characterization as "mercenaries" who ruin the presumed "team chemistry" of an ethnically homogenous national team. These arguments are based largely on classic nineteenth-century arguments regarding citizenship and national identity.

Governments of all stripes sought to capitalize on football's popularity. However, scholars have taken a particular interest in its role in authoritarian governments. Trained in journalism and psychology, respectively, Jim O'Brien and Kevin Simpson question how football is used to create complicity, whether from outsiders attempting to chastise the Nazi regime or from within the Spanish dictatorship. Simpson's article analyzes a propaganda film that featured a football match in the Nazi concentration camp of Terezín. The Nazi government hoped to harness the popularity of football to frame its propaganda piece, intended to satisfy the Danish government and International Red Cross, who had expressed concerns about the conditions in the camp. Jim O'Brien's essay analyzes the role of football in Spain during the twentieth century, with a particular interest in its significance during the Franco dictatorship. Always contested, Spanish nationalism appears as a fragile construct divided by deep regional loyalties. This article takes a journalistic approach to soccer's history with a focus on a long time period and big questions. Beginning in the 1920s and following the trajectory of the national team until today, O'Brien finds that the national squad has created moments of cohesion that masked the regional and political struggles. Without such a powerful state apparatus, many former colonial territories have found football to be a powerful vehicle in their quest for nationhood. Steve Menary examines the varying degrees of success of former colonies in working within FIFA's governance to gain recognition.

The sixth section explores the relationship between civil society and the state in three distinct cases: Brazil, Italy, and Sierra Leone. These relationships are central to understanding the nature of violence and pleasure in football participation and spectatorship. Each author uses the lens of football to analyze the interaction between the state, nationalism, and the public. Bernardo Buarque traces a dramatic shift from traditional fan groups to the grassroots organizations, sometimes quite violent, during the Brazilian dictatorship. Buarque approaches the subject of fan identity and violence from a historical perspective, which is sorely needed to understand the social significance of these groups. In quite a different case, Tamba M'bayo demonstrates how the state's mismanagement and corruption in Sierra Leone has strangled its football clubs. This is striking given that one could assume it was the civil war (1991–2002) that hampered football's development. Instead, M'bayo argues, "Sierra Leone's regression in the sport has been due mainly to the misplaced priorities of government officials rather than structural damages resulting from the war." This has important implications for understanding the country today. Likewise, Rosario Forlenza's work cautions us against commonsense assumptions about the role of football. Placing the importance of football to Prime Minister Silvio Berlusconi's career in historical context, Forlenza analyzes the relationship between shipping magnate Achille Lauro and Napoli during the 1950s. Thus, it is historical in seeking out a comparison, not across space, but time. Forlenza uses Lauro's career as a lens on Italy's struggle with the challenges of the post-War period.

In "Political Science and International Relations," Mauricio Borrero and Aaron Horton explore two countries with declining football fortunes, the Soviet Union and North Korea, respectively. Despite its availability to authoritarian governments, football on the pitch could not provide the fairy tale stories that governments hoped it would. Through their study of the national football teams and their performance in international sport, Aaron Horton and Mauricio Borrero analyze how we can understand changing political goals and diplomatic efforts of two "closed" societies during the Cold War period. Because of their isolation from US governments and the Cold War media climate, many long-standing assumptions about the monolithic and unchanging nature of the post-World War II period have remained entrenched. Football created avenues for relationships beyond politics for two societies with heavy ideological surveillance.

In the final section, two philosophers use football as a lens to consider classical questions, such as the nature of irony and representation. Both are interested in contemporary governance of football, which has been riddled by corruption by the world governing body, FIFA. Historians typically shy away from making recommendations for the future. These essays make clear how a critical analysis of the past can help to inform policy. Jason

Burke Murphy calls on creative fans to embrace virtue, irony, and glory and insists the game be organized with these three ideas in mind. Walters argues that the governance of the top tier of elite men's professional soccer is today in an unprecedented state of disrepair, moral bankruptcy, and public disrepute such that hitherto unimaginable transformations have become possible. There are widespread instances of corruption, collusion, and vote buying among almost all of the bidding nations, although apparently not enough of it to be a problem by FIFA's reckoning. Ignoring or covering up corruption is emblematic of FIFA's general comportment as an institution, and also reflects identical dynamics that beset other major soccer governance bodies.

This anthology represents a sample of presentations given at a conference in New York in 2014; thus they bear the mark of a particular moment. On the cusp of the 2014 World Cup in Brazil, many of the scholars expressed deep concern over the massive public expenditures laid out for the tournament, the private security forces established, and the changes to civil laws demanded by the organizing committee. Their concerns were not unfounded. Moreover, the following year, on the eve of the 2015 Women's World Cup in Canada, FIFA officials were arrested as part of an investigation spearheaded by the US Department of Justice. FIFA President Sepp Blatter ambiguously announced his resignation in the vaguely distant future. In December 2015, another round of officials were arrested. At the very moment when football is enjoyed, unprecedented popularity and influence around the world we are reminded yet again of the complicated intersection of politics, history, and the world's most popular sport.

NOTES

1. For memoir see C. L. R. James, *Beyond a Boundary* (Durham: Duke University Press, 1993); Critical biographies include Mike Marqusee, *Redemption Song: Muhammad Ali and the Spirit of the Sixties* (London and New York: Verso, 2005); Susan Ware, *Game, Set, Match: Billie Jean King and the Revolution in Women's Sports* (Raleigh: University of North Carolina Press, 2011).
2. Lynne Truss, *Get Her Off the Pitch: How Sport Took Over My Life* (London: Fourth Estate, 2009).

3. Eduardo Galeano, *Soccer in Sun and Shadow*, revised and updated edition (New York: Nation Books, 2013). David Goldblatt, *The Ball is Round: A Global History of Soccer* (New York: Riverhead, 2008).

4. Peter Alegi, *African Soccerscapes: How a Continent Changed the World's Game* (Miami: Ohio University Press, 2010); Gregg Bocketti, *The Invention of the Beautiful Game: Football and the Making of Modern Brazil*, (Gainesville: University Press of Florida, 2016); Roger Kittleson, *The Country of Football: Soccer and the Making of Modern Brazil* (Berkeley: University of California Press, 2014); Joshua H. Nadel, *Fútbol!: Why Soccer Matters in Latin America* (Gainesville: University Press of Florida, 2014).

5. Pierre Bourdieu, "Sport and Social Class," *Social Science Information* 17 (1978): 819–840.

6. Immanuel Wallerstein, *Unthinking Social Science: The Limits of Nineteenth-Century Paradigms* (Cambridge, MA: Polity Press, 1991); Geoff Eley, *A Crooked Line: From Cultural History to a History of Society* (Ann Arbor: University of Michigan, 2005); William Sewell, *Logics of History: Social Theory and Social Transformation* (Chicago: University of Chicago, 2005).

7. Paul Blackledge, *Reflections on the Marxist Theory of History* (Manchester: University of Manchester Press, 2006).

8. Pierre Bourdieu, "Program for a Sociology of Sport," *Sociology of Sport Journal*, Vol. 5 Issue 2, (1988): 153.

9. Holly Thorpe and Rebecca Olive, ed. "The Power, Politics, and Potential of Feminist Sports History: A Multi-Generational Dialogue," *Journal of Sport History* 39 (2012): 379–394; Jean Williams, *A Game for Rough Girls?: A History of Women's Football in Britain* (London: Routledge, 2003); Ibid., *A Beautiful Game: International Perspectives on Women's Football* (London: Bloomsbury Academic, 2007).

10. William Sewell Jr., *Logics of History*, 164.

11. For example, see the Football Scholars Forum at http://footballscholars. org/

PART I

Art Criticism

CHAPTER 2

Drawing the Foul: Diving and Visuality in Contemporary English Football

Luke Healey

On April 2, 2014, the Twitter representatives of German soccer magazine *11Freunde* posted one of their occasional "Bei der Geburt getrennt" ("separated at birth") vignettes, which typically attempt to milk humour out of visual similarities between a footballer and some other, culturally disparate figure.

The diptych concerned the European Champions League quarterfinal tie between Manchester United and Bayern Munich played earlier that evening. Controversy had surrounded the referee's decision to send off Bayern's Bastian Schweinsteiger for a second bookable offence late in the game, a sliding tackle on United's Wayne Rooney. The latter was widely judged to have made the Bavarian's tackle look more brutal than it really was. Rooney thus stood accused of an offence that is officially prohibited in professional soccer under the rubric of "simulation," following a ruling of the International Football Association Board (IFAB) in March 1999.

As of that year, Law 12 of the Fédération Internationale de Football Association's (FIFA) official Laws of the Game document contains a clause stating that "any simulating action anywhere on the field, which is intended to deceive the referee, must be sanctioned as unsporting behav-

L. Healey (✉)
Art History and Visual Studies, University of Manchester, Manchester, UK

© Hofstra University 2017
B. Elsey, S. Pugliese (eds.), *Football and the Boundaries of History*,
DOI 10.1057/978-1-349-95006-5_2

iour."[1] As such, a player guilty of simulation must be shown a yellow card. Although the clause covers deception *tout court*, the range of advantages which could plausibly be gained through "simulating action" is so small that the offence is synonymous with attempts to hoodwink the referee into recognising fair tackles as fouls. Simulation is thus associated with the type of agonised leap that we see in the *11Freunde* image, to the extent that in the United Kingdom it is referred to almost exclusively as "diving." Diving is by no means exclusive to late-twentieth- and early-twenty-first-century football, although it is in the decades immediately preceding and following IFAB's ruling that the majority of Anglophone commentary on the phenomenon is located. Accounting for the lag between diving's earliest recorded appearances in the game and its recognition both by FIFA and IFAB and by the mass media is an interesting scholarly challenge, though it falls beyond the scope of this particular chapter.

The wags behind *11Freunde*'s social media activity rendered their accusation of simulation in the form of a suggestion of kinship between Rooney and a well-known American pacifist poster from the time of the Vietnam War. The two images do indeed contain a common gesture: like the soldier, Rooney's arms are extended behind his body, his knees buckled and his face arranged in a grimace. Assuming some awareness of twenty-first-century soccer, the spirit of this gag is clear: it suggests that Rooney has no right to assume the heroic posture of a dying brother-in-arms, and is a pompous fraud for having done so.

From the perspective of somebody weaned on the English Premier League, which supplanted the old Football League Division One in 1992, there is an irony here. With increased television revenues making it easier for English clubs to recruit talented foreign players, aided in turn by the so-called Bosman Ruling of 1995, which prohibited leagues in the European Union (EU) from placing restrictions on the number of EU-raised players their teams were permitted to sign, German footballers were the first foreign group to be saddled with a blanket reputation as divers by the English press. The caption to a photograph of Jürgen Kohler, used to illustrate an article by Simon Barnes from the June 29, 1994, issue of *The Times*, describes the defender "executing a nine-point dive in the accepted German manner."[2] When Göppingen-born striker Jürgen Klinsmann signed for Tottenham Hotspur in 1994, his deceitful reputation was so entrenched that he was driven to acknowledge it through goal celebrations in which he dived theatrically onto his stomach and slid along the turf.

English footballers on the other hand have long been seen as untainted by the kind of tactical duplicitousness that is manifest in diving. The notion of diving as a foreign contagion was notoriously espoused by the likes of Manchester United manager Sir Alex Ferguson and former England national captain John Terry, who in 2009 opined that "we're a very honest country and it's a very honest league we play in."[3] The act is antithetical to the national game's self-ascribed characteristics of "strength, power, energy, fortitude, loyalty, courage."[4] Diving's reputation as a recent, alien and debasing influence on the English game elides domestic discussions of the phenomenon dating back as far as 1975.[5] Regardless, the German magazine's target is well chosen: there could be few greater scandals in English football than a dive from the decidedly less-than-cosmopolitan Rooney, a rumbustious and powerful forward known at his peak for demonstrating the highest virtues of the national game.

11Freunde's satirical intervention contains the seed of this essay's argument. Both the vignette and my own work share an assertion—albeit articulated on rather different terms—that when footballers dive they echo figures from visual culture more broadly. The magazine's social media editors might have equally invoked the classical Greek sculpture *Laocoön and his Sons* as a visual doppelgänger; Rooney's posture as caught in this snapshot mimics that of the eponymous Trojan priest in a number of respects. I will elaborate the details of *this* echo shortly.

First, however, it is worthwhile pausing to consider the methodological attachments that underpin this study. In seeking to draw such a parallel between high art and mass media material, I reproduce a fundamental claim which animates a wide range of scholarly practices dedicated to exploring visual material in a manner distinct from the connoisseurial bent associated with traditional Art History; namely, that forms, techniques and ideologies of visual representation frequently cross borders between disparate cultural fields, rendering questionable the assumed pre-eminence of any single given field.[6] This principle, which forms the basis of the still-nascent discipline known in Anglophone academia as Visual Studies, is crucial here in two respects. Firstly, this principle is what dismantles the Humanities' traditional interdict against serious contemplation of the species of material at hand, drawn as it is from outside the field of elite visual production. Secondly, it allows one to pose the question as to how representations shared by disparate fields are differentiated by the broader forces of relation between those fields.[7] My suggestion that the press snapshot of the footballer Rooney and the *Laocoön* share a common visual theme is not neutral; rather, it is vexed by a sense of awkwardness which is produced by the socio-cultural formations that maintain football and high art as separate fields. As is clear from the *11Freunde* vignette, Rooney's capacity for mimicry is inflected with guilt and recrimination. It is precisely this inflection, this sense that Rooney's performance is not just an echo of some other visual material but also an *illegitimate* echo, that forms the crux of this chapter.

***

I contend that scholarly frameworks derived from disciplines dedicated to visual material are essential to understanding the reactions that diving provokes. As an issue of sporting ethics, diving is profoundly tied up with questions over the status of images and image-making. Given football's current articulation to a vast and febrile media economy, one could be forgiven for thinking that the game's relationship with apparatuses of image production is devoid of tension. Complicating this somewhat is an article from the September 1981 edition of FIFA's in-house publication *FIFA News*, which demonstrates that the organisation entertained a distinct *iconophobia* at a certain point in its history. Written by Rene Courte, then PR and Press Officer for the Federation, the piece describes the resolutions of a meeting of FIFA's Technical Committee, placing particular emphasis on players as role models. As Courte recounts,

> Members of the FIFA Technical Committee expressed their concern about the excessive demonstrative attitude of some players and teams when a goal is scored. For several years various National Associations have attempted to subdue the un-manly behaviour of some football players who embrace, kiss and hug each other in an over-emotional fashion after scoring a goal.[8]

To identify an "excessive demonstrative attitude" in goal celebrations denotes a certain feeling for visuality as a subversive force, one which FIFA in its official capacity feels compelled to police and regulate. Horst Bredekamp notes that Courte's ideas were at the time badly received, arguing, "Barely one announcement of recent times has been met with such unanimous refusal as this ban on body contact."[9] Yet one can see the effects of FIFA's policing attempts today in the rules which exist against players removing their shirts to celebrate goals, added to FIFA's Laws of the Game in 2004, and the notion of an *excess of demonstrativity*, along with the gendered connotations with which Courte saddles it, persists in commentaries on diving to this day.

In spite of this, it is clearly the case that football always was *demonstrative*. Public visibility of the sport may have intensified and metamorphosed throughout the course of football's ongoing *rapprochement* with the media industry and with the forces of capitalism more broadly, but the game has for almost the entirety of its history possessed an aesthetic dimension by dint of being a popular sport played for the sake of an audience. Sport in general has a right to be considered a part of visual culture: in her essay "Stilling the Punch," art historian Lynda Nead argues the case for incorporating boxing photography into the narratives of art history without subjugating the former to the latter. While accounts of the aesthetics of boxing imagery exist, Nead notes, "in nearly all of these accounts it is assumed that the category of the aesthetic is a given, that its meaning is understood and shared and that it simply implies a degree of formalization or that it involves visual pleasure."[10] Far from simply conferring on an object the quality of being "a bit like art," however, "aestheticization" for Nead is "ambiguous and disputed"; one cannot simply talk of the aestheticisation of boxing imagery as if this did not open up more questions than it answers.[11]

Rather, Nead proposes to utilise techniques derived from art history in order to carry out examinations of boxing imagery, aiming ultimately "to use the contradictions within boxing itself to redefine our understanding of the aesthetic and to allow the tensions to feed into what we might imagine as the aesthetic in this context."[12] In Nead's argument, boxing itself is seen to possess its own visual structures, standards and debates which must be made to inflect any interpretation of the sport through art historical methodologies.

A similar approach is clearly required when discussing football photography in light of art history, in order to avoid a simplistic presentation of the relationship between its own visual vernacular and the high cultural imagery with which it resonates, and which it might otherwise be tempting to elevate to the status of "master signifier."[13] The observation that a diving footballer shares iconographic features with the classical marble figure group *Laocoön and his Sons* is not the end of the analysis. The context of this resonance—a context in which Rene Courte's identification of an excess of demonstrativity in football finds support from similar *iconophobic* sentiments elsewhere in the game—demands to be addressed. First, though, it is worth considering this resonance in more detail, a task for which Nead's essay has already equipped us.

* * *

As Nead relates, the *Laocoön* occupies a privileged position in German aesthetics, and was discussed in detail by Gotthold Ephraim Lessing, Johann Joachim Winckelmann and Johann Wolfgang von Goethe.[14] For the former two, the central figure, who is depicted desperately trying to fight off the serpents that are in the process of strangling his sons, represents a supreme achievement on the part of Classical art's "noble simplicity and tranquil grandeur" (Fig. 2.1).[15]

This phrase belongs to Winckelmann, but Lessing cites it approvingly in the first chapter of his own essay on the *Laocoön*.[16] Lessing venerates the sculpture on the basis that its creator balanced the need to show Laocoön's suffering with the need to adhere to the fundamental aesthetic rule that art must not be a turn-off: "The master," Lessing writes, "strove to attain the highest beauty in given circumstances of bodily anguish," on which basis "it was impossible to combine the latter in all its disfiguring vehemence with the former."[17] Had Laocoön's torment been represented carelessly, the work would have been incapable of arousing the requisite levels of sympathy, becoming instead "a hideous horrible creation from which we gladly turn away our face."[18] In this respect, Nead notes, Lessing and Winckelmann were aligned in focusing on the way in which "the pain revealed in…the body of the central figure is transfigured by the still expression of the face, representing a mastery of suffering that allows the spectator a calm and detached contemplation of the work."[19] Elsewhere in the *Laocoön* essay, Lessing emphasises the importance for figurative sculptors of choosing the correct single moment into which to distil the depicted unfolding action, a feat accomplished by the creator of the *Laocoön*: "if this single moment obtains through Art an unchangeable duration, then it ought to express nothing which in our conception is transitory."[20] For Lessing, the ideal artistic depiction of violence is based on an imaginary sequence from which the most harmonious possible "freeze-frame" has been selected: a second either way and all aesthetic value may be usurped by the merely *transitory*.

These concepts are useful in dealing with certain standout images of diving footballers. A second example of the genre is provided by the image

Fig. 2.1 *Laocoön and His Sons*, ca 27 BC–AD 68, Vatican Museums, photo credit Asier Villafranco Velasco/ThinkStock

of Didier Drogba wearing the orange shirt of his native Ivory Coast, taken during Ivory Coast's FIFA World Cup group stage match against Argentina on June 10, 2006 (Fig. 2.2).

In this photograph, the violent effects of the player's leap are mitigated by a certain grace and harmony in the composition. While not flawless on Lessing's terms, this image is certainly superior to one which it

Fig. 2.2 Didier Drogba, Cote d'Ivoire (Photo credit: Dusan Vraniel, Press Association, UK)

almost completely resembles, and which we can identify—unlike its close cousin, which has been widely circulated online to illustrate blog posts on the subject of diving but which always appears uncredited–as the work of Associated Press photographer David Hecker. In the latter image, which can clearly be read as captured from a different position on the touchline owing to the arrangement of advertising hoardings in the bottom half of the frame, the legs are a touch further apart and the head and shoulders have not been thrown back all the way. Hecker's image as such falls into the Lessingian category of the *transitory*, in contrast to the anonymous image, which offers both a sense of bodily torment and the impression of a body curving elegantly and artfully backwards. The photographer behind each of these images must be credited with a measure of authorial control over these effects, since their relative ability to capture the incident close to its apex, as well as their decision of what to include and what to leave out of the frame, both when shooting and when subsequently wiring pictures to their agency, decides what kind of composition we see.

In addition to the photographer, and the journalistic apparatus that turns the raw images it receives into scandalous artefacts, we must, however, consider a third creative agent, and that is the player himself. The harmony and communicability of diving images rests to a great deal upon the relative degree of enveloping circularity effected by the tackled party. Another example of an image which conveys violence but which also possesses enough formal regularity to not merely be dismissed as a *hideous horrible creation* is Neal Simpson's photograph of Harry Kewell, taken during a 1999–2000 Premier League match between Leeds United and Manchester United (Fig. 2.3).

The partial intrusion of the referee and the tackling player into the frame are disruptive elements in the composition as a whole, but Kewell's posture is otherwise a tour de force of gracefully presented agony. Kewell's mouth is open, unlike the *Laocoön*, and his mid-length hair effects a degree of violence that is mercilessly uncomposed, but there is a conventionality to Kewell's body shape which helps the image to stand out from many dozens of similar images accessible in the archives of the major photographic agencies: extended contemplation, as Lessing suggests, is contingent on a certain stylisation and attendant familiarity of form, created here in the overlap between the respective agencies of player and photographer.[21]

Alongside the *Laocoön*, both the Kewell image and the Drogba image summon a number of resonances from outside the domains of fine art. *11Freunde* drew a comparison between Wayne Rooney's simulated fall against Bayern Munich in April 2014 and the fall of the soldier depicted on a pacifist poster from the time of the Vietnam War; these images of Drogba and Kewell might further remind us of another military-themed depiction of tragic collapse, that of Willem Dafoe's character in the 1986 film *Platoon*, a sequence from which the cover image of the current DVD release was extracted. What is clear in all of these images is a conventional sense of the male body pushed into an extreme of vulnerability: arms are thrown up into the sky in surrender or behind the torso in a negation or denial of self-protection mechanisms; eyes are closed, cancelling the controlling powers of sight; and the mouth hangs open like a wound. The stylised vulnerability communicated in these images is compounded by our expectations of what a soldier, or a footballer, should look like: these are men we anticipate will be strong, powerful and in control of their bodies. This is what lends the war images their pathos, though, as the *11Freunde* cartoon communicates, the application of this kind of iconography in the world of football is more comic than tragic, based on an understanding of the falsified, *autopoietic* nature of the depicted collapse.

Fig. 2.3   Harry Kewell (Photo credit: Neal Simpson)

Nead credits well-timed sporting snapshots with offering "a delay, an extraction from the ceaseless motion of the fight that allows a contemplative and perhaps critical spectatorship."[22] What is most noteworthy about images of diving, given what we know about the activity, is the extent to which the diving players themselves are complicit in opening up and maintaining this extraction. In pretending to have been fouled, diving players quite literally make an exhibition of themselves, demanding to be visually evaluated by an external source, the referee. This accounts both for the interest which diving presents for Visual Studies and for the unease around diving within certain footballing communities: it is the diving players themselves, at least as much as the photographer that captures the moment, that are responsible for producing the effects of bodily violence captured in these photographs.

We can refer to one of the few academic interventions in the subject of diving in support of this notion. In Paul H. Morris and David Lewis's behavioural psychology study "Tackling Diving: The Perception of Deceptive Intentions in Association Football," the researchers compiled clips and conducted a series of experiments in order to offer a taxonomy of simulation in football. Their coding consists of four categories, all of which offer clear guidance in deciding between simulation and genuine foul play. In order to be safely identified as a dive, Morris and Lewis suggest, the incident in question must lack "temporal contiguity," "ballistic continuity" and "contact consistency."[23] In addition, Morris and Lewis identify a fourth category, which they call the "Archer's Bow," and which is noted as a behaviour "unique to deception."[24] In "its most complete form," the authors state, "the tackled player resembles a drawn bow: the chest is thrust out; the head is back; the arms are fully raised and pointing upwards and back; the legs are raised off the ground and bent at the knee."[25] Morris and Lewis' identification of this fourth category advances the notion that diving has its own proper form of expression, arising independently of the forms of expression employed in the rest of the game in which it is found, and which is occasionally "perfected," as caught, for instance, in the Drogba and Kewell images.

Morris and Lewis confess that "the origin of the set of behaviours we name the 'archer's bow' is to a degree puzzling," before noting that the most straightforward motivation is communicability: "The behaviour is clearly noticeable."[26] Remarking that the position adopted in players performing the archer's bow is contrary to the momentum which challenges would ordinarily create in the tackled player, as well as offering little by way of self-protection, the researchers surmise that "the 'archer's bow' is used by the player to convey the extreme nature of the collision; the collision is so extreme that all the normal self-protection mechanisms involved with preparing for the fall cannot be utilized."[27] They subsequently compare examples of the "archer's bow" to Robert Capa's photograph "Loyalist Militiaman at the Moment of Death, Cerro Muriano, September 5, 1936," a famous image of a dying Spanish Republican soldier which has at least since 1975 been implicated as staged.[28]

Setting aside lingering controversies over the veracity of this image, it is clear that the authors' citation of Capa's photograph is intended to connect their own material to a work seen in some circles to belong, through imitation of the throes of violent death, to a visual tradition of heroic suffering. This, of course, is the same gesture made by the *11Freunde* vignette referenced at the beginning of this chapter, and by my own comparison to the *Laocoön*. As has already been claimed, however, there is a disconnect between the two families of imagery which renders the sporting snapshots distinct in their affect. At best, the similarity between the dying hero and the diving footballer is a source of comedy; at worst it is a point of scandal. I will now outline how certain conservative voices in the English tabloid press have sought to frame diving's unique expressive capacity as a figure of degeneracy.

***

I have already shown that certain figures in the FIFA establishment have explicitly articulated *excessive demonstrativity* to errant masculinity. Rene Courte's words merely conform to the societally ingrained notion that concern for one's own appearance is an intrinsically feminine trait. In *Ways of Seeing*, John Berger represents this cultural trope in the form of an axiom, "*men act* and *women appear*."[29] Diving, which we have established aspires to conditions of powerful visual communicability, and can clearly be considered as a demonstration in excess of the action most required in that moment (namely, the movement of hands to the front of the body, to break the eventual fall), is discussed by English commentators with unsurprising frequency in terms beholden to this logic.

Consider an article written by Des Kelly for the January 22, 1999, issue of *The Mirror*. Kelly's subject is the French midfielder David Ginola, then running the wing for Tottenham Hotspur, a player whose long hair and silky skills made him a suspiciously exotic persona in the years of increasing cosmopolitanism that marked the first decade of the English Premier League. That Ginola was also known to dive transformed this suspicion into a full-blown crisis of masculinity. In this article, Kelly calls Ginola's heterosexuality into question as the player is described as having gone "down faster than Monica Lewinsky in the Oval Office."[30] He criticises the player for possessing the "morals of a pop tart," and finds a way of intimately tying his Frenchness to his suspect masculinity by referring to him, in an appropriation of the name of a famous French children's character, as "Little Ponce."[31]

A cartoon that depicts Ginola in swimming trunks, plummeting elegantly from a high diving board as a pair of opposition players look on in bemusement, accompanies the article. It is a neat fit that the match which Kelly focuses on featured Wimbledon, who were, at this stage in their history, well-known for a violent and fancy-free brand of football that saw them labelled "The Crazy Gang." Kelly does not exactly take issue with Ginola's contrastingly stylish technique, however; what is taboo here is the player's awareness that he is one of the best, with all that this entails:

> The Spurs fans revere Ginola, not because he has mastered the careful flick of the locks, the Gallic shrug, or the winning smile for the camera. He is lauded at the club because he is a footballer who has the ability to make the White Hart Lane admission charge seem worthwhile with one scintillating run, a jaw-dropping turn or a searing shot.
> Sadly, he does not seem to understand that one pitiful somersault with pike over an imaginary leg destroys that magic.[32]

Kelly draws a line in the sand here: Ginola rewards those who invest in the spectacle of his performances when he demonstrates his skills. The player's absorption and his ability to make good use of this leads to an absorbing spectacle for the gathered crowd. When Ginola loses absorption with the game at hand and dives, however—and Kelly ties this expressly to the player's exotic sense of vanity—he dismantles the crowd's sense of absorption. He pulls back the curtain to "destroy the magic." When Ginola's performance dissolves into a form of demonstration which implicitly acknowledges the presence of an audience, he debases the game and feminises himself.[33] Ginola's feminisation is furthermore ambient: if norms dictate that *men act and women appear*, then Ginola's dives dismantle football's "magic" by drawing in unacceptable clarity the player's exhibition value. This critical act of *autopoiesis* reflects the audience's viewing back on itself, bringing to light a massive, non-normative circuitry of men-watching-other-men, one that can be found anywhere that sport is followed.

A second spread from a national newspaper helps to reinforce this point. The article in question is an opinion piece by Gideon Brooks from an issue of the *Daily Express* dated March 13, 2006, and prompted by Didier Drogba's admission during the week that he "sometimes dives."[34] Brooks considers the idea that diving has become an accepted part of the game to be "a thoroughly depressing view," but commends Drogba for taking a step towards "stopping the rot."[35] Cartoonist Graham Allen, who provides an illustration for Brooks' piece, is decidedly less sympathetic.

Here, Drogba is depicted, like Ginola, in swimming trunks, about to jump from the diving board into a pool of ordure, from which the word "Cheating" bubbles up in lumps. In preparing his dive, Drogba offers his rear to the befuddled-looking BBC reporter who stands on the poolside, holding out a large, phallic microphone in a suggestive manner. Movement lines give the impression that Drogba is not just offering his behind to the reporter, but waggling it invitingly, an impression bolstered by the striker turning his head to face the reporter. This perhaps incidental or accidental evocation of anal eroticism is striking. As with Ginola in Kelly's Oval Office scenario, Drogba is imagined here not just as homosexual, but as homosexual in a specifically submissive, pleasure-giving capacity. The solicitation of gazes that Drogba employs when he dives, in other words, finds in this cartoon a defensive, homophobic expression. Drogba's tendency, in diving, to acknowledge the gaze of the viewer puts into crisis a basic tenet of English football: that it is not a *spectacle*, which is sexually dubious, but a *competition*, which is masculine, heteronormative and homosocial.

* * *

Kelly's article and Allen's cartoon strike similar notes to the *11Freunde* vignette that opened this essay. In each case, diving is scrutinised for its errant visual productivity, and in each case this productivity is associated with a lack of heteronormative, masculinist moral fibre. The humour of the *11Freunde* post lies in our ability to recognise the fraudulent basis upon which Wayne Rooney's pleas of bodily torment are founded; his attempt to replicate with his own body the gravity that is summoned by the dying soldier in the American propaganda poster with which the image is compared casts the Englishman as a hysterical coward. Meanwhile, Kelly's article and Allen's illustration each seek to draw an air of scandal around their subject by highlighting their perceived hypertrophic tendency to actively solicit the gaze of others through expressive bodily performances, a tendency which we are invited to consider as intrinsically effeminate or homosexual. As has been demonstrated, this characterisation of diving as fundamentally unmanly finds support in words offered more than two decades earlier by FIFA Press Officer Rene Courte concerning so-called *excessive demonstrative attitudes.*

The characteristic diving image is thus an artefact steeped in guilt. Diving is an act of extracurricular visual *autopoeisis* on the part of the given player, and is thereby inexorably bound up in *iconophobic* discourses that continue to see masculinity in terms of authenticity over appearance, praxis over performance. Well-timed snapshots like those of Drogba and Kewell give supreme expression to these illegitimate bodily displays.

While this illegitimate *autopoiesis* is liable to lend diving players a bad reputation in the sporting press, it is simultaneously what makes them a valuable case study for scholars seeking to approach sport through the lens of disciplines centred on the visual. Divers are, in their own way, akin to those advocates of Visual Studies who seek to contest the purist orthodox-ies which have traditionally divided visual culture up into high and low, eternal and ephemeral, legitimate and illegitimate: it is, after all, in a sense the divers themselves that drew the first connection between their own bodies and the *Laocoön.* In producing the "archer's bow," divers strike a compact between their own immediate requirements on the pitch and the rehearsal of age-old iconographies of violence. Morris and Lewis' research suggests that such actions are in fact reflective and considered, even if it does not necessarily follow that every footballer who dives is intimately familiar with the Greek Classical canon.

***

It has been demonstrated over the course of this chapter that diving sheds light on football's multifarious, intimate and idiosyncratic investment in aesthetic discourse in numerous ways. We stand to learn a great deal by focusing on situations where the game's sense of its own aesthetic consti-tution becomes ambivalent and contested. Following Lynda Nead's suggestion, I contend that it is precisely these situations that may enable us to *redefine our understanding of the aesthetic* through traditionally marginalised material. Further studies into football's visual by-products would thus not only enrich our understanding of the history of the game, but make an invaluable contribution to Visual Studies more broadly.

NOTES

1. Fédération Internationale de Football Association. *Laws of the Game 1999* (Zurich: Fédération Internationale de Football Association, 1999), 27.
2. Simon Barnes, "Bizarre moments attract coveted awards," *The Times*, June 29, 1994: 40.
3. Mikey Stafford, "England v Slovenia: England are too honest to dive, says Terry: Playing fair can go against us, says Capello's captain: 'England lads get contact but try to stay on feet'," *The Guardian*, September 5, 2009: 3.
4. David Winner, *Those Feet: A Sensual History of English Football* (London: Bloomsbury, 2005), 7.
5. Alan Thompson, "Now hit them hard," *Daily Express*, November 3, 1975: 18.
6. References here are too numerous, but for a canonical introduction to this approach the reader may wish to turn to Roland Barthes' *Mythologies*, Mieke Bal's *Reading Rembrandt: Beyond the Word-Image Opposition* or to the works of Stuart Hall and the Birmingham School of Cultural Studies.
7. The language of "fields" in this chapter is indebted to the influence of Pierre Bourdieu; for a concise introduction to Bourdieu's concept of cultural fields see David Swartz, *The Sociology of Pierre Bourdieu* (Chicago: University of Chicago Press, 1997).
8. René Courte, "Editorial," *FIFA News*, 220 (September 1981): 461.
9. Horst Bredekamp, *Bilder bewegen: Von der Kunstkammer zum Endspiel Aufsätze und Reden* (Berlin: Wagenbach Klaus, 2007) 159. My translation.
10. Lynda Nead, "Stilling the Punch: Boxing, Violence and the Photographic Image," *Journal of Visual Culture*, 10, no. 3 (December 2011): 305–323. http://vcu.sagepub.com/content/10/3/305. Accessed 04 Dec 12. p. 313.

11. Nead, 2011: 314.
12. Ibid.
13. Georges Didi-Hubermann, "Dialektik des Monstrums: Aby Warburg and the Symptom Paradigm," *Art History*, 24, no. 5 (November 2001): 621–645. http://onlinelibrary.wiley.com/doi/10.1111/1467-8365.00289/abstract. Accessed 28 Aug 14, p. 631.
14. Nead, 2011: 315.
15. Ibid., p. 317.
16. Gotthold Ephraim Lessing, *Laocoön*, trans. Robert Phillimore (London: George Routledge & Sons, 1905), 59.
17. Lessing 1905: 68.
18. Ibid.
19. Nead 2011: 317.
20. Lessing 1905: 71.
21. The Czech-Brazilian philosopher Vilém Flusser has written persuasively on the relationship between visual familiarity and contemplation. Flusser notes that one easy way for a mass media photograph to stand out in the daily flow of "redundant" new images is to present something which demonstrates some degree of continuity with the past, and which thereby offers a "standstill situation." See: Vilém Flusser, *Towards a Philosophy of Photography*, trans. Martin Chalmers (London: Reaktion, 2000), 65.
22. Nead 2011: 317.
23. Paul H. Morris and David Lewis, 'Tackling Diving: The Perception of Deceptive Intentions in Association Football (Soccer), *Journal of Nonverbal Behaviour*, 34, no. 1 (March 2010): 1–13. http://link.springer.com/article/10.1007/s10919-009-0075-0?no-access=true. Accessed 01 Nov 12, p. 8.
24. Morris; Lewis, 2010: 8.
25. Ibid.
26. Ibid., 11.
27. Ibid., 12.
28. Ibid.
29. John Berger, *Ways of Seeing* (London: Penguin, 1990), 47.
30. Des Kelly, "The Dive Artist Formerly Known as Prince," *The Mirror*, January 22, 1999: 53. Kelly refers here to the scandal over then-US President Bill Clinton's sexual relationship with White House intern Monica Lewinsky, the details of which had been revealed in January 1998, and which had led to an ultimately

unsuccessful attempt to impeach the President in December of the same year.
31. Kelly, 1999: 53.
32. Ibid.
33. Kelly's theory of performativity, such as it is, finds here a strong resonance in the ideas of the French Enlightenment critic and writer Denis Diderot. For a breakdown of Diderot's ideas regarding absorption and theatricality, see Michael Fried, *Absorption and Theatricality: Painting and Beholder in the Age of Diderot* (Berkeley: University of California Press, 1980).
34. Brooks, 2006: 77.
35. Ibid.

Works Cited

11Freunde_de (11Freunde_de). 2014. Knapp an der Ikone vorbei, Wayne! #MUFCFCB #rooney #schweinsteiger #why. 2 April 2014, 2:03 a.m. Tweet.
Berger, John. *Ways of Seeing.* London: Penguin, 1990.
Bredekamp, Horst. *Bilder bewegen: Von der Kunstkammer zum Endspiel Aufsätze und Reden.* Berlin: Wagenbach Klaus, 2007.
Brooks, Gideon. "Hand It to Didier." *Daily Express,* March 31, 2006: 77.
Courte, René. "Editorial." *FIFA News,* September 1981, 220: 461.
Didi-Hubermann, Georges. "Dialektik des Monstrums: Aby Warburg and the symptom paradigm." *Art History* 24, no. 5 (2001, November): 621–645. http://onlinelibrary.wiley.com/doi/10.1111/1467-8365.00289/abstract. Accessed 28 Aug 2014.
Fédération Internationale de Football Association. *Laws of the Game* 1999. Zurich: Fédération Internationale de Football Association, 1999.
Kelly, Des. "The Dive Artist Formerly Known as Prince." *The Mirror,* January 22, 1999.
Lessing, Gotthold Ephraim. *Laocoon.* Translated by Robert Phillimore. London: George Routledge & Sons, 1905.
Morris, Paul H., and David Lewis. "Tackling Diving: The Perception of Deceptive Intentions in Association Football (Soccer)." *Journal of Nonverbal Behaviour* 34, (March 1, 2010): 1–13. http://link.springer.com/article/10.1007/s10919-009-0075-0?no-access=true. Accessed 1 Nov 2012.
Nead, Lynda. "Stilling the Punch: Boxing, Violence and the Photographic Image." *Journal of Visual Culture* 10, (December 3, 2011): 305–323. http://vcu.sagepub.com/content/10/3/305. Accessed 04 Dec 2012.
Winner, David. *Those Feet: A Sensual History of English Football.* London: Bloomsbury, 2005.

CHAPTER 3

From Galáctico to Head Butt: Globalization, Immigration and the Politics of Identity in Artistic Reproductions of Zidane

Daniel Haxall

In 2013, an international committee of journalists and former players named "the best eleven players of all time" for *World Soccer* magazine.[1] Zinedine Zidane was selected for a midfield consisting of Alfredo di Stefano, Johann Cruyff and Diego Maradona; however, this recognition fails to reflect his legacy and cultural significance. Revered as a symbol of a racially integrated France due to his Algerian heritage, Zidane has been celebrated as a diplomat, "good Muslim" and inspiration to many throughout the world. Yet no discussion of Zidane is complete without mentioning the penultimate match of his career, the 2006 World Cup final where he was expelled for head-butting Italian defender Marco Materazzi. Thus, a player who dazzled the world with his footballing brilliance became immortalized through an act of violence, and a career marked by championships and personal honors became associated

D. Haxall (✉)
Department of Art History, Kutztown University of Pennsylvania,
Kutztown, Pennsylvania, USA

© Hofstra University 2017
B. Elsey, S. Pugliese (eds.), *Football and the Boundaries of History*,
DOI 10.1057/978-1-349-95006-5_3

with failure. The complicated and enigmatic nature of "Zizou" perhaps accounts for his iconic status. His kit remains a bestseller nearly a decade after his retirement and he appears as a frequent subject in contemporary art.[2] Representations of Zidane extend beyond fan eulogies; instead, these artworks offer critical reflections about fame and publicity, gender norms and social taboos, the commodification of athletes and the politics of sport. In diverse ways, Zidane has become emblematic of globalization and contemporary life, a footballer utilized by artists to unpack histories of representation, immigration and colonization.

THE LEGEND OF "ZIZOU"

In order to understand the surfeit of artworks featuring Zidane, it is first necessary to appreciate his prominence as a footballer and place it in the collective imagination of sports fans. Zinedine Zidane was born in Marseille, France, in 1972 to immigrants from the Kabyle region in Algeria. The youngest of five, he grew up in La Castellane, a suburb, or *banlieue*, of Marseille known for high rates of crime and poverty. He entered the soccer academy at Cannes, making his professional debut with the club at age 17 before signing with Bordeaux. There, Zidane rose to international prominence, being named the Ligue 1 Player of the Year and making his first appearances for the French national team. He then transferred to one of Europe's most storied clubs, Juventus of Italy, winning the Serie A title twice while being awarded the league's top foreign player two times. Despite his accolades, Zidane demonstrated a violent streak, receiving a five-match ban for head-butting a player and accumulating 14 red card ejections throughout his career. Nonetheless, his reputation skyrocketed in 1998 when he led France to the World Cup title, scoring twice in the final against Brazil.

The French squad featured a diverse roster of players from its former colonies, rendering their victory culturally and politically significant.[3] As such, the media projected the soccer pitch as a site of integration, and the visibility of Zidane altered some perceptions of French citizenry. In the press, the team nickname of *Les Bleus*, based on the color of their jerseys, became *black–blanc–beur* ("Black–White–Arab"), an updated tricolor configuration that reflected the heterogeneity of the squad. Not everyone welcomed this diversity as National Front leader Jean-Marie Le Pen labeled the team "artificial" for including the children of immigrants. Despite such protests from the political right, most viewed the World Cup as a harbinger of the future with Zidane best representing its potential. He became the most famous person in France, and as Geoff Hare commented, "a symbol of a multicultural France at ease with itself, and to others a role model of what could be achieved in a socially fractured society, he came to represent the central social and political issues of post-colonial France."[4] Laurent Dubois also noted that Zizou represented a larger interrogation of French identity, observing: "Since 1998 the question of 'Who is Zidane?' has been a crucial way of asking 'What is France?'" (Fig. 3.1).[5]

On the strength of his performance at the World Cup, Zidane was awarded FIFA's (Fédération Internationale de Football Association) World Player of the Year as well as the European Player of the Year. His legend grew further as France won the European Championship in 2000, advancing to the final on Zidane's overtime goal against Portugal. Firmly cemented as one of the world's pre-eminent footballers, he left Juventus for Real Madrid in the most expensive transfer in history at the time. The midfielder cost $64 million and made an immediate impact, scoring a legendary volley to win the UEFA (Union of European Football Associations) Champions League in his first season. Despite a disappointing showing in the 2002 World Cup where he was injured and missed the first two matches, Zidane won FIFA World Player of the Year again after leading Real Madrid to the Spanish title. Zidane announced he would retire after the World Cup in 2006, and he excelled while leading France to the championship game, scoring three times in the tournament including the decisive goal in the semifinals. He tallied again in the final and earned the Golden Ball for outstanding player of the tournament. It looked as though Zidane might end his career as World Cup champion, but with the game in extra time he was expelled for headbutting Italian defender Marco Materazzi, an act that stunned the world.

Responses to Zidane's head butt flooded the media and varied considerably. One of the most popular reflections about the incident is "Zidane's Melancholy" by Jean-Philippe Toussaint. In attempting to comprehend the head butt, Toussaint wrote that Zidane carried the "painful perception of the passing of time...the sadness of the ordained end, the bitterness of the player who is contesting the last match of his career and cannot resolve to finish." The French captain understood that his career could not end beautifully by winning the World Cup because that would include an acceptance of closure, and by extension, death. Feeling "broken" and "vulnerable," and no longer capable of artistic "form," the melancholic Zidane sought escape, an abrupt counter to nullify his pending fate.[6] Witnessing the match in Berlin's Olympic Stadium, Toussaint, like

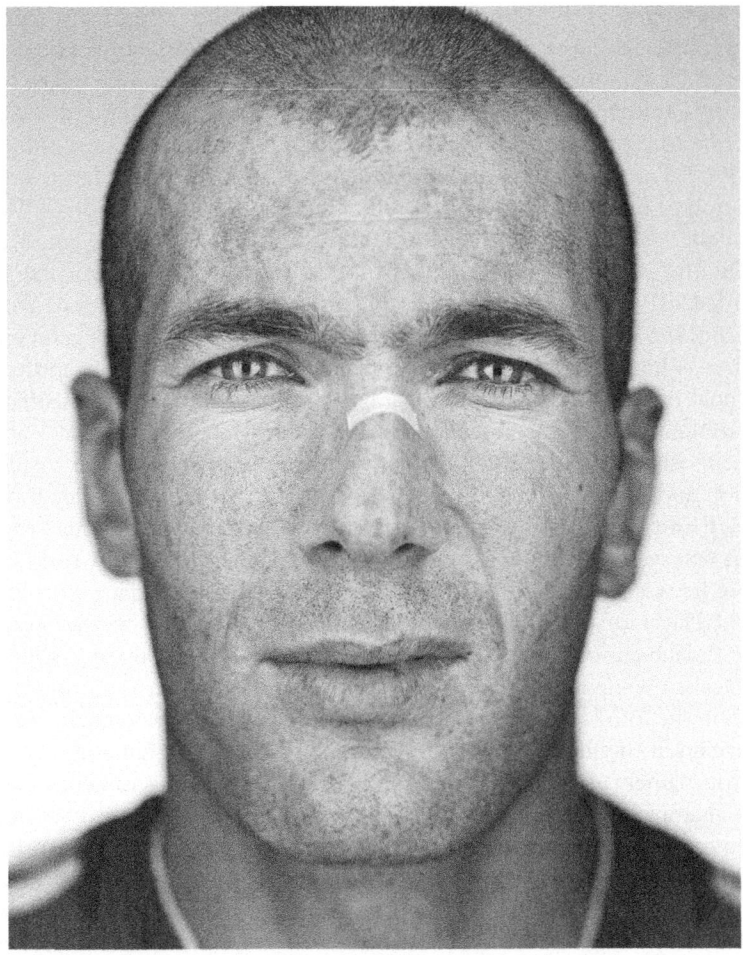

Fig. 3.1   Martin Schoeller, *Zinedine Zidane*, © August Images, LLC

the 715 million watching on live television, missed the head butt in real time since it occurred away from the action.[7] With replays the only means to access the event, Toussaint concludes that Zidane's gesture never took place; it was not observed, thereby existing only as an impulse.[8]

A few days after the World Cup, Roger Cohen wrote in the *New York Times* that Zidane "killed a certain narrative of his life," and compared the Frenchman to Camus' *The Stranger*, in which the French-Algerian Meursault senselessly murdered an Arab. In Cohen's estimation, Zidane produced an enigmatic drama with "all the complexity of a great novel."[9] Indeed, many scholars utilized literature and philosophy to understand the head butt, with Antonis Coumoundouros interpreting Zidane platonically in an essay tracing the four cardinal virtues through soccer.[10] Ahmer Nadeem Anwer further deconstructed the head butt through literary tropes, in particular the "Resurgence and Fall of Zinedine Zidane," which follows trajectories of mythmaking ranging from "moral judgment and deserved damnation" to "'Romantic' mad genius" and Othello-like Other. Casting the Italian Materazzi as "compatriot of Machiavelli and *Mafiosi*," Anwer suggested an alternate reading of Zidane through "near-Eastern cultural traditions, where slights unto the 'honour' of family women will not be pardoned."[11] For many, Zidane's ethnic and religious heritage became the lens through which they interpreted his persona and behavior on the pitch. Nacira Guénif-Souilamas argued that he became emblematic of issues connected to colonialism, simultaneously signifying the French republic through its egalitarian meritocracy and cultural goodwill toward its former colonies; Islamic extremism by the machismo of his head butt; the archetypal Arab whose body becomes "the site of a performance of ambivalence and multiplicity"; an objectified Adonis-like body; and, finally, the docile Kabyle.[12] Further complicating these varied readings is Zidane's public silence, as some have criticized him for failing to publicize significant social and political issues.[13] Ultimately, Zidane's enigmatic character developed through components varied and complex: his binational background, championship-winning goals and propensity for violence.

PICTURING ZIDANE: THE FETISHIZED FOOTBALLER

Prior to the infamous head butt, Zidane's talent made him one of the world's most coveted players. Rodolfo de Florencia (b. 1968, Morelos, Mexico) explored the commodification of such footballers by framing Zidane's record-breaking transfer from Juventus to Real Madrid within the language of commodity fetishism (Fig. 3.2).

This painting isolates Zidane's muscular legs while his name and $64 million dollar transfer fee appear in the top right corner. No other features identify the midfielder, yet the blue background and red socks evokes the French national team. In the series *Star Players*, de Florencia frames ath-

Fig. 3.2   Rodrigo de Florencia, *Star Player #1*, 2002 (acrylic on canvas, 20 × 16 in) Courtesy of the artist

letes like Zidane, Ronaldo and Batistuta as physical traits and monetary values, fragmenting their bodies to render them as merchandise. While this association is clear, the artist's rhetorical devices expose the machinations of fetishism in sports marketing and player contracts. By isolating particular anatomical features, such as the legs, de Florencia's paintings resemble Jean Baudrillard's notion of the "fetish-beauty," the abstraction of a sought-after object, in this case the body, into a system of representation. Since the fetish refers to a surrogate, or proxy for that which is desired, the body becomes separated into partial units, a montage of sorts that Baudrillard considers consumable. The divided body loses agency, and stripped of its totality and power, becomes an object safe for consumption.[14] Without contextual references beyond the transfer fee, the disjointed bodies appear salable, reducing Zidane and others to a code of activity defined solely by physique and price tag. Where Marx and Engels believed that monetary value typically conceals the social character of labor, de Florencia diminishes his *Star Players* to a code of physical performance and net worth, reminding audiences of these players' iconic status and value while criticizing their commodification in advertising and the transfer market.[15]

The desire attached to Zidane's fetishized body extends beyond commodity and performance; instead, artworks about the former French captain reframe him as an object of sexual desire. Lyle Ashton Harris (b. 1965, New York City, United States) began documenting soccer's gender codes during a fellowship at the American Academy in Rome in 2001.[16] While photographing games in Italy, the artist became intrigued by intersecting displays of masculinity, class and power that occurred on match days. His black-and-white prints feature *ultras*, or extreme fan groups, as well as players and riot police. While working on this series, Harris discovered an Adidas advertisement featuring Zidane reclining on a training table with a young man tending to his feet. Harris expanded the image into a series of mural-sized collages, *Blow Up*, that include his match day photographs alongside press images depicting fan violence (Fig. 3.3).

For his installation of *Blow Up* in Seville, Spain, he added images from bullfights, stills of Zidane's head butt and the cover from *Artforum* that featured reviews of Douglas Gordon and Philippe Parreno's film about the soccer star. Situated adjacent to the oversized image of Zidane's pedicure is a reproduction of Manet's *Olympia* (1863, Musée d'Orsay, Paris, France), a maneuver that reverses our relationship to the canonical reclining nude. Critics in the nineteenth century protested the representation of the prostitute in her boudoir as well as her black servant, suggesting that Manet had breached standards of artistry and decorum. By replacing Olympia with Zidane, Harris contests the objectifying male gaze of art history, offering a male body as the source of our desire while complicating the circumstances surrounding this scopic encounter. Yet the dark-skinned

Fig. 3.3 Lyle Ashton Harris, *Blowup IV* (Sevilla), 2006 (collage installation) Courtesy of the artist

trainer's position remains the same as Olympia's black maid, acknowledging the expected subservience of the racial Other and continuity of biased hierarchies.

Throughout the collage, Harris pasted his previous photographic work that examines race, gender norms and sexual orientation, opposing the hyper masculinity of soccer hooligans with images of the artist in drag. An advertisement for Calvin Klein underwear features former Arsenal star Freddie Ljungberg, a campaign that made him a "gay icon" and target of harassment from female admirers and opponents alike. Where the former allegedly groped him in nightclubs, the latter directed homosexual slurs to the Swedish winger, thus indicating the sexualized and gendered systems within athletic competition.[17] Additional images in the collage include photographs of Michael Jackson, an artist known for gender and racial mutability, stills from Harris' performance as "MJ" at Yale University and sculptures depicting Antinous, Hadrian's young lover who was deified by the emperor after his death. Throughout the work, Harris conflates desire with soccer, a sport that privileges physical fitness from sex symbols such as Ljungberg and David Beckham. The title, *Blow Up*, underscores this connection, referencing Michelangelo Antonioni's critically acclaimed yet sexually provocative 1966 movie about a fashion photographer. Like the film's protagonist who expands his photographs to uncover hidden details, Harris modifies the format and scale of images to locate narratives of contested identity. While his compilation mimics the format of a bulletin board, Harris' juxtaposition of images evokes far more than a fan's scrapbook. Instead, the artist offers layers of conflations, from the ritualized violence of the Spanish bullfight to the orchestrated antics of Italian *Ultras*, and the same-sex interaction between Zidane and his trainer to the homo-social culture of soccer clubs and fans. At the center of this menagerie is Zidane in roles ranging from endorsing Adidas to head-butting Materazzi, a microcosm of the diverse positions he occupies in football and as a subject in contemporary art.

ZIDANE IN ACTION: GLOBALIZATION AND THE TELECRACY

The best-known and most-discussed artwork about the midfielder remains Douglas Gordon (b. 1966, Glasgow, Scotland) and Philippe Parreno's (b. 1964, Oran, Algeria) *Zidane, a 21st Century Portrait* (2006). For this project, the filmmakers trained 17 cameras on Zidane while he played for Real Madrid in April of 2005. Each utilized different types of film from a variety of positions throughout Madrid's Bernabéu Stadium—13 in high-definition 35mm format, a Super-16mm handheld camera, and 2 with cutting-edge telephoto lenses—yet all of them remained focused solely on Zidane's movements and not the match at large. With television feeds spliced into a soundtrack provided by the band Mogwai, audiences witnessed a match-long, or 90-minute, montage that tracked every pass, tackle and foul by Zidane. At times moments of great artistry occur when Zidane skillfully traps the ball or assists on a goal, but in other instances Zidane jogs around the pitch, dragging his cleat and wiping sweat from his deeply focused brow. Subtitles relay his reflections on soccer, a sparse monologue variously interrupted by crowd noise, players calling to each other or the thud of a struck ball. Without the context of the match to ground Zidane's performance, viewers become confused as to his whereabouts on the field, and he often seems removed from the action altogether.

While audiences might have difficulty following the progress of the game, they clearly identify Zidane's intense focus and determination. In a review for *Artforum*, Michael Fried questioned whether the film could be taken seriously as a "portrait." The art historian previously wrote about nineteenth-century portraiture, claiming that the medium of painting could not compete with photography in generating an accurate likeness. To compensate for this shortcoming, painters such as Manet depicted their subjects candidly, capturing their personality while engaged in activities beyond posing for a picture. Applying this idea to Gordon and Parreno's film, Fried celebrated *Zidane* for successfully portraying the footballer "absorbed in the action."[18] The film also includes moments when his focus breaks down and Zidane becomes aware of the fans in the stadium. The theatricality of public performance should rupture the absorptive model constructed by Fried; however, he claimed that Zidane's "double consciousness" elucidates the problematic nature of representation. Ultimately, Fried praised Gordon and Parreno for revealing the instability of portraiture and critically engaging one of the major precepts of modernist art.

The filmmakers drew inspiration from Hellmuth Costard's *Football Like Never Before*, a 1971 movie that followed George Best during a 1970 match for Manchester United. Despite the similarities in concept, the technology available to Gordon and Parreno easily surpassed the six cameras used by Costard. Notwithstanding telephoto lenses and high-definition equipment, close-ups fail to deliver the intimacy such techniques claim to offer. Paul Myerscough criticized the film because "the *galáctico*, like any modern celebrity, is available to us only through his mediation, and the more pervasive his image, the more frustratedly we recognize that he remains finally opaque, unreachable."[19] Tim Griffin wrote that this distance from Zidane, as well as his distance from teammates while focused on the match, produces "an impression of melancholy or isolation."[20] The fragmentation of time and reality that unfolds during *Zidane* serves to defamiliarize the athlete even while we gain impossible proximity to his person. Rather than knowing and understanding the man, we consume him like the advertisements lining the pitch, making the "portrait" one of contemporary marketing and its infiltration of the sport spectacle. Framed before a backdrop of billboards, "Zidane now operates in the densest microcosm of contemporary post-Fordist society—a spectacularized workplace designed almost exclusively for sight; a landscape premised on immanent reproducibility."[21] Simon Critchley noted how the midfielder becomes fetishized to the point of commodity, transforming into "a product with rights owned by Adidas, Siemens, or his whole panoply of sponsors."[22] The transnational identities of these labels reflect today's globalized world, one connected by consumption and sport and represented by Gordon and Parreno. The filmmakers themselves are Scottish and French-Algerian, the corporate sponsors and club teams multinational and commentary of the film polyglot. The dynamics of globalization inform how we understand Zidane and this film exemplifies the "graphic unconscious," in which advertising frames our daily experiences.[23] Indeed, the portrait offered in *Zidane* is not of a footballer per se, rather the visage of a world interconnected by technology and commerce.

Beyond portraiture and globalization, Andy Birtwistle read the film as a meditation about cinematic experience in the age of television, one that restores the materiality of film by "placing its qualities on display."[24] The filmmakers achieved this by alternating from television feeds, defined by low-resolution images, to spectacular, high-definition cinema footage. According to Birtwistle, "at the point of transition we are struck by the visceral, affective power of *cinematic* experience, momentarily overwhelmed by cinema's materiality and the sheer power of its audiovisuality."[25] While high-definition technology increasingly offers a similar experience at home, television broadcasts continually reestablish the significance of a soccer match through overlays of the score, statistics, replays and analysis from announcers. However, Gordon and Parreno offer a 90-minute montage devoid of such contextual information, disrupting traditional spectatorship through the technological sublime. In this way, *Zidane* epitomizes Baudrillard's critique of televised events, where the context of the "real" is replaced by the "terroristic hyperrealism" of its broadcast.[26] Ultimately, direct experience becomes controlled by the "telecracy," Eduardo Galeano's term for our mediated consumption of soccer through television.[27] As such, game times become determined by viewership opportunities and the stadium evolves into a televisual playground of jumbotrons and digitized advertising banners.

Soccer's media saturation overwhelms visitors in Harun Farocki's (b. 1914, Nový Jičín, Czech Republic; d. 2014, Berlin, Germany) *Deep Play* (2007), a 12-channel installation that presents the entire World Cup final between France and Italy through diverse platforms. Each channel displays different feeds: television footage, surveillance recordings from Berlin's Olympic Stadium, the artist's view of the arena from his adjacent hotel, animation sequences depicting the match, charts and statistical analysis of the game and isolated shots of players and coaches. The video projections engulf us with information that unfolds over the duration of the match, prompting reflection about the sport spectacle, role of data in soccer and televisual systems that govern our consciousness. The detailed graphs and digital simulations of *Deep Play* reflect the prominence of science and technology in contemporary sport; for example, "sabermetrics" revolutionized baseball through "objective" analytics and soccer coaches increasingly utilize cutting-edge software to analyze performance and optimize results. Farocki's installation acknowledges the manner in which this information shapes players' behavior, but perhaps more importantly, our experience of the game.

Farocki's oeuvre might be considered an extended meditation on the telecracy that dictates our lives. His previous work examined war and consumerism and the various ways media manipulates public engagement in society. *Deep Play* exposes the limits of the televisual because, despite being inundated with images and information, viewers fail to gain complete understanding of the match as it unfolds. For example, statistical data offers no insight into the causes of Zidane's head butt, and those watching the final in "real time" missed the event altogether. Many critics observed how the omnipresence of the camera does not equate to full knowledge. As Holland Cotter noted, "in seeing more, Mr. Farocki seems to ask, are we seeing better, or are we missing the real picture, the actual event?"[28] Indeed, most of us see only the montage produced by a television company under the authority of FIFA. When considered with the accompanying surveillance footage, the mechanisms of control and influence dictating media consumption become apparent. While *Deep Play* might not focus solely on Zidane, he remains complicit in this arrangement because as viewers watch his performance, they digest hours of footage exploited by the current televisual regime.

BLACK–BLANC–BEUR: ZIDANE AND IMMIGRATION

Where Farocki ponders the implications of the telecracy, Haig Aivazian (b. 1980, Beirut, Lebanon) constructs a different kind of video that employs the mythology of the head butt to interrogate French immigration issues, stereotypes of Arab and Muslim identity and codes of masculinity. For his 26-minute film, *How Great You Are, O Son of the Desert!* (2013), Aivazian links speculation about what Materazzi said to Zidane to social disorder and racial profiling. The artist spliced together footage from the World Cup final with animations and photographs depicting riots, bombings and the death of children at the hands of overzealous police. The narrative begins with the well-publicized notion that Materazzi called Zidane the "son of a terrorist whore," an insult Aivazian uses to fictionalize him as a religious or political extremist. Likening the head butt to a suicide car bombing, the narrator traces such behavior to Zidane's upbringing in La Castellane, labeling him a "*racaille*" or "thug." Traversing from sport to class, discussion of riots in the *banlieues* of Paris is followed by a joke told by Zidane that presumptively includes a punch line about terrorism. When Zidane's anecdote does not include a violent ending, it reveals our biased expectations about his North African ancestry, an aspect of his identity highlighted in the film's title. Such typing or profiling is further explored through the deaths of two Islamic teenagers who were accidentally electrocuted while fleeing cops enforcing an identification law. The bizarre interpretive links made throughout the video reflect those made by the media, assumptions that "astounded" the artist with their "flawed logic." Riots in Paris had nothing to do with the head butt, and Aivazian thinks Zidane simply "could not control his macho urges."[29] Accordingly, the maneuver was neither terroristic nor anticolonial, and it certainly did not prevent Zidane from making millions in endorsements or being hailed as an international hero. Instead, as the artist asserts, the media overhyped the significance of one player's ejection from a soccer match through essentializing rhetoric and fears about immigration.

Chris Beas (b. 1971, Sierra Madre, United States) similarly explores the politics of sports and fandom, referencing sports memorabilia to contest national identity and spectator behavior. While his favorite team Manchester United and their former star George Best feature prominently in his oeuvre, Zidane recurs as a metaphor for transnationalism and political history. For Beas, soccer offered a "rejection of American xenophobia" that mars debates surrounding immigration in many places, particularly his hometown of Los Angeles. As noted in a recent review, Beas' installations interrogate the notion of American exceptionalism, with soccer an appropriate tool because of its global popularity. "Football is this sort of cauldron of different aspects of life, whether it's violence, beauty, politics or economics," he explains. "There are all these social aspects of the game outside of the physical act of playing, so for me, it's a great place to gather information."[30] In a series of tabletop tableaux subtitled *Pitch Invasions*, Beas appropriated small plastic figurines of the game's biggest stars, including Zidane, and arranged them into complex groupings. Set on simulated turf, these athletes compete in a cluster without the ball, leading us to question their activity. Is this scrum a brawl, the type of behavior football struggles to prevent? The inclusion of Roger Milla of Cameroon rising triumphantly atop the tangled mass of French, English and Spanish footballers suggests the political potential of the sport, with competition a means of contesting complicated histories.

Beas wryly fused these aspects in the small bronze statue, *No That Really is El Cid, He Only Thinks He's Zizou* (Fig. 3.4). Here Zidane assumes the pose from his famous goal in the Champions League final; however, rather than striking the ball he kicks a prone combatant reminiscent of Materazzi. Thus, Beas collapses two iconic moments into one, the volley and the head butt, reflecting the problematic nature of Zidane's legacy. The use of bronze recalls the art historical tradition of statuary commemorating great deeds or historically significant individuals; however, the scale of the work suggests minor trophies rather than public monuments. The work's title offers a surprising connection, suggesting that El Cid, the noted military leader and hero of Spain, aspires to be Zidane. This statement carries complex associations because of Zidane's Berber heritage and El Cid's record of fighting Muslims in the eleventh century. In addition, El Cid might offer a historical context for appreciat-

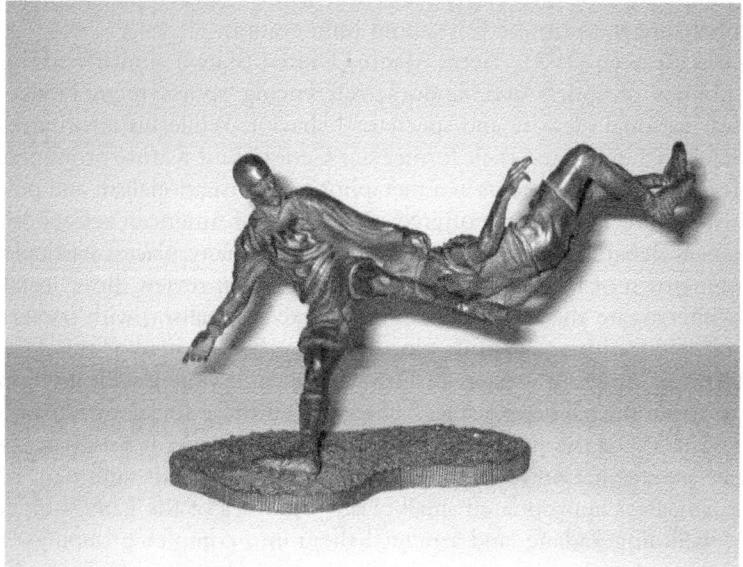

Fig. 3.4   Chris Beas, *No, That Really Is El Cid, He Only Thinks He's Zizou*, 2007 (bronze, edition of 3 with 2 artist proofs, 5 ¼ × 10 ½ × 5 ¼ in) Courtesy of the artist

ing Zidane and his sociopolitical significance because the general fought to unite Spain whereas Zidane supposedly unified France and forged a new conception of its nationhood, receiving two knighthoods like his medieval counterpart in Spain.

LE NIF: ZIDANE AS A POSTCOLONIAL HERO

Zidane's accomplishments and Algerian ancestry made him an international icon, particularly in Africa, where he represents the potential to achieve success despite humble origins.[31] Adel Abdessemed (b. 1971, Constantine, Algeria), however, immortalized Zidane's head butt with a statue cast in bronze five meters tall (Fig. 3.5). This work lays bare the aggressive masculinity that has come to dominate sports while acknowledging the fallibility of today's athletes, an aspect of Zidane that attracted him:

> When the episode of the head-butt happened I felt as if I had experienced that head-butt on my own body. Zidane is Algerian like me and he has been caught up by his culture. But I think that Zidane's gesture expressed freedom. I was interested in dealing with it as a counter-celebration. The Greeks made sculptures of glory, of gods, demigods and Olympic athletes. *Headbutt* is an icon celebrating a moment of weakness, a defeat.[32]

The monumental sculpture carries various interpretive possibilities. Where the artist empathized with Zidane and found his "moment of weakness" humanizing, others considered it offensive. The National Association of French Football Districts protested the work's display at the Centre Pompidou in Paris for tarnishing Zidane's reputation and corrupting French youth. In a letter to Zidane seeking his help in their efforts to remove the work, chairman Michel Keff wrote that the negative representation of football undermined the "sporting ethics and values" taught in the academy system.[33]

While the Centre Pompidou refused to censor the work, a similar controversy erupted after *Headbutt* was purchased by the Qatar Museums Authority and displayed along the Corniche in Doha. Intended to reside permanently along the promenade, the sculpture was removed after four weeks because of its contentious subject. Some echoed the complaints of the French soccer organization by claiming the statue promoted violence and illustrated negative values. Others protested its idolatrous

Fig. 3.5 Adel Abdessemed, *Coup de tête*, 2011–12. Installation at the Centre Georges Pompidou, Paris (bronze, approx. 210 ¼ × 137 × 85 ⅞ in) © 2015 Artists Rights Society (ARS), New York/ADAGP, Paris

nature and implications for Islamic culture. In response to a *New York Times* story about the controversy, Omar Chatriwala, publisher of *Doha News*, remarked that Abdessemed's original meaning was lost in the debate and that Qataris objected to the work because "we don't put up statues of anyone...only animals and inanimate objects."[34] The Qatar Museums Authority stated that the work was moved to accompany an exhibition of Abdessemed's work at the Museum of Modern Art rather than the result of the protests;[35] however, media representations of Zidane following the World Cup suggest otherwise. In tracking coverage of the incident, Yasmin Jiwani argued that the press "not only reproduced Orientalist frames (animal imagery, violence and irrationality) but also underscored associations between Muslims and terrorists in its speculations regarding what Marco Materazzi had said to provoke Zidane's actions."[36] Although Abdessemed insisted his sculpture is based on Zidane's action and not media responses or political ideologies, the footballer remains socially charged by virtue of his complicated character and multiethnic identity.[37]

The ramifications of Zidane and the head butt surfaced in other works by Abdessemed's contemporaries, notably Hassan Musa (b. 1951, El Nuhud, Sudan). One of his painted textiles, *Jacob Wrestling the Angel*, restages Zidane's gesture as Delacroix's painting of the same title (Fig. 3.6).

Wearing the number ten jersey, the footballer lowers his head and drives into the angel while a ball rests between the combatants' feet. Gothic text radiates around the pair, verbiage borrowed from a lawyer's blog about the lack of consequences in sporting violence. Potentially criminal as an assault, athletes like Zidane avoid legal prosecution because, as the blog notes, football authorities determine the fate of the assailant rather than the justice system.[38] For Musa, Zidane's head butt carried particular significance as a heroic rejection of European hegemony, calling it "the colonized people answer to the colonists!"[39] Despite being born in and playing for France, Zidane represents Africa through his Algerian parents; making the "gesture of freedom" mentioned by Abdessemed a rebuttal to colonialism and exploitation. Soccer historically functioned as a platform for Algerian political action, with nationalists utilizing the sport to mobilize independence efforts and a pitch invasion disrupting a match between France and Algeria in 2001.[40]

This association became more pronounced when Musa converted the painting into a print for FIFA's World Cup portfolio, a collection of posters by prominent international artists selected by a German art-marketing

Fig. 3.6 Hassan Musa, *Jacob Wrestling with the Angel*, 2008 (ink on cloth, 207 × 160 cm) © Pascal Polar Gallery, Brussels

firm. Musa drew upon a tradition of Asafo war flags for the print, war emblems created by the Akan people to illustrate their resistance to European rule. The artist wrote that he "wished to bring this composition of Delacroix close to an Asafo flag," adding, "Africans would give everything for football to be [a] continuation of politics."[41] The reference to Asafo textiles renders soccer a platform for political activism, a recurrent theme in Musa's oeuvre as he often appropriates iconic works from the history of art to critique racial fetishism, colonization and contemporary political events. Musa, like many Muslims and Algerians, believed that with his head butt, Zidane demonstrated "*le nif*," an Arabic expression for protecting the honor of oneself or one's family.[42] Several, including David Winterstein and Jiwani, have documented how in the press he became perceived as the "good Muslim" for defending his family from insult and "acting out a hegemonic chivalric masculinity."[43] Ironically, the midfielder was praised by the presidents of both Algeria and France, celebrated for representing Algerian success and values as well as French integration and exceptionalism.

CONCLUSION

In reflecting upon the 2006 World Cup, Eduardo Galeano wrote that Zidane "was the best player of the tournament, despite that final act of insanity or integrity, depending on how you look at it. Thanks to his beautiful moves, thanks to his melancholy elegance, we could still believe that soccer was not irredeemably condemned to mediocrity."[44] Indeed, an athlete known for brilliance led France to victory and became a hero in the process. His portrait was projected on the Arc de Triomphe and he represented the complexities of national identity in an age of globalization and immigration. Yet his career ended in infamy, complicating the legacy of a revered sportsman who became muse to numerous contemporary artists. Ultimately, Zinedine Zidane remains an icon of sporting success, colonization and its discontents, ethnicity and the fetishized male body, a complex set of associations for a player renowned for excellence and failure on the pitch.

NOTES

1. "The Greatest," *World Soccer,* Summer 2013: 41–54.
2. This essay concentrates on the diverse ways Zidane has been represented in contemporary art. Rather than including examples from

commercial art or graphic design, I have included only those who exhibit as professional artists within a gallery or museum setting.

3. The roster included Thuram born in Guadeloupe, Karembeu born in New Caledonia, Lama born in Guyana, Desailly born in Ghana, Zidane born to Algerian immigrants, Djorkaeff born to an Armenian mother and Kalmouk father, Lizarazu with three Basque grandparents and Barthez with a Spanish grandmother. Marks, "French National Team and National Identity," 52–53.

4. Hare, *Football in France*, 2, 188.

5. Dubois, *Soccer Empire*, 136.

6. Touissant, "Zidane's Melancholy," 12–13.

7. http://www.fifa.com/mm/document/fifafacts/ffprojects/ip-401_06e_tv_2658.pdf

8. Touissant, "Zidane's Melancholy," 14.

9. Roger Cohen, "Camus and Zidane Offer Views on How Things End," *New York Times,* 12 July 2006, http://www.nytimes.com/iht/2006/07/12/sports/IHT-12globalist.html.

10. Coumoundouros, "Plato and the Greatness of the Game," 72–74.

11. Anwer, "Zizou's Cup of Woe," 101–103.

12. Guénif-Souilamas, "Zidane: Portrait of the Artist as Political Avatar," 205–226.

13. For example, Philippe Auclair criticized Zidane's self-marketing and political apathy, particularly his support of Qatar's campaign to host the 2022 World Cup and failure to intervene when Kabyle protestors were violently suppressed in Algeria in 2001. Philippe Auclair, "The Dark Lord within Zinedine Zidane," *Eight by Eight* 3 (2014): 64–67; 109.

14. Jean Baudrillard, *For a Critique of the Political Economy of the Sign*, trans. Charles Levin (Candor: Telos Press, 1981): 94–97.

15. Karl Marx and Friedrich Engels, *Capital*, vol. 1. trans. Samuel Moore and Edward Aveling; reproduced in *The Norton Anthology of Theory and Criticism*, ed. Vincent Leitch (New York and London: Norton, 2001): 777, 779; Santiago Espinosa de los Monteros, "Rodolfo deFlorencia," http://www.rodolfodeflorencia.com/texts.html.

16. Coblentz, "Multiplicities and Singularities," 49–50.

17. Freddie Ljungberg interview with Alex Thomas, *CNN World Sport,* 21 September 2012, http://www.cnn.com/video/data/2.0/video/sports/2012/09/22/ws-ljungberg-sitdown-thomas-intv.cnn.html.

18. Fried, "Absorbed in the Action," 332–335, 398.
19. Myerscough, "Short Cuts," 22.
20. Griffin, "The Job Changes You," 338.
21. Ibid., 336.
22. Critchley, "Working-Class Ballet," 64.
23. Beugnet and Ezra, "A portrait of the twenty-first century," 84.
24. Birtwistle, "Douglas Gordon and Cinematic Audiovisuality," 104.
25. Ibid., 108.
26. Simonyi and Van Tomme, "Real-Time Spectacles," 5–11.
27. Galeano, "The Telecracy," in *Soccer in Sun and Shadow.*
28. Holland Cotter, "Art in Review," *New York Times,* 1 February 2008, http://www.nytimes.com/2008/02/01/arts/design/01gall.html?pagewanted=all&_r=0.
29. Mohaiemen and Aivazian, "Six-Shooters and Nationalist Stamps," 285–286.
30. Chris Beas, as quoted in Rhea Mahbubani, "Soccer Is Artist's Muse," *Coastline Pilot,* 28 May 2014, http://www.coastlinepilot.com/entertainment/tn-cpt-et-0530-laguna-art-museum-chris-beas-20140529,0,889409.story.
31. For a study of artists from the African diaspora engaging the politics of soccer, including earlier forms of my analysis of Adel Abdessemed, Lyle Ashton Harris, and Hassan Musa, see Daniel Haxall, "Pitch Invasion: Football, Contemporary Art, and the African Diaspora," *Soccer and Society* 16, nos. 2–3 (March–May 2015): 259–281.
32. Adel Abdessemed, as quoted in Dessanay, "Adel Abdessemed," 93.
33. Adam Sage, "Fans furious as Zidane's Moment of Madness Is Immortalized by Artist," *The Times,* 23 October 2012: 30–31, http://www.thetimes.co.uk/tto/news/world/europe/article3576239.ece.
34. Robert Mackey, "Qatar Removes Statue of Zidane's Head Butt After Complaints," *The Lede: New York Times,* 30 October 2013, http://thelede.blogs.nytimes.com/2013/10/30/qatar-removes-statue-of-zidanes-head-butt-after-complaints/.
35. Victoria Scott, "QMA Moves Zidane Head-Butt Statue from Corniche to Mathaf," *Doha News,* 28 October 2013, http://dohanews.co/qma-moves-zidane-head-butt-statue-from-corniche-to-mathaf/.
36. Jiwani, "Sports as a Civilizing Mission," 11.
37. Email correspondence with the artist, 18 September 2014.

38. English translation from Hassan's Musa website, http://www.pascalpolar.be/site/oeuvresview.php?no_inv=musa-01-18. The original appeared on: http://www.maitre-eolas.fr/post/2006/07/10/397-le-coup-de-boule-de-zidane-est-il-passible-de-la-correctionnelle.
39. Ibid.
40. For histories of football within the political history of France and Algeria, see: Dine, "France, Algeria and Sport," 495–505; Dubois, *Soccer Empire*, 177–197.
41. Hassan Musa's website, http://www.pascalpolar.be/site/oeuvresview.php?no_inv=hm-01-059.
42. Winterstein, "The Other Algeria," http://www.ohio.edu/sportsafrica/journal/Volume3/theotheralgeria_winterstein.htm.
43. Jiwani, "Sports as a Civilizing Mission," 26, 28.
44. Galeano, "The 2006 World Cup," in *Soccer in Sun and Shadow*.

Works Cited

Anwer, Ahmer Nadeem. "Zizou's Cup of Woe: A Mythic Moment Re-Read." *Social Scientist* 34, no. 9/10 (September–October, 2006): 94–103.

Beugnet, Martine, and Elizabeth Ezra. "A Portrait of the Twenty-First Century." *Screen* 50, (Spring 1, 2009): 77–85.

Birtwistle, Andy. "Douglas Gordon and Cinematic Audiovisuality in the Age of Television: Experiencing the Experience of Cinema." *Visual Culture in Britain* 13, no. 1 (2012): 100–113.

Coblentz, Cassandra. "Multiplicities and Singularities: Lyle Ashton Harris Takes a Picture." In *Lyle Ashton Harris: Blow Up*, edited by Cassandra Coblentz, 49–68. Scottsdale/New York: Scottsdale Museum of Contemporary Art/Gregory R. Miller & Co, 2008.

Coumoundouros, Antonis. "Plato and the Greatness of the Game." In *Soccer and Philosophy: Beautiful Thoughts on the Beautiful Game*, edited by Ted Richards, 63–74. Chicago/La Salle: Open Court, 2010.

Critchley, Simon. "Working-Class Ballet." In *The Sports Show: Athletics as Image and Spectacle*, edited by David E. Little, 60–68. Minneapolis: Minneapolis Institute of Arts, 2012.

Dauncey, Hugh, and Geoff Hare, eds. *France and the 1998 World Cup: The National Impact of a World Sporting Event*. Abingdon/New York: Routledge, 1999.

Dessanay, Margherita. "Adel Abdessemed: Art with a Hammer." *Elephant* 14, (2013): 88–99.

Dine, Philip. "France, Algeria and Sport: From Colonisation to Globalisation." *Modern & Contemporary France* 10, no. 4, (Spring 2002): 495–505

Dubois, Laurent. *Soccer Empire: The World Cup and the Future of France*. Berkeley: University of California Press, 2010.

Fried, Michael. "Absorbed in the Action." *Artforum* 45, (September 1, 2006): 332–335, 398.

Galeano, Eduardo. *Soccer in Sun and Shadow*. Translated by Mark Fried. New York: Open Road, 2014; Revised ed 1995.

Griffin, Tim. "The Job Changes You." *Artforum* 45, (September 1, 2006): 336–339

Guénif-Souilamas, Nacira. "Zidane: Portrait of the Artist as Political Avatar." Translated by Naomi Baldinger. In *Frenchness and the African Diaspora: Identity and Uprising in Contemporary France*, edited by Peter Bloom, Ch. Didier Gondola, and Charles Tshimanga, 205–226. Bloomington: Indiana University Press, 2009.

Haree, Geoff. *Football in France: A Cultural History*. Oxford/New York: Berg, 2003.

Jiwani, Yasmin. "Sports as a Civilizing Mission: Zinedine Zidane and the Infamous Head-butt." *Topia: Canadian Journal of Cultural Studies* 19, (Spring 11, 2008): 11–33.

Marks, John. "The French National Team and National Identity: 'Cette France d'un 'bleu metis.'" In *France and the 1998 World Cup: The National Impact of a World Sporting Event*, edited by Hugh Dauncey and Geoff Hare, 41–57. London/New York: Routledge, 1999.

Mohaiemen, Naeem, and Haig Aivazian. Six-Shooters and Nationalist Stamps: A Conversation Between Naeem Mohaiemen and Haig Aivazian." *The Arab Studies Journal* 18, (Spring 1, 2010): 270–287.

Myerscough, Paul. "Short Cuts." *London Review of Books* 28, (October 19, 2006): 22.

Simonyi, Sonja, and Niels Van Tomme. "Real-Time Spectacles: Two Artworks and the Representation of Soccer." *Afterimage* 36, (May/June 6, 2009): 5–11.

Touissant, Jean-Philippe. "Zidane's Melancholy." Translated by Thangam Ravindranathan and Timothy Bewes. *New Formations* 62, (Autumn, 2007): 12–14.

Winterstein, David. "The Other Algeria: Zidane, World Cup Soccer, Globalization, and the Media." *Impumelelo: the Interdisciplinary Electronic Journal of African Sports* 3, (2008). http://www.ohio.edu/sportsafrica/journal/Volume3/theo-theralgeria_winterstein.htm.

PART II

Collective Psychology and Group Identity

Soccer in the Shadow of Death: Propaganda and Survival in the Nazi Ghetto-Camp of Terezín

Kevin E. Simpson

As the world's game, soccer captivates the imagination, stokes the competitive nature, and arouses intense emotion. And the political manipulation of these passions has a long history. One of the most notorious examples of the exploitation of the game of soccer is found in the story of a competitive league created by Jewish prisoners within one of the most infamous camps in the Nazi concentration camp system, Terezín, in former Czechoslovakia. Most accounts of the corruption of soccer in this era have been exclusively historical and political. The present essay addresses the legacy of the Holocaust through a unique, cross-disciplinary approach. The field of social psychology enhances historical interpretation though an exploration of the interplay between the sociocultural phenomenon of soccer in a wartime concentration camp and the psychology of the victims held captive in the Nazi terror state.

Originally named Theresienstadt, Terezín was a garrison town built in the nineteenth century during the reign of the Habsburg Empire.[1] Created

K.E. Simpson (✉)
Department of Psychology, John Brown University,
Siloam Springs, Arkansas, USA

© Hofstra University 2017
B. Elsey, S. Pugliese (eds.), *Football and the Boundaries of History*,
DOI 10.1057/978-1-349-95006-5_4

as a citadel-style fortress, the provincial town of Theresienstadt existed for nearly two centuries as a casern for royal armies but it wasn't until the middle of the twentieth century that the fortress was used not as a defensive barrier but instead as a prison. As part of Germany's expansionist war in Europe, Terezín served for three-and-a-half years as a ghetto-camp unique in the Nazi sphere. Located 40 miles north of Prague in the German "Protectorate" of Bohemia, Terezín was both a transit camp and a collection center for Jews eventually destined for "re-settlement to the east," the cryptic euphemism for transport to the killing centers in Poland. Intended to camouflage the true nature of Nazi policy, Terezín was a settlement ghetto where thousands perished due to starvation and disease. The vast majority of those who managed to survive the deplorable living conditions were eventually deported to their deaths in the east. Presented to the world as a model ghetto, Terezín also had the remarkable distinction of being a place of culture and profound artistic expression. The strength of the human spirit was on full display in the theatrical, musical, artistic, and sporting endeavors pursued by the prisoners. Situated at the heart of these acts of survival and rebellion was the "beautiful game."

Within this tragedy are two seemingly incompatible stories of corruption and heroism. Labeled by the inhabitants, *Liga Terezín*, organized soccer flourished in the worst conditions imaginable. The story rightly begins with a brief history of the camp and an explanation of why soccer was allowed to exist in this prison at all. To this end—and essential to the ruse of the camp as a "paradise" destination—was the use of propaganda film.[2] Nazi propagandists saw a unique opportunity to manipulate the most popular ball-sport in Europe and images from the last match of *Liga Terezín* were incorporated heavily into this propaganda film intended to mask the murderous purposes of the camp. The final section of the chapter will then address the legacy of the soccer in Terezín, as a memorial both to those who were lost in the Holocaust and to those who see soccer as a means by which society might combat modern-day racism and anti-Semitism.

Background on Terezín: Life in a Ghetto-Camp

To understand the existence of organized league soccer in one of the most unimaginable places, a Nazi concentration camp, one must begin with a description of the ghetto-camp of Terezín. Terezín was a show-camp in occupied Czechoslovakia, cynically designed to mask the genocidal actions of the Nazi regime in Eastern Europe. Declared by the occupiers as an "autonomous ghetto" under Jewish self-administration, Terezín is notorious as being a transit point on the deportation route to Auschwitz and other killing centers. This was the case particularly for Jews deported from the greater German Reich who were led to believe that they were relocating to a "spa-town" where they would spend their days in comfortable retirement. Created to hold "Jews who would be missed," Terezín contained prominent Jews from across Europe, many of whom were elderly and had served in the military or who had celebrity status in the arts or other areas of cultural life. Typically, these Jews came from major European cities, most notably Berlin, Prague, and Amsterdam. Regardless of their land of origin, all of these luminaries fell prey to the lie that they would be spared forced labor. This elaborate deception engulfed a wide range of gifted artists, musicians, scientists, writers, and, relevant to this analysis, footballers.

Initially built to accommodate a civilian population of 7000, Theresienstadt reached a peak of 58,497 persons in 1942 as transports bringing thousands of aged and war-disabled Reich Jews arrived, flooding the ghetto and presenting camp officials with unsolvable problems.[3] Not surprisingly, living conditions in the ghetto-camp quickly deteriorated with available housing, food and water, and medical facilities made intentionally inadequate. Scientist-designed feeding schemes were designed to keep prisoners barely alive. Ultimately, overcrowding, pestilential disease, hard labor, and starvation diets made survival all but impossible except for the young and the healthy. If one survived the abhorrent living conditions, there still remained the casual cruelty of the SS guards, which often meant beatings and executions for the most minor of offenses.

At the close of 1942, the deadliest year in the history of the ghetto-camp, the first steps were being taken to organize the well-known visit of the International Red Cross (IRC) to Theresienstadt. This is also the period in which organized soccer emerged in Terezín. In response to the deportation of nearly 500 Danish Jews to Terezín in October 1943, the Danish government immediately and relentlessly demanded inspection of the camp. International pressure had mounted on the Nazi regime after these deportations and within a few months, a visit by the IRC was arranged. After lengthy negotiations, delegates from the IRC and the Danish Red Cross visited the ghetto of Theresienstadt on June 23,

1944. To ready the camp for the Red Cross inspection, the SS ordered a major beautification project (also known as the "embellishment" in the camp) and deportations intensified immediately including the transport of 5000 prisoners starting in April 1944 to reduce the appearance of overcrowding.

Jewish prisoners were then enlisted to help create the façade of a "model ghetto" to the outside world. Buildings were cleaned up and painted, streets were cleaned, and park benches and flower gardens appeared from nowhere. New facilities were also created which included a children's playground and a music pavilion in the town center, along with a refurbished café, a ghetto bank, and a transformed gymnasium made to look a performance stage with accompanying prayer hall and library.[4] When it came time for the inspection, the representatives of the IRC followed a predetermined path (marked with a red line on maps provided them) through the ghetto and the group never deviated from the tour route prepared by the Germans. The tour lasted a mere 8 hours and any questions directed to camp residents were ignored, per the instructions given to the residents by the SS guards.[5] Despite the highly orchestrated nature of the tour, the visit of the IRC represented a major propaganda victory for the Nazi occupiers. Ultimately, the deception was made complete: the favorable reports which followed prevented inspection of the more extensive killing center at Auschwitz-Birkenau when that death camp was operating at maximum efficiency.

In the four years that the ghetto-camp of Terezín was in operation, just over 155,000 people entered this walled town with nearly 88,000 sent to their deaths in the camps in the East. In fact, of those who were deported to extermination camps, just 3097 survived.[6] Another 35,000 died within the ghetto itself and most of these victims were children and the elderly. At the end of the war, Terezín's role changed to that of a reception center for those in mixed marriages from the Reich, Jews from Hungary and Slovakia, and after April 1945, prisoners forced on the infamous death marches. On May 9, 1945, the Soviet Red Army liberated Theresienstadt. At the time of liberation there were about 30,000 Jews in Theresienstadt, most of who were concentration camp survivors. Those who had survived had arrived at Terezín when deportations had largely stopped and living conditions had marginally improved. Clearly, Terezín played an extraordinary role in the imperialist and propaganda operations of Nazi Germany. The story of how these propaganda messages were created follows.

The Propaganda Films

Coinciding with the summer 1944 visit of the IRC, the initial planning of the propaganda film started in December 1943. At the same time, the beautification program was initiated and it wasn't until seven weeks later, after the visit of the IRC on June 23, 1944, that actual filming began. The cruel irony is that Jews were not only forced to make a film designed to obscure their own suffering and devastation, but they were also forced to fund the film as well using wealth stolen from them as they originally entered them camp. After 11 days, the filming was completed in early September 1944.[7]

Officially called *Theresienstadt: A Documentary Film from the Jewish Settlement Area*, the film was directed by the famous German actor and cabaret star Kurt Gerron, a one-time costar with Hollywood legend Marlene Dietrich. In collaboration with Prague newsreel company *Aktualita*, the film wasn't fully completed until March 1945, only two months before the German surrender that ended the war in Europe. Produced predominately for foreign consumption, the film went missing after the war but not before there was a limited screening for high-ranking SS officers and, at a separate viewing, to a select group of delegates of the IRC.[8] Thinking that his involvement would save his life, Gerron poured himself into the project. But tragically, Kurt Gerron was sent on the very last transport from Terezín to Auschwitz, where he soon perished in the gas chambers.

Consisting of more than a quarter of the running time for the 90-minute film, the final match of the professional-level soccer league at Terezín dominates the propaganda effort. The September 11, 1944, match between the *Kleiderkammer* (used clothing store) and the *Jugendfursorge* (children's care unit) is featured and individual players are easily identified. Both teams emerge from the tunnel for the warm-up, the pre-match handshakes, and the coin toss with the referee. Children and other spectators, likely numbering close to 2000, ring the courtyard pitch, devoid of grass. Arcades, three stories high, are filled to capacity with onlookers. Much of the play on the dirt field appears to be at a high level as the competitors give a genuine spirited effort.

The power of propaganda has long captivated psychologists and historians alike. Professionals from both fields share an interest in revealing the mechanisms of influence in mass persuasion. A foremost expert on the propaganda films of Terezín is Dutch historian Karel Margry. In an interview for a 2010 Israeli-produced documentary on the main league at Terezín, he observed: "The surprising thing is how long the football sequence is. It makes football in Theresienstadt look more important than it was, which is part of the propaganda idea behind it. The SS realized that football is something that not just the people in the ghetto, but people all over the world liked."[9] Clearly, the SS overlords recognized the propaganda value by featuring soccer so prominently in the film, which also includes other sporting activities such as swimming, women's handball, and select track and field events. Altogether, the film creates a "summer camp effect,"[10] reinforcing the myth that the Jews had arrived at a vacation destination, replete with rich leisure and cultural opportunities. Though no complete copies of the film have ever been found, the sobering reality is that the vast majority of those people involved in the creation of the film, both as players and as spectators, were murdered mere days after the end of filming.

In a likely prologue to the main film, an earlier Terezín film was directed by Jewish inmate Irene Dodalova and filmed by German security police (SD) cameramen in late 1942. This time period in the ghetto-camp was the apex of suffering and death for the prisoners at Terezín as overcrowding, disease, and starvation devastated the captives. Soccer appears briefly in this film as prisoners played pick-up games on elevated embankments around the fortress. Matches were played on cold, muddy ground with a few spectators gathered, and the newly constructed crematorium ominously visible in the background of these scenes from the film. Intended to reflect a more realistic "normality," the amateur soccer from late October of 1942 coincided with the worst period of the ghetto when the death rate was the highest (e.g., nearly 4000 perished in the month prior to the filming of the soccer scenes).[11]

Curiously, the dated black and white film remains a powerful piece of propaganda, incomplete as it is. Yet, when final editing had been completed, several months after the filming, neither of the propaganda films from Terezín was shown to any audience outside of Germany, as was the original plan. One player who survived this madness was Honza Burka, a star player of *Liga Terezín*. Burka played at left-back and long after the war he recalled the great difficulty he encountered when trying to relate to his ghetto experiences in his post-Holocaust life: "We didn't try to explain, because nobody would understand us," he recalls. "I'm very lucky that in this film, I see myself playing football. (This means) that everything was true, not a story I was telling to somebody."[12] Even 70 years after the events, the power of Nazi propaganda to corrupt remains evident. Witness the easy access of the surviving film clips on Internet websites such as

YouTube, so readily employed by Holocaust deniers in their grotesque perversion of historical fact for many years after the war.

Liga Terezín

Prior to the outbreak of war in Europe, soccer captivated the collective imagination of the sporting public across the continent. But during World War II, the great majority of the domestic European leagues ceased playing. Well before the Nazi takeover of their country, soccer in Czechoslovakia was among the very best in the world. At the 1934 World Cup held in Italy, the Czech national team narrowly lost the cup final to the host Italians, 2:1. And presaging what the Nazis would do at Terezín, it was the Italians who used the 1934 World Cup as an ideological platform for the purported successes of fascism. With this history as a prologue, competitive soccer continued to flourish in the most unlikely of places: the Nazi concentration camp of Terezín.

The great majority of the players in the highest league at Terezín were of Jewish descent but many nationalities across Europe were represented, including German, Dutch, Slovak, and Danish prisoners. Within the concentration camp, teams were organized by the professions represented in the camp. For example, teams were drawn from groups such as ghetto police and guards, electricians, butchers, and kitchen workers, and because this was a highly desired pursuit within the camp due to the additional food rations given to players, a spot on one of these teams was highly desired. Therefore, it is not surprising that those teams with ready access to food and sustenance, like the kitchen and butchers' teams, were among the league leaders during the time the league was in operation, from 1942 to late fall 1944 (Fig. 4.1).

Without a doubt, Liga Terezín was an escape and a type of resistance against a death sentence. When one reads the few survivor accounts from this time period, there was pronounced enjoyment found in playing the sport regardless of the amateur or professional status of the player. A number of national team players from the Czechoslovakia national team, along with a handful of professional level soccer players drawn from Olympic and professional teams prior to the war, all competed in the top ghetto league. Soccer was also played among the youth and amateur captives of the camp. In fact, the youth players were very excited about the possibility of such a diversion in a place designed to strip them of their dignity and, ultimately, of their lives. Interestingly, the art created by the children of

Fig. 4.1 Souvenir poster of the Liga Terezín ghetto team, "Aeskulap" (From Herrmann´s Collection of the Terezín Memorial, Czech Republic, watercolor by W. Thalheimer. © Zuzana Dvořáková)

Terezín also became well known, even outside of Holocaust studies, and league soccer shows up in the newspapers, drawings, collages, and journals kept by children in the ghetto. Moreover, children particularly loved to watch and to compete. In the aforementioned (final) propaganda film, you can readily see numerous children seated in the garrison's arcades watching the final match.

It is remarkable to realize that in the final year in the operation of the ghetto-camp, there were nearly 3000 men and women who played soccer, often on the ramparts atop the earthen walls of the fortress. Typically, at the highest level there would be 12 teams competing, usually playing in the spring and autumn seasons when the weather was most suitable for play. For the elite-level players, tournaments were held in the courtyard of the Dresden barracks and matches typically included seven-a-side with three strikers, a midfielder, two defenders and a goalkeeper. Not surprisingly, teams were required to have the yellow star on their new uniforms, which were often created by other inmates within the ghetto. Professional referees were recruited and matches usually lasted 60 to 70 minutes. Games were often high-scoring affairs and at the highest level of play, team captains sometimes traded team flags before matches.

Practical considerations were also evident in the administration of Liga Terezín. Because of the transitory nature of the camp, as it was a transfer camp for extermination centers such as Auschwitz-Birkenau in southern Poland, team composition changed frequently. Replacing deported and deceased players presented a challenge for organizers and bizarrely, survivors reported that there was a transfer window session on Mondays from 10 to 2 p.m. to replace players who had been lost during the previous week. Results from the matches were posted in a public place, usually at the seat of the Jewish council of elders, also known as the *Judenrat* (Fig. 4.2).

The council of elders supported the league and often the championship matches were opened by a delegate of this council. The *Judenrat* also set up discipline commissions and awarded prizes to the winners of the league in a given season. Makeshift ghetto newspapers, often published by the Jewish children in the ghetto, provided match results, game statistics, and league standings.

It was in the early fall of 1943 that the league continued during a peak period of deprivation and suffering. Players competed with a profound physical hunger and under daily threats of beatings and deportation.

	Arb. Zentr.	Elek- triker	Fleischer	Gärt- ner	Hagib. Prag	Hagib. TTherac.	Jugend Fürs.	Kader	Kleid. Kamm.	Köche	Praga	Wien	Punkte +e	Gesamt score
Arb. Zentr.		5:2	3:3	1:6	4:2	6:1	3:4	2:2	3:8	1:7	8:3	14:2	12	50:40
Elek- triker	2:5		2:0	2:4	6:8	4:2	0:7	2:2	3:5	1:6	7:3	4:2	9	33:44
Flei- scher	3:3	0:2		4:3	4:0	5:2	4:12	8:1	1:2	2:7	8:3	11:3	13	51:38
Gärt- ner	6:1	4:2	3:4		3:4	4:5	1:8	4:1	1:9	3:4	4:3	7:1	10	40:42
Hagib. Prag	2:4	8:6	3:4	4:3		8:3	6:5	1:6	6:11	5:8	2:1	3:3	11	48:59
Hagib. Theres.	1:6	2:4	2:6	5:4	3:8		1:15	4:3	0:8	3:15	2:5	1:3	4	24:77
Jugend Fürs.	4:3	7:0		8:1	5:6	15:1		5:4	3:9	3:3	2:3	4:3	15	68:37
Kader	2:2	2:2	1:8	1:4	6:1	3:4	4:5		2:5	4:9	2:2	4:4	6	31:46
Kleid. Kamm.	8:3	5:3	2:1	9:1	11:6	8:0	9:3	5:2		4:6	7:2	9:3	20	77:30
Köche	7:1	6:1	7:2	4:3	8:5	15:3	3:3	9:4	6:4		5:3	12:2	21	82:31
Praga	3:8	3:7	3:8	3:4	1:2	5:2	3:2	2:2	2:7	3:5		6:1	7	34:48
Wien	2:14	2:4	3:11	1:7	3:3	3:1	3:4	4:4	3:9	2:12	1:6		4	35:67

Fig. 4.2 Final table from the autumn 1943 Liga Terezín football league in Ghetto Terezín (From Herrmann's Collection of the Terezín Memorial, Czech Republic. © Zuzana Dvořáková)

Among the spectators there were SS officers who had reserved special box seats in the center of the barracks courtyard. By many survivor accounts, these torturers and murderers often applauded loudly and enthusiastically during the matches.[13] But in the end, the vast majority of the players at the professional and at the amateur levels were ultimately deported to other camps as the Allied armies closed in on Terezín at the close of the war. Yet, one famous survivor of Liga Terezín is the one-time Czech national team goalkeeper Jirka Taussig, well known to the prisoners and their Nazi captors even before his arrival in the camp in 1943. Taussig recalled that one of the few ways to survive the camp was to play soccer (Fig. 4.3).

Of his playing days with the remnant clothing department team (the *Kleiderkammer* squad), Taussig remembers fondly: "We were the stars of Terezín; every Sunday afternoon 3,500 fans came to watch the league matches. Youth saw us as a model to imitate, we gave them hope, and we represented life. In all the misery and suffering hope was a rare thing! We played for them, because we knew that shortly they would be sent East and we felt that we gave them a little spark of light before their death."[14]

Fig. 4.3 Czech goalkeeper Jirka Taussig making a save in the final match of Liga Terezín (Photo taken from Nazi propaganda film. © Chronos-Media, Germany.)

LEGACY OF *LIGA TEREZÍN*

Sport has the power to change the world. It has the power to inspire, it has
the power to unite people in a way that little else does. It speaks to youth in
a language they understand. Sport can create hope, where once there was
only despair. It is more powerful than governments in breaking down racial
barriers. It laughs in the face of all types of discrimination.

*Speech by Nelson Mandela at the Inaugural Laureus Lifetime Achievement
Award*[15]

By documenting the story of soccer in places like Terezín, we honor the
memory of those lost during the Holocaust. We remember those who
chose sport as a means of hope and inspiration. We also challenge, in the
most forceful manner, Holocaust denial, so easily disseminated in this digital age. Football also serves as a medium, especially with younger genera-
tions, passionate about the game, who often cannot comprehend the scale
of death and destruction contained in the Holocaust. Football bridges
this generation gap. In light of the fact that the firsthand witnesses to the
Holocaust are rapidly decreasing in number with each year that passes, the
urgency of sharing this legacy becomes more evident.

Today, the modern-day Dresden Barracks, where most of the *Liga
Terezín* matches were once played, are dilapidated and in significant disrepair, off limits to the numerous visitors who come to Terezín each year.
In contemporary Prague, another important memorial to the thousands
of Czechs lost in the Holocaust is the Pinkas Synagogue. Inscribed on
the walls of this once-active synagogue are 77,297 names of souls lost
to Nazi aggression, drawn from registration lists, transport papers, and
survivor accounts. In our day, the victims have a name. And one name in
particular stands out, located in the Brno section of the memorial wall:
Pavel Breda, a player from *Liga Terezín* and one who materializes from
the past when the opening scenes of the football montage are shown
from the propaganda film. Breda is the second player seen as the teams
run on to the field for the match. The heroism of the persecuted, captured on film, creates many evocative images that powerfully reverberate
forward into history.

In the years after the war, Europe has witnessed a number of demo-
graphic revolutions, many of them originating in post-colonial migrations
from Africa and Eastern Europe to countries in Western Europe. The
steady flow of new immigrants from the south and east has challenged

long established national identities. Consequently, there is wide variation in how well these immigrant groups have been incorporated into mainstream society. In many cases, these trends give rise to political extremes in the last two decades of activist groups espousing right-wing nationalism and anti-immigration views.[16]

Likewise, football reflects these reactionary movements as foreign players have increased in number across many European domestic leagues, in what might be called a football migration.[17] For instance, elite clubs like Chelsea and Arsenal in England recently fielded teams comprised entirely of foreign players. In Eastern Europe, the old prejudices against Jews and Roma have been easily generalized to newly arriving African and Asian football migrants and against black players on visiting teams.[18] However, racist and fascist organizing on the terraces largely disappeared by late 1990s across Europe.[19] Some of this progress may be attributed to the anti-racism campaigns set up at the same time to combat such prejudice and discrimination (e.g., English footballers appearing in the *KICK IT OUT* campaign). Yet, before a 2010 Polish premier league contest, an anti-Semitic banner was unfurled in the stands without consequence for the home club. Much more recent examples of racism are also rampant in Italian and Spanish soccer, with the most visible and egregious examples including "monkey taunts" and bananas thrown onto the field from the stands on a regular basis.[20]

Though most football associations have in place punishments for racist chanting by spectators and players alike, these policies are not consistently enforced nor do any resulting punishments bring any lasting effect. In an incident from October 2004, a Dutch referee was the first to abandon a game when sexist and anti-Semitic chants at The Hague versus PSV Eindhoven match persisted despite crowd warnings.[21] Regrettably, within the last decade, a fan awaiting the start of a match in the Dutch first division would not be surprised to hear anti-Semitic chants rising up from the crowd, including the sounds of hissing gas meant to recall the Nazi gas chambers and others giving the Hitler salute as select visiting teams arrive at the stadium.[22] Chants such as these are frequently used against fans of teams with historical links to Jewish communities: Ajax of Amsterdam, Argentina's Atlanta, and Tottenham Hotspurs of north London.[23] Though anti-Semitism has been appropriated by opposing fans, especially in Holland, it is important to note that these displays are not usually about anti-Judaism. Amid these recent trends in immigration, Jews themselves have eased into the background as primary targets of genuine hate and derision.[24]

Through narrative accounts and rare photographs from Terezín capturing the prisoner experience we are provided the moral rationale for rejecting the indifference of the "bystander effect" studied so richly by psychologists for decades. With a commitment to resist indifference found in the lives and choices of the footballers at Terezín, we also recognize that soccer has the potential to break down racial, ethnic, and religious barriers. It allows people to unify in a modern age that continues to see anti-Semitism and racism run unabated in the sport. In these stories, we witness the endurance of the human spirit in vigorous competition. And human agency is given a voice again as we consider the psychology of the victim. Soccer in Terezín aroused the competitive drive in a place calculated to strip it away from the individual. In a time when hope was used against the prisoners themselves and deception was a cynical lie told through film and masquerade, football provided resistance and an escape. When confronted with the "pitiless, faceless malevolence of the Nazi death machine,"[25] soccer shined as a humanitarian response to brutality.

NOTES

1. Ludmila Chladkova, *The Terezín Ghetto* (Prague: Pamatnik Terezín, 2005), 4.
2. Karel Margry, "Theresienstadt (1944–1945): The Nazi Propaganda Film Depicting the Concentration Camp as Paradise," *Historical Journal of Film, Radio and Television* 12, no. 2 (1992): 145.
3. Chladkova, *The Terezín Ghetto*, 15.
4. Margry, "Theresienstadt," 146.
5. *Voices of the Holocaust Project*, "David P. Boder Interviews Friedrich Schlaefrig, 23 August 1946," http://voices.iit.edu. Accessed 1 Feb 2014.
6. Martin Winstone, *The Holocaust Sites of Europe: An Historical Guide* (London: IB Taurus, 2010), 169.
7. Margry, "Theresienstadt," 153.
8. Ibid, 154.
9. Mike Schwartz and Avi Kanner, *Liga Terezín* directed by Avi Kanner (2013; Givat Haim Ihud, Israel: Beit Theresienstadt, 2013), DVD.
10. Ibid.

11. Chladkova, *The Terezín Ghetto*, 48.
12. Schwartz and Kanner, *Liga Terezín*.
13. Karpel Dahlia, "Even SS Officers Applauded the Jewish Players of the Soccer League in Terezín," *Haaretz*, April 17, 2009, http://haaretz.com/. Accessed 14 Jan 2014.
14. Beit Terezin Memorial, "Newsletter from the Memorial Archives," August 2009.
15. Nelson Mandela, Inaugural Address, Laureus Lifetime Achievement Award Ceremony, May 25, 2000, Monaco, http://www.laureus.com/.
16. Goldblatt, *The Ball is Round*, (New York: Riverhead Books, 2008), 700.
17. Franklin Foer, *How Soccer Explains the World* (New York: HarperCollins, 2004), 84.
18. Goldblatt, *The Ball is Round*, 769.
19. Gabriel Kuhn, *Soccer vs. the State: Soccer Tackling Football and Radical Politics* (Oakland: PM Press, 2011) 146.
20. Foer, *How Soccer Explains the World*, 85.
21. Kuhn, *Soccer vs. the State*, 95.
22. Simon Kuper, *Ajax, the Dutch, the War: The Strange Tale of Soccer During Europe's Darkest Hour* (New York: Nation Books, 2012), 224.
23. Ibid, 94.
24. Foer, *How Soccer Explains the World*, 85.
25. Norbert Troller, *Theresienstadt: Hitler's Gift to the Jews* (Chapel Hill: UNC Press, 1991), xxx.

Works Cited

Beit Terezin Memorial (Israel). *Newsletter from the Memorial Archives*. August 2009, no. 67 (2009), http://bterezin.org.il. Accessed 1 Feb 2014.
Chladkova, Ludmila. *The Terezín Ghetto*. Prague: Pamatnik Terezín, 2005.
Foer, Franklin. *How Soccer Explains the World*. New York: HarperCollins, 2004.
Goldblatt, David. *The Ball Is Round: A Global History of Soccer*. New York: Riverhead Books, 2008.
Hájková, Anna. "The Fabulous Boys of Theresienstadt: Young Czech Men as the Dominant Social Elite in the Theresienstadt Ghetto". In *Im Ghetto: Neue Forschungen zu Alltag und Umfeld* [Contributions to the History of National Socialism], edited by Christoph Dieckmann and Babette Quinkert, Vol. 25. Göttingen: Wallstein Verlag, 2009.

Hoffmann, Hilmar. *The Triumph of Propaganda: Film and National Socialism.* Providence: Berghahn, 1996.

Karpel, Dahlia. "Even SS Officers Applauded the Jewish Players of the Soccer League in Terezín". *Haaretz,* 2009. http://haaretz.com/, April 17, 2009. Accessed 14 Jan 2014.

Kuhn, Gabriel. *Soccer vs. the State: Soccer Tackling Football and Radical Politics.* Oakland: PM Press, 2011.

Kuper, Simon. *Ajax, The Dutch, the War: The Strange Tale of Soccer During Europe's Darkest Hour.* New York: Nation Books, 2012.

Mandela, Nelson. Inaugural Address, Laureus Lifetime Achievement Award Ceremony, May 25, 2000, Monaco, 2000. http://www.laureus.com/. Accessed 12 Feb 2014.

Margry, Karel. "The First Theresienstadt Film (1942)". *Historical Journal of Film, Radio and Television* 19, no. 3 (1999): 303–337.

———. "Theresienstadt (1944–1945): The Nazi Propaganda Film Depicting the Concentration Camp as Paradise". *Historical Journal of Film, Radio and Television* 12, no. 2 (1992): 145–162.

———. "The Concentration Camp as Idyll: Theresienstadt – A Documentary from the Jewish Settlement Area. In *Geschichte, Rezeption und Wirkung: Jahrbuch 1996 zur Geschichte und Wirkung des Holocaust,* 319–352. Frankfurt: Fritz Bauer Institut, 1996.

Schwartz, Mike, and Avi Kanner. *Liga Terezín,* DVD. Directed by Avi Kanner. Givat Haim Ihud. Israel: Beit Theresienstadt, 2013.

Steiner, Frantisek. *Fotbal Pod Zlutou Hvezdou ("Soccer Under the Yellow Star").* Prague: Olympia, 2009.

Troller, Norbert. *Theresienstadt: Hitler's Gift to the Jews.* Chapel Hill: UNC Press, 1991.

Voices of the Holocaust Project. *David P. Boder Interviews Friedrich Schlaefrig, 23 August 1946.* http://voices.iit.edu. Accessed 1 Feb 2014.

Volavkova, Hana. *I Never Saw Another Butterfly...Children's Drawings and Poems from Terezín Concentration Camp, 1942–1944.* New York: Schocken Books, 1993.

Winstone, Martin. *The Holocaust Sites of Europe: An Historical Guide.* London: IB Taurus, 2010.

CHAPTER 5

In the Shadow of the State: The National Team and the Politics of National Identity in Spain

Jim O'Brien

Spain is not a nation, National Unity was a reality historically imposed by the Absolute Monarchy and has been maintained all along by the political regimes of contemporary Spain.[1]

Spanish national identity is complex and difficult to define. It has been and continues to be subject to political and ideological intervention and persuasion, as Solís suggests. The success of the Spanish national team in recent years, confirmed by the 2010 World Cup victory in Johannesburg and secured by Iniesta's winning goal, suggested the unifying capacity of football in fusing symbols and rituals of shared identity, bringing together the historically contested ethnicities and nationalisms of the contemporary Spanish state as a focal point expressing what Quiroga has termed "dual identity" through which support for *La Selección*[2] can be reconciled with deeply rooted traditions of allegiance to regionally and locally based football identities and rivalries.

J. O'Brien (✉)
Department of Journalism, Southampton Solent University,
Southampton, England

© Hofstra University 2017
B. Elsey, S. Pugliese (eds.), *Football and the Boundaries of History*,
DOI 10.1057/978-1-349-95006-5_5

73

This success has led to a burgeoning literature examining the historic, political and cultural aspects that have shaped contemporary Spanish football. Both Phillip Ball's *Morbo: The story of Spanish football* and Jimmy Burns, *La Roja: A journey through Spanish Football* and Burns *La Roja* cover similar ground in their studies, contextualizing the development of the Spanish game from its genesis in the last decades of the nineteenth century within wider political and societal dynamics. Their studies present valuable perspectives on Spanish club football while explaining the paradoxes surrounding *La Selección*. Quiroga examines Spanish football as a metaphor for contested identities and alternative nationalisms, critically assessing the relationship between *La Roja* and cultural sensibilities around national and regional ethnicities in contemporary Spain. Indeed, as Burns asserts, the achievements of *La Roja* struck a rare note of harmony amidst the discordant voices of protest, recession and resurgent claims for separatism and independence which have reverberated around Spain since Iniesta's iconoclastic goal, as the team embraced a mix of Spain's regional identities.[3]

While the player has been lauded every time he enters or leaves the pitch, the complex interplay of history, politics and culture persists within the framing and representation of the national team and its relationship to the rich tapestry of club and regional identities in Spain. The success of *La Roja* is set against a backdrop of frequent failure for *La Selección*, so that concepts of nation and nationhood remain keenly contested, with the historic legacy of the perception of a lack of patriotism and empathy for Spain due to their deeply embedded identification with ethno-regional peripheries within the cultural synthesis of the game's folklore in the Spanish state.[4] Football was and is at the core of these debates.

The game's foundation in the late nineteenth century drew on the developing significance of the educational value of sport, particularly in the regions of Catalonia, Navarre and the Basque Country.[5] Football became associated with defining regional identities within these parameters. As the structure of the Spanish state was ideologically contested in the 1920s and 1930s, the game's gradual expansion became a more important aspect of its apparatus.[6] Under Franco, the synthesis involving sport, football and ideology defined state centralism and control permeating every level of Spanish society. The fortunes of *La Selección* have always operated in the shadow of the Spanish state, whatever its political and ideological predilection.

The central tenet of this chapter is to examine the development of the national team since its debut in the 1920 Antwerp Olympic Games. From that folkloric participation it has served as a catalyst for the complexities surrounding constructions of "Spanishness," raising questions pertaining to the coherence, legitimacy and governance of the Spanish state per se. Football's intricate involvement in these processes has been a political barometer of archetypal center–region tensions. The game's burgeoning role as a mass spectacle has been exploited by both the Spanish state and its opponents as cultural articulations of distinctive ethnicities and identities, notably in defining the dichotomy between Madrid, Catalonia and the Basque Country. The history of *La Selección* in the Spanish political landscape reinforces the notion of an interwoven pattern of regionalism, nationalism, globalism and glocalism defining Spain as a group of nations.[7]

This chapter considers a set of case studies in order to shed light on the role of the Spanish national team in reflecting, framing and expressing the political and cultural debate around Spanish identity; it begins with an evaluation of *La Selección* in the Antwerp Olympics, a seminal moment regarding the team's success and in the symbolism and iconography surrounding the dualism of the fabled *La Furia* as the legacy of the tournament, and the subsequent framing of El Fatalismo to define the mold in which the national team was historically cast, and concludes with the contemporary branding and representation of *La Roja* to contextualize a contemporary, mature, democratic Spanish nation, in which "Spanishness" could be celebrated alongside Spain's divergent ethnicities.[8] Consideration is also accorded to Spain's participation in the Brazil 1950 World Cup, Franco's triumph in the 1964 European Nations Cup, Spain's hosting of the 1982 World Cup and achievement in reaching the final of the 1984 Nations Cup in France. The relationship between nation, state and region and the capacity of the game to reflect political and cultural cohesion, division and fragmentation has permeated the landscape of Spanish football from the factionalism unleashed by the renaissance of the historic communities in 1898 to contemporary claims for autonomy in the Basque Country and Catalonia. Football has defined both continuity and change around its constructions and representations of contested nationalisms, in its regional power centers and as the national side started to emerge in the 1920s. As the Spanish state has embraced monarchy, republic, civil war, dictatorship and democracy changing political contexts allowed football to be in the vanguard of resurgent regionalism in the 1980s and to symbolize the contemporary debates around separation and independence since 2008. The recent successes of La Roja both reassert the historic debates around *La Selección* as a focal point of center–region tensions and provide a contemporary resonance due to the complex synthesis between

Catalonia, FC Barcelona and the national team. The emotions, representations and distinctive identities underscored by constructions of Spanish,
Basque, Catalan and Galician nationalisms is embedded in these political
and cultural foundations, finding potent expression in the development of
the game. In football terms the success of *La Roja* is set against a historic
backdrop of failure in international competition, in stark contrast to the
repeated success of clubs in European competition since the 1950s, con-
firming the national side's lack of achievement.[9]

LA FURIA AND THE LIONS OF ANTWERP 1920

As prototype of virility on the pitch, "Basque Fury" was transformed into
"Spanish Fury," a concept which was taken up with great delight by the
falange ideology led by Primo de Rivera.[10]

Gomez astutely pinpoints the early capacity of political leaders to utilize
the iconography of football to project wider cultural values. At the time
of the Antwerp Olympics, the Spanish game was amateur and regional in
nature, reflecting the center–regional complexities which had defined the
political landscape since 1898.[11] Football's genesis ushered in regionalism, modernity and a set of socioeconomic developments in the 1880s
and 1890s, with the pivotal year of 1898 witnessing a humiliating military defeat in the loss of Cuba, Imperial Spain's last colonial outpost,
which triggered a crisis of confidence impacting on Spain's political and
cultural life, as the nation struggled to define a new identity. While 1898
was framed as the "Year of Disaster" in Madrid, the eclipse of Empire
was paralleled by cultural renaissance and political turmoil in Catalonia
and the Basque Country. The year was powerfully symbolic for the center–regional dichotomy.[12] By the time the RSFF (Royal Spanish Football
Federation) was set up in 1913[13] club football was already significant in
expressing distinctive nationalisms.

Even as the game gradually evolved in Madrid, it was subject to Basque
and Catalan influences.[14] When *La Selección* first emerged it was subject
to latent fissures around constructions of nation and nationhood, so that
1920 became a metaphor for all the embryonic divisions in the Spanish
psyche, with divergent concepts of nationhood transferred to the game.[15]
Moreover, the team's participation in the Antwerp tournament foreshadowed the dictatorship of Primo de Riviera after the collapse of Alfonso

XIII's monarchy. Any sense of national cohesion and unity was fragile, so that *La Selección* was fraught with difficulties surrounding the composition of the team and its leadership.

Though born in Madrid, Coach Paco Bru had been successful for several years as trainer of FC Barcelona, his approach embodying the spirit of Catalanism. His authority was challenged both by the political intervention of the RSFF in Madrid because the squad was based on Basque and Catalan players, reflecting the strength of club football at the time, and by a player rebellion before the match against Denmark, demanding that only Basque players be included. In the end, Bru refused to capitulate in the face of the competing pressures of centralism and regionalism, so the team, while based on a majority of Basque players, also included Zamora and Samitier, the two Barcelona stars of the period. The strengths and weaknesses of the country were reflected in the performances, both on and off the pitch.[16] "The fact that *La Selección* encompassed most of his choices asserted independence from the centralism of Madrid, but without any notion that the team really represented Spain, though the press of the time attempted to whip up a sense of national pride by asserting that everyone should put the interests of the nation above other more trivial interests and remember that it is not about going to Antwerp as tourists, but playing as ambassadors, to show the world that there is more to Spain than bulls."[17] This reinforced one of the traditional Spanish cultural stereotypes, that of "*pan y toros*" (bread and bulls).

In the tournament the team excelled, winning the Silver Medal, albeit in controversial circumstances, reflecting the complex regulations governing the competition.[18] Two crucial elements emerged from Antwerp 1920.It provided the first international, mediated icons of Spanish football with the team's captain Belauste immortalized as one of the "Lions of Antwerp," exemplifying the team's values and spirit with the decisive goal in the match against Sweden, which he dedicated to Sabino Arana, the founder of the PNV (Basque Nationalist Party). It also witnessed the folkloric genesis of *La Furia Española*, a set of Basque core values which epitomized the team's efforts—hard work, courage, spirit and physical strength. These became synonymous with the framing of "Spanish" values to forge a sense of national identity in the exploitation of the team's success, to become a defining element of Spanish football identity.[19] This created an enduring reference point for *La Selección* to engender an emotive sense of nationhood, based on iconic symbols, rituals and myth building, drawing on the heroic events of the sack of Antwerp (1576) to fuse football with positive legacies of a glorious past. Belauste, whose goal and values embellished the birth of *La Furia*, was paradoxically a political activist and supporter of the PNV. In the labyrinth of football's historical development in Spain, the events of 1920 set the template for much of what transpired in the subsequent development of *La Selección*.[20] This was accompanied by the darker specter of *El Fatalismo*, a combination of bad luck, injustice and poor officiating perceived as characterizing many of the team's displays in international competition, especially against Italy, as evidenced by the World Cups of both 1934 and 1994[21] by which time the master narrative around the national side had become synonymous with failure, fatalism and decadence.[22]

THE GHOST OF ZARRA AND BRAZIL 1950

Zarra was a reference for youth in the fifties, a brilliant decade for Spanish football; not only for his personality as a footballer representing *La Furia Española*, but also for his image as an honest man.[23]

The celebrated achievements of Zarra, as evidenced in Vinolo's study of Spain in the 1950s, cast a shadow across the decade, both within the game itself and in its wider representations. By the time Spain participated in the Brazil World Cup (1950) football and politics had become inextricably linked within rival constructions of ethnicity and identity in the volatile history of the first decades of the twentieth century Spanish state.[24] After the post-civil war years of repression in the 1940s, the tournament in Brazil constituted both the opportunity for the Franco regime to exploit football's potential as a focus of populist mass distraction and a chance to end Spain's isolation from the international stage.[25] The competition was the first occasion for the regime to utilize the burgeoning potential of football to legitimize the notion of a unitary Spanish state to both internal and external publics within the parameters of centralized control and regulation. The success of the team in finishing fourth began a decade in which the exploitation and manipulation of the game as a mass spectacle consolidated the homogenization process of national identity.[26] Although *La Selección* ultimately lost heavily to the hosts, the 1-0 victory over England at the Maracanã in Rio de Janeiro was portrayed in hyperbolic terms by Madrid to celebrate the defeat of the old colonial adversary and the game's ancestral foundation. Zarra, the Basque scorer of the winning goal, became one of Spanish football's iconic figures in the 1950s, reflecting the courage, pride and spirit of *La Furia*.[27] His stardom allowed Franco to use the earlier success of *La Furia Española* so that the Basque values of the Antwerp team became culturally assimilated to express core values of Franco's Spain. As the repression of the 1940s evolved into the austerity of the 1950s, football became critical within the regime as a focus of distraction and diversion. The folkloric deeds of the Antwerp team were merged with the success of the team in Brazil to foster "Spanish" values in the construction of national identity. The attributes of courage, spirit, hard work and the capacity to overcome adversity which epitomized *La Selección* to national and international audiences were adopted by the regime for propagandist purposes to engender a feeling of national pride.

Paradoxically, the 1950 squad contained a majority of Basque and Catalan players, once again highlighting the fragility of the link between football, the nation and *La Selección*. The hard work and team spirit defined in overcoming adversity became interwoven with manufactured "Spanishness" to epitomize those values *El Caudillo* expressly admired; so *La Furia* became interwoven with bullfighting and flamenco as part of the regime's cultural populism and representation of Spanish nationhood.[28] Press and radio coverage of the event was slavishly manipulated by a centralized state apparatus, with talisman Zarra raised to the status of Churchill because of his heroic deeds.[29] In a similar vein, the postvictory telegram sent to Franco by Spanish football official Calero eulogized "Excellency: we have vanquished the perfidious Albion," dedicating the success "to the best *Caudillo* in the world."[30] The goal scored by Zarra became one of the defining moments of the national team embellishing consensus and unity, as No-Do news glorified and constantly replayed this aesthetically ugly goal to engender patriotism and national pride.[31]

In the austere 1950s, football became crucial in the implementation of No-Do as the autocracy's mechanism of cultural control, from the homogenization of club nomenclature in the 1940s to the rise of Real Madrid from the mid-1950s in projecting a positive iconography around the regime in winning the first five European Cups.[32] While the representation of *La Selección* was aimed primarily at domestic consumption, Real Madrid had both an external and an internal function in representing the unitary, centralized state.[33] Ironically, their success was based largely on a cluster of international stars, including Di Stefano, Puskas, Kopa and Santamaria, although television projected the club into the international domain as symbols of a unified Spanish nation, with an ambassadorial role and status. Football was further used in the period as a safety valve in which resistance to the center was contained, especially in the Basque Country and Catalonia, where club flags and symbols were used to express historically rooted alternative nationalisms, as focal points of ethnicity and identity. For Athletic Bilbao and FC Barcelona these rituals replaced proscribed national flags as articulations of dissidence and opposition to Franco.[34] In this sense the regime's exploitation of club rivalry was more sophisticated than its manipulation of *La Selección* to define Spanish unity and division, reflecting the complexity of state intervention in the governance and structures of football.

By the end of the decade, Real Madrid, carefully recast as Franco's team, and the national side, had capitalized on football's growth to constitute a crucial site of political and cultural cohesion, so that "Spanishness" and the nation became juxtaposed within a vortex of Catholicism, control and manufactured consensus within the fabric of the state's apparatus. In the 1940s Real Madrid had been relatively unsuccessful, with the Franco regime supporting Atlético Aviación (subsequently Atlético Madrid). The growth of the club under President Bernabéu and their subsequent success in the 1950s meant that it became a key factor in projecting a positive international profile of Spanish national identity.[35] Moreover, Real Madrid represented the unitary Spanish state, the primacy of center over region. The image of success identified the club with Franco's Spain, so that whenever El Caudillo attended a match at the Bernebéu, the press invariably linked his presence to the profile of Real Madrid. In football's lexicon, *los oriundos*[36] and foreigners were incorporated into the "Spanish" identity of *La Selección*, so that the squad taking part in the Chile World Cup of 1962 contained Di Stefano, Santamaria and Puskas. Their failure to progress beyond a tough group (which included Brazil and Czechoslovakia, the two eventual finalists) incurred press criticism, with *Marca* asserting that "the team is so full of foreigners…that it no longer plays like a team of real Spaniards, with passion, with aggression, with virility, and above all, fury."[37] This brought about a purification process whereby the RSFF acted in tandem with the regime to ban foreigners from the Spanish game until the protracted signing of Johan Cryuff by FC Barcelona in 1974.

MADRID 1964; FOOTBALL AND FRANCO'S NEW SPAIN.

Under Franco, the notion of a single Spanish identity and the promotion of its image were encouraged via football and thus sport's role as a vehicle for frustrated nationalism was contained.[38]

Crolley and Hand define the dual sensibility surrounding Spanish football under Franco. Constructs of nationalism and the role of *La Selección* in framing it became more homogenized, resulting in the genesis of the "New Spain" which played in the semifinals and final of the 1964 European Nations Cup, given credence by the perceived failure of foreign influences in the team.[39] The Madrid final at the Bernabéu, with Franco and his ministers in attendance, cemented the game's politicization in promoting a series of images around the reaffirmation of a coherent Spanish national identity, in which the social drug of football generated interclass appeal within the emergent economic development of Franco's Spain.[40]

By 1964, the autocracy had become astute in recognizing the capacity of football to be exploited for political and cultural objectives. The fascist anthem *Cara al Sol* was sung before matches, and *La Selección* saluted and chanted *¡Arriba Espana! ¡Viva Franco!* to support the regime. Matches were televised to distract the public, especially at politically sensitive times.[41] The 1960 competition had brought about a politically motivated boycott when Spain refused to play the Soviet Union in the quarterfinals.[42] As Spain gradually moved from austerity to economic growth, underpinned by technological and educational expansion, football was used to project fascist Spain as a successful nation at ease with itself and its leadership, promoting Franco as popular and populist so that any victory for *La Selección* was represented as a victory for Francoism.[43] The 2-1 victory over the Soviet Union by the new, young "Spanish" team was extensively exploited for propagandist purposes as the ideological triumph of Fascism over communism, while attempting to soften the harsh image of Spain in the international arena. Franco realized that by utilizing football to reestablish links with opposing ideologies a more positive set of images around Spain were being fostered. This challenged traditional stereotypes of fascist Spain, at least to the outside world.[44]

Internally the tone was set by the slavishly loyal daily newspaper, *ABC*, which enthused that "in this quarter of a century there has never been displayed a greater popular enthusiasm for the state born out of victory over Communism and its fellow travelers."[45] Progress and success was fused with the archetypal values of *La Furia* to define contemporary Spanish nationhood with the added spice of victory over the ideological enemy of communism. In football terms, the team was an unexciting outfit, lacking in flair and being rather fortunate to win, particularly in the semifinal against Hungary. Fascism tended to eschew art and elegance, preferring masculine machismo stereotypes of strength and force, personified by the ethos of the 1964 team, in which the talent of players such as Amancio and Suarez was stifled by the rugged approach of Fuste, Pereda and others.[46] Success in the final was a stage-managed, mediated event, broadcast live to a national and international audience, the climax coming when Union of European Football Associations (UEFA) President Stanley Rous gave the cup to Olivella, the Spanish captain, in a flag-waving Bernebéu. This was a display of state nationalism on a huge scale, an orchestrated portrayal of a unified Spain, maximizing the political symbolism of the game in the reinforcement of legitimacy and the mass distraction of escapist popular culture,[47] underpinned by a triumphal and patriotic media.[48]

In retrospect, the victory of *La Selección* in 1964, the national side's sole success in international competition until the emergence of *La Roja* over 40 years later, represented the zenith of the Franco dictatorship's capacity to utilize football's potential to both engender national identity and keep latent regionalism under control, effectively neutralizing the separate identities of FC Barcelona and Real Madrid, while boosting Franco's delusion of his domestic popularity and his acceptance on the international stage.[49] The regime mercilessly exploited football to define the sovereignty of a centralized, unified Spain, with the simultaneous aim of containing nationalist aspirations in the regions.[50] Containment, consensus and control were the leitmotifs underpinning state manipulation of the game. In Franco's later years, and in the transition to democracy between 1975 and 1982, football was a barometer of continuity and change.[51] The resurgent nationalisms precipitated by the emergence of the autonomous communities arising out of the 1978 Constitution paved the way for the renaissance of club football in the Basque Country and Catalonia in the early 1980s with the clubs "being significant symbols of the democratic process itself, because of their distinctive histories and politics."[52] The success of Athletic Bilbao in 1984 and 1985 symbolized a rejection of Madrid's centralism and the reaffirmation of the national identity of Euskal–Herria.[53] These sites of separate ethnicities for the embryonic Spain of the Regions challenged the established orthodoxies that had shaped the politico-football synthesis for the previous four decades, weakening the traditional juxtaposition of *La Selección* with Spanish identity. This enabled the cultural power of sport to be assimilated into a devolved political system of regional identities (Fig. 5.1).[54]

Fig. 5.1 La Liga 2015–2016 team emblems; Nation, Locality, History and Identity ©Jim O'Brien

La Selección Spain 1982—Unity and Division

> The 1982 World Cup in Spain, top heavy with twenty-four teams and ill organized by its hosts, ill augured from the farcical moment of the draw, beset by heat and displeasing incidents, nonetheless ended in a dramatic crescendo.[55]

Glanville's comprehensive history of the World Cup highlights many of the negative aspects surrounding Spain's hosting of the 1982 event. Italy's victory over West Germany in a pulsating final in Madrid obscured the fact that for the host nation, symbolically celebrating an end to autocracy and embarking on a democratic future, the tournament was a disaster which failed to paper over all the old cracks and tensions underlying the feeble unifying power of *La Selección* in the Spain of the autonomous regions. The side's failure aptly demonstrated a cluster of different ethnicities and allegiances around football.

When a fledging democratic Spain hosted the World Cup, the relationship between center and region was fluid and volatile. Both the tournament and *La Selección* itself reflected all the nascent tensions around football's traditional and changing roles in articulating the emergent constructions around contested nationalisms within the fragile Spanish state.[56]

The buildup to *El Mundiespaña* was interwoven with complex processes of political and cultural change. The powerful symbolism of awarding Spain the tournament recognized the reintegration of the country into the international community in the post-Franco era, culminating in the accession to the European Community in 1986, a process which Prime Minister González couched as being a historic reorientation with Europe. Montalban has suggested that football was crucial in the uncertain transition period following the death of Franco in 1975 in that it opened up both the renaissance of regional languages and more democratic structures within club football, while maintaining a sense of national cohesion through *La Liga*'s infrastructure.[57] The Constitution (1978) paved the way for the Spain of the autonomous communities in which suppressed notions of alternative nationhood found expression in the resurgent regionalism celebrated by the success of Basque and Catalan football in the early 1980s. These oscillating paradoxes meant that that the capacity of *La Selección* to frame "Spanishness" was limited once the imposed cohesion of Francoism had dissipated.

After the opening ceremony and first match, featuring King Juan Carlos as the image of unity in the *Camp Nou*, the RSSF's hosting of the tournament was dominated by uneasy compromises and attempts to mask the deep divisions between center and region. This was reflected in contemporary coverage of the event by the Spanish press.[58]

Consequently, although the nucleus of Uruguayan coach Santamaria's team was drawn from Real Sociedad, winners of *La Liga* in the two previous seasons, the original plan was that *La Selección* would play all matches leading up to the final in Valencia. This decision revealed the incoherence underlying the framing of the squad, and the contrast between the team and the sentiments of supporters. It was difficult to imagine that Valencia's stadium, *La Mestalla*, noted for its support for a unitary Spain, would fully endorse a side containing many Basque players.[59] The poor performances of the team, only just squeezing into the second round after drawing with Honduras and losing memorably to Northern Ireland, meant that later matches were played in Madrid, giving rise to a crescendo of justified criticism in the Spanish media.[60] From its much-ridiculed mascot, *el naranjito*,[61] to a style of play embedded in the outdated values of *La Furia*, dour and hardworking, but without courage and spirit, and lacking in technical and tactical aplomb, the team's displays constituted the nadir of the national side in international competition. The hype surrounding the "Spanishness" of the event was in direct contrast to the sense of dislocation and apathy enshrouding the side, especially in the earlier matches, typified by goalkeeper Arconada's error against Northern Ireland, seeming to reflect a deeper malaise. This gave rise to conspiracy theories that the Real Sociedad player was involved in a Basque plot to intentionally lose the match, indicating how deeply the fractures reverberated around overt expressions of alternative nationalisms at the time. In comparison to the strength of club football in the regions the national side lacked cohesion, cast in the mold of an oppressive past, resonant of the pessimism and fatalism that had underscored football's niche in the shaping of Spanish national identity. Their performances found little support in a skeptical public, once the initial flag waving in Valencia had given way to the harshness of media scrutiny, with low key support, particularly in Catalonia and the Basque Country,[62] in contradistinction to the vibrancy of support for club football in the newly established autonomous regions. The criticism of *La Furia*, the traditional representation of the national side, suggested a deeper rejection of one of the defining images of Francoism. The harsh, physical style of play harked back to the regimented, controlling impulses of the dictatorship. Spain's new democracy contextualized the game as a focal point of regional values and divergent ethnicities. For the Basque Country this was marked by a reclaiming of traditional values recast in the success of its major clubs. In Catalonia, FC Barcelona reasserted its cultural power as a unifying force for Catalanism, the team's style of play starting to evolve as an alternative to *La Furia*. In this sense, the values of *La Furia* started to appear anachronistic, crystallizing a critique of Madrid and State centralism.

The first signs of the gradual reframing of *La Selección* became evident in the European Nations Cup of 1984, when the team finished runners up to a Platini-inspired France. The stewardship of Miguel Muñoz ensured that a mixture of pragmatism and some of *La Furia*'s traditional values produced a more inclusive, balanced squad suggesting an increasing confidence in the New Spain's socialist, democratic consensus of growth and modernity, though still rather reliant on the collective spirit in its style of play.[63] The team was more cohesive and tactically coherent after the debacle of 1982.[64] Yet by 1991, the very existence of *La Selección* and its capacity to represent the central Spanish state was under threat, with *ABC*, among others, starting a media and public debate calling for the national side to be disbanded. In the subsequent World Cup (1994), this perspective gained credibility through the inability of the national team to defeat their old adversary Italy, the unlucky curse of *El Fatalismo* failing to deflect criticism that the team still represented a mixture of the Catalans and the PNV.[65]

LA ROJA AND LA SELECCIÓN—FOOTBALL'S NATIONAL CONSENSUS

La Roja transformed the somewhat negative and destructive *La Furia* of old into something as vital as but more life giving than wine or even blood, transfused rather than spilled.[66]

Burns graphically describes the transformation which took place in respect of *La Selección* between 2008 and 2012, both in terms of on-field success and in the framing of the iconography surrounding the national side as *La Furia* faded into the annals of Spanish football history, to be replaced by *La Roja*, in what appeared to be a radical break with the past. What took place was more evolution than revolution, the catalyst for change being the poor performance of *La Selección* in the 1980s and 1990s, when all the regional diversity of the New Spain were reflected in the lack of coherence and identity in the national team. While Spanish club football continued to produce excellent players and the clubs themselves prospered in European competition, *La Selección* struggled to carve a niche in international football, without *La Furia* to instill unity.[67]

Seminal changes in the game itself and within Spanish society during the 1990s laid the foundations for the emergence of *La Roja*. The impact of the Bosman Ruling (1995) together with the game's increased mediatization and globalization impacted on the political and cultural traditions of Spanish football to engender a more fluid set of dynamics while opening up the game to a burgeoning global television audience as entertainment and spectacle.[68] Club football's rivalries became the dominant expression for this expansion, so that *La Selección* had to create a new identity in the context of the global game of the late 1990s and post-millennium period. While this was not translated into results, developments in tactics and coaching permeated the game, crystallizing a break with past rigidity. Moreover, the changes in football were paralleled by wider political and cultural nuances. The stability of competitive party politics, the economic boom of the 1990s and the early millennium and the devolved regional dichotomy of the Spanish state reflected a maturing democracy that masked some of the traditional divisions within Spanish society. *La Roja* was able to positively exploit these.

Set against this backdrop, the pinnacle of the national side's achievement in securing Spain's first World Cup in South Africa 2010 finally laid to rest the perception of *La Selección* as the failures of international football and suggested that political, ethnic and cultural divisions had been blunted by the unifying process of sporting success. The tournaments prior to *La Roja*'s breakthrough in Euro 2008 mostly reinforced the notion of the national side as underachievers in international competition, with recurrent incidents reflecting traditional center–region tensions. *La Selección* was still negatively associated with the memory of the dictatorships of Primo de Rivera and Franco in the public psyche, particularly in the Basque Country and Catalonia. From the 1950s club football at national and European levels became more dominant and increasingly mediatized in the iconography of the Spanish game. By the 1980s and 1990s underlying dynamics of change can be perceived, reflecting the wider political canvas of evolution, coalition and protracted debates between center and region. The influence of the 1995 Bosman Ruling[69] defined shifting mosaics of migration, ethnicity and identity. Allied to economic growth and the maturing of Spanish democracy, these challenged the old orthodoxy and stereotyping of *La Furia* so that its cultural framing of *La Selección* was gradually eroded. The globalization and further mediatization of the traditional constructs of the Spanish game underwent cultural, political and football-centered change, notably through the foundation of *La Masia* to become the core of FC Barcelona's embodiment of Catalanism and the development of the tiki-taka style of play for which it became globally renowned. These factors were instrumental in the evolution of *La Furia* into *La Roja*, with profound implications for the image, construction and identity of the national side from 2006 onwards, with the consequence that *La Roja* entered a golden period which harnessed the brilliant talents of a number of Catalan and Basque players.[70]

The term *La Roja* was first coined by former national team coach, José Luis Aragones in the buildup to Euro 2008. Although he subsequently denied any politically cynical motive behind the change, pointing out that the Spanish team had played with red shirts and blue shorts during the latter years of the Franco regime.[71] Its adoption as a key component of media marketing suggested a significant shift away from the core values of *La Furia* that had historically been associated with *La Selección*. The framing of *La Roja* embraced a rebranding process to shake off the ghost of the Francoist past in order to stimulate mass support, particularly from younger consumers, around the team's participation in Euro 2008 and 2012, and the World Cup (2010). The Adidas-inspired motif *Nace de Dentro*[72] projected corporate globalization to juxtapose past and current iconography, framing *La Furia Roja* to position the team at the core of popular "Spanish" mass culture while embellishing the late 1990s and post-millennium renaissance of patriotism in the buildup to Euro 2012, so that Vicente del Bosque was able to forge, temporarily at least, a national consensus in a country that historically has struggled to agree on what constitutes the common good.[73] This evolution highlighted issues concerning the construction and representation of the national side, suggesting that nuances of ethnicity and identity remained as contested as ever, challenging consensual "Banal Nationalism"[74] in shaping a cluster of rival constructs in the nexus between football, Catalanism, Basqueness and Spanishness.[75] This reframing of a positive sense of Spanish identity around football success was reflected in the attitude of *La Roja* itself, with the team able to vanquish the traditional roots of discord, particularly between the Real Madrid and FC Barcelona players, to represent a mature, democratic sense of Spanish nationalism underpinned by the success of *La Selección*.[76]

Spain's success in winning three consecutive tournaments was based on a sophisticated coaching and training system, modeled on a fusion of *La Cantera*[77] and *La Masia*[78] producing a generation of exceptional players, including Xavi, Iniesta, Busquets and others. The foundation of *Las Rozas*[79] allowed the Spanish Federation to instigate a system that inculcated personal, training and playing values in attempting to turn out homogenized products.[80] The nucleus of the squad and its playing style were based on Pep Guardiola's FC Barcelona. This led to an interlocking process in which *La Selección* was Catalanized and "Spanishness" was globalized through the diversity of global media platforms to construct an apolitical squad based extensively on the players of FC Barcelona.[81] Support for *La Roja* developed in Catalonia due to this interconnectivity, challenging the previously held apathy toward the national side. The continued success of the side projected an inclusive fabric of "Spanishness," creating new unity in diversity.[82] The approach of Coach Del Bosque showed an awareness of how this success might be exploited for political and cultural purposes.

The fluency, technical excellence and artistry of the team certainly banished the shackles of *La Furia*, but a closer analysis of the recent manifestations of *La Selección* reveals more than the kudos of sporting success. Beneath the break with folkloric football tradition and the euphoria of winning, the game's lexicon tapped into regionalism, alternative nationalisms and cultural/political identities within the vortex of the impulse of globalization. This gave further complexity to the traditional mores shaping Spanish football, in which the dualism of historic discourse had associated Catalans with modernity, culture and democracy, while framing Spaniards as naturally backward, unrefined and authoritarian.[83]

Due to its recent high global media profile, *La Selección* remains under scrutiny, with potential challenges to its fractured history of representing the Spanish state. For all the discourse around *La Roja*, club football in the global market economy remains critical to patterns of alliance, rivalry and ethnicity. As political campaigns for independence have gathered momentum in Catalonia and the Basque Country, questions about the future of the national team continue to resonate. The future realization of separate statehood by Spain's regions creates issues of governance for UEFA and the Fédération Internationale de Football Association (FIFA), threatening the hegemony of the RSFF as custodian of the Spanish game. The lexicon of Spanish football at the club and national level could face radical changes. The basis for alternative nationalisms and separate statehood already exists in the "national" teams of Catalonia, the Basque Country and Galicia. Although these are rooted in the historical framework of Spanish football and predate the genesis of the national team,[84] the fusion of independence movements with the regional hue of football's political populism have provided a contemporary focus for these traditions. Under UEFA and FIFA jurisdiction only a small number of friendly matches are currently sanctioned. Nevertheless, there is a groundswell of fan support for these games, especially with the appointment of Johan Cryuff, who until recently was the coach of the Catalan *selección*. Recent matches involving the Basque Country and Catalonia[85] are testimony to this. Should the central unitary Spanish state disintegrate, enabling the regional power bases of Spanish football to fully compete in international competitions, both the legitimacy and the playing strength of *La Selección* would be severely compromised. The capacity of Catalonia and the Basque Country to participate as independent self-governing states would have significant football and non-football consequences. Some precedents for this can be noted in the emergence of national teams in the wake of the disintegration of Yugoslavia in the 1990s. The success of Croatia in the 1998 World Cup and the subsequent achievements of Slovenia and Bosnia–Herzegovina in international competition are potent symbols of distinctive nationhood and ethnic diversity. These examples act as sources of inspiration for the contemporary independence campaigns in Spain's historic regions; for Madrid they are evidence of Europe's shifting geopolitical landscape and football's power to define the unity and division of the nation-state, posing a real threat to Spain's continued existence.

At present, the Spanish state stands at uneasy crossroads, the success of *La Selección* being rare moments of cohesion and distraction set against a backdrop of economic meltdown and political factionalism at all levels of state infrastructure. The recent failure of Del Bosque's team to progress beyond the first stage of the Brazil 2014 World Cup intensifies debates around nationhood and the capacity of *La Selección* to frame it. In football terms it suggests the eclipse of one of the game's truly great sides. It also highlights how *La Roja* was able to fuse art, science and sport into an underpinning philosophy to define a cultural cohesion in which political and historic traditions were contained. Cast in this light, the interlocking synthesis of Guardiola's FC Barcelona and Del Bosque's Spain can be witnessed as the burnout of tiki-taka in Brazil 2014, foreshadowed by the relative failure of Gerardo Martino's side to maintain FC Barcelona's recent dominance of Spanish club football. Within these contexts, *La Roja* acted as a veneer, masking and remolding the turbulence of center–region tensions. *La Selección* remains a source of tension because of the reemergence of regional teams and related symbols.[86] While affection for the achievements of the national team is genuine and warm in Catalonia and the Basque Country, the empathy is a subdued and muted one in contrast to the flag-waving excitement celebrating the team's success in the traditional Spanish hotbeds of Madrid, Valencia and Seville. *La Roja* represented more than the game itself as both a cultural and a political phenomenon in contemporary notions of Spanish identity.[87] Given that *La Selección* has not played in the Basque Country since 1968, and rarely visits Barcelona, the divided sensibilities surrounding the synthesis between football, politics and ethnicity remain indelibly potent in the Spanish psyche.

The role of *La Selección* has been reappraised in the wake of Brazil 2014, as football's cyclical nature continues to be contextualized within the political and cultural dynamic of the Spanish state. Since the constitutional settlement of 1978[88] sports policy has been decentralized under regional control, a seminal contrast with the rigidity of centralism under Franco. Football's place within this political and cultural vortex is complex and ambivalent. While there has never been a national stadium as a focal point of national identity, since 1928 the top two tiers of Spanish club football have operated on a national level, while the governance of the game remains largely centrally controlled. These paradoxes cut across the thematic landscape of Spanish football, maintaining balance between cohesion and fragmentation. The kudos emanating from the successes of *La Selección*, whether framed as *La Furia* or *La Roja*, have been exploited for political capital by the Spanish state while the failures of the national side have prompted intense debates around the constructions of Spanish nationhood. In the current atmosphere of political and cultural uncertainty, the state continues to use football to prop up unity while the Camp Nou, the new San Mames and the Bernabéu stadia reinforce the game's historic regional power bases, functioning increasingly as nexus of cultural identity within the parameters of global fandom.

NOTES

1. Fernando Leon Solís, *Negotiating Spain and Catalonia* (Bristol: Intellect Books, 2003), 13.
2. *La Selección Nacional*—The name historically given to the Spanish National team since 1920, revealing tensions, ambiguities and conflict surrounding the framing of Spain as a nation.
3. Philip Ball, *Morbo: The Story of Spanish Football,* (London: WSC, 2011), 220.
4. Vic Duke and Liz Crolley, *Storming the Bastille; Football, Nationality and the State.* (London: Longman, 1998), 26–30.
5. Francisco Caspistegui and Santiago Leoné, *Cien años de relación entre los navarros y eldeporte.* (Pamplona: Eunsa, 2010), 107–109.

6. David Goldblatt, *The Ball is Round: A Global History of Football* (London: Riverhead, 2006), 210–213.

7. Michael Richards, "Collective Memory: The Nation State and Post-Franco Society," in *Contemporary Spanish Cultural Studies,* eds. Barry Jordan and Tamosunas, Rikki-Morgan. (London: Arnold, 2000), 40–42.

8. Daniel Gomez, *La Patria Del Gol; Futbol y política en el Estado Español.* (Madrid: Astiro, 2007), 101.

9. Ball, *p. 230–233.*

10. Ibid., Gomez, p. 41.

11. Liz Crolley and David Hand. *Football and European Identity; Historical Narratives Through the Press.* (London: Routledge, 2006), 98–100.

12. José Alvarez Junco and Adrian Shubert, eds. *Spanish History Since 1808.* (London: Hodder Education, 2005), 101.

13. Royal Spanish Football Federation—Originally founded in 1909, with the prefix 'Royal' added in 1913. It became a member of FIFA in 1914, and UEFA in 1954.

14. Madrid FC was founded in 1902 by two Catalan brothers, Juan and Carlos Patros; the following year Basque students in Madrid set up a branch of Athletic Bilbao, which became Atlético Madrid in 1907.Football was very strong in the Basque Country and Catalonia at this time, so that the first *selección nacional* was bound to draw on these roots.

15. Ball, 221–224.

16. Ball, 222.

17. Caro, *Madrid Sport 1920;* cited in Ball, p. 223.

18. Belgium won the Gold Medal in the tournament, though their opponents Czechoslovakia were subsequently disqualified for protests against refereeing decisions during the match against the hosts. A complex play-off system took place to decide the Silver Medal. In this match Spain beat the Netherlands 3-1.

19. Crolley and Hand, 2006, 100.

20. Ball, 223–224.

21. In the 1934 World Cup, Spain lost controversially to Italy 1-0 in a replay following a 1-1 draw the previous day. In both matches *La Selección* had a goal disallowed. In 1994, in the United States, Spain lost 2-1 in the quarterfinals to Italy. These defeats symbolized the curse of fatalism around the national team, only van-

quished by *La Roja's* victories over Italy in the quarterfinals of Euro 2008 (on penalties) and in the final of Euro 2012 (4-0).

22. Alejandro Quiroga, *Football and National Identities in Spain; The Strange Death of DonQuixote.* (London: Palgrave Macmillan, 2013), 43.
23. Juan Soto Vinolo, *Los años 50; Una historia sentimental de cuando España era diferente* (Madrid: La Esfera, 2009*), 152.
24. Jim O'Brien, "Shades of Basqueness" in Dashper et al: *Sports Events, Society and Culture.* (London: Routledge, 2014), 164, and Gomez, 49–52.
25. Juan Soto Vinolo, *Los años 50; Una historia sentimental de cuando España era diferente.* (Madrid: La Esfera, 2009), 155.
26. Ibid., p. 156.
27. Burns, *La Roja; A Journey Through Spanish Football,* (London: Simon and Schuster, 2012), 145–147.
28. Ibid., p. 202.
29. Ball, p. 239.
30. Eduardo Galeano, *Soccer in Sun and Shadow.* (New York: Nation Books, 2013), 102.
31. Enrique Paradinas, *La Roja en La Copa del Mundo.* (Madrid: T&B Editiones, 2010), 67.
32. No-Do—*Noticiarios y Documentales Cinematographias* (1943–1981). This was the name given to the official monopoly control of cinema newsreels by the Spanish state. It allowed the Franco regime to utilize output for propaganda purposes.
33. Vic Duke and Liz Crolley. *Storming the Bastille; Football, Nationality and the State.* (London: Longman, 1998), 34–36.
34. Quiroga, p. 65.
35. Ball, pp. 126–127.
36. *Los Oriundos*—The term was first coined by Mussolini to incorporate South American players of Italian descent into the 1934 World Cup team. It was adopted by the Franco regime to incorporate Di Stefano and Santamaria for the 1962 World Cup.
37. Goldblatt, p. 415.
38. Duke and Crolley, p. 35.
39. Burns, *La Roja,* pp. 199–203.
40. Mary Vincent, Spain *1833–2002* (Oxford: Oxford University Press, 2010), p. 179.

41. In 1962, after the rejection of Spain's application to join the EEC, TVE frequently broadcasted best goals of *La Selección*.

42. Galeano, p. 131.

43. Duke and Crolley, p. 34.

44. Ball, p. 242.

45. *ABC*, June 1964, cited in Ball, p. 242.

46. Paradinas, p. 139.

47. Duke and Crolley, p. 33.

48. James Riordan and Kruger Arnd, eds. *European Cultures in Sport; Examining the Nations and Regions*. (Bristol: Intellect Books, 2003), 130.

49. Burns, *La Roja*, p. 200–202.

50. Crolley and Hand, p. 105–106.

51. Montalban, *El País*, June 8, 1998.

52. Carlos Santacana, personal communication, Barcelona, March 2010.

53. Quiroga, p. 218.

54. Riordan and Kruger, p. 131–133.

55. Brian Glanville, *The Story of the World Cup* (London: Faber and Faber, 2012), 238.

56. Crolley and Hand, 2006, p. 111.

57. Manuel Vazquez Montalban, Futbol; *un religión en busca de un dios*. (Barcelona: Arena Abierta, 2005), 179–183.

58. The day following the defeat by Northern Ireland (Valencia, June 25, 1982), press headlines exclaimed *España, un desastre* (Spain, a disaster), *Lamentable partido* (woeful match).

59. The antipathy of Valencia fans toward Basque and Catalan teams is well known, as is their support for *La Selección*. This tradition was apparent as recently as November 2014, when the club hosted Athletic Bilbao in *La Liga*—throughout the game the home fans sang '¡*Viva España!*' as a response to the current debate surrounding autonomy and independence.

60. Paradinas, p. 224–225.

61. '*El naranjito*' (the little orange)—the official world cup mascot for 1982 was a little orange dressed in the football kit of *La Selección*. It both alienated alternative nationalisms and seemed to represent an unimaginative stereotype of Spanish national identity, locked into the Francoist past.

62. Duke and Crolley, pp. 41–42.

63. Burns, *La Roja*, pp. 277–279.
64. Quite apart from the extraordinary result of the final qualifying match, in which *La Selección* defeated Malta 12-1 in December 1983 (a result which echoed the values of *La Furia*, and re-established some sense of national pride within the contemporary landscape of the Spain of the autonomous communities), West Germany was beaten 1-0 and a talented Denmark team was defeated 6-5 on penalties in the semifinals.
65. Solís, p. 44.
66. Burns, *La Roja*, p. 350.
67. In the World Cups from 1990 to 2006, in spite of impressive qualifying campaigns, *La Selección* did not progress beyond the quarter-final stage.
68. Timothy Ashton, *Soccer in Spain; Politics, Literature and Film.* (Toronto, Scarecrow Press, 2013), 48.
69. The Bosman Ruling (1995) allowed freedom of movement for players at end of contract, without a transfer fee being paid (Article 39, EC Treaty). It followed a dispute between Jean-Marc Bosman and the Belgian Football Association.
70. Ian Hawkey "Catalan and Basque Country reignite call for independent national football identities," December 2013, www.telegraph.co.uk.
71. Burns, *La Roja*, .p. 306.
72. "*Nace de Dentro*" (Born from within) was the shirt logo adopted by *La Selección* for Euro 2012. It was promoted through a huge advertising campaign video which stressed the strength, feeling and pride of the team.
73. Burns, "What's Behind La Roja?", (www.Time.Com, June 2012).
74. Billig, pp. 21–25.
75. Banal nationalism refers to the central tenet of Billig's thesis; that nationalism is expressed by the symbols and rituals of everyday life, principally through the media. The articulation of the folklore, images and symbols of football dovetail neatly with his ideas.
76. Gomez, pp. 117–119.
77. *La Cantera* (The Quarry). Term used by clubs to define players coming either from their academies or from the local geographical area/region. It is part of the folkloric tradition of Spanish club football.

78. *La Masia*—The eighteenth-century farmhouse adjacent to the Camp Nou which was developed into FC Barcelona's training academy by Cryuff in the late 1980s.The philosophy adopted produced the players which came to symbolize the style of the club, and *La Roja*.

79. *Las Rozas* is the headquarters of the RSFA. Located outside Madrid, it is the academy and training complex for *La Selección*.

80. Ian Hawkey, "Catalonia and Basque Country Reignite Call for Independent National Football Identities," December, 2013, www.telegraph.co.uk

81. Ball, p. 234.

82. Mariann Vaczi, "The Spanish Fury; a political geography of soccer in Spain," in *The International Review for the Sociology of Sport*, Online Article, accessed February 25,*2013*.

83. Quiroga, p. 179.

84. Catalonia had its first *selección* in 1904, playing against club sides before making its international debut in 1912. The Basque Country (*Euskal-Herria*) played combined matches with Cantabria from 1915, before having its own *selección* in1922.

85. The Basque Country defeated Peru 6-0 at the new San Mames on December 28, 2013, in front of 27,000 spectators whilst Catalonia won 4-1 against the Cape Verde Islands at the Olympic Stadium on December 30, 2013, watched by a crowd of 23,000.

86. Vaczi, (2013).

87. Burns, *La Roja*, pp. 376–378.

88. Riordan and Kruger, p. 130–131.

WORKS CITED

Ashton, Timothy. *Soccer in Spain; Politics, Literature and Film. Toronto*: Scarecrow Press, 2013.

Ball, Philip. *Morbo: The Story of Spanish Football*. 2nd ed. London: WSC, 2011.

Billing, Michael. *Banal Nationalism*. London: Sage, 2004.

Burns, Jimmy. *La Roja: A Journey Through Spanish Football*. London: Simon and Schuster, 2012a.

Burns, Jimmy. "What's Behind La Roja: The Politics and Poetry of Spanish Soccer (June 2012)," *Time.com*, New York, 2012b.

Caspistegui, Francisco and Santiago Leone. *Cien años de relación entre los navarros y el deporte*. Pamplona: Eunsa, 2010.

Crolley, Liz and David Hand. *Football, Europe and the Press*. London: Frank Cass, 2002.

Crolley, Liz and David Hand. *Football and European Identity; Historical Narratives Through the Press*. London: Routledge, 2006.

Duke, Vic and Liz Crolley. *Storming the Bastille; Football, Nationality and the State*. London: Longman, 1998.

Galeano, Eduardo. *Soccer in Sun and Shadow*. New York: Nation Books, 2013.

Glanville, Brian. *The Story of the World Cup*. London: Faber and Faber, 2012

Goldblatt, David. *The Ball Is Round: A Global History of Football*. London: Riverhead, 2006.

Gomez, Daniel. *La Patria Del Gol; Futbol y política en el Estado Español*. Madrid: Astiro, 2007.

Hawkey, Ian. *"Catalonia and Basque Country Reignite Call for Independent National Football Identities"*. December, 2013. www.telegraph.co.uk

Hunter, Graham. *Spain: The Inside Story of La Roja's Historic Treble*. London: Backpage Press, 2013.

Junco, José Alvarez and Adrian Shubert, editors. *Spanish History Since 1808*. London: Hodder Education, 2005.

Montalban, Manuel Vazquez. *Futbol; un religión en busca de un*. Barcelona: Arena Abierta, 2005.

O'Brien, J. "Shades of Basqueness." In *Sports Events, Society and Culture*, edited by Katherine Dashper et al. London: Routledge, 2014.

Paradinas, Enrique. *La Roja en La Copa del Mundo*. Madrid: T&B Editiones, 2010.

Quiroga, Alejandro. *Football and National Identities in Spain; The Strange Death of Don Quixote*. London: Palgrave Macmillan, 2013.

Richards, Michael. "Collective Memory: The Nation State and Post – Franco Society." In *Contemporary Spanish Cultural Studies*, edited by Barry Jordan and Rikki Morgan – Tamosunas. London: Arnold, 2000.

Riordan, James, and Kruger Arnd, editors. *European Cultures in Sport; Examining the Nations and Regions*. Bristol: Intellect Books, 2003.

Shaw, Duncan. "The Politics of 'Fútbol'." *History Today* 35, (August 8, 1985): 1–4.

Solís, Fernando Leon. *Negotiating Spain and Catalonia*. Bristol: Intellect Books, 2003.

Sutherland, Claire. *Nationalism in the Twenty-first century: Challenges and Responses*. New York: Palgrave Macmillan, 2012.

Vaczi, Mariann. "The Spanish Fury; A Political Geography of Soccer in Spain." In *The International Review for the Sociology of Sport*. Online Article. Accessed 25 Feb 2013.

Vincent, Mary. *Spain 1833–2002*. Oxford: Oxford University Press, 2010.

Vinolo, Juan Soto. *Los años 50; Una historia sentimental de cuando España era diferente*. Madrid: La Esfera, 2009.

PART III

Political Science and International Relations

Beyond the Unfulfilled Promise of Soviet International Football, 1945–1991

Mauricio Borrero

After several decades of relative isolation, Soviet football (soccer)[1] made a memorable entry onto the international scene in November 1945 when the Dynamo Moscow club toured Great Britain, gaining praise from a demanding British public and press with its attractive style and dominant results. The ensuing emergence of Soviet international football occurred in the context of budding Cold War rivalries and coincided with the broader opening of Soviet society that followed the death of Joseph Stalin in March 1953. Throughout the mid-1960s, Soviet football teams continued to build on the promise of the 1945 Dynamo tour, winning a gold medal at the 1956 Melbourne Olympics, reaching the quarterfinals of the 1958 World Cup, winning the inaugural European Championship in 1960, before securing fourth place at the 1966 World Cup. Led by a world-class goalkeeper, Lev Yashin, Soviet football seemed ready to permanently join the top echelons of international football. But by the end of the Soviet period in 1991, despite a few occasional high points, a distinct feeling of underachievement and unfulfilled promise surrounded Soviet international football.

M. Borrero (✉)
Department of History, St. John's University, Queens, NYC, USA

© Hofstra University 2017
B. Elsey, S. Pugliese (eds.), *Football and the Boundaries of History*,
DOI 10.1057/978-1-349-95006-5_6

The failure of Soviet football to achieve a level of dominance similar to that of Soviet Olympic sports preoccupied and frustrated Soviet athletic officials. Robert Edelman, the leading scholar of Soviet sports, has noted "three enormous handicaps in seeking international glory," which placed Soviet football at a competitive disadvantage. Severe winters forced a three-month winter break on the Soviet football calendar, longer than that of most European nations. In the hyper-competitive Cold War environment where the Olympic Games became a surrogate for the larger rivalry between superpowers, football—with only a few prestigious annual and quadrennial trophies—could not compete equally for budgetary resources and top athletes against sports with large medal counts and greater rewards such as track and field, gymnastics, boxing, and weightlifting. Finally, the Soviet Union's claim that its athletes were amateurs despite the existence of an extensive network of financial support may have benefited Soviet athletes at the Olympic level, but hurt them in international football competitions where they competed against true professionals, the best their rivals had to offer.[2]

Soviet national teams and clubs may have failed to live up to their initial promise in terms of results, victories, and trophies, but the history of Soviet international football opens up intriguing research windows, two of which are the subject of this chapter. Data from postwar football tours suggests that Soviet football was an integral participant in the post-World War II internationalization of football while the growing importance of non-Russian players and clubs in Soviet football after 1961 prompts us to explore the links between football and national identity in Soviet society.

The history of Soviet international football provides a valuable counterpoint to the image of the "Big Red Machine" that has dominated Cold War narratives of international sport. The model of sport as a surrogate for superpower competition is a valid one, but applies best to the Cold War-era Olympic Games, beginning with the 1952 Helsinki Olympics, the first to field Soviet teams. Besides providing real competition, sport also created a space for contact between the Soviet bloc and other countries at a time when other venues were closed or under tight ideological supervision. This was especially true of football, a sport with true mass global appeal and a deeply rooted history of international competitions and barnstorming foreign tours by clubs and national sides. The world of international football was a multipolar one where neither superpower had great power status, and small nations such as Uruguay had attained greater prestige than either the United States or the Soviet Union.

Soviet International Football: A Brief Narrative

Soviet teams had traveled abroad in the prewar period, but it was the 1945 Dynamo tour that first put Soviet football on the international map.[3] Over three weeks in November 1945, Dynamo Moscow—reinforced by a few players from other Dynamo regional teams—played four matches in the United Kingdom, two in London against Chelsea and Arsenal, one in Wales against Cardiff City, and one in Scotland against Glasgow Rangers. The results—two draws against Chelsea and Rangers, a ten to one mauling of Cardiff City, and a tight 4-3 victory over Arsenal—were in hindsight less important than the validation the tour gave to Soviet football.[4] But, from the point of view of international competition, the 1945 Dynamo tour proved to be a false dawn. The goodwill generated by the joint Allied victory over Nazi Germany dissipated within a year, soon to be replaced by a Cold War among former allies. The domestic Soviet game reached new heights in terms of attendance and entertainment value, but Soviet clubs or teams were infrequently seen beyond their borders until after Stalin's death in March 1953. One exception was the national team that participated in the football competition at the 1952 Helsinki Olympics, the first Olympic Games the Soviet Union had ever attended, but failed to get out of the first round.

The first postwar decade might have indeed been the "Golden Era" of Soviet domestic football, but if there was a golden era in Soviet international football it was the decade between 1956 and 1966.[5] It began with the gold medal that the Soviet team won at the 1956 Melbourne Olympics with a team that included some of the finest players the Soviet Union ever produced, including the goalkeeper Lev Yashin, the midfielder Igor Netto, the forward Nikita Simonian and the star-crossed, but immensely talented striker Eduard Strel'tsov, then only 19 years old. The Soviet Union qualified for its first World Cup in 1958, repeating the feat for the next three World Cups in Chile, England, and Mexico. A Soviet team won the inaugural European Championship in 1960 in Paris, with a small assist from Francisco Franco's government that refused to allow Spain to travel to Moscow to play one leg of their quarterfinal match. Four years later the Soviets reached the finals of the second European Championship in Madrid, but lost to the Spanish hosts. In the meantime, in 1963, Lev Yashin had become the first Soviet player and, so far only, goalkeeper to win the prestigious Ballon d'Or or European Footballer of the Year award given by the French sports magazine *France Football*. The highest achievement of a decade that a history of Soviet football would later capture with the slogan "Paris gold, Madrid silver, and London bronze" came at the end during the 1966 World Cup in England, where the Soviet team finished in fourth place.[6]

It was a dazzling decade, but one that proved to be the peak of Soviet international football rather than the foundation for consistent future success. The quarterfinal elimination by Uruguay in the 1970 Mexico World Cup in extra time marked the end of a cycle of four continuous World Cup appearances with relatively good results (three quarterfinal appearances and a fourth place in 1966). Yashin's retirement in 1971, commemorated by the Fédération Internationale de Football Association (FIFA) with a testimonial match in Moscow in May 1971, removed the star appeal that had helped attract audiences worldwide to Soviet football, even if after 1967 he had ceased to be the automatic starting goalkeeper for his club or the Soviet national team.

The 1970s proved to be a barren decade for the Soviet national team. The Soviet Union continued to produce talented players, such as the Ukrainian striker Oleg Blokhin, winner of the 1975 European Footballer of the Year award, but the national team entered a long cycle of under-achievement, which arguably, it never overcame. It failed to qualify for both the 1974 and 1978 World Cups and, after a second-place finish in the 1972 European Nations Cup, the Soviet team missed all the subsequent tournaments until 1988.

On the surface, the Soviet absence from the 1974 World Cup was due to the decision to boycott the return leg of a home-and-away playoff with Chile following the military coup that overthrew the leftist government of Salvador Allende on September 11, 1973. With the World Cup still at only 16 teams, FIFA had reserved a spot for the winner of a two-game playoff between a European team and a South American team. The first match was played in Moscow on September 21, 1973, and ended in a 0-0 draw, an advantageous result for the Chilean squad. The Soviets forfeited the return match on November 21, protesting the fact that the site of the game, Santiago's Estadio Nacional, had been used for the torture and executions of political prisoners rounded up in the aftermath of the recent military coup. They would later point to the forfeited game as the main reason for their failure to qualify, but on football terms there was no guarantee that they would have qualified had they played the game, given that the first match had ended in a draw.[7]

The Soviet absence from the 1974 World Cup could be explained on the basis of political principle, but the same could not be said of the failure to qualify for the 1978 World Cup in Argentina. As with the 1974 qualification, the Soviet Union was placed in a European group (with Hungary and Greece) whose winner would face a South American team in a playoff for a World Cup spot. This time, however, the Soviet Union did not even make it to the playoff stage, finishing second to Hungary, who in turn defeated Bolivia to reach the 1978 World Cup.

The Soviet national team returned to the World Cup in 1982 for the first of three successive, but ultimately forgettable, appearances. Only toward the end of the 1980s, in what proved to be the twilight of the Soviet Union, did Soviet national teams come close to recapturing their earlier glories and promise. In the 1988 European Championship a surprising Soviet team embraced the role of underdog, defeating England and the Netherlands in the group stage and Italy in the semifinal, before bowing out to a talented Netherlands squad in the final match. Four months later at the Seoul Olympic Games, the Soviet Union defeated Italy and Brazil on the way to a gold medal, its first in football since the 1956 Melbourne Olympics, a bittersweet full circle from what had appeared to be the dawn of Soviet international football.

Soviet Football on Tour

The growing internationalization of Soviet football after 1953 was part of the domestic "thaw" that followed Stalin's death. It was also part of an increasingly internationalized landscape in football itself. The 1948 London Olympics and the 1950 World Cup hosted by Brazil marked the resumption of the two premier international quadrennial sporting events which World War II had interrupted. Other international football competitions took root between 1956 and 1960, all of which survive to this day with slight variations: the annual European Champions' Club Cup (now the Champions' League), the annual Copa Libertadores for South American clubs, and the quadrennial European Nations Cup or European Championship for national squads.[8] Moreover, the growth of passenger air travel after World War II facilitated the rapid expansion of the well-established tradition of post-season international tours by clubs who played friendly matches while gaining exposure, goodwill, and revenue. Soviet teams and clubs were very much a part of this new international football landscape. Soviet clubs had visited European nations in the 1930s, while clubs from neighboring countries such as Turkey and Czechoslovakia occasionally visited the Soviet Union.[9] In tune with the Soviet Union's political orientation there were some well-publicized visits that provided the ideal balance between quality football and political correctness. Such was the case of the all-star Basque team that arrived in Moscow in June 1937 on a fundraising trip at the height of the Spanish Civil War. The visit was a memorable one and the Basques proved to be a far more skilled team than their Soviet hosts. Only Spartak managed to defeat them, with the help of several questionable refereeing calls.[10] But those pre-1954 tours had been infrequent and limited to European countries. After 1954, tours of Soviet teams differed from earlier ones in their growing frequency and in their range of destinations. Western Europe and Eastern Europe continued to be the primary destinations for traveling Soviet teams, but travel to Latin America, Asia, and Africa became more frequent, a reflection of the growing Soviet interest in the non-Western world.

As the number of Soviet football's foreign trips increased, the destinations became more varied. Data for the travels of the five main Moscow clubs (Dynamo, Spartak, TsSKA, Torpedo, and Lokomotiv) during the period 1954–1973 gives us insight into the changing picture of Soviet international football travel. During these two decades, the five Moscow teams played in a total of 229 matches in foreign cities. Seventy percent of the trips they made were to Western and Eastern Europe, a reflection of geographical proximity, historical tradition, and the political realities of close contacts between the countries of the Soviet bloc. The remaining trips were to Asia, Africa, and Latin America, with Asian destinations accounting for slightly over one-half of these trips.

A closer look at Soviet football travel to Asia, Africa, and Latin America suggests that "pragmatic" goals (testing Soviet teams against high-level competition and earning hard currency) coexisted with "ideological" goals (propaganda and cultural relations), with Latin American trips mostly "pragmatic" and Asian and African trips mostly "ideological." Given the high demand for quality football and a relatively stronger football market in Latin America, it is not surprising to find evidence of several tours by Soviet clubs to the region. The better-known Moscow clubs, Dynamo and Spartak, visited the region five times, while Dynamo Tbilisi, a lesser-known but rising power in Soviet football, visited four countries in November and December 1961.[11]

Soviet football trips to Africa and Asia are best viewed within the context of Soviet–Third World cultural relations rather than in terms of football itself. If the goal was to use foreign exposure to improve its overall quality, Soviet football had less to gain from travel to Africa and Asia than to Latin America, a sign that "ideological" factors prevailed over "pragmatic" ones, given that Asian and African football was not then at the same level of European or Latin American football. The timing of Dynamo's 1960 tour of Ghana, Togo, and Nigeria and Lokomotiv's 1961 tour of Ghana, Mali, and Guinea suggests that they were goodwill visits, linked to decolonization. African newspapers, such as the Lagos newspaper *Daily Times*, treated Soviet visits as major events, as shown by the front page for December 3, 1960, where the headline "Nigeria Meets Moscow Dynamos Today" overshadowed a smaller one that read "Lumumba Arrested."[12] "Ideological" considerations may have played an even greater role in determining the schedules and frequency of Soviet football tours of Asia. Between 1954 and 1973, the five Moscow teams visited Asian countries 34 times, including newly independent nations, such as Indonesia, Cambodia, Burma, India, Pakistan, Lebanon, Syria, and Jordan, all relative minnows in international football.

A further look into the preparation and organization of these tours reveals a Soviet sports bureaucracy seeking to balance Stalin-era behaviors and traditions with the new opportunities of international football.[13] Soviet football teams generally toured during the summer break in the annual championship (late July–early August) or at the end of the football season (November–December).[14] In deference to Soviet planning preferences, exchange visits were scheduled several years in advance, with some flexibility for last-minute additions. A six-year agreement between French and Soviet teams for the 1954–1959 period led to annual visits of four French clubs, while Dynamo Moscow and Dynamo Tbilisi visited France.[15] The principle of reciprocity was still in evidence in 1963 when the Soviet and Algerian football federations arranged for a 16-day tour of Algeria by an "all-star" team drawn from Moscow clubs to be followed in 1964 by an eight-day tour of Algeria by a Soviet club, and a 12-day visit by an Algerian club. Soviet football federation officials welcomed the interest of foreign teams, such as the Brazilian club Botafogo to visit the Soviet Union, but firmly reminded them of the need to organize a return visit by a Soviet team to Brazil.[16]

The growing opportunities for international travel and visits from foreign teams also brought Soviet officials into greater contact with the world of football promoters and agents, who played an important role in contacting foreign football federation officials and making travel arrangements for extended tours. The Soviet archives provide a few glimpses of what must have been a fascinating, but occasionally frustrating culture clash between Soviet bureaucrats schooled in the ways of the planned economy and administrative *fiat* and businessmen representing the more dynamic capitalist ethos of international football.

Earning hard currency helped determine travel destinations, but profit motives did not always prevail. In 1962, Juliusz Ukrainczyk, a businessman affiliated with the Dutch Football Federation, tried to convince Soviet football officials of the "very advantageous" economic possibilities of sending Spartak Moscow on a nine-match, six-week Latin American tour. Spartak was the defending Soviet champion, had already toured Latin America in 1959, and had substantial international recognition. But Ukrainczyk's suggestion fell on deaf ears; in fact, Spartak did not return to Latin America for the rest of the 1960s or early 1970s.[17]

Bureaucratic obtuseness may have been at the heart of another case that showed that Soviet football officials were not always on the same page as their international counterparts. In late spring 1963 the Chilean sports agency Viamundi and the Soviet football federation agreed on a South American by a Soviet team by the end of the year. Correspondence between the two sides reveals that the Chileans assumed the team would be Dynamo Moscow with its star, Lev Yashin, while the Soviets never confirmed nor denied this would be the case. As the tour dates neared, the Soviets began to propose other alternatives, infuriating the Chilean agency, until it pulled out of the deal. Eventually, the Soviet Olympic team made the trip to South America, a solution that did not please the various South American hosts, who had expected a healthy profit from matches featuring Yashin and his Dynamo Moscow club.[18] Usually Soviet officials played a strong hand in determining which teams they would send on tour and where, but in this case their secrecy, delays, and highhandedness made them appear unprofessional. The consequences of such mishandling were not long-lasting. Football, after all, was good business and Soviet football, with Yashin as a drawing card, was in great demand from the late 1950s through the mid-1960s.

TANGLED IDENTITIES

Issues of identity have long provided a rich vein for football-related research. Fans have often seen their football teams as standard-bearers of urban, regional, or national identity or as vehicles for its expression. The early linkage between football and factories contributed to teams whose identity was defined by their workplace or a neighborhood's industries. Peñarol, one of the powerhouses of Uruguayan and South American football, was originally the Central Uruguay Railway Cricket Club, and its fans are still known as *carboneros* (coalmen). Employees of the Buenos Aires Western Railway were the original founders of the club Ferrocarril Oeste in 1904, while the Chilean clubs Cobreloa and Cobresal—both founded in the late 1970s—are linked to that country's copper mining regions. Ethnically defined football teams have historically served as magnets for immigrant communities, particularly in Latin America. In Brazil, the club Vasco da Gama was founded by Portuguese immigrants to Rio de Janeiro, while the Italian communities of São Paulo and Belo Horizonte supported the modern-day clubs Palmeiras and Cruzeiro.[19] Raanan Rein's work on Club Atlético Atlanta highlights the large extent to which Buenos Aires Jews expressed their identity through the club.[20] Chile, in particular, features a large number of clubs, originally founded along ethnic immigrant lines, ranging from Audax Italiano to Unión Española to Palestino.[21] Club identities that corresponded to class, trade, or profession in a city were in greater evidence in the early stages of football club formation, although social and geographical mobility and intermarriage have somewhat diluted these original identities.

Of the triad of class, ethnicity, and nation, the latter has perhaps retained the greatest defining power with regard to the identities of football clubs or national teams. The best-known example of the powerful equivalence between football club and national identity is perhaps the case of FC Barcelona, which during the twentieth century became closely identified with Catalonian identity and nationalism, particularly in the decades of the Franco dictatorship when they were suppressed by the centralizing Castilian policies.[22] The notion that the Brazilian national team, the *seleção*, greatly contributed to the articulation of a Brazilian *nation* is widely accepted in scholarly and journalistic accounts of Brazilian football.[23] On the negative side, the expression of nationalism through football identities was an integral element of the unraveling of the former Yugoslavia, as captured by the veritable riot that took place during the match between Dynamo Zagreb and Red Star Belgrade in May 1990 when "ultras" from each team battled each other on the field in Zagreb.[24]

With some adjustments, the interpretive lens of identity can be applied to Soviet football, particularly with the numerous clubs whose identity was tied to the workplace. Lokomotiv and Torpedo, both from Moscow, were linked to the city's railroad and automobile workers, respectively, while the names of clubs such as Shakhtar Donetsk, Metallist Kharkiv, and Neftchi Baku speak to the miners, metalworkers, and oil workers of the dominant industries in those three cities. Soviet clubs' identities were more likely to have been assigned from above than adopted from below, a fact that helps explain the emergence of Spartak Moscow as the "people's" team in the Soviet Union. Unlike its main rivals Dynamo Moscow and CSKA Moscow, sponsored by the police and the army, Spartak was originally sponsored by the food workers' trade union, a relatively minor one in the constellation of Soviet ministries, trade unions, and industries.[25]

The lens of identity can also enrich our understanding of the complicated dynamics of nationality and ethnicity in the Soviet Union, a state founded on internationalist principles—the fundamental unity of workers worldwide—but structured on national lines: 15 republics with numerous ethnically defined autonomous republics, regions, and districts. But this lens has not been consistently applied to the Soviet case, where issues of national identity are complicated by the coexistence of particular individual nationalisms (Ukrainian, Georgian, Lithuanian, etc.) and an overarching "Soviet" nationalism.

The topic is an important, but complex, one that requires more research. For now two issues stand out in the context of the present discussion about Soviet international football. First is the changing composition of Soviet international teams from the 1950s to the 1990s. The Soviet team that won the gold medal in Melbourne was composed entirely of players from four of the five leading Moscow teams. Three decades later, at the 1986 World Cup, the Soviet team had only 5 players drawn from teams in the USSR's Russian Republic, and 17 from the non-Russian republics, 11 of whom played for Dynamo Kiev. While we can safely assume that Ukrainians played for Moscow-based clubs and that not all of Dynamo Tbilisi's players were ethnically Georgian, this shift in the composition of Soviet national teams can shed light on subtle changes in the balance of power among nationalities and republics and ethnic identity in the latter years of the Soviet Union.

A second issue that football can help illuminate is the connection between individual Soviet nationalisms (i.e. Ukrainian, Georgian, Armenian, or Lithuanian) and an all-encompassing Soviet (not Russian) nationalism. Football, with a long tradition of variable fan loyalties (single, multiple, staggered), provides an interesting platform from which to observe these issues, particularly as many Soviet households became less ethnically homogeneous due to geographical mobility and intermarriage.

The year 1961 is an important watershed in assessing the growing importance of non-Russian clubs and football within the Soviet Union. It was the year when Dynamo Kiev won the first of its 13 Soviet championships, signaling a shift in the overall balance of power between Russian teams (from the Russian Republic) and teams from the other 14 constituent republics of the USSR. Prior to 1961, only teams from Moscow had won the USSR championship and the top rungs of Soviet had been reserved for Moscow teams. From 1961 to 1991, Russian teams (all from Moscow except Zenit Leningrad, the 1984 champion) won 11 titles, while non-Russian teams won 20. Although Dynamo Kiev unquestionably dominated this period, capturing 13 of the 20 titles won by non-Russian clubs, enough other non-Russian teams were crowned Soviet champions to suggest that the shift in the balance of power was not simply due to the emergence of one dominant non-Russian team (Fig. 6.1).[26]

The growing importance of non-Russian teams in Soviet football is also evident from the number of players from non-Russian clubs selected for the Soviet national team at major competitions, such as the World Cup,

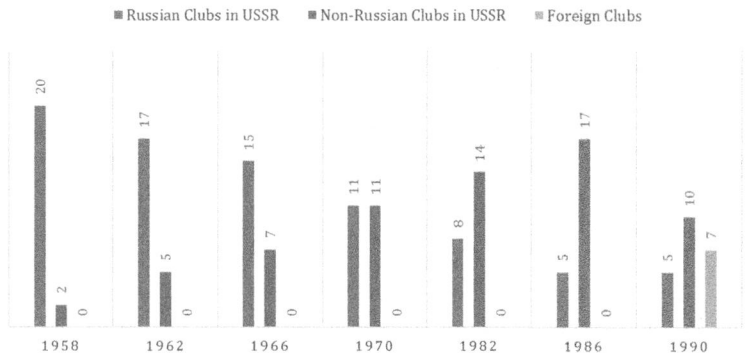

Fig. 6.1 Club composition of USSR World Cup teams, 1958–1990 (http://rsssf.com/tablesu/ussr-wc.html; accessed August 14, 2015)

as shown in Table 6.1.[27] The table shows the declining contribution of Russian clubs (based in the USSR's Russian Republic) to the composition of the squads that represented the Soviet Union in seven World Cups between 1958 and 1990. With only a few exceptions, Russian club players essentially came from the five main Moscow clubs (Spartak, Dynamo Moscow, CSKA Moscow, Torpedo, and Lokomotiv). What began in 1958 as primarily an all-Moscow affair by the 1980s became a more inclusive all-Soviet affair with players recruited from a broader range of Soviet clubs. The 1990 squad included for the first time Soviet players based in teams outside the Soviet Union, a factor that became even more prominent in the composition of the 1994 World Cup team, where only 10 of the 22 players in the squad hailed from Russian clubs.

The changing balance between Russian and non-Russian clubs in the composition of Soviet World Cup teams also reflects the long shadow cast by the *eminence gris* of late Soviet football, Valery Lobanovsky (1933–2002). A decent winger with a talent for taking corner kicks, Lobanovsky played on the record-making 1961 Dynamo Kiev side, before retiring in 1968. After four years managing Dnipro Dnipropetrovsk, Lobanovsky became the coach of Dynamo Kiev in 1973, a position he held almost continuously until 1990. His main claim to fame was as a coach, first of Dynamo Kiev and then of the Soviet national team, where he used his Dynamo Kiev as the foundation of the Soviet national team. The tactic had been used earlier to greater effect by Guzstav Sebes, coach of the Hungarian *Aranycsapat*—the "Golden Squad" or "Magical Magyars"—which dominated international football in the early to mid-1950s.[28]

Difficult to quantify or systematize, fan allegiances provide a fascinating, but often frustratingly elusive, window into football identities. Manfred Zeller's recent exploration into Soviet-era football fandom contains an interview with an Armenian fan that suggests the many layers at work in the minds and hearts of Soviet fans living in a multiethnic society. Zeller's interviewee states that in the 1950s "'internationally oriented' Armenians in Tbilisi [felt they] should silently oppose Dynamo Tbilisi, around which the nationalist mentality of its Georgian fans was entwined." Instead, he supported the Soviet Army team (CSKA), and when the team was disbanded in 1952 after its failure to win the gold medal at the Helsinki Olympics, he switched loyalties to Spartak Moscow, a team that had signed two Armenians in the late 1950s and benefited from the aura of underdogs.[29]

On paper, Ukraine's Dynamo Kiev and Georgia's Dynamo Tbilisi were the two most likely Soviet-era clubs to play the role of FC Barcelona's surrogate vehicle for suppressed nationhood. Both were the dominant team within their Soviet republics and both attained a large measure of international respectability through participation in European club competitions and by providing players to the Soviet national teams.[30]

But there are important differences between the two clubs. Dynamo Kiev was only one of several frequently competitive Ukrainian-based Soviet clubs, in part a reflection of Ukraine itself, a well-populated state with five or six important urban centers. Besides Dynamo Kiev, Ukrainian fans could choose from Chernomorets Odessa, Metalist Kharkiv, Dnipro Dnipropetrovsk, and Shaktar Donetsk as objects of their support. Dynamo Kiev may have dominated Ukrainian football and gained the allegiance of Ukrainians as the team best equipped to stand up to the Moscow teams, but within Ukraine fan allegiances were frequently fragmented.

Much like Ukraine, Georgia had made important contributions to Soviet football from the very outset of the Soviet football league, especially through its flagship club, Dynamo Tbilisi. The rosters of the Soviet Union's World Cup teams are dotted with important Georgian players from the defenders Murtsi Khurtsilava and Aleksandr Chivadze to the forwards Mikhail Meskhi and Slava Metreveli. It may have been Dynamo Tbilisi that came closest to replicating FC Barcelona's role within Catalonia and Spain. As Jonathan Wilson notes, Dynamo Tbilisi quickly became the dominant team within Georgia, enjoying both official favor and popular support, outflanking smaller rivals.[31]

To better understand Dynamo Tbilisi's role as a conduit for Georgian identity, we can briefly look at football in the other two Caucasus republics, Armenia and Azerbaijan. Armenia had no single dominant, high-performing team of the caliber of Dynamo Tbilisi. Instead, early fan allegiances were split between Dynamo Yerevan and Spartak Yerevan, before the emergence of Ararat Yerevan in the 1970s as a strong, regularly competitive Armenian club in the Soviet league that won the double (Soviet league and USSR cup) in 1973, coached by the great Nikita Simonian.[32] In Azerbaijan, Neftchi Baku was linked to Baku's extensive oil industry, which in Soviet times featured large numbers of ethnic Russian workers, thus minimizing the club's potential as a vessel for national identity.[33] Moreover, Neftchi Baku itself was at best a mid-table team, with few major victories to its name.

Conclusion

The first post-Soviet decade, rightly called Russia's "Great Depression," brought new challenges to Soviet football.[34] Once-powerful clubs lost the benefits of state patronage and were forced to resort to sometimes dubious self-financing methods until rescued by oligarchs seeking investment opportunities.[35] Top-level talent left for Western Europe, but with rare exceptions (Andryi Shevchenko) failed to significantly impact their new teams. Internationally, the Russian national team continued the slide of the late Soviet era, qualifying for only three of the six World Cups held between 1994 and 2014, and in all three cases failed to make it out of the group stage while the Olympic team failed to qualify for any of the competitions held between 1992 and 2012. The Soviet performance in the European Cup was better, qualifying for four of the five tournaments held between 1996 and 2012, and reaching the semifinals in 2008 with a surprising and entertaining squad led by the talented but inconsistent Andrei Arshavin that lost to the eventual champion, Spain. Russian clubs did not progress deep into the UEFA-sponsored competitions. Of the newly independent former Soviet republics only Ukraine has made a dent in international football, qualifying for its first World Cup in 2006 coached by its former star Oleg Blokhin, and its first European Cup in 2012, which it co-hosted with Poland.

Soviet international football may not have fulfilled its early promise. But beyond that veneer of disappointing results lies a rich history that provides insights into the tentative internationalization of Soviet society in the post-Stalin years, the changing dynamics of Russian and non-Russia clubs in Soviet football, and the extent to which non-Russian football clubs served as vessels of national identity.

Notes

1. I will use the term "football" instead of "soccer," since it is used more commonly internationally and corresponds more to the Russian term "футбол" (futbol).
2. Robert Edelman, *Serious Fun: A History of Spectator Sports in the USSR* (New York: Oxford University Press, 1993), 129–130.
3. Edelman, *Serious Fun*, 60, 63–64; for a history of Soviet football through the end of the Stalin era, see Mario Alessandro Curletto, *I piedi dei Soviet: il futból dalla Rivoluzione d'ottobre alla morte di Stalin* (Genoa: Il melangolo, 2010).

4. Edelman, *Serious Fun*. 87–91.
5. Robert Edelman, *Spartak Moscow: A History of the People's Team in the Workers' State* (Ithaca: Cornell University Press, 2009) 136–162.
6. *Sto let rossuuskomu futbolu* (Moscow: Rossiiskii futbol'nyi soiuz, 1997), 124–157.
7. Edelman, *Serious Fun*, 127–128. See also, Brenda Elsey, "'As the World is my Witness: Transnational Chilean Solidarity and Popular Culture," in Jessica Stites Mor, ed. *Human Rights and Transnational Solidarity in Cold War Latin America* (Madison: University of Wisconsin Press, 2013), 177–178.
8. Brian Glanville, *A Book of Soccer* (New York: Oxford University Press, 1979), 293–298.
9. Edelman, *Serious Fun*, 85–110 and Downing, *Passovotchka: Moscow Dynamo in Britain 1945* (London: Bloomsbury, 2000).
10. Edelman, *Serious Fun*, 63–64; *Spartak Moscow*, 104–110.
11. Esenin, *Moskovskii futbol*, pp. For Dynamo Tbilisi, see GARF (Gosudarstvennyi Arkhiv Rossiiskoi Federatsii—State Archive of the Russian Federation) f. 9570, op. 1, d. 809, l. 2.
12. *Daily Times* (Lagos), December 3, 1960, p. 1.
13. Jenifer Parks has researched this topic in far greater detail. See Jenifer Parks, "Red Sport, Red Tape: The Olympic Games, The Soviet Sports Bureaucracy, and the Cold War, 1952–1980"; unpublished Ph.D. dissertation, University of North Carolina—Chapel Hill, 2009.
14. GARF f. 9570, op. 1, d. 948, l. 50.
15. GARF f. 9570, op. 1, d. 948, l. 48.
16. On Algeria, see GARF f. 9570, op. 1, d. 1099, l. 45; on Botafogo, see GARF f. 9570, op. 1, d. 809, l. 13.
17. GARF f. 9570, op. 1, d. 948, ll. 72–73; Esenin, *Moskovskii futbol*, pp. 160–161.
18. GARF f. 9570, op. 1, d. 1088, ll. 1–80.
19. Janet Lever, *Soccer Madness* (Chicago/London: University of Chicago Press, 1983), 77.
20. Raanan Rein, *Fútbol, Jews, and the Making of Argentina* (Stanford: Stanford University Press, 2014).
21. For Palestino and other clubs from Middle Eastern immigrant communities in Chile, see Brenda Elsey, *Citizens and Sportsmen Futbol & Politics in 20th-Century Chile* (Austin: University of Texas Press, 2011), 149–164.

22. The literature on FC Barcelona is extensive. A good introduction is found in Jimmy Burns, *Barça: A People's Passion* (London: Bloomsbury, 1999).

23. Alex Bellos, *Futebol: the Brazilian Way of Life*. Updated edition (London: Bloomsbury, 2014); David Goldblatt, *Futebol Nation: The Story of Brazil through Soccer* (New York: Nation Books, 2014).

24. Franklin Foer, *How Soccer Explains the World: An Unlikely Theory of Globalization* (New York: Harper Perennial, 2010), 7–34.

25. Edelman, *Spartak Moscow*, 63–66.

26. In addition to Dynamo Kiev's 13 titles, non-Russian Soviet champions included Dynamo Tbilisi from Georgia (1964, 1978), Ararat Erevan from Armenia (1973), Dynamo Minsk from Belarus (1982), and the Ukrainian teams Dnepr Dnepropetrovsk (1983, 1988), Zarya Voroshilovgrad (now Luhansk) (1972). For the full list of Soviet-era champions, see http://www.rsssf.com/tablesu/ussrchamp.html. Accessed 14 Aug 2015).

27. The team-specific breakdown of players was as follows: In 1958, two players from Dynamo Kiev. In 1962, two from Dynamo Kiev and three from Dynamo Tbilisi. In 1966, four players from Dynamo Kiev, two from Dynamo Tbilisi, and one from Neftchi Baku. In 1970, five players from Dynamo Kiev, five from Dynamo Tbilisi, and one from Chernomorets Odessa. In 1982, eight players from Dynamo Kiev, four from Dynamo Tbilisi, and one each from Ararat Yerevan and Dynamo Minsk. In 1986, eleven from Dynamo Kiev, two from Dynamo Tbilisi, three from Dnepr Dnepropetrovsk, and one from Dynamo Minsk. In 1990, nine from Dynamo Kiev, and one from Dynamo Minsk, while seven team members were playing professionally in Spain, France, Italy and West Germany. http://www.rsssf.com/tablesu/ussr-wc.html. Accessed 14 Aug 2015).

28. Hungary won the gold medal at the 1952 Olympics and finished second to West Germany in the 1954 World Cup. On Hungary's years at the summit of international football, see Andrew Handler, *From Goals to Guns: The Golden Age of Soccer in Hungary, 1950–1956* (Boulder: East European Monographs, 1994).

29. Manfred Zeller, "'The Second Stalingrad': Soccer Fandom, Popular Memory and the Legacy of the Stalinist Past," in *Euphoria and Exhaustion: Modern Sport in Soviet Culture and Society*, ed. Nikolaus Katzer, et al. (Frankfurt/New York: Campus Verlag, 2010), 207–210.

30. For introductory profiles to both clubs, see Jonathan Wilson, *Behind the Curtain*, 14–23, 232–233.
31. Wilson, *Behind the Curtain*, 233–234.
32. Wilson, *Behind the Curtain*, 244–246.
33. Wilson, *Behind the Curtain*, 256. The team was known as Neftiannik Baku from its foundation in 1937 until 1967, when it was renamed Neftchi Baku. Both are terms for oil worker; *neftiannik* is Russian, *neftchi* is Azeri.
34. Donald Raleigh, *Soviet Baby Boomers: An Oral History of Russia's Cold War Generation* (Bloomington: Indiana University Press, 2012), 312–313.
35. Wilson, *passim*, See also, Marc Bennetts, *Football Dynamo: Modern Russia and the People's Game.* (London: Virgin Books, 2009).

Works Cited

Bellos, Alex. *Futebol: The Brazilian Way of Life.* Updated edition. London: Bloomsbury, 2014.

Bennetts, Mark. *Football Dynamo: Modern Russia and the People's Game.* London: Virgin Books, 2009.

Burns, Jimmy. *Barça: A People's Passion.* London: Bloomsbury, 1999.

Curletto, Mario Alessandro. *I piedi dei Soviet: il futból dalla Rivoluzione d'ottobre alla morte di Stalin.* Genoa: Il melangolo, 2010.

Downing, David. *Passovotchka: Moscow Dynamo in Britain 1945.* London: Bloomsbury, 2000.

Edelman, Robert. *Serious Fun: A History of Spectator Sports in the USSR.* New York: Oxford University Press, 1993.

———. *Spartak Moscow: A History of the People's Team in the Workers' State.* Ithaca: Cornell University Press, 2009.

Elsey, Brenda. *Citizens and Sportsmen: Futbol and Politics in 20th-Century Chile.* Austin: University of Texas Press, 2011.

Esenin, K.S. 1974. *Moskovskii futbol.* Moskovskii rabochii: Moscow.

Foer, Franklin. *How Soccer Explains the World: An Unlikely Theory of Globalization.* New York: Harper Perennial, 2010.

Glanville, Brian. *A Book of Soccer.* New York: Oxford University Press, 1979.

Goldblatt, David. *The Ball is Round: A Global History of Football.* London: Penguin, 2007.

———. *Futebol Nation: The Story of Brazil Through Soccer.* New York: Nation Books, 2014.

Handler, Andrew. *From Goals to Guns: The Golden Age of Soccer in Hungary, 1950–1956.* Boulder: East European Monographs, 1994.

Lever, Janet. *Soccer Madness.* Chicago/London: University of Chicago Press, 1983.

Parks, Jenifer. *"Red Sport, Red Tape: The Olympic Games, The Soviet Sports Bureaucracy, and the Cold War, 1952–1980.* Unpublished Ph.D. dissertation. Chapel Hill: University of North Carolina, 2009.

Prozumenshchikov, M. Iu. *Bol'shoi sport, bol'shaia politika.* Moscow: RO. SSPEN, 2004.

Raleigh, Donald. *Soviet Baby Boomers: An Oral History of Russia's Cold War Generation.* Bloomington: Indiana University Press, 2012.

Rein, Raanan. *Fútbol, Jews, and the making of Argentina.* Stanford: Stanford University Press, 2014.

Sto let rossiiskomu futbolu. Moscow: Rossiiskii futbol'nyi soiuz, 1997.

Vasil'ev, Pavel. *Poslednii kumir: Rossiiskii futbol ot Iashina do Gazzaeva.* Moscow: Eksmo, 2008.

Wilson, Jonathan. *Behind the Curtain: Travels in East European Football.* London: Orion, 2006.

Zeller, Manfred. "'The Second Stalingrad:' Soccer Fandom, Popular Memory and the Legacy of the Stalinist Past". In *Euphoria and Exhaustion: Modern Aport in Soviet culture and society,* edited by Nikolaus Katzer, et al., 207–210. Frankfurt/ New York: Campus Verlag, 2010.

CHAPTER 7

Post-colonial Outcomes: FIFA, Overseas Territory and National Identity

Steve Menary

The effect of external rule has nearly always been both to cultivate and to prohibit nationalist activity. Partly in consequence of this, nationhood, as a positive expression of a unique collective identity, has proven the most successful strategy through which to resist and express a difference from the fixings and hierarchies of colonial power.[1]

No sport has proven better at helping establish a sense of nationhood than football. As Guilianotti and Finn assert, football is the most important setting within popular culture for displaying a national identity that can then be mediated through mass communication.[2] A nation can be created, even if the teams on the field represent anything but in a political sense. This is illustrated by the number of sovereign states accepted by the United Nations (UN) and those admitted to the Fédération Internationale de Football Association (FIFA) (193 countries against 209 football states). With nine sovereign states still outside of FIFA, that provides an even wider divergence between real countries in a political sense and those seeking nationhood on the football field. A large proportion of this discrepancy is the legacy of the colonial era, particularly the imperialist expansion

S. Menary (✉)
Department of Journalism, University of Winchester, Winchester, UK

© Hofstra University 2017
B. Elsey, S. Pugliese (eds.), *Football and the Boundaries of History*,
DOI 10.1057/978-1-349-95006-5_7

of France, Great Britain and the Netherlands. Many of these territories have subsequently accepted a status less than full independence and still resist colonial power culturally. Football is a powerful tool in this quest for an identity and 2013 was to prove a significant year in this struggle.

After a battle that began 15 years earlier, the British holding of Gibraltar was admitted as the 54th member of UEFA. Prior to their admission by UEFA, Gibraltar's last competitive matches had been in the football competition at the 2011 Island Games in the Isle of Wight, where opposition included the tiny Channel island of Alderney. After being admitted by UEFA in May 2013, Gibraltar's first opponent was the 2010 World Cup qualifier Slovakia. For the remnants of the French empire, 2013 proved even more meaningful both on and off the pitch. Tahiti—part of the overseas collective of French Polynesia—became the first post-colonial remnant to appear at a senior FIFA competition for more than half a century. Tahiti suffered three heavy defeats in the Confederations Cup at Brazil, but Tahiti had earned the right to take part by winning the 2012 Oceania Nations Cup. Gibraltar and Tahiti proved their worth on the pitch and illustrated the benefits of official recognition from football's governing bodies, but this recognition of overseas territories is uneven.

Some territories are able to benefit from FIFA's significant largesse yet others, where nationhood is equally as unlikely as Gibraltar in a political sense, are left on the sidelines. This dislocation can be seen in the last competition that Tahiti participated in prior to the 2013 Confederations Cup. The Coupe de l'Outre-Mer, the Overseas Cup, was a biannual tournament staged in Paris and funded by the Fédération Française de Football (FFF). In their first match at the 2012 Overseas Cup, Tahiti played Mayotte, a French overseas collective in the Indian Ocean, whose organising body, the Ligue de Football de Mayotte, is not recognised by any footballing body apart from the FFF: Mayotte triumphed.

NEDERLANDS-KOLONIALE RIJK

Attempts to create a sense of sporting uniqueness in overseas territories through membership of FIFA pre-dated both decolonisation and the Second World War, which brought about the end of the European colonial empires. This process of sporting independence was pioneered, albeit reluctantly at first, by the Dutch. An association was formed in the Dutch Caribbean holding of Curaçao in 1921. Initially known as Curaçao Voetbalbond (CVB), this association was not recognised by the colonial political administration or the Koninklijke Nederlandse Voetbalbond (KNVB) back in the Netherlands for political reasons, yet in 1932 the CVB was accepted as a full member by FIFA.[3] This situation was resolved after a year and the Dutch approach to footballing independence has since been one of a more relaxed decentralisation. In 1938, the Dutch East Indies (now Indonesia) qualified for the finals of the 1938 FIFA World Cup and Curaçao reached the finals of the football tournament at the 1950 Olympic Games in Helsinki. Though focused on Curaçao, this team included players from Aruba and Bonaire over the years and became known as the Netherlands Antilles during the 1958 World Cup qualifiers, reflecting an earlier change in political title. In the immediate post-colonial era, the Netherlands Antilles was amongst the strongest sides in the region and won the Caribbean championships in 1950 and 1962.

The islands of the Dutch Antilles are the Netherlands' last colonial holding. Their status is mostly as autonomous countries within the Kingdom of the Netherlands. They are not one of the 17 territories identified by the UN as non-self-governing territories.[4] However, players from the Antilles are still able to play freely in the Netherlands. The Antilles began to fracture in a sporting and political sense when Aruba became a separate state within the Kingdom of the Netherlands in 1986. Two years later, the Arubaanse Voetbal Bond secured full membership of FIFA and in 2010 the rump Netherlands Antilles was finally dissolved with Curaçao taking the FIFA membership held by the Netherlands Antilles. In 2013, Sint Maarten was admitted as a full member of the Confederation of North, Central American and Caribbean Association Football and Bonaire became a CONCACAF associate member. Of the Dutch Antilles, only Bonaire remained affiliated to the KNVB and that tie would need to be severed if full CONCACAF status was to be achieved.[5]

Bonaire won the inaugural ABCS Cup (the competition is an acronym of Aruba, Bonaire, Curaçao and Suriname, formerly Dutch Guiana until securing independence in 1975) in 2010 for Dutch-speaking Caribbean territories but the admission of Sint Maarten was a surprise as there is little evidence of organised football and two years previously the KNVB described the state of organised football in Sint Maarten as a "mess."[6] Sint Maarten's admission to full CONCACAF membership did bolster an organised bloc of Dutch-speaking Caribbean territories, which began to emerge in 2010 through the annual ABCS Cup. Etienne Silee, the coach of Curaçao, explains: "The ABCS Cup is more the continuity of the historical bond and the close relationship of the Dutch speaking island (sic) in the CFU [Caribbean Football Union]."[7] Although the KNVB trains coaches from the Dutch colonies and Surinam and has helped develop pitches in Antriol, Rincon and North Salina, the relationship on the field is less developed. The Netherlands played the Netherlands Antilles on three occasions in full internationals but the last match was an 8-0 win in Europe by the colonial masters in 1962.

FRANCE: DÉPARTEMENTS ET TERRITOIRES D'OUTRE-MER

Sport was imported to the French colonies at the end of the nineteenth century and has been central to the cultivation of the notion of soft power by the French state. Football in particular has played a key role in both disseminating a view to the rest of the world of strong modern nation and uniting a multi-ethnic country. France's triumph at the 1998 World Cup final is routinely cited as an example of this unifying effect. The 1998 French World Cup victory has been much remarked for the background of players from former colonies, but less attention has been on those from existing colonial holdings: Christian Karembeu (New Caledonia) and Lilian Thuram (Guadeloupe). Thuram came to France during his childhood but Karembeu moved at 17 and is an example of many other players recruited from overseas territories to French professional clubs.

Football in the French colonies was being taken up enthusiastically by the 1930s and often in opposition to the colonial power's insistence on a military education and gymnastics, with Combeau-Mari writing that "multisport societies only played football, much to the despair of colonial administrators."[8] Today Marc Kanyan is better known as a New Caledonian politician but in 1968 he was a member of the French team that reached the quarter-finals of the 1968 Olympic football tournament. Krasnoff argues that the unifying effect of football in France stretches back further still, in particular to the 1958 World Cup finals, where France finished third: "There was one public culture, one language and one shared history of the team's triumphs and trials, especially the legacy of 1958, which grew into mythic lore."[9]

In 1960, France hosted the Jeux de la Communauté (Community Games) for French-speaking African nations plus overseas departments and territories as a new structure called Communauté was brought to allow overseas peoples to decide themselves whether their own status should be with the state, a territory, department, federation or member of the Communauté.[10] Initially, the Communauté included four overseas departments, French Guiana, Guadeloupe, Martinique and Réunion, and six overseas territories, French Somaliland, the Comoros, New Caledonia, French Polynesia, Wallis and Futuna and Saint Pierre and Miquelon. At the 1960 Jeux de la Communauté, football was included with France beating Cameroon in the final, 3-1, thus ensuring that Les Bleus conveniently stayed at the top of the French colonial pyramid.[11] In 1962, metropolitan France began to engage even more directly with the Outre-Mer over football with Guadeloupe, and Martinique was permitted to send a team to mainland France at the expense of the FFF to compete in the Coupe de France, which caused "great excitement in the islands."[12] Of those ten territories or departments to attend the Jeux de la Communauté, only French Somaliland (now Djibouti) and the Comoros are no longer attached to France, although Mayotte voted to remain French when the Comoros sought independence. In 1989, France began hosting the Jeux de la Francophonie, the translation: Francophone Games, for French-speaking territories as a counterweight to Britain's pursuit of soft power through the Commonwealth Games, which—as the Empire Games—began in 1930 and has become a post-colonial sporting mega-event.

In common with the remaining Dutch overseas holdings, players in the last vestiges of France's colonial empire benefit from access to European passports, but in return the best players are creamed off by the FFF to play for France. Typically, players from French overseas departments and territories play first for the representative teams from places such as Guadeloupe, and then those showing the most promise are recruited for Les Bleus to represent the modern-day French empire. As these territories had representative teams that only played at a local level, this did not represent a problem. Any players wishing to take the journey in reverse, such as Jocelyn Angloma of Guadeloupe, could only do so once five years had elapsed since their last senior international appearance for Les Bleus.

In 1990 and only a year after being formed, the Fédération Tahitienne de Football (FTF) was admitted to FIFA after the extension of the autonomy given by Paris to the local authorities in these holdings for education and sport. This was also recognition of the distance between Paris and colonial outposts such as Papeete and Noumea, the capital of New Caledonia, which was admitted to FIFA in 2004 on the grounds that a ballot on independence was due in 2012.[13] After the 1998 World Cup victory, a more centralised inclusive approach to a French identity in the Outre-Mer emerged as the FFF set up a competition solely for teams from colonial holdings to take local representation to a new level. The Overseas

Cup was first staged in 2008 and featured seven representative teams from French Guiana, Guadeloupe, Martinique, Mayotte, New Caledonia, Réunion and Tahiti (French Polynesia). The week-long competition was hosted by lower league professional teams from the Parisian suburbs with the cost of the tournament, including flights and accommodation for 18 players and 7 officials, all borne by the FFF. The Overseas Cup became biannual and in 2010 St Pierre and Miquelon was invited to form a representative team from the three clubs on the North American islands to make the numbers up to an even eight teams. Saint Martin was a member of the Caribbean Football Union and had participated in regional competitions but in 2012 the FFF limited the competition to eight teams. At this time, the FFF estimated the cost of staging the event to be around €900,000. Although Parisian-based members of the larger Caribbean diaspora attended matches, crowds were not large and income from matches for the FFF must have been low (Fig. 7.1).

The aim of the tournament was not to make money but again to bolster the notion of the French sporting empire and a wider French identity in the Outre-Mer. This Overseas Cup also provided a clear message: of all the old colonial empires, only France could stage its own mini-World Cup. The Overseas Cup played to the ideals of sport for development and

Fig. 7.1 2012 Overseas Cup winners Reunion. © Steve Menary

peace (SPD), that "sport is not socially or politically fixed in its organisation or its development mobilization, orientation or implementation."[14] By engaging the places outside any organised sporting framework such as Mayotte and St Pierre and Miquelon, but also with FIFA members, the FFF was acknowledging the need for fluidity, yet at the heart of French engagement with the Outre-Mer is a need to service the needs of metropolitan France. Players in the Overseas Cup could only take part if they were playing in leagues of their department or territory. So, for example, Lesly Malouda could—and did—represent French Guiana in Caribbean regional competitions, but could not play for his department's team in the Overseas Cup as he played professionally in France. Teams taking part in the Overseas Cup were also described as representatives of the individual local leagues, such as the Ligue Guadeloupéenne de Football (LGF) rather than "national" teams even though places such as Guadeloupe and Martinique regularly fielded national teams in regional competitions. Combeau-Mari argues there is no contradiction because Guadeloupe along with French Guiana, Martinique and the Indian Ocean island of Réunion has a "deep attachment" to France.[15] Yet the stimulus for the Overseas Cup came not from these old colonies but from New Caledonia and Christian Karembeu, who explains:

> We know where we come from and we want to give back what Guadeloupe or Martinique or New Caledonia gave to the national team. We know our background. I wanted to be close to them but also to try to give another visibility of how we are, our tradition, our culture, this is the way we are and the tool is sport.[16]

Karembeu was a regular visitor to the competition, whilst many other famous French players from the Outre-Mer also attended from Thuram to Florent Malouda and Frédéric Piquionne (born in New Caledonia, but who played for Martinique). These players were not able to compete and even those who had been subsequently asked to do after the required time lag were keen not to devalue the credibility of their birthright by making worthless guest appearances. Steve Marlet of Fulham was a visitor to the 2012 Overseas Cup. In 2012, he said: "I am from Martinique. That's why I [went]. The tournament is a good thing for football to get a chance to see this kind of selection. It's important to organise this kind of competition in France because so many players play professionally in France from the West Indies. Two years ago, the trainer of Martinique called me as five years had passed and I could play but I said I was too old."[17]

The acceptance of New Caledonia into FIFA was to prove the last by a French territory, department or collective as the FFF sought to unite the Outre-Mer through the Overseas Cup but the ambitions for sporting nationhood in these territories had outstripped those of their French sponsors. In February 2013, the new president of CONCACAF, Jeffrey Webb, proposed that the football associations in French Guiana, Guadeloupe, Martinique and Saint Martin and also Dutch Sint Maarten be admitted to the confederation as full members at the body's next congress in April 2013. The reasoning behind this decision was described by CONCACAF as "fully integrating the Caribbean region culturally and economically through football."[18] The admission duly took place and was partially in recognition of advances made on the pitch by some of those French possessions now welcomed into CONCACAF. Even with the best players regularly stolen by various French representative teams, Guadeloupe was strong enough to reach the semi-finals of CONCACAF region's premier tournament, the Gold Cup, in 2007 and the quarter-finals two years later. Martinique won the Caribbean Cup in 1993 and has qualified for the Gold Cup on three occasions, reaching the quarter-finals in 2002, while French Guiana qualified for the 2013 Caribbean Cup finals. Admitting Saint Martin, their Dutch-speaking neighbours Sint Maarten and another Dutch holding, Bonaire, as an associate, had less justification on the pitch but took membership of CONCACAF to 41 associations. This number was closer to the 46 full members and one associate member achieved by the Asian Football Confederation, which like CONCACAF has three full places at the World Cup finals and the chance of a fourth through an intercontinental play-off. In February 2013, Jocelyne Sapotille, President of the Sports Commission in Guadeloupe, said: "It is also of great value for France to have us integrated into the CONCACAF region, as it is our intention to make French football shine through our Caribbean experience."[19]

Admitting the four French territories strengthened the sporting soft power of France as a voting bloc of French-controlled territories from the old territories was created yet all the best players remained available for Les Bleus. The FFF subsequently cancelled the Overseas Cup in March 2014. Alain Soreze, general secretary of the LGF, says: "No more Coupe de l'Outre-Mer because too expensive and not a lot spectators, merchandising and media TV for the event."[20] Instead, the FFF proposes to offer clubs in the Outre-Mer more places in the Coupe de France, so any inadvertent attempts by metropolitan France to fund nationhood in a sporting sense have essentially ended. In club versus country, club has triumphed. The French Caribbean holdings are unable to enter larger events, such as the World Cup, and the associations there do not expect to progress to full FIFA membership due to the political objections of France. This appears to typify the approach by France to nationhood in overseas holdings, allowing territories, departments and collectives to advance footballing standards yet ensuring that France keeps the option to recruit the best players from the most fertile territories for Les Bleus.

THE BRITISH EMPIRE

Contradictions between English sporting identity and Great Britain's political status have meant there has been little emphasis in developing sporting soft power in the remnants of the British empire. In the Caribbean territories, the British colonial sporting legacy has been overwhelmed by the globalising impact of satellite television from the United States. Briton Tom Smith arrived in the Turks and Caicos Islands in 1984 and went on to found the Turks and Caicos Football Association (TCIFA). He reflects: "You went into a school and all the children played basketball and wanted to be Michael Jordan."[21]

In these remnants of the British empire, the creation of sporting nations amongst these British overseas territories has been for more prosaic reasons. Membership of CONCACAF for associations such as the TCIFA came as now discredited leader Jack Warner sought to establish a sizeable power bloc. Tiny Caribbean islands where the game barely existed and governance would prove fatally weak were ushered first into CONCACAF then FIFA to justify greater World Cup representation and boost the power of Warner and his immediate entourage. A failure by the English Football Association (FA) to engage with the tiny British holdings in the region was a major reason why nascent associations in these islands were so susceptible to approaches from Warner.

In 1996, Jack Warner made the British territory of the Turks and Caicos Islands an associate member of CONCACAF even though no Turks and Caicos Islands Football Association even existed. Football in the Turks and Caicos then comprised a four-team league featuring a team of British expatriate workers, a side drawn from workers at the island's Club Med resort and two teams of Haitian immigrants. The league was organised by Tom Smith, a former referee from Bedfordshire, who only after being contacted by Warner formed the TCIFA. Two years later, the TCIFA was admitted to FIFA and since then more than US$5 million has flowed into the islands from the world body to provide grass and artificial pitches and much more. CONCACAF and Warner insisted that the Turks and Caicos fielded a national side, but appearances are intermittent and hardly representative of the island's racial profile.

Between 2000 and 2010, the Turks and Caicos senior team played just ten games yet received US$3.1 million from FIFA's financial assistance programme and US$800,000 in funding for capital projects from the world body's GOAL scheme. Only the tiny former Portuguese colony of Sao Tome et Principe played fewer international matches over this period. [22] In this league of non-appearances, the sides that ranked third and fourth after playing just 13 and 17 senior international matches, respectively, were also British overseas territories. Another difficulty to effective development of football has been that British passports are issued by the British government and not the local administrations. In the British Virgin Islands, around 90% of adult players are not able to obtain a British passport.[23] These players are classed as "Belongers," which provides full citizen's rights such as voting and residency but no passport, so these players are not eligible to represent the islands under FIFA rules. British Caribbean islands that are in FIFA not only are amongst the most reclusive national teams in the world but also suffer from poor governance. Monserrat's population is little more than 5000; the island has no football league or even a properly functioning club and was accused in 2012 of failing to pay two former managers, Scott Cooper and Ruel Fox, around US$100,000 in wages.[24] In Anguilla, half of the island's six clubs were banned from voting in Anguilla Football Association (AFA) meetings, not shown financial accounts and not given an explanation as to why the AFA president, Raymond Guishard, was banned from football for 45 days and fined £200 by FIFA in November 2011.[25] The Dutch Caribbean holding of Aruba was also amongst the world's least active international teams in this period, illustrating that a laissez-faire policy to encouraging and developing sport at overseas holdings does not always boost the aspirations of SPD at a micro sporting level.

The approach to sporting governance and development at the remaining territories within the British empire is partly clouded by the paradox of four national football associations existing as FIFA members within the nation of the United Kingdom Great Britain and Northern Ireland. Certainly, the associations in Northern Ireland, Scotland and Wales would be unlikely to devote time and resources to developing football in overseas holdings that were also subject to invasions by the English/British. In June

2012, the British government published a White Paper aimed at strengthening links with the overseas territories after political scandals caused by poor governance in holdings such as the Cayman Islands.[26] There is no mention of sport in that report, which illustrates the dichotomy of the post-colonial outcome in British sport. There is no soft power strategy, as funding and developing the game is left to the local representatives, who are then unable to field their strongest teams at the international level due to political restrictions from the Mother Country.

In cricket, the ideal of a pan-Caribbean West Indies team has successfully survived the twin impacts of decolonisation and globalisation. The footballing equivalent, which surely had less support amongst the public school elite at the heart of British government, proved less successful. The British Caribbean Football Association (BCFA) was formed in 1957, based in Jamaica, and included Barbados, Bermuda, British Guiana (now Guyana), Dominica, Grenada, Jamaica, St Vincent and Trinidad. A BCFA tour of Britain took place in 1959, but as constituents gained independence enthusiasm for the pan-Caribbean association petered out amongst players and officials in a sport predominantly played by the working classes in the metropole and the colonial holdings. As independence was achieved, step by step the members of the BCIFA joined FIFA yet their cricketing counterparts were happy to stay within the framework of the West Indies and the success that brought.

When those remaining British overseas territories did seek competition overseas, this was not with England or even North America. The Bermuda Football Association (BFA) joined FIFA in 1962 but the national team's first opponents were another small cold island in northern Europe: Iceland. Even when the BFA needed funds to help develop the game, these came not from Britain or the FA but through a £3000 grant from the Bermuda government.[27] Bermuda went on to eliminate the United States from the qualifiers for the football tournament at the 1968 Olympic Games. The Bermudan government subsequently advanced another £10,000 to help the BFA stage one of the first international youth tournaments in the Caribbean region.[28] Even more recently, when the BFA attempted to regain some momentum in Bermudan football and tried to draw young Bermudians away from a growing gang culture, the linkup was not with Britain but the United States. The Bermuda Hogges franchise was launched in 2006 and entered the Mid Atlantic Division of the Eastern Conference of USL (United Soccer League) Premier Development League in the United States, though this club folded in 2013.

There is evidence of organised football on Ascension Island and St Helena, but outside of Bermuda and the Caribbean the only remaining British colonies with functioning associations to seek engagement overseas have been Gibraltar and the Falkland Islands. In both cases, attempts at greater footballing development have been stymied by their political heritage. Gibraltar has been claimed by Spain since the 1713 Treaty of Utrecht, while Argentina's claims to the Falkland Islands also date back hundreds of years. As befits a colonial garrison, much of Gibraltar's sporting heritage is based on sports steeped in British public schools and Empire—cricket, hunting, rowing, rugby and yachting—but a "mass following of football by the services" resulted in the formation of the Gibraltar Football Association (GFA) in 1895.[29] In 1909, the GFA was accepted as a member of the FA on similar terms to English county associations. Initially Gibraltar's footballing status was on similar grounds and engagement was generally sought with clubs, rather than national associations or other representative teams.

Conversely, given what drove Gibraltar onto the international footballing stage, there was even a long shared football heritage with Spain and support for Spanish clubs, though Archer writes that this was, not unsurprisingly, for Catalan Barcelona rather than Franco-ist Real Madrid.[30] As early as 1913 a GFA team played in Madrid and Seville visited the colony in 1935. Between 1949 and 1955, other Spanish teams visited including Malaga and Seville again and the Gibraltar representative team even toured Germany and Luxembourg in 1954, culminating in a 4-2 win over the Luxembourg national side.[31] In 1954, Queen Elizabeth II visited the British enclave and the following year the Spanish government ruled that written permission was needed by Spanish sports teams playing in Gibraltar, thus heralding a long and escalating period of isolation for Gibraltarian sport culminating in Spain closing its border in 1969. The border would not reopen for 16 years, during which time Gibraltarian sports teams looked elsewhere for opportunities as a siege mentality festered in all walks of life on the Rock against Spanish influence.

In 1985, the Island Games Association (IGA), an organisation founded on an often-esoteric British love of islands, staged the first Island Games on the Isle of Man and featured 15 teams, including 6 that were part of the wider British empire. Only St Helena was an overseas territory, but as membership of the IGA grew to 24 islands, Gibraltar was admitted on the basis that the border with Spain was closed so the Rock was classed, in a moment of quixotic support for past notions of Empire, as an island and welcomed into the IGA.[32] In 1989, football was introduced to the Island Games and this biannual tournament was to provide the only regular competition for Gibraltar, who first took part in 1993 and won in 2007, and also the Falkland Islands, who made their debut in 2001. Attendance is at the expense of the athletes involved and a trip to Europe, where all but one of the Island Games tournaments has been held, typically costs footballers from the Falkland Islands around £2000 each. The only assistance comes from the Falkland Island government and there has been no help for the Falkland Islands Football League from the English FA and the only overseas engagement, outside of the Island Games, has been in Chile.[33] This is in stark contrast with France and the FFF, which paid out around €2.7 million to stage three Overseas Cups and continues to cover expenses of clubs from the Outre-Mer taking part in the Coupe de France.

Historically, the FA has engaged with the Empire but unlike the Netherlands, where matches between the Oranje and the Antilles were classed as full internationals, games between England and British overseas holdings are not. The then British colony of Hong Kong joined FIFA independently of the FA in 1954 when England played Hong Kong twice in May 1961 at the Government Stadium in Wan Chai; neither of the matches were given full international status, nor were matches against Gibraltar in 1965 and 1973 and Bermuda in 1955. England has also been careful not to confer nationhood on territories soon to leave the Empire. England visited Hong Kong in 1996, a year before the Asian territory was due to be handed back to China. The Hong Kong Football Association had been admitted to FIFA in 1954, yet the match is described in FA records as a game between England and Hong Kong XI. More recently, the only engagement has been through the involvement of England C, which is a representative team for players playing outside the Football League and the heir to the old England amateur team that was disbanded after the amateur credo was abolished in 1974. England C visited Gibraltar in 2011 and Bermuda in 2013. The British approach to sport in its former empire contrasts starkly with the Gallic drive for soft power, or the more laid-back Dutch approach. In what remains of the British empire, there appears to be a complete abrogation of responsibility as territories are left to regional domestic political machinations that may support the notion of independence on one level, but do little to foster the aims of SPD.

POST-POST-COLONIAL LEFTOVERS

Of the 17 non-self-governing territories identified by the UN, 9 are British overseas holdings and 2 are French and only Gibraltar and the Falkland Islands remain unrecognised by FIFA. Outside the remnants of the British, French and Dutch empires and the two relics of Denmark's former empire, Greenland and the Faroe Islands, are associations in other small territories or micro domains with a sporting inheritance stemming from a combination of post-colonial times and the new world order. Here too, recognition from sporting bodies is erratic. At the 2001 UN conference on decolonisation, dependencies of the United States, including American Samoa and Guam, argued that like the Gibraltarians their residents prefer the political status quo yet American Samoa and Guam are members of FIFA and enjoy myriad benefits in terms of development, opportunities and finance. So too does the federation in Macau, which joined the world body four years after the overthrow of the Salazar regime in 1974, when Portugal's colonial policy was reversed, yet Macau never achieved independence. Instead, Macau, like Hong Kong, reverted to Chinese rule, albeit indirectly.

The main global superpower to emerge after the end of the Second World War and the post-colonial era is the United States. In the post-post-colonial world, there are five national teams competing that are either under the sway of the United States or ultimately an extension of the United States, including one—Puerto Rico—that could potentially become the 51st state, yet has been a member of FIFA since 1960. In this new post-colonial empire, the absurdity of football's recognition criteria means that all the players fielded in the teams representing the US Virgin Islands—a FIFA member since 1998—have US passports and even the local newspaper cannot bring itself to describe the USVI XI as a national team.[34]

CONCLUSION

In some of the remaining protectorates and overseas holdings, full independence is neither practical nor, in many cases, even desired by the local population. Instead, loose affiliation with a larger country provides benefits such as political security, passports and a currency, whilst allowing for greater footballing independence. Yet lack of a coherent global sporting policy created this current uneven situation, where some French holdings and British territories are able to enjoy and even misuse the benefits of international acceptance, while others are left undeveloped. Typically, those holdings claimed by another country—Mayotte (the Comoros), Gibraltar (Spain) and the Falkland Islands (Argentina)—suffer the most, as greater political recognition is more contentious. The result is sporting isolation from the rest of the international community and even the "mother country". This is the troubling and seemingly unsolvable dichotomy of the post-post-colonial sporting outcome. Although FIFA ruled in 2011 that priority for membership be given to the remaining independent countries outside of the world body and then independent territories, the only recognition—and then only partial—has come for Kosovo. [35]

Hoolihan argues that the issue of differentiation is "likely to be more important than integration" for sport in small states and this also applies to those remaining overseas territories where there is a need to be seen in a sporting and wider cultural sense as independent.[36] Certainly, sporting freedom must surely be beneficial to those British overseas territories that are significant players in offshore finance, as a "national team" can serve to validate an independence that does not exist. In these territories, adopting football rather than cricket, the most prevalent sport amongst existing and British colonial holdings in the Caribbean, or the American sports that are widely viewed on cable television, is illustrative of the independent strategy that Hoolihan cites as helping small states assert nationhood through sport. However, Darnell and Hayhurst argue that elite competitive football, such as overseas territories competing in FIFA tournaments such as World Cup qualifiers, actually hampers in SPD and that mobilising football development cannot solve political and social constraints and limitations.[37] This can be borne out through the example of British Caribbean territories, where football has been introduced and developed yet significant numbers of players are unable to play, which would surely only serve to hamper the aims of SPD. In his theory of community, Baumann argues for communities that explode then become extinct but also introduces a third category of the "cloakroom community." Baumann argues that these communities "need a spectacle which appeals to similar interests dormant in otherwise disparate individuals and so bring them all together for a stretch of time when other interests—those which divide them instead of unite—are temporarily laid aside, put on a slow burner or silenced altogether."[38]

As the world's most popular sport, football has the potential to achieve just this. Trying to solve colonial-era disputes solely through the development of football is misguided, but greater consistency in the recognition and development of football both from the colonial power and also from FIFA itself is surely possible. For all those cloakroom communities left over from the colonial era and struggling to find a sporting identity against the social and cultural pressures of historical antecedents, an even playing field in terms of recognition and development from the political and sporting powers must be essential.

NOTES

1. Peter Childs and Patrick Williams, *An Introduction to Post-Colonial Theory* (Abingdon: Routledge, 1997), 205.
2. Richard Giulianotti and Gerry P. T. Finn, "Old Visions, Old Issues: New Horizons, New Openings? Change, Continuity and Other Contradictions in World Football," *Sport in Society* 2, no. 3: 257.
3. *World Soccer*, January 1962, p. 14.
4. http://www.un.org/en/decolonization/nonselfgovterritories. shtml. Accessed 3 July 2014.
5. Remco Van Dam, historical co-ordinator at the KNVB, April 3, 2014.
6. http://www.playthegame.org/news/detailed/cas-ruling-puts-new-focus-on-small-football-nations-5218.html. Accessed 28 March 2014.
7. Interview with Etienne Silee, coach of the Curaçao national football team, June 25 2013.
8. Evelyne Combeau-Mari, "Sport in the French Colonies (1880–1962): A Case Study," *Journal of Sport History*, 33, no. 1 (Spring 2006): 42.
9. Lindsay Sarah Krasnoff. *The Making of Les Bleus: Sport in France 1958–2010* (Maryland: Lexington, 2012), 84.
10. Evelyne Combeau-Mari, 2011. "Sport and Decolonisation: The Community Games," *The International Journal of Sport History*, 28, no. 12 (April 1960):1717.
11. Ibid., 1721.
12. *World Soccer*, January 1962, p. 14.
13. Steve Menary, *Outcasts: The Lands That FIFA Forgot* (Studley: Know The Score, 2007), 1.
14. Simon C. Darnell and Lindsay M. C. Hayhurst, "Sport for Decolonization: Exploring a New Praxis of Sport for Development," *Progress in Development Studies*, 11, no. 3 (2011): 193.

15. Combeau-Mari, "Sport in the French Colonies," p. 28.
16. Christian Karembeu, Born in New Caledonia and a 1998 World Cup winner with France. September 22, 2012.
17. Steve Marlet, Former professional player at Lyon and Fulham and French international. September 24, 2012.
18. http://www.concacaf.com/team/french-guiana. Accessed 28 March 2014.
19. Ibid.
20. Alain Soreze, General Secretary of the Ligue Guadeloupéenne de Football, March 20, 2013.
21. *World Soccer*, March 201, p. 42.
22. Steve Menary, "What's A Vote Worth?" *The Blizzard* no. 3, 151.
23. http://www.cfufootball.org/index.php/latest-news/9302-cfu-to-support-efforts-to-have-fifa-reconsider-competition-eligibility-rules-for-overseas-territories. Accessed 28 Mar 2014.
24. http://www.playthegame.org/news/detailed/players-launch-attack-on-caribbean-football-leaders-5491.html?type=98&cHash=e52b22e31f3f0b51373c0626ea095f83. Accessed 28 Mar 2014.
25. Ibid.
26. Foreign & Colonial Office. *The Overseas Territories: Security, Success and Sustainability*, 2012.
27. *World Soccer*, March 1969, p. 17.
28. Ibid.
29. E. G. Archer, "Imperial Influences: Gibraltarians, Cultural Bonding and Sport," *Culture, Sport Society* 6, no. 1 (Spring 2003): 58.
30. Ibid., 59.
31. *World Soccer*, September 1969, p. 21.
32. Admitted in interview with Brian Partington, Island Games Association president, July 13, 2005.
33. Menary, 54.
34. CNN – http://edition.cnn.com/2011/SPORT/football/09/13/football.us.virgin.islands/. Accessed 2 Apr 2014.
35. http://www.playthegame.org/news/detailed/cas-ruling-puts-new-focus-on-small-football-nations-5218.html 31 Accessed Mar 2014.
36. Barrie Hoolihan, "Small States: Sport and Politics at the Margin," presentation at the 2013 annual conference of the Political Studies Association (Sports Special Interest Group) at the University of Bath, February 1, 2013.

37. Darnell and Hayhurst, 189.
38. Zygmunt Baumann, *Liquid Modernity* (Cambridge: Polity, 2000), 200.

WORKS CITED

Archer, E.G. "Imperial Influences: Gibraltarians, Cultural Bonding and Sport. *Culture, Sport, Society* 6, no. 1 (Spring 2003).

Baumann, Zygmunt. *Liquid Modernity*. Cambridge: Polity, 2000.

Childs, Peter, and Patrick Williams. *An Introduction to Post-colonial Theory*. Abingdon: Routledge, 1997.

Combeau-Mari, Evelyn. "Sport and Decolonisation: The Community Games". *The International Journal of Sport History* 28, no. 12 (1960, April): 1717.

———. "Sport in the French Colonies (1880–1962): A Case Study". *Journal of Sport History* 33, no. 1 (Spring, 2006).

Foreign & Colonial Office. *The Overseas Territories: Security, Success and Sustainability*. London: Stationery Office, 2012.

Giulianotti, Richard, and Gerry P.T. Finn. Old Visions, Old Issues: New Horizons, New Openings? Change, Continuity and Other Contradictions in World Football. *Sport in Society* 2, no. 3 (1999): 256–282.

Krasnoff, Lindsay Sarah. *The Making of Les Bleus: Sport in France 1958–2010*. Maryland: Lexington, 2012.

CHAPTER 8

The Hermit Kingdom versus the World: North Korea in the 2010 World Cup

Aaron D. Horton

The Democratic People's Republic of Korea (DPRK), better known as simply "North Korea," is, without a doubt, one of the most secretive states in the world. Until recently, North Koreans had almost no access to information from the outside world, and likewise that outside world had relatively little knowledge of the domestic situation inside the DPRK. The state's ongoing isolationism has led some modern observers to label North Korea "the Hermit Kingdom,"[1] a term used in reference to the entire Korean peninsula since the nineteenth century, when Western missionaries and would-be imperialists encountered stiff and sometimes violent resistance to outsiders.[2]

The modern DPRK's intense resistance to outside information and, therefore, influence, is tied closely to Korea's recent history, in which it had been, more often than not, a pawn to greater powers such as China or Japan, which ruled the peninsula as a colony from 1910 to 1945. In a situation remarkably similar to that in post-World War II Germany, Korea found itself divided into American and Soviet zones of occupation until 1948, when the United States installed hardcore anti-communist Syngman Rhee as president of the newly constituted Republic of Korea (ROK) in the South. The Soviets responded by establishing Kim Il-sung,

A.D. Horton (✉)
Department of History, Alabama State University, Montgomery, AL, USA

© Hofstra University 2017
B. Elsey, S. Pugliese (eds.), *Football and the Boundaries of History*,
DOI 10.1057/978-1-349-95006-5_8

an anti-Japanese resistance fighter who had spent most of the war in Russia, as leader of the DPRK. Upon taking power, Kim began constructing a cult of personality around himself that ultimately would rival those even of Hitler and Stalin. Kim ("The Great Leader") and his successors, son Kim Jong-il ("The Dear Leader") and now grandson Kim Jong-un ("The Supreme Leader"), have constructed an alternate narrative of history that exalts the Kims as gods among men who have successfully defied the imperialist ambitions of Japan and the United States (whose "unprovoked" invasion started the Korean War in 1950) while building a perfect society (indeed, the best in the world, according to official claims) on the principle of *Juche*, or self-reliance.

Outside observers know, of course, that for all of North Korea's bellicose bluster, especially its recent and seemingly ceaseless threats about using its nuclear weapons, all but the very elite of the country's population suffer from extreme material privation. Many scholars, including B.R. Myers in his excellent study of DPRK propaganda, *The Cleanest Race*, believe that North Korea will soon face a "mass legitimation crisis" due to increasing awareness among its people of conditions in South Korea and beyond, thanks to smuggled DVDs and black market radios that can receive broadcasts from China and South Korea.[3] Even moderate reform would likely result in a "dam-bursting" flood of popular demands for greater change, so the regime's only recourse is to maintain its ongoing saber-rattling hostility to the outside world, especially the United States and its "puppet," South Korea.

How would this belligerent, isolationist country fare in the world's greatest international sporting competition? Along with the Olympics, the World Cup is usually celebrated for its emphasis on peaceful, friendly competition, even when political relations between competitors may be less than ideal. For example, the United States and Iran played a group match in the 1998 Finals without incident; in fact, Iran's players offered white roses to the Americans, and the teams posed for a group photo before the contest.[4] Such friendly episodes are thankfully common in recent international competitions, but how would the secretive "Hermit Kingdom" of North Korea fare when forced to put its alleged superiority to the test in the world's most popular sporting event? Given the country's political behavior, it is unsurprising that North Korea's involvement in the 2010 World Cup in South Africa was a bizarre affair, from qualification to the Finals and beyond. Exploring this episode in DPRK history will demonstrate that the national team's fortunes on the field at the 2010

Finals were a microcosm of their nation's circumstances. How does soccer contribute to complicating media polemics? Using media and secondary historical sources to new ends. Utilizing a broad array of media reports as well as official statements from the Korea Central News Agency, the DPRK's official online news organ, this chapter will demonstrate that the North Korean national team's 2010 World Cup campaign was effectively an extension of its country's ongoing tendency to construct and subscribe to its own, often bizarre, narratives of its history and relationship to the outside world. In this context, the national soccer team was simply another means for North Korea to promote its superiority, both to its own people and to the outside world, however unusual its many strange claims appeared in media coverage leading up to and during the World Cup. Despite hopes among some observers that North Korea's participation in the competition would somehow lead to greater dialogue and understanding between the "Hermit Kingdom" and the outside world, the following discussion will demonstrate that the national soccer team's campaign was largely "business as usual" for a country steeped in secrecy and outlandish propaganda.

Past Glory

The 2010 World Cup was not the DPRK's first appearance in a World Cup Finals. In the months and weeks before the South Africa Finals, many observers looked to the team's one other World Cup appearance as a possible indication of their prospects. In the 1966 England Finals, the team shocked the world by defeating Italy 1-0 in a group match to advance to the quarterfinals. In that contest, North Korea led Portugal 3-0 at halftime, but surrendered a whopping five goals (four of them scored by legendary forward Eusébio) in the second half to lose 5-3.[5] The team captured imaginations with its relentless attack; Michael Elliot of *Time* magazine, who attended the quarterfinal against Portugal, remarked that "defense didn't seem to be in their plan." Elliot adds that the Koreans captured the hearts and minds of the people of Middlesbrough, where their group matches were held, and that their loss to Portugal was one of the "most extraordinary games of soccer ever."[6] Indeed, the *Chollima* (a mystical winged horse and nickname of the DPRK national squad) had left such an impression on the footballing world that nearly 50 years later, in 2002, Daniel Gordon and Nick Bonner produced a BBC documentary, *The Game of Their Lives*, featuring interviews with the seven remaining members of the 1966 squad. Louise Taylor of *The Guardian* argues that the team's bond with the people of Middlesbrough (aided, no doubt, by their red jerseys' similarity to those of the city's club) is a testament to soccer's ability to "bring the unlikeliest people together." Indeed, when the surviving members of the team were allowed to return to the United Kingdom in 2002, a rare opportunity for North Koreans to travel abroad, their bus, adorned with the sign "North Korea World Cup Squad Tour 2002," was met in Middlesbrough with enthusiastic honking and waving from motorists.[7] Though we do not have access to any internal sources to confirm its reasons for doing so, one might plausibly surmise that the DPRK government granted the team permission to revisit the location of the country's greatest soccer triumph as part of the larger process of détente stemming from South Korean president Kim Dae Jung's "Sunshine Policy" of engagement with the ROK's reclusive and often-hostile northern neighbor. North Korea's success in 1966 foreshadowed the emergence of Asian soccer; the DPRK team had advanced further than any Asian side, a fact that certainly contributed to their underdog status and enthusiastic reception among fans in England and beyond. In recent years, with the expansion of the Finals and inclusion of more teams from the region, Asian sides such as Japan and South Korea are staples of the tournament, and usually bring with them high hopes and expectations of advancing to the knockout rounds.

North Korea's surprising performance in 1966 reflected the country's early economic successes in the decade and a half following the Korean War. Modern observers usually envision repression, material deprivation and economic stagnation when they think of North Korea. In the 1950s and 1960s, the state was certainly repressive, but its economy, driven largely by heavy industry and steel in particular, was superior to South Korea's in terms of annual growth and standard of living. In fact, American officials worried that the North's relative prosperity would endanger the political stability of their southern ally.[8] The DPRK's economic bubble had burst by the end of the 1960s, but even in the 1980s its capital Pyongyang was still, according to Bruce Cumings, among the "most efficient, best-run cities in Asia."[9] The greatest calamity for North Korea's economy was the collapse of communism in Eastern Europe, beginning with the peaceful revolutions in East Germany, Czechoslovakia, Hungary and others in 1989 and ending with the dissolution of the Soviet Union at the end of 1991. Russian "trade" (thinly veiled aid) with North Korea declined sharply as the private entrepreneurs who purchased formerly state-run industries had little interest in economic ties to the DPRK, particularly since they would receive little of value in return. Trade between the countries decreased from $2.56 billion in 1990 to a mere $0.14 billion in 1994.[10] DPRK agriculture was reliant on chemical fertilizer, whose production was dependent on discount fuels from Russia and China. This situation, had North Korean citizens known of it, could have illustrated perfectly the inherent failure of Kim Il-sung's *Juche* philosophy, which boasts that North Korea can be completely self-reliant and therefore free of dependence on *any* foreign power, ally or otherwise. Facing a perpetual energy shortage, North Korea was ripe for disaster when a series of torrential rains struck the country in 1995, flooding fields and washing away precious soil. With its agricultural production reduced approximately by half in 1996, it is unsurprising that the DPRK experienced a catastrophic series of famines that killed, even by conservative estimates, at least 2.5 percent of its population.[11] Since then, the country has repeatedly extorted aid from South Korea and the United States through a seemingly endless cycle of confrontation and détente, a protection racket on a national scale, with North Korea promising "good behavior" in exchange for economic assistance.

From 1966 to 2010, North Korea's attempts to qualify for the Finals had been unsuccessful and hardly worth mentioning, with the exception of one incident. In the qualifying campaign for the 2006 Finals in Germany, North Korea played Iran in Pyongyang on March 30, 2005, in front of approximately 60,000 fans at Kim Il-sung Stadium (nearly every major structure, monument or institution is named for Kim Il-sung or his successors). The contest was not going well for the *Chollima*; they trailed Iran 2-0 when tensions erupted. Syrian referee Mohammed Khousa failed to award a penalty after North Korean player Nam Song Chol fell in Iran's penalty area, and the DPRK players rushed him to complain. Nam shoved Khousa, leading to a red card. But the more interesting action took place in the stands, as fans threw bottles and chairs onto the pitch, causing a 5-minute delay following the ejection.[12] After order was (mostly) restored, the match continued and Iran held its lead to the end. The spectators' rage didn't subside with the referee's final whistle, however. Fans surrounded the exits to prevent the Iranian team from leaving, and soon began fighting with riot police in the surrounding streets. It took the authorities roughly two hours to restore order and facilitate the Iranian team's departure. This was most likely the first riot in North Korean history,[13] but what exactly did it signify? One is tempted to interpret the explosion of fan violence against both the opposing team and their own police as a sign of brewing frustration with the regime. In recent years, North Koreans have been more willing to confront or resist police and military officials, at least when it concerns "misdemeanor" offenses,[14] but does that equate to a willingness to oppose the regime itself? There seems to be a growing sense among North Koreans that the regime is largely responsible for their material struggles,[15] but as far as we know there is no broad, organized resistance to the regime. Most likely, this episode is akin to scenes repeated countless times around the footballing world: fans, whipped into an irrational frenzy by a perceived injustice on the pitch, lash out at everything in sight. While there may have been an underlying element of rage against the Kim machine in the riot, there simply isn't enough evidence to prove this conclusively. Nonetheless, this episode is at the very least suggestive of widespread passions lurking under the surface among many North Koreans, passions that in this particular instance may have been channeled into a more "acceptable" venue (nationalistic anger at the perceived unjust treatment of the national team) than direct political protest, which the Kim regime has consistently and thoroughly suppressed through mass internment in labor camps and outright executions of more egregious offenders.

QUALIFICATION

The *Chollima* would fare much better in the 2010 qualifying campaign, earning a place in the Finals in South Africa. As the 2010 Finals approached, the question naturally arose: would the 2010 DPRK squad repeat the surprising success of their 1966 predecessors? The 1966 team represented a nation undergoing a period of surprising economic growth and prosperity, but the 2010 team would represent one hamstrung by decades of isolation, poor leadership and material privation. Would its performance mirror the country's circumstances, as the 1966 team's had? The 2010 qualification campaign indicated that the North Korean team would indeed be a microcosm of the recent "state" of the DPRK.

The North Koreans easily defeated Mongolia 9-2 in the preliminary round of the Asian Football Confederation (AFC) qualifiers, securing automatic qualification for the third round. As fate would have it, they were drawn randomly into Group 3 (of 5), with Jordan, Turkmenistan and, most importantly, South Korea. The Korean Central News Agency (KCNA), the DPRK's official online news organ, issued cursory reports about each match's result, albeit in typical KCNA idiosyncratic fashion, labeling every single opponent a "rival."[16] Of course, for a state so steeped in nationalism, perhaps the label is not so inappropriate. Most of the reports are uninteresting, merely reporting location and result of the contests, but the matches against South Korea were a different matter entirely.

The *Chollima* began their third round campaign with a 1-0 away win against Jordan in Amman on February 8, 2008, a positive start before their first encounter with South Korea on March 26. The KCNA report on the match, a 0-0 draw, is unremarkable save for the fact that the contest took place in Shanghai, China, rather than in Pyongyang as originally scheduled. The official report does not address the reason for a neutral venue, but it was due to North Korea's refusal to display South Korea's flag or play its national anthem before the match. In international matches, the Fédération Internationale de Football Association (FIFA) requires that both nations' flags be displayed and that both anthems be played. The North Korean government refused, suggesting instead the playing of a traditional Korean folk song and the display of the joint flag that the countries had marched under in the opening ceremonies of the Olympic Games from 2000 to 2006, which is a blue silhouette of the Korean peninsula on a white background.[17] Their fourth round contest in Pyongyang would be moved to Shanghai for the same reason.[18] Each nation has long insisted that it is the only legitimate government on the peninsula, although since Kim Dae-jung's presidency (1998–2003), South Korea had maintained a conciliatory stance toward their northern neighbor, a stance that included displaying the North Korean flag and playing its anthem at qualifying matches in Seoul, in addition to the aforementioned joint marching in the Olympics. This did not, however, prevent the North Koreans from causing a stir. The remainder of the AFC third round matches proceeded without incident, with North Korea drawing 0-0 away against both Turkmenistan and South Korea on June 2 and 22, respectively, and securing home wins, 1-0 on June 7 against Turkmenistan and 2-0 on June 14 against Jordan, to finish their group level with South Korea at 12 points, securing a spot in the fourth round of AFC qualifiers.

As fate would have it, North Korea was once again drawn in the same group as South Korea in round four, along with Iran, the UAE and Saudi Arabia. The campaign began well, with a 2-1 win against the UAE on September 6, 2008, and an uneventful 1-1 draw against South Korea on September 10, a would-be home contest once again played in Shanghai. Following a 2-1 setback against Iran on October 15, the *Chollima* picked up six points from consecutive home matches, a 1-0 win against Saudi

Arabia on February 11, 2009, and a 2-0 victory against the UAE on March 28. With ten points and only three matches remaining, North Korea was in a good position to reach the Finals in South Africa.

On April 1, 2009, in Seoul, South Korea defeated the North 1-0. Four days later, the KCNA posted an angry demand for FIFA to investigate a "serious incident" that happened before the match: the North Korean players had been poisoned by the South Koreans, incapacitating them mere minutes before the opening whistle. This "deliberate act perpetrated by adulterated foodstuff," along with a referee from Oman "so biased...he insisted the ball headed by our player into the goal mouth...at 6 minutes... was not the [sic] goal," led to the team's defeat in this crucial qualifying contest. Outlandish as it was, the article suggested the true reason for its accusations in its closing statements, which attributed South Korea's "plot-breeding and swindling" to new ROK president Lee Myung-bak, who had taken office in February 2008. Lee, a conservative politician and former Hyundai CEO, had been elected partly due to his platform of taking a harder line with North Korea by demanding that ROK financial aid be met with political concessions by the DPRK.[19] The alleged poisoning of North Korean players was merely part of Lee's larger strategy of "anti-reunification and treacherous moves to incite confrontation with the DPRK."[20] Even if we allow that several North Korean players may legitimately have been ill (striker Jong Tae-se claimed to the media that he had symptoms resembling stomach flu), in blaming Lee Myung-bak's government for the supposed incident the DPRK sought to cast aspersions on a regime far less agreeable than previous ones to the unrestricted provision of aid. This fits the larger pattern of provocative behavior on the part of North Korea, including the sinking of a South Korean naval vessel, the *Cheonan*, in March 2010 and the artillery bombardment of Yeongpyeong Island that November.[21] Almost without exception, such incidents are intended to force South Korea and its allies, particularly the United States, to increase economic and food aid in exchange for North Korea's "good behavior." This would not be the last time North Korea would make unusual excuses for a soccer loss against a hated rival nation. In the 2011 Women's World Cup, the North Korean government blamed their 2-0 loss to the United States on June 28 on the fact that several of their players had been struck by lightning while training in Pyongyang.[22] Five players later tested positive for steroids, which North Korean officials explained away as natural remedies used to help them recover from the lightning strike.[23]

Aside from its predictable problems with South Korea, the remainder of North Korea's qualifying campaign was uneventful. The team secured a place in South Africa with a pair of 0-0 draws, at home against Iran on June 6 and away against Saudi Arabia on June 17. According to the KCNA, the team, returning from Riyadh, was welcomed at the airport in Pyongyang with bouquets and garlands.[24] In a review of 2009, a year "filled with miraculous events," the KCNA hinted at hopes of a 2010 repeat of North Korea's famous 1966 run, stating that the *Chollima* had earned a spot in the Finals "to create a great sensation again after 44 years."[25] The North Korean team would certainly create a sensation, though not quite the one DPRK officials had anticipated.

THE FINALS

As the 2010 Finals approached, the international media was rich with speculation about the North Korean team. Foreigners are usually banned from domestic matches in North Korea, and find it difficult to obtain tickets even for international contests, despite FIFA requirements that foreign journalists be allowed to attend.[26] Tim Hartley of BBC News, one of only a handful of foreign journalists to have attended DPRK domestic league matches, described at length his bizarre experience at a club contest between Pyongyang FC and army club Amrokgang in Pyongyang in 2013, noting that the crowd, many of whom were in military uniform, was eerily silent, a far cry from the usual raucous atmosphere at soccer matches. Not even the goals were enough to evoke a noisy reaction from the crowd in what Hartley described as "the most bizarre game [he'd] ever watched."[27] As the 2005 riot after the home match against Iran demonstrated, North Korean crowds seem more passionate about international matches, likely due to the regime's intense anti-foreign nationalist propaganda.

For most members of the 2010 DPRK squad, journalists had only their names and what little could be gleaned from their televised qualifying matches. Information regarding clubs, amateur backgrounds and so forth was sketchy at best. There were, however, a handful of players who were not only well-known, but not even residents of North Korea. These players were *Chongryon*, pro-DPRK ethnic Koreans who live in Japan. This community numbers around 600,000, and most are descendants of immigrant laborers who came to Japan when it ruled Korea as a colony prior to 1945.[28] Their ideological devotion to North Korea stems, therefore, either from geographic origin in the North or from attraction to the DPRK's intense anti-colonial (and therefore anti-Japanese) rhetoric. Ironically, many *Chongryon* who chose to immigrate back to North Korea after 1945 ended up regretting the decision, especially because they were subject to the same travel restrictions as other North Koreans, and have become dependent on periodic financial and material assistance from relatives still living in Japan.

According to FIFA regulations, *Chongryon* living in Japan may choose to represent North Korea, South Korea or Japan. Striker Jong Tae-se was not only a *Chongryon*, but also North Korea's star player, nicknamed "The People's Rooney" in the football media. Prior to the 2010 Finals, Jong was playing for Blackburn Rovers in England. Jong, who has never actually resided in North Korea but did attend a DPRK-funded school in Japan, grew up idolizing the famous 1966 team. Jong's father, evidently to ensure more opportunities for his son both in Japan and abroad, had registered him for a South Korean passport, but after watching the DPRK's loss to Japan in a qualification match for the 2006 Germany Finals, Jong decided he wanted to represent North Korea and help them qualify for the 2010 Finals. Because he had already been issued a South Korean passport, Jong fought a lengthy (and DPRK-funded) legal battle to renounce it in favor of a North Korean one, allowing him to play for the *Chollima*.[29]

Aashish Gadhvi of *London Korean Links* suggested that Jong and other *Chongryon* were "slowly lifting up the iron curtain," and indeed one is tempted to view Jong's inclusion in the North Korean squad as a crack in the seemingly impregnable wall of secrecy that surrounds the DPRK, especially so given the North's usual efforts to limit its citizens' exposure to the outside world. Jong's familiarity with the material prosperity of Japan and South Korea could be considered dangerous, even if the only North Koreans he spoke with regularly were his teammates, who were completely enthralled by the games on his smartphone, a luxury few if any of them had ever seen or perhaps even heard about.[30] North Korea's use of *Chongryon* players is more likely due to the practical need to utilize foreign players with better talent and foreign club experience if the DPRK is to have any hope of international success. Interestingly, the KCNA qualifying match reports made a rather obvious habit of *not* mentioning Jong, despite the fact that their success was largely due to his 17 goals in 23 matches prior to the 2010 Finals.[31]

The inclusion of both Koreas in the Finals also raised the question of whether South Koreans would also support their northern brethren in the tournament. Reactions were mixed. Oh Kyu-wook of the *Korea*

Herald said he would support the North Koreans because "they are part of Korea" and that he doesn't think about politics when watching football.[32] Park Ji-sung, Manchester United and South Korea midfielder, said he would watch North Korea's matches because "[we] speak the same language and are actually the same country," and that "maybe we can get closer to North Korea through the World Cup."[33] Such sentiments are unsurprising, despite the fact that mere months before the Finals 46 South Korean sailors had died when a North Korean submarine sank the *Cheonan*, a navy vessel. As B.R. Myers argued in *The Cleanest Race*, many Koreans view ethnicity, not nationality, as the primary feature of their culture. Former European Parliament member Glynn Ford offered a similar assessment, noting that both North and South Koreans are very nationalistic, and would probably support each other's teams except in the unlikely event of a head-to-head contest at the Finals.[34] Not all South Koreans were enthused about their northern neighbor's participation in the Finals, however. Choi Hyun-duk of Seoul said "North Korea [isn't] our country and...we [don't] have to support them." She did add, however, that most people she knew probably would have supported the DPRK squad if not for the *Cheonan* incident.[35] Unfortunately, it is impossible to know with any certainty how North Koreans felt about the South Korean team, or even how much they knew about the details of the tournament itself given the DPRK's tight control of information.

In the days leading up to North Korea's opening group-stage match against Brazil, the team represented its poverty-stricken country well by using public exercise facilities to save money (footage of which appeared quickly on YouTube) while avoiding all press conferences. The sole exception was Jong Tae-se, who spoke briefly to the media following the DPRK's disastrous friendly match against Nigeria in Johannesburg on June 6. Tickets were free, and fans outside stampeded in a rush to enter the 10,000-seat Makhulong Stadium.[36] North Korea lost the match 3-1 amidst the chaos that saw at least 14 people seriously injured, but Jong took the opportunity to make a rare statement to the media in which he guaranteed that his team would defeat Brazil.

Prior to their opening match, four of North Korea's players, Kim Myong-won, Kim Kyong-il, An Choi-hyok and Pak Sung-hyok, went missing, leading to widespread speculation that they had attempted to defect. Apparently the four players were listed as "absent" on the official squad list for the Brazil match, though there was never any official confirmation of attempted defection. FIFA issued an official statement on June

18, claiming no knowledge of the situation and that the DPRK coaching staff denied the rumors. The players evidently reappeared in training camp a few days later, with no further explanation provided.[37] While we may never know what transpired during the week or so that the players were supposedly missing, it would not be surprising if they had indeed attempted, albeit unsuccessfully, to defect. Since the famines of the mid-1990s, tens of thousands of North Koreans have left the country, with most ending up across the border in Manchuria living among the numerous ethnic Koreans in the region. Sports offer one of the only opportunities for North Koreans to travel abroad, a privilege reserved only for athletes or high-ranking officials, and the temptation for these four players to use the opportunity to defect must have been tremendous.

On June 15 North Korea surprised many by holding Brazil to a 0-0 tie at halftime. Brazil scored twice in the second half, though Ji Yun-nam added a goal for the *Chollima* in the 89th minute to end the match as a respectable 2-1 loss. The KNCA praised the team for "not losing [its] confidence" after going down 2-0.[38] Non-DPRK observers were also impressed by the team's performance. Robin Bairner of *Goal* praised Jong Tae-se's "gusto" in attacking the Brazilian defense, as well as the team's "committed defending" that held Brazil scoreless until halftime, adding that North Korea's performance had given their upcoming group opponents, Portugal and Ivory Coast, a "great deal of food for thought."[39] Matthias Krug of ESPN also commended Jong's performance, adding that North Korea had "made a statement of intent in South Africa."[40] The result emboldened North Korean authorities, who decided to televise the next group match, against Portugal, live instead of on the 12-hour delay used for the contest against Brazil.[41]

During the first match, viewers, including me, became curious about the strangely wooden group of around 1000 fans wearing identical North Korea gear. Their artificial smiles and awkward behavior seemed to indicate that few if any of them had ever actually seen a football match in their lives. ESPN television commentator Martin Tyler informed viewers that these North Korean supporters were in fact Chinese actors who had been paid to cheer for the DPRK. While no one familiar with North Korea could have been surprised by this, given the state's reluctance to allow its citizens to travel abroad, the story had actually been broken over a month earlier by Malcom Moore of *The Telegraph*, who learned from China's state-run media that Chinese fans would receive North Korea's ticket allotment (Fig. 8.1).[42]

Even more strangely, North Korea's coach, Kim Jong-hun, announced that during the Brazil match, he had been receiving "regular tactical advice during matches" from Kim Jong-il via a mobile phone "not visible to the naked eye." Naturally, Kim added that the Dear Leader had invented this invisible phone himself.[43] As preposterous as this assertion sounds, such exaggeration is merely another manifestation of the Kim family's cult of personality, which often makes outrageous claims, including that Kim Jong-il invented the hamburger or that he shot multiple holes-in-one in his first round of golf. Such statements are intended to create an impenetrable mystique surrounding the Kim family, though B.K. Myers argues that these boasts are merely an extension of the DPRK's broader myths about the unique purity of the Korean race, a "childlike" race that requires exceptional "parental" guidance from the Kims.[44]

On June 17, a KCNA article claimed that citizens of Pyongyang were "confident" that their team would win its remaining group matches and "live up to the expectation of the Korean people."[45] In reality, North Korea's second group match against Portugal on June 21 was an unmitigated disaster, especially given the live broadcast back home. The team lost 7-0, leading to an abrupt cut to factory workers praising Kim Jong-il.[46]

Fig. 8.1 North Korean "fans" at the team's group-stage match against Brazil (Photo credit: Kim Kyung Hoon/Reuters)

Kim Jong-hun had evidently left his invisible phone back at the hotel. Unsurprisingly, the KCNA made no mention of the match whatsoever. It also ignored the team's third and final match at the Finals, which they lost 3-0 to Ivory Coast.

Shortly after their final loss, both Jong Tae-se and Kim Jong-hun spoke to the media. Jong admitted to a FIFA media representative that "there was a real gulf in class between us and our opponents…they definitely possess an edge over us mentally, physically, and technically…our lack of elementary skill made it impossible to win." Jong's assessment, shaped partly by his extensive international experience, was surprisingly honest, given the team's reputation for secrecy. Of course, Jong was not facing the prospect of returning to North Korea, as he planned to return to Japan after leaving South Africa. Kim Jong-hun, on the other hand, sounded positively apologetic in his statement by admitting that he "failed to come up with a proper strategy to counter our rivals' fierce attacks." He then praised his players for "put[ting] in all their efforts until the last minute," perhaps hoping to absolve them of the team's failure in the eyes of the North Korean government.[47] Kim may have been anticipating a possible punishment upon the squad's return home, and he was not alone.

After such an inglorious showing, many observers speculated about whether the North Korean team would be punished for embarrassing their nation and leader. In late July, reports began to surface that the team had indeed been publicly humiliated in a so-called "grand debate" on July 2, in which they were forced to endure six hours of "shaming" for failing in their "ideological struggle" in South Africa. This is unsurprising, given that ordinary North Koreans usually attend weekly "self-criticism" meetings during which they are expected to confess to their neighbors any ideological or personal failings in the previous week. Jong Tae-se and An Yong-hak both escaped the session by flying directly back to Japan after the tournament, a luxury unavailable to DPRK-based players. Especially troubling were the reports that head coach Kim Jong-hun had been stripped of his party membership and sent to perform hard labor on a building project.[48] FIFA soon launched an inquiry into the rumors, and reported that the DPRK's football association had assured them that neither the coach nor the team had been punished in any way for their World Cup performance.[49] Given North Korea's secrecy and outright lies in other matters, one is naturally inclined to doubt the veracity of the DPRK's official statement, though apparently Kim Jong-hun made several public appearances to reassure outside observers that, at the very least, he had not been locked away in a coal mine or prison camp. Of course, his and the team's appearances after reports of punishment do not mean it did not occur, only that it did not cause any visible permanent damage.

For all the anticipation and speculation about North Korea's participation in the 2010 World Cup, including suggestions by some that the team might repeat the 1966 squad's surprising and inspiring performance, in the event we witnessed exactly what one might have expected. The DPRK's participation in the 2010 World Cup was a microcosm of the nation's circumstances. A secretive, repressive and poverty-stricken state steeped in often-preposterous propaganda confronted the outside world, only to be humiliated by teams with superior talent and experience. All of the fake fans, invisible phones and Japanese-based star strikers in the world could not get the *Chollima* a single point in group play. The team's struggles are evocative more broadly of the DPRK's precarious conundrum in recent years: its leaders realize that the country will fail without foreign aid and reform, but any move toward reform or openness would likely facilitate the regime's downfall. Thus the country is stuck in a constant cycle of threats and appeasement in order to obtain more aid from South Korea and the United States, while its citizens are gradually becoming more aware of their relative poverty and misery through bootleg DVDs and foreign radio. How long before the regime faces a catastrophic "7-0 defeat" of its own in a case of life imitating football? No one can say for sure, but like North Korea's World Cup campaign, defeat is likely inevitable.

NOTES

1. "The Secret State of North Korea," *Frontline* (PBS). Aired January 14, 2014.
2. Bradley K. Martin, *Under the Loving Care of the Fatherly Leader: North Korea and the Kim Dynasty.* (New York: Thomas Dunne, 2006), 125.
3. B.R. Myers, *The Cleanest Race: How North Koreans See Themselves— and Why it Matters.* (New York: Melville House, 2011), 170–171.
4. Neil Billingham, "98: The most politically charged game in World Cup history," *FourFourTwo,* June 2, 2010. http://www.fourfourtwo.com/features/98-most-politically-charged-game-world-cup-history. Accessed 17 Jan 2014.
5. David Goldblatt, *The Ball is Round: A Global History of Soccer".* (New York: Penguin, 2008), 425–427.

6. Michael Elliot, "Go North Korea!" *Time*. June 3, 2010. http://content.time.com/time/specials/packages/article/0,28804,1991933_1991952_1993809,00.html. Accessed 20 Jan 2014.

7. Louise Taylor, "How little stars from North Korea were taken to Middlesbrough's heart." *The Guardian*. June 8, 2010. http://www.theguardian.com/football/2010/jun/08/north-korea-world-cup-middlesbrough. Accessed 20 Jan 2014.

8. Bruce Cumings, *Korea's Place in the Sun: A Modern History*. (New York: Norton, 2005), 434.

9. Cumings, *Korea's Place in the Sun*, 405.

10. Andrei Lankov, *The Real North Korea: Life and Politics in the Failed Stalinist Utopia*. (Oxford: Oxford University Press, 2013), 76.

11. Lankov, *The Real North Korea*, 78–79.

12. "Soccer: Iran wins amid riot in North Korea." *New York Times*. March 31, 2005. http://www.nytimes.com/2005/03/30/sports/30iht-soccer.html?_r=0. Accessed 22 Jan 2014.

13. Lankov, *The Real North Korea*, 107.

14. "The Secret State of North Korea."

15. Gordon Chang, *Nuclear Showdown: North Korea takes on the World*. (New York: Random House, 2006), 86.

16. Various KCNA Match Reports. *Korea Central News Agency*. http://www.kcna.co.jp/index-e.htm.

17. Mark Ledsom, "Koreas match moved to Shanghai after anthem row." *Reuters*. March 7, 2008. http://uk.reuters.com/article/2008/03/07/uk-soccer-fifa-koreas-idUKL0789295820080307. Accessed 16 July 2014.

18. Austin Peters, "Clash of North and South Koreas ends all square." *The Telegraph*. September 10, 2008. http://www.telegraph.co.uk/sport/football/international/2779037/Clash-of-the-Koreas-ends-all-square-Football.html. Accessed 22 Jan 2014.

19. Lankov, *The Real North Korea*, 174.

20. "FIFA Urged to Take Appropriate Measure." *Korea Central News Agency*. April 4, 2009. http://www.kcna.co.jp/index-e.htm. Accessed 15 Jan 2014.

21. Lankov, *The Real North Korea*, 179.

22. John Ashdown, "North Korea blame lightning strike for defeat by USA." *The Guardian*. June 28, 2011. http://www.theguardian.

com/football/2011/jun/28/north-korea-usa-womens-world-cup. Accessed 16 July 2014.

23. "N. Korea Manufacturing Banned Drugs for Athletes, Defector Claims." *Chosun Ilbo.* July 20, 2011. http://english.chosun.com/site/data/html_dir/2011/07/20/2011072000809.html. Accessed 16 July 2014.

24. "DPRK Players Return Home." *Korea Central News Agency.* June 20, 2009. http://www.kcna.co.jp/index-e.htm. Accessed 15 Jan 2014.

25. "Year Filled with Miraculous Events." *Korea Central News Agency.* December 22, 2009. http://www.kcna.co.jp/index-e.htm. Accessed 15 Jan 2014.

26. Marc Bennetts, "If North Korea go out of the World Cup, will anyone hear them fall?" *The Guardian.* November 8, 2011. http://www.theguardian.com/football/blog/2011/nov/08/north-korea-world-cup-qualifying. Accessed 24 Jan 2014.

27. Tim Hartley, "North Korea's silent football matches." *BBC News.* May 10, 2013. http://www.bbc.com/news/magazine-22470430. Accessed 16 July 2014.

28. Barbara Demick and Yuriko Nagano, "North Korea's star at the World Cup." *Los Angeles Times.* June 14, 2010. http://articles.latimes.com/2010/jun/14/world/la-fg-north-korea-soccer-20100614. Accessed 16 July 2014.

29. Demick and Nagano, "North Korea's star at the World Cup."

30. Aashish Gadhvi, "The curious case of Jong Tae-se." *London Korean Links.* November 13, 2009. http://londonkoreanlinks.net/2009/11/13/the-curious-case-of-jong-tae-se/. Accessed 24 Jan 2014.

31. James Montague, "The secret machine: Inside North Korea's World Cup squad." *CNN.* June 15, 2010. http://www.cnn.com/2010/SPORT/football/06/08/north.korea.secret.team/index.html. Accessed 16 July 2014.

32. Rose Raymond, "South and North Korea Both Made History This World Cup." *National Public Radio.* June 22, 2010. http://www.npr.org/blogs/showmeyourcleats/2010/06/22/128014731/south-and-north-korea-both-made-history-this-world-cup. Accessed 24 Jan 2014.

33. John Duerden, "Park Ji-sung hopes World Cup can help unite a divided Korea." *The Guardian.* May 27, 2010. http://www.the-

guardian.com/football/2010/may/28/park-ji-sung-south-korea?INTCMP=ILCNETTXT3487. Accessed 24 Jan 2014.

34. David Bartram, "World Cup will be good for Koreas." *The Guardian*. May 19, 2010. http://www.theguardian.com/commentisfree/2010/may/19/north-south-korea-world-cup?INTCMP=ILCNETTXT3487. Accessed 24 Jan 2014.

35. Raymond, "South and North Korea Both Made History This World Cup."

36. Dave Middleton, "Policeman crushed as thousands stampede Nigeria-North Korea friendly." *The Guardian*. June 6, 2010. http://www.theguardian.com/football/2010/jun/06/nigera-north-korea-fan-stampede. Accessed 27 Jan 2014.

37. Zack Wilson, "Four DPKR men are believed to be AWOL." *Goal*, June 18, 2010. http://www.goal.com/en/news/1863/world-cup-2010/2010/06/18/1983029/fifa-has-no-information-on-missing-north-korean-players. Accessed 15 July 2014.

38. "Match between DPRK and Brazil." Korea Central News Agency. June 16, 2010. http://www.kcna.co.jp/index-e.htm. Accessed 27 Jan 2014.

39. Robin Bairner, "The Selecao didn't have it easy from the Chollima." *Goal*, June 15, 2010. http://www.goal.com/en-us/news/67/world-cup-2014/2010/06/15/1978448/brazil-2-1-north-korea-hard-work-but-maicon-elano-give. Accessed 15 July 2014.

40. Matthias Krug, "North Korea worthy of world stage." *ESPN*, June 15, 2010. http://www.espnfc.com/world-cup/columns/story?id=797238&cc=5901. Accessed 25 May 2014.

41. John Sudworth, "North Korea TV Viewers see Cup Loss." *BBC News*, June 21, 2010. http://www.bbc.co.uk/news/10371350. Accessed 27 Jan 2014.

42. Malcolm Moore, "Chinese actors to cheer for North Korea during World Cup." *The Telegraph*, May 13, 2010. http://www.telegraph.co.uk/sport/football/world-cup/7719050/Chinese-actors-to-cheer-for-North-Korea-during-World-Cup.html. Accessed 27 Jan 2014.

43. Russell Goldman, "North Korean Soccer Coach Talks to 'Dear Leader' Via Invisible Phone." *ABC News*, June 17, 2010. http://abcnews.go.com/International/world-cup-2010-north-korean-coach-talks-kim/story?id=10931655. Accessed 27 Jan 2014.

44. Myers, *The Cleanest Race*, 77.

45. "Expectations Reposed in Korean Football Team." *Korea Central News Agency*. June 17, 2010. http://www.kcna.co.jp/index-e. htm. Accessed 27 Jan 2014.
46. Sudworth, "North Korea TV Viewers see Cup Loss."
47. "Chollima reflect on miserable campaign." FIFA.com, June 26, 2010. http://www.fifa.com/tournaments/archive/worldcup/southafrica2010/news/newsid=1259112/. Accessed 15 July 2014.
48. Justin McCurry, "North Korea's failed World Cup footballers undergo public mauling." *The Guardian*, July 30, 2010. http://www.theguardian.com/world/2010/jul/30/north-korea-footballers-public-mauling. Accessed 27 Jan 2014.
49. "FIFA Statement on Korea DPR." FIFA.com, August 25, 2010. http://www.fifa.com/aboutfifa/organisation/footballgovernance/news/newsid=1289561/index.html. Accessed 27 Jan 2014.

WORK CITED

Ashdown, John. "North Korea Blame Lightning Strike for Defeat by USA. " *The Guardian*, June 28, 2011. http://www.theguardian.com/football/2011/jun/28/north-korea-usa-womens-world-cup.

Bairner, Robin. "The Selecao Didn't Have It Easy from the Chollima." *Goal*, June 15, 2010. http://www.goal.com/en-us/news/67/world-cup-2014/2010/06/15/1978448/brazil-2-1-north-korea-hard-work-but-maicon-elano-give.

Bartram, David. "World Cup Will be Good for Koreas." *The Guardian*, May 19, 2010. http://www.theguardian.com/commentisfree/2010/may/19/north-south-korea-world-cup?INTCMP=ILCNETTXT3487.

Bennetts, Marc. "If North Korea Go Out of the World Cup, Will Anyone Hear Them Fall?." *The Guardian*, November 8, 2011. http://www.theguardian.com/football/blog/2011/nov/08/north-korea-world-cup-qualifying.

Billingham, Neil. 98: "The Most Politically Charged Game in World Cup History." *FourFourTwo*, June 2, 2010. http://www.fourfourtwo.com/features/98-most-politically-charged-game-world-cup-history.

Chang, Gordon. *Nuclear Showdown: North Korea Takes on the World*. New York: Random House, 2006.

Cumings, Bruce. *Korea's Place in the Sun: A Modern History*. New York: Norton, 2005.

Demick, Barbara, and Yuriko Nagano. "North Korea's Star at the World Cup." *Los Angeles Times*, June 14, 2010. http://articles.latimes.com/2010/jun/14/world/la-fg-north-korea-soccer-20100614.

Duerden, John. "Park Ji-sung Hopes World Cup Can Help Unite a Divided Korea." *The Guardian*, May 27, 2010. http://www.theguardian.com/football/2010/may/28/park-ji-sung-south-korea?INTCMP=ILCNETTXT3487.

Elliot, Michael. "Go North Korea!" *Time*, June 3, 2010. http://content.time.com/time/specials/packages/article/0,28804,1991933_1991952_1993809,00.html.

FIFA Statement on Korea DPR. FIFA Official Website, August 25, 2010. http://www.fifa.com/aboutfifa/organisation/footballgovernance/news/newsid=1289561/index.html.

Gadhvi, Aashish. "The Curious Case of Jong Tae-se." *London Korean Links*, November 13, 2009. http://londonkoreanlinks.net/2009/11/13/the-curious-case-of-jong-tae-se/.

Goldblatt, David. *The Ball Is Round: A Global History of Soccer*. New York: Penguin, 2008.

Goldman, Russell. "North Korean Soccer Coach Talks to 'Dear Leader' Via Invisible Phone." *ABC News*, June 17, 2010. http://abcnews.go.com/International/world-cup-2010-north-korean-coach-talks-kim/story?id=10931655.

Hartley, Tim. "North Korea's Silent Football Matches." *BBC News*, May 10, 2013. http://www.bbc.com/news/magazine-22470430.

Korea Central News Agency. Various reports. http://www.kcna.co.jp/index-e.htm.

Krug, Matthias. "North Korea Worthy of World Stage." *ESPN*, June 15, 2010. http://www.espnfc.com/world-cup/columns/story?id=797238&cc=5901.

Lankov, Andrei. *The Real North Korea: Life and Politics in the Failed Stalinist Utopia*. Oxford: Oxford University Press, 2013.

Ledsom, Mark. "Koreas Match Moved to Shanghai After Anthem Row." *Reuters*, March 7, 2008. http://uk.reuters.com/article/2008/03/07/uk-soccer-fifa-koreas-idUKL0789295820080307.

Martin, Bradley K. *Under the Loving Care of the Fatherly Leader: North Korea and the Kim Dynasty*. New York: Thomas Dunne, 2006.

McCurry, Justin. "North Korea's Failed World Cup Footballers Undergo Public Mauling." *The Guardian*, July 30, 2010. http://www.theguardian.com/world/2010/jul/30/north-korea-footballers-public-mauling.

Middleton, Dave. "Policeman Crushed as Thousands Stampede Nigeria-North Korea Friendly." *The Guardian*, June 6, 2010. http://www.theguardian.com/football/2010/jun/06/nigera-north-korea-fan-stampede.

Montague, James. "The Secret Machine: Inside North Korea's World Cup Squad." *CNN*, June 15, 2010. http://www.cnn.com/2010/SPORT/football/06/08/north.korea.secret.team/index.html.

Moore, Malcolm. "Chinese Actors to Cheer for North Korea During World Cup." *The Telegraph*, May 13, 2010. http://www.telegraph.co.uk/sport/football/

world-cup/7719050/Chinese-actors-to-cheer-for-North-Korea-during-World-Cup.html.

Myers, B.R. *The Cleanest Race: How North Koreans See Themselves—and Why It Matters.* New York: Melville House, 2011.

"N. Korea Manufacturing Banned Drugs for Athletes, Defector Claims." *Chosun Ilbo,* July 20, 2011. http://english.chosun.com/site/data/html_dir/2011/07/20/2011072000809.html.

Peters, Austin. "Clash of North and South Koreas Ends All Square." *The Telegraph,* September 10, 2008. http://www.telegraph.co.uk/sport/football/international/2779037/Clash-of-the-Koreas-ends-all-square-Football.html.

Raymond, Rose. "South and North Korea Both Made History This World Cup." *National Public Radio,* June 22, 2010. http://www.npr.org/blogs/showmeyourcleats/2010/06/22/128014731/south-and-north-korea-both-made-history-this-world-cup.

"Soccer: Iran Wins Amid Riot in North Korea." *New York Times,* March 31, 2005. http://www.nytimes.com/2005/03/30/sports/30iht-soccer.html?_r=0.

Sudworth, John. "North Korea TV Viewers See Cup Loss." *BBC News,* June 21, 2010. http://www.bbc.co.uk/news/10371350.

Taylor, Louise. "How Little Stars From North Korea Were Taken to Middlesbrough's Heart." *The Guardian,* June 8, 2010. http://www.theguardian.com/football/2010/jun/08/north-korea-world-cup-middlesbrough.

"The Secret State of North Korea." *Frontline* (PBS), Aired January 14, 2014.

Wilson, Zack. "Four DPKR Men Are Believed to Be AWOL." *Goal,* June 18, 2010. http://www.goal.com/en/news/1863/world-cup-2010/2010/06/18/1983029/fifa-has-no-information-on-missing-north-korean-players.

PART IV

Race and Ethnic Studies

Fausto dos Santos: The Wonders and Challenges of Blackness in Brazil's "Mulatto Football"

Roger Kittleson

The death of Fausto dos Santos in March 1939 was replete with moral messages for his contemporaries. A player of skills that earned him the nickname "Maravilha Negra" (Black Wonder) at the first World Cup of 1930 and of a vigorous style that intimidated opponents and teammates alike, he, nonetheless, spent his last weeks wasting away in the interior of Minas Gerais. A late marriage must have brightened this period for him, and newspapers eagerly reported rumors that his illness might abate, but in the end he succumbed to tuberculosis at the age of 34.[1]

He was far from the only player whose life was cut short by disease in this era. As a footballer who had won "glory, fame, and money," though, he served as a reminder of the damage that tuberculosis and other maladies wreaked preferentially upon the *povo* (common folk), even its most physically gifted representatives.[2] At the same time, his fellow players and former clubs raised money to fund his medical care and, later, to provide support to his surviving family. Some of these gestures were the heartfelt actions of former teammates and rivals, while others came across as public

R. Kittleson (✉)
Department of History, Williams College, Williamstown, MA, USA

© Hofstra University 2017
B. Elsey, S. Pugliese (eds.), *Football and the Boundaries of History*,
DOI 10.1057/978-1-349-95006-5_9

relations initiatives by officials with whom he had clashed almost until the end of his playing days.[3] All, though, suggested that the growing world of *futebol* was trying to take care of its own but needed to do more.[4]

Because his demise drew attention to the plight of footballers in the tumultuous 1920s and 1930s, it also took on complex political implications. He had lived with an independence that exasperated *cartolas* (club and federation directors); the pathos of his final year made it easier for not only officials but also journalists to celebrate him as a true *craque* (star player, from the English "crack"). This consecration, however, required a great deal of historical revision, for Fausto had lived the conflicts that characterized *futebol* of his age—and lived them fully. A self-conscious Afro-Brazilian man who wanted to play his own way on and off the field, who moved decisively to try to earn a decent living before the official professionalization of soccer in his country, he raised hackles as often as he elicited praise. Above all, his rebellious nature posed a challenge to the emerging discourse of a mixed-race national style of *futebol* and depictions of the sport as a practice that exemplified the "racial democracy" forged in post-abolition Brazil.[5]

FAUSTO AND "BROWN PROFESSIONALISM"

The idea of a peculiarly Brazilian way of playing soccer appeared in fragmentary form as soon as the nation's teams began to take on foreign opposition in the 1910s. It was in the 1920s and especially the 1930s, though, that the notion of a "mulatto football" came together more definitively. By these latter decades, the sport had undergone a massive popularization, attracting widespread interest among spectators of all social classes and incorporating new sorts of players in what had been a game of the largely white elite. By the time that Fausto took the field for Bangu, his first big club, "the British game" had been Brazilianized, its pretensions of gentlemanly amateurism giving way to an illegal but de facto professionalism. This shift involved not only profit seeking by club directors and merchants but also the entrance of men of the *povo* who wanted to turn a pastime into a living.

The acclaim that Afro-Brazilian players earned in the world press and the titles they helped bring home contributed to the forging of a new, more inclusionary sense of the nation. Writers, scholars, and journalists—from José Lins do Rego to Gilberto Freyre to Mário Filho and beyond—formulated a notion of "mulatto football" that celebrated the contributions of "the African" and "the indigenous" to national culture. This praise contained unmistakable paternalism. The mixed-race *povo* was hailed for primitive, mostly corporal traits: the "plasticity" that showed up in *futebol* as it had long done in popular dance, the *ginga* (or swing) and the playfulness that Brazilian footballers used to concoct a beautiful game of dribbles, feints, and improvised shots. *Futebol*, in this vision, emanated naturally from the physical and psychological nature of the mostly non-white majority; although they worked at the level of instinct—and not on some higher intellectual plane—Afro-Brazilians were thus fundamental parts of Brazil. This vision of the nation as a distinctively and organically mixed race was thus inclusive but it also exoticized the very people it ostensibly celebrated.[6]

In this way, the new visions of a mixed-race nation represented on the soccer pitch imposed terms of inclusion on people of color.[7] Membership in the reformulated nation offered individuals a positive way of feeling themselves part of the national community. But mixed-race national identity also presupposed the exclusion—and indeed the repression—of competing, separate racial identities. Anyone insisting on their difference and thereby questioning the integrity of the revamped sense of *brasilidade* (Brazilianness) would be met with suspicion and often hostility. A player who dared to contest the power of the paternalistic *cartolas* who ruled soccer clubs and confederations, moreover, faced more concrete penalties, from the denial of bonuses to expulsion from leagues or banishment from the national team.[8]

Long before he entered the pantheon of Brazilian footballing greats, Fausto sparked doubts, disdain, and anger among soccer officials. Born in the small city of Codó in the northern state of Maranhão in 1905, he arrived in Rio as a young child.[9] His family made the long journey to the national capital in search of better prospects, and it paid off for their son when he caught the eye of soccer scouts at the age of 12. Despite the "devilish" moves he had displayed on the right side of his neighborhood club, Campo Grande, he later slid into the heart of midfield.[10] By 1926 he found a place in the team of Bangu, where he gave hints of his ability to dominate an entire game from his central position.[11] Located in the Rio hinterlands, Bangu was the classic factory club, having been founded by Scottish and English managers of a Brazilian-owned textile mill in the suburb a half-hour's train ride outside the city of Rio. Like other such clubs, Bangu drew at first on its workforce for its team and then began to recruit more widely. This made the Bangu side very different in its composition from the teams of traditional social and sports clubs of the Rio elite. While Fluminense, most notoriously, tried to keep its membership white and wealthy, Bangu and other factory clubs fielded Afro-descendant working-men alongside their white colleagues. Despite conflicts with city league officials on this point, the British directors of Bangu steadfastly continued to put out multiracial squads.[12] Thus the tall, lanky Fausto stood out at Bangu for the abilities he showed on the pitch and not for his race.[13]

Soon enough, another team that had dared to break the race bar-rier lured the young Fausto into the city. Vasco da Gama, a historically Portuguese club, had carried out a "revolution" in the early 1920s by ven-turing into the lower reaches of Rio society in its recruitment of players. Bolstered by talented Afro-Brazilian players, Vasco won back-to-back Rio championships in 1923 and 1924.[14] Threatened with expulsion by the city league, Vasco directors swore to obey the regulations. Their actions soon contradicted their words, though, as they brought Fausto and more Afro-Brazilians to the club. As a hard-tackling and smooth-passing "pivot" in the midfield, Fausto helped Vasco to the first two of the four consecutive Rio titles it won between 1929 and 1932. In the process he became a legendary figure at the club.

Like Bangu—and most clubs—Vasco paid its players in these years, although legal professionalization of the game came only in 1933. Rather than wages, though, the players received payment in the form of "bonuses" or "tips" (*bichos* or *gorjetas*). This false amateurism was known, tellingly, as "*profissionalismo marrom*," or brown professionalism. Disciples of the old football, with its ideals of genteel amateurism, cracked down on Vasco not only because of the presence of Afro-Brazilians in the club, but also because these working-class men were playing for hire.[15] Indeed, some large clubs in Rio and São Paulo kept up their protests against profession-alism well after 1933. Like the great goalie Marcos de Mendonça, a few clubs even opted to remove themselves from the game, so great was the disgust they felt at a *futebol* played not for pure sport but rather for the base motive of earning a living.[16]

Fausto's commitment to making soccer his career was always evident. Indeed, it led him to take an extraordinary step in late 1931. Trying to bank on their successes in Rio, the directors of Vasco organized an excur-sion to Europe, the first ever by a Rio club and the second by any Brazilian team.[17] Reinforced with new players like Fernando, who had been at Fluminense, and Nilo, hired from Botafogo, the team dazzled in most of the 12 exhibition matches it played in Spain and Portugal. Along with the attacker Russinho and the goalie Jaguaré, Fausto showed European audiences "extraordinary" speed and technique.[18] Among those most impressed were officials from F.C. Barcelona, who offered contracts to Fausto and Jaguaré. Not only were the promised salaries double what they could have earned in Brazil, they would be entirely legal in Spain. The promise of a steady and respectable income was too much to turn down. A Vasco official accompanying the team admitted that by playing in Europe, Fausto and Jaguaré would be able "to guarantee their futures."[19] The two became the first in a long line of Brazilians to play for Barcelona, joining an exodus of stars fleeing the poverty and dependency that characterized Brazilian *futebol* to try their luck in Spain or France or Italy or wherever they might work in a less "confusing professionalism."[20]

This is not to say that the choice was easy in all respects. The tearful goodbyes that marked Vasco's departure for Brazil suggest that remaining in Europe had its drawbacks.[21] Still, when he reflected later on his time in Spain, Fausto declared that he thought that "the life of a professional footballer" was "the best possible" since it delivered not only good pay but also respectful treatment. This ideal slipped from his grasp at Barcelona very quickly. Jaguaré had already found his salary lower than expected, since he had trouble winning a spot in the team and thus earning bonuses based on the number of games played; he left to play in Marseille. Fausto, though, excelled on the field, winning plaudits in the press and reportedly being used to teach Barcelona's B team to play at a greater pace.[22] When Barça hit a patch of poor performances, Fausto found himself one of four players voted out of the squad by the club's board of directors.[23] With the Rio press speculating hopefully that the professionalization of *futebol* would bring Fausto home, the *craque* unexpectedly moved to the Swiss club Young Fellows. Rio had to wait until 1934 for the return of this prodigal son.[24]

Fausto's reintegration into Rio's football proved more difficult, however, than journalists and *cartolas* anticipated. The directors of Vasco counted on the Black Wonder as a key piece who would line up alongside other noted *craques* like Domingos da Guia, Rey, Gradim, and Leônidas da Silva; the hope was that this remarkably expensive squad could return the club to championship form. The reconquest of the Rio title did not satisfy Fausto, who set off again in search of better pay for his labors. His short spell in Uruguay failed to provide the security he desired; most distressingly, he never received a house for his mother, a long-held desire of his that club directors at Nacional promised to fulfill.[25] After leaving Nacional he traded barbs with the Montevideo club's director, who accused him of match fixing.[26] Once more he headed back to Rio, where he forced his way out of Vasco and into another club trying to build a super-team. This time it was Flamengo, in an attempt to establish itself as a popular club, both by winning on the field and by doing so with a squad composed almost entirely of men of color. Once again, Fausto joined Domingos and Leônidas as headliners; once again, Fausto fell out with management.[27]

STARDOM AND ROGUERY

The disputes and transfers that marked Fausto's decade of club *futebol* were far from abnormal. Other stars of the era shared his frustration with what Domingos da Guia called "the regime of tips" (*o regime de bichos*) before full professionalization and the manipulation and deceit of *cartolas* afterward.[28] The quest for steady and respectful employment led not only Fausto, but also many other stars of his era to sign for clubs in Europe, Argentina, and Uruguay. The driving force behind such moves, though, went beyond regular payment of salaries and bonuses. For Fausto as for Domingos and others, the goal was as much autonomy over their lives, even their bodies, as it was sheer profit. Dependence on the whims of a club boss who might decide to pay a bit less on a given day, who would play favorites, and who would almost always demand some show of sub-servience was demeaning.[29]

Knowing of his sad end, it is difficult not to think of Fausto's battles for control over his life as self-destructive. Until illness forced him off the pitch, though, he made great use of his athletic abilities while enjoying himself in his leisure hours. Not only was he tremendously skilled, but Fausto also worked hard and thoughtfully during games. Whether positioned just in front of his team's central backs or drifting back into defense, he handled the ball marvelously and passed it deftly. Moreover, in addition to technical "precision," Fausto played with a steel nerve that impressed most opponents and observers.[30] Indeed, although his touch on the ball was spectacular, he also threw himself into tackles ferociously. More than once his challenges started fights on the pitch. Even teammates found themselves the targets of his vigorous challenges, with a few reporting injuries caused—on at least one occasion intentionally—by Fausto.[31]

Shrugging off complaints about particular incidents, Fausto declared that he played with the virility that soccer required. Particularly at the international level, he asserted, men had to be aggressive and willing to do battle. After his exploits at Vasco earned him a spot on the Brazilian team that participated in the first World Cup, held in 1930 in Uruguay, he went so far as to criticize individual teammates as well as Brazilians more generally for transforming soccer "into a game for ladies." His honesty was as striking as the harshness of his judgments he offered after Brazil's opening defeat to Yugoslavia. Some members of the Seleção, like the goalie Joel, had performed adequately. A few, like the defender Itália, had "fought back with security, worked, and slid a great deal." Others, in his opinion, had failed to overcome their fears, with Poly "afraid of his own shadow" and Nilo "cowardly." Worst of all, in his estimation, was the renowned attacker Araken, who had shown only "the game of a ballerina."[32]

The public nature of these declarations was extraordinary, but they revealed the sort of masculine pose that Fausto maintained until the last year of his life. He famously told a masseur from the national team, "Losing is no disgrace...The shame is in being afraid."[33] On the pitch he certainly showed the fearlessness that he demanded of others. In that realm as well as others, he also strongly held true to his own sense of self. Unlike those Afro-Brazilians who tried to whiten their physical image, he resisted. That is, he refused to straighten his hair, as the great Friedenreich had done, and certainly never applied rice powder in an attempt to whiten his skin tone, as Carlos Alberto had while playing for Fluminense in 1914.[34] When the press condemned his rubbing spit on the ball as a sign that he was revealing his primitive nature, "feeding his racial tendencies in a gesture of superstition," he likewise ignored the criticism.[35] He was not just a tough man, but also a tough black man, "a hard black to knock down" (*um preto duro na queda*), as he once told a team doctor.[36]

When it came to the medical and coaching staff of the various teams for which he played, Fausto's confidence often turned into intransigence. He had had troubles with his chest since the start of his time at Bangu. His repeated bouts of "flu" and chest colds worried his physicians, who cautioned him to lead a quieter life. Fausto, though, was an inveterate Bohemian, a "friend of *cachaça*" (cane liquor), and a lover of nightspots. When he left Bangu for Vasco he did so not only to transfer to a bigger club but also to move closer to the cafés, bars, and *gafieiras* (dance halls) he habitually frequented. Living in the city he would no longer have to take the train in before meeting up with his friends. He maintained his commitment to this lively socializing as long as his health permitted.[37] Returning from Barcelona, for instance, he warmly recalled his social life there, focusing particularly on the attractions of the Spanish women, of whom he had "good impressions." Indeed, he said playfully, "I fell a little bit in love."[38] At Flamengo he became a regular at the Café Rio Branco, a meeting-place where players and club officials alike indulged in a few beers and a lot of conversation, often before heading out on livelier pursuits.[39] Indeed, he persisted in what his doctor called "dissipation," staying out late and drinking, when his body was giving out on him. On a trip with Flamengo to Bahia in March 1938, he went out with Domingos da Guia and Leônidas da Silva "to take advantage of their popularity." Their late night out ended with a brawl at a cabaret and criticism in the local press.[40]

By the time of this incident in Salvador, Fausto had also lived out a full-scale war with the board of directors of Flamengo and the coach they had brought in to revolutionize the team. As happy as Fausto was to be back in Rio, he found the ideas of innovative Hungarian manager Dori Kruschner threatening. Since his time at Bangu, Fausto had played in the center of the field, as an axis or pivot, and enjoyed the freedom the position gave him to dominate the flow of the game. Kruschner, though, sought to implant the "W-M" model that had become popular in Europe. This system required Fausto to withdraw to the center of the three *beques* (backs) who formed the base of the "W." It may well have been that the coach merely wanted to preserve Fausto, whose stamina was clearly waning. In Fausto's eyes, however, the change was an insult. As his previous coach at Flamengo, Flávio Costa, later recalled, Fausto had been "an artist" and "[w]hen he saw himself transformed into a *beque*, he felt diminished." Fausto was unwilling to admit that he had lost any of his vigor, proclaiming, "I'm still the same, see? The same!"[41]

For several months Fausto certainly showed that he had not lost his fighting spirit. He resisted Kruschner by taking his case directly to club president José Bastos Padilha, only to find Padilha in full support of his new manager.[42] In response, Fausto sought out higher legal authorities who might cancel his contract with Flamengo. When these efforts failed to produce the desired results, he threatened to arrange a transfer to the club São Cristóvão, which would have been a step down in prestige though it might have given him a greater sense of autonomy.[43] Thwarted once more, he simply skipped practices. All of these actions, to the *cartolas*, were clear evidence of Fausto's truculence and bad faith. To punish him, they fined him and banned him from the team, which left him feeling that they wanted "to cook him over a low fire" (*cozinhá-lo em fogo frio*).[44]

Although rumors suggested that he would carry on with his legal battle, Fausto soon gave up the battle in an uncharacteristic manner. By the end of 1937 he publicly admitted defeat, going so far as to sign a letter full of apology to Flamengo's directors and ostentatious praise of Kruschner's "superior and efficient" coaching. A note of pride crept out at the close of the generally obsequious document; after promising to show up and work hard at all practices and to adhere to the manager's methods, Fausto (or whoever wrote the letter for him) added that this behavior would leave the *cartolas* "unable to say anything about his discipline."[45] His concession may have come across in the press as a swallowing of pride, but it also meant that Fausto could rejoin the team. Moreover, not only was he welcomed back to the starting 11, he returned to his preferred position in central midfield.[46]

In the end, then, Fausto's apparent surrender may have been a savvy political maneuver. Soon enough, though, the importance of the matter faded as his health began to decline dramatically. Fausto had always been aware of his respiratory weakness. His curious move from Barcelona to Young Fellows may have been motivated by a desire to benefit from the healthy air he might find in Switzerland.[47] But whether out of stoicism or self-delusion, he kept his health concerns to himself until they were too obvious to deny. From that point on, he put himself in the hands of his doctors and faded quietly from the scene.

Conclusion: "Head Held High on the Field and in Life"[48]

Fausto dos Santos was a star in life, the only Brazilian to earn a spot on the all-tournament team at the 1930 World Cup and hailed from that time on as the "Black Wonder."[49] His achievements made him a hero not only for the general public but also for the Afro-Brazilian press.[50] Long after his death, moreover, other promising, dark-skinned players would be dubbed "the new Black Wonder," though none proved his equal on the field.[51] During his decade-long career, he inspired admiration with his play but also provoked irritation among those who put themselves in charge of the game. His approach to *futebol*, as a means of making a living that did not interfere with his Bohemianism, confounded both the *cartolas* whose paternalism he resisted and also the scholars and journalists who formalized the dominant discourse about the Brazilian style of *futebol* beginning in the 1920s and 1930s.

This style, initially called "mulatto football" but later made famous as "the beautiful game" (*o jogo bonito*), located the source of all that was authentically Brazilian in the ranks of the mixed-race, largely poor common folk. A theoretically democratic ideal, this conception of a national culture derived from the *povo*, nevertheless, hailed certain figures more passionately than others. Fausto proved rather difficult for even the great promoters of the new *brasilidade* to welcome into the nation. In his hugely influential work, *O negro no futebol brasileiro* (The Black Man in Brazilian Soccer), Mário Filho wrote admiringly of Fausto's athletic gifts but lamented that he had been too much of a "rebel" (*revoltado*) to find a constructive way of responding to the unfair demands of *cartolas*. As a result of his inflexibility, that is, Fausto isolated himself and fell short of achieving his potential influence.[52]

Of course, few if any *craques* lived up to the standards that the creators of new national myths imposed. Even indisputable stars like Leônidas da Silva, whose performance at the 1938 World Cup thrilled the nation and made him a symbol of the fluid and technical Brazilian style in the telling of Mário Filho, José Lins do Rego, and Gilberto Freyre, were at times perceived as impertinent.[53] What is perhaps most telling is that these unruly stars retained prominence in the hegemonic narratives of Brazilian *futebol*. They challenged racial and other injustices during their careers, but such contestations only rarely appeared in dominant accounts of the rise of a great national cultural form—*futebol*—from the *povo*. Willing to confront his social betters legally, to proudly display his Afro-Brazilianness, and to question the manliness of national team members, Fausto was an uncomfortable fit for the assimilationist Brazil that was emerging during his short career.[54] In the complex and contradictory racial politics of Brazilian soccer, his determination to define himself as an Afro-Brazilian man and as an independent professional faded into the background as ill health took him out of public view. The more palatable and patriotic vision of this early star as the "Black Wonder," hailed by the world press, hid his rebel past.[55]

NOTES

1. "Melhora o estado de saude de Fausto," *Jornal dos Sports*, 25 Feb. 1939; "Morreu Fausto dos Santos!," *Jornal dos Sports*, March 28, 1939.

2. "Eles ainda vivem por esse mundo de Deus," *Mundo Esportivo*, September 5, 1947; Plínio Labriola Negreiros, "A nação entra em campo: O futebol nos anos 30 e 40," PhD diss., Pontifícia Universidade Católica, São Paulo, 1998, 106–7; "O caso Fausto— Uma lição para os novos," *O Globo Sportivo*, May 4, 1939.

3. "A renda do treino de sabbado será em benefício de Fausto e Quintanilha," *Gazeta de Noticias*, February 28, 1939; "O ultimo aprompto dos Cariocas,"*Gazeta de Noticias*, 4 Mar. 1939; "Pelo amparo da familia de Fausto," *Jornal dos Sports*, March 31, 1939; "Fausto irá ao Judiciario!," *Jornal dos Sports*, May 25, 1937.

4. Edson Leite, "Um grito de alerte!," *Mundo Esportivo*, February 28, 1947.

5. Mário [Rodrigues] Filho, *O negro no futebol brasileiro*, 4th ed. (Rio de Janeiro: Mauad, 2003), 173.

6. On this exoticizing of the people more generally, see Florencia Garramuño, *Primitive Modernities: Tango, Samba, and Nation*, trans. Anna Kazumi Stahl (Stanford: Stanford University Press, 2011), 40–1; Roberto Ventura, *Estilo tropical: História cultural e polêmicas literárias no Brasil* (São Paulo: Companhia das Letras, 1991), 36–41.

7. Paulina L. Alberto, *Terms of Inclusion: Black Intellectuals in Twentieth-Century Brazil* (Chapel Hill: University of North Carolina Press, 2011); Renato Ortiz, *Cultura brasileira e identidade nacional*, 3rd ed. (São Paulo: Brasiliense, 1985), esp. 43–4; Brian Owensby, "Towards a History of Brazil's 'Cordial Racism': Race Beyond Liberalism," *Comparative Studies in Society and History* 47, no. 2 (2005): 318–47.

8. Roger Kittleson, *The Country of Football: Soccer and the Making of Modern Brazil* (Berkeley: University of California Press, 2014), 31–42.

9. Francisco Xavier Freire Rodrigues, "Modernidade, disciplina e futebol: Uma análise sociológica da produção social do jogador de futebol no Brasil," *Sociologias* 6, no. 11 (Jan./June 2004): 274–5.

10. "Escreve Lula: 'Fausto foi maravilhoso e sempre pensei em jogar com ele,'" *Mundo Esportivo*, January 9, 1948.

11. "O *caso Fausto*—Uma lição para os novos," *O Globo Sportivo*, May 4, 1939.

12. Fatima Martin Rodrigues Ferreira Antunes, "O futebol nas fábricas," *Revista USP* 22 (1994): 102–9.

13. "O Bangú não pode gastar mais de cento e cincqoenta contos de réis com o seu team," *O Globo Sportivo*, November 5, 1938.

14. João Manuel Casquinha Malaia Santos, "Revolução Vascaína: A profissionalização do futebol e a inserção sócio-econômica de negros e portugueses na cidade do Rio de Janeiro (1915–1934)," Ph.D. diss., Universidade de São Paulo, 2010.

15. Mário [Rodrigues] Filho, *O negro no futebol brasileiro*, 4th ed. (Rio de Janeiro: Mauad/FAPERJ, 2003), 120–42.

16. "O amor entrou em campo," *Correio da Manhã*, 13 Apr. 1970; Leonardo Affonso de Miranda Pereira, "Pelos campos da nação: um *goal-keeper* nos primeiro anos do futebolbrasileiro," *Estudos Históricos* 19 (1997): 23–40; Claudio Nogueira, *Futebol Brasil memória: De Oscar Cox a Leônidas da Silva (1897–1937)*(Rio de Janeiro: Editora SENAC Rio, 2006), 185–90.

17. Tomás Mazzoni, *História do futebol no Brasil (1894–1950)* (São Paulo: Edições Leia, 1950), 181–90, 231. C.A. Paulistano made a famous trip in 1925, wonderfully described in Araken Patusca, with Marinho U. de Macedo, *Os reis do futebol* (São Paulo: n.p., 1945), 73.

18. "O Vasco em Lisboa," *Jornal dos Sports*, July 31, 1931; "O Vasco da Gama em Lisboa," *Correio da Manhã*, 5 Aug. 1931; "O Vasco da Gama em Portugal," *Correio da Manhã*, August 13, 1931.

19. "Fausto, Jaguaré e Fernando ficarão na Europa," *O Globo*, August 3, 1931; "Fausto e Jaguaré choraram quando se despidiram dos companheiros," *O Globo*, September 17, 1931.

20. "Criemos o profissionalismo," *Jornal dos Sports*, August 4, 1931; "As excursões de footballers nacionaes ao estrangeiro e o perigo do profissionalismo," *A Noite*, December 14, 1932; Santos, "Revolução Vascaína," 380–5; Marcos de Castro and João Máximo, *Gigantes do futebol* brasileiro (Rio de Janeiro: Civilização Brasileira, 2011), 46–7; Leonardo Affonso de Miranda Pereira, *Footballmania: Uma história social do futebol no Rio de Janeiro, 1902–1938* (Rio de Janeiro: Nova Fronteira, 2000), 303–41.

21. "Fausto e Jaguaré choraram quando se despidiram dos companheiros," *O Globo*, September, 17 1931.

22. "Fausto e Jaguaré não poderão jogar partidas officiaes," *Correio da Manhã*, 1 Sep. 1931; "Fausto treinador do Barcelona F.C.," *A Batalha*, December 19, 1932; Castro and Máximo, *Gigantes*, 48;

23. "A situação de Fausto," *Jornal dos Sports*, January 29, 1933; "Fausto—valor inestimavel que o football brasileiro reconquistou," *Jornal dos Sports*, March 9, 1933.

24. "O regresso de Fausto e Jaguaré," *Correio da Manhã*, August 23, 1931; "O que há sobre a vinda de Fausto," *Jornal dos Sports*, January 27, 1933.

25. Robert M. Levine, "Sport and Society: The Case of Brazilian *Futebol*," *Luso-Brazilian Review* 17, no. 2 (1980): 242; Castro and Máximo, *Gigantes*, 52; Edson Leite, "Uma cruz para Fausto," *Mundo Esportivo*, March 14, 1947; Domingos da Guia, "A tragédia do futebol brasileiro: Kruschner foi o 'coveiro' do Fausto," *Ultima Hora*, June 6, 1957.

26. "Fausto defende-se das acusações do Sr. Narancio," *Jornal dos Sports*, January 7, 1936.

27. "Fausto colloca em cheque à Censura," *Jornal dos Sports*, February 22, 1936; Pereira, *Footballmania*, 328.

28. Quoted in Aidan Hamilton, *Domingos da Guia: O Divino Mestre* (Rio de Janeiro: Gryphus, 2005), 71.

29. Domingos da Guia, "Passe: Mercado de escravos" and "Concentração: Prisão sem grades," *Última Hora*, June 14 and 17, 1957; Domingos da Guia, Depoimentos para a posteridade, Museu da Imagem e do Som, Rio de Janeiro (1967); [Rodrigues] Filho, *O negro*, 170–1.

30. "Como a imprensa paulista aprecia a partida," *A Batalha*, December 24, 1929; "Porque Fortes vae jogar no lugar de Molla," *A Batalha*, December 21, 1929; "Os brasileiros vão medir suas forças, amanhã, com os bolivianos," *A Noite*, June 20, 1930; "O Vasco da Gama em Lisboa," *Correio da Manhã*, August 5, 1931; Pereira, *Footballmania*, 313.

31. "Iniciando a concentração, os jogadores nacionaes realisaram, hontem, um proveitoso ensaio nocturne," *A Noite*, June 20, 1930; "Fausto, Brilhante e Almeida estão sendo processados," *A Critica*, October 5, 1930; Roberto Assaf and Clóvis Martins. *Flamengo x Vasco: O clássico dos milhões* (Rio de Janeiro: Relume Dumará, 1999), 39.

32. "Fausto fala á A NOITE sobre as causas da derrota brasileira," *A Noite*, July 18, 1930.

33. Castro and Máximo, *Gigantes*, 41.

34. [Rodrigues] Filho, *O negro*, 60–1.

35. "As superstições do football," *Jornal dos Sports*, November 20, 1931; Hamilton, *Domingos*, 62.
36. Castro and Máximo, *Gigantes*, 43.
37. Edson Leite, "Uma cruz para Fausto," *Mundo Esportivo*, 14 March 14, 1947; Castro and Máximo, *Gigantes*, 38, 43.
38. "Fausto—valor inestimavel que o football brasileiro reconquistou," *Jornal dos Sports*, March 9, 1933.
39. Castro and Máximo, *Gigantes*, 53.
40. *A Gazeta*, March 23, 1938.
41. Edson Pinto, *O futebol no jogo da verdade: Flávio Costa* (Rio de Janeiro: Cape, 1996), 48.
42. Castro and Máximo, *Gigantes*, 54–5; Mário [Rodrigues] Filho, *Histórias do Flamengo*, 4th ed. (Rio de Janeiro: Mauad X, 2014), 44–6.
43. "Somente a Judiciaria vae decidir!," *Jornal dos Sports*, February 24, 1937.
44. "Displicencia e pouca solicitude," *Jornal dos Sports*, April 15, 1937; "Fausto não compareceu ao individual de hontem," *Jornal dos Sports*, April 17, 1937; [Rodrigues] Filho, *O negro*, 223.
45. "Fausto comprometteu-se a cumprir as ordens de Kruschner," *Jornal dos Sports*, May 8, 1937.
46. Domingos da Guia, "A tragédia do futebol brasileiro: Kruschner foi o 'coveiro' do Fausto," *Ultima Hora*, June 6, 1957; Castro and Máximo, *Gigantes*, 55–7.
47. Castro and Máximo, *Gigantes*, 49.
48. Antonio Falcão, quoted in *90 minutos de sabedoria: A filosofia do futebol em frases inesquecíveis*, ed. Ivan Maurício, 5th ed. (Rio de Janeiro: Garamond, 2008), 36.
49. Solange Bibas, *As Copas que ninguém viu: Histórias e bastidores* (São Paulo: Catavento, 1982), 26.
50. Bruno Otávio de Lacerda Abrahão and Antonio Jorge Soares, "A imprensa negra e o futebol em São Paulo no início do século XX," *Revista Brasileira de Educação Física e Esporte* 26, no.1 (2012): 72.
51. Domingos da Guia, Depoimentos; "Coluna dos consulentes," *Mundo Esportivo*, March 28, 1947; "A Maravilha Negra," *Placar*, October 29, 1976.
52. [Rodrigues] Filho, *O negro*, 173.

53. Four years after Fausto faced off against Kruschner and his bosses, Leônidas ended up serving time in jail because of his disputes with the Flamengo leadership. Leônidas da Silva, "O famoso caso do exército," *Última Hora*, April 8, 1964; André Ribeiro, *Diamante Negro: Biografia de Leônidas da Silva*, 2nd ed. (São Paulo: Cia dos Livros, 2010), 170–89.

54. Matthew G. Shirts, "Literatura futebolística: Uma periodização," in *Futebol e cultura: Coletânea de estudos*, ed. José Carlos Sebe Bom Meihy and José Sebastião Witter (São Paulo: IMESP/DAESP, 1982), 52–3; Joel Rufino dos Santos, *História política do futebol brasileiro* (São Paulo: Brasiliense, 1981), 125; and con. Anatol Rosenfeld, *Negro, macumba e futebol* (São Paulo: Editora Perspectiva, 2000), 100–1.

55. But con. "Grandes vultos do esporte brasileiro—Brandão," *Mundo Esportivo*, August 15, 1947.

WORK CITED

PERIODICALS

A Batalha, 1929, 1932
A Critica, 1930
Correio da Manhã, 1931, 1970
A Gazeta, 1938
Gazeta de Noticias, 1939
O Globo, 1931
O Globo Sportivo, 1939
Jornal dos Sports, 1931, 1933, 1936, 1937, 1939
Mundo Esportivo, 1947–1948
A Noite, 1930, 1932
Placar, 1976
Ultima Hora, 1957, 1964

ARTICLES, BOOKS, AND THESES

Abrahão, Bruno Otávio de Lacerda, and Antonio Jorge Soares. "A imprensa negra e o futebol em São Paulo no início do século XX." *Revista Brasileira de Educação Física e Esporte* 26, no.1 (2012): 63–76.
Alberto, Paulina L. *Terms of Inclusion: Black Intellectuals in Twentieth-Century Brazil*. Chapel Hill: University of North Carolina Press, 2011.

Antunes, Fatima Martin Rodrigues Ferreira. "O futebol nas fábricas." *Revista USP* 22 (1994): 102–109.

Assaf, Roberto, and Clóvis Martins. *Flamengo x Vasco: O clássico dos milhões*. Rio de Janeiro: Relume Dumará, 1999.

Bibas, Solange. *As Copas que ninguém viu: Histórias e bastidores*. São Paulo: Catavento, 1982.

Castro, Marcos de, and João Máximo. *Gigantes do futebol brasileiro*. Rio de Janeiro: Civilização Brasileira, 2011.

Garramuño, Florencia. *Primitive Modernities: Tango, Samba, and Nation*. Translated by Anna Kazumi Stahl. Stanford: Stanford University Press, 2011.

Guia, Domingos da. Depoimentos para a posteridade. Rio de Janeiro: Museu da Imagem e do Som, 1967.

Hamilton, Aidan. *Domingos da Guia: O Divino Mestre*. Rio de Janeiro: Gryphus, 2005.

Kittleson, Roger. *The Country of Football: Soccer and the Making of Modern Brazil*. Berkeley: University of California Press, 2014.

Levine, Robert M. "Sport and Society: The Case of Brazilian *Futebol*." *Luso-Brazilian Review* 17, no. 2 (1980): 233–252.

Maurício, Ivan, ed. *90 minutos de sabedoria: A filosofia do futebol em frases inesquecíveis*, 5th ed. Rio de Janeiro: Garamond, 2008.

Mazzoni, Tomás. *História do futebol no Brasil (1894–1950)*. São Paulo: Edições Leia, 1950.

Negreiros, Plínio Labriola. A nação entra em campo: O futebol nos anos 30 e 40. PhD dissertation, Pontifícia Universidade Católica, São Paulo, 1998.

Nogueira, Claudio. *Futebol Brasil memória: De Oscar Cox a Leónidas da Silva (1897–1937)*. Rio de Janeiro: Editora SENAC Rio, 2006.

Ortiz, Renato. *Cultura brasileira e identidade nacional*. 3rd ed. São Paulo: Brasiliense, 1985.

Owensby, Brian. "Towards a History of Brazil's 'Cordial Racism': Race Beyond Liberalism." *Comparative Studies in Society and History* 47, no. 2 (2005): 318–347.

Patusca, Araken, and Marinho U. de Macedo. reis do futebol. São Paulo: n.p, 1945.

Pereira, Leonardo Affonso de Miranda. "Pelos campos da nação: um *goal-keeper* nos primeiro anos do futebol brasileiro." *Estudos Históricos* 19 (1997): 23–40.

Pereira, Leonardo Affonso de Miranda. *Footballmania: Uma história social do futebol no Rio de Janeiro, 1902–1938*. Rio de Janeiro: Nova Fronteira, 2000.

Pinto, Edson. *O futebol no jogo da verdade: Flávio Costa*. Rio de Janeiro: Cape, 1996.

Ribeiro, André. *Diamante Negro: Biografia de Leónidas da Silva*. 2nd ed. São Paulo: Companhia dos Livros, 2010.

Rodrigues, Francisco Xavier Freire. "Modernidade, disciplina e futebol: Uma análise sociológica da produção social do jogador de futebol no Brasil." *Sociologias* 6, no. 11 (January/June, 2004): 260–299.

[Rodrigues] Filho, Mário. *O negro no futebol brasileiro.* 4th ed. Rio de Janeiro: Mauad, 2003.

[Rodrigues] Filho, Mário. *Histórias do Flamengo.* 4th ed. Rio de Janeiro: Mauad X, 2014.

Rosenfeld, Anatol. *Negro, macumba e futebol.* São Paulo: Editora Perspectiva, 2000.

Santos, Joel Rufino dos. *História política do futebol brasileiro.* São Paulo: Brasiliense, 1981.

Santos, João Manuel Casquinha Malaia. *Revolução Vascaína: A profissionalização do futebol e a inserção sócio-econômica de negros e portugueses na cidade do Rio de Janeiro (1915–1934).* Ph.D. dissertation, Universidade de São Paulo, 2010.

Shirts, Matthew G. "Literatura futebolística: Uma periodização." In *Futebol e cultura: Coletânea de estudos,* edited by José Carlos Sebe Bom Meihy and José Sebastião Witter, 45–69. São Paulo: IMESP/DAESP, 1982.

Ventura, Roberto. *Estilo tropical: História cultural e polêmicas literárias no Brasil.* São Paulo: Companhia das Letras, 1991.

CHAPTER 10

Who Counts as a Real American? Dual Citizenship, Hybridity, and the U.S. Men's National Team

Jon D. Bohland

Since the early twentieth century, the US Men's National Soccer Team (USMNT) has featured players from immigrant and transnational backgrounds. Following their first qualification to the FIFA World Cup in 1990 in 40 years, the USMNT began to regularly compete in international competitions at the highest level. As part of their effort to become a successful and competitive national team, USMNT managers began to recruit dual nationals for the United States. These players, largely drawn from dual national families with German and Latino heritage, chose the USMNT despite being eligible for other national team programs. In this chapter, I argue that dual national players face unfair characterization as "mercenaries" who ruin the presumed "team chemistry" of an ethnically pure national team. I contend that such arguments are based largely on nineteenth-century discourses of citizenship and national identity.

My study analyzes 15 years of sports media discourses within the American soccer community focused on American players with dual citi-

J.D. Bohland (✉)
Department of Political Science, Hollins University, Roanoke, VA, USA

© Hofstra University 2017
B. Elsey, S. Pugliese (eds.), *Football and the Boundaries of History*,
DOI 10.1057/978-1-349-95006-5_10

zenship, including articles written by professional journalists, blog and message board postings by American soccer fans, as well as interviews with current and former players and coaches. Using a critical discourse analysis informed by postcolonial theory and scholarship on national identity, I analyze these sources for examples of nativism and classic nationalistic tropes. For example, dual national players are framed by some important soccer media members as threats to the "team chemistry," outsiders who threaten to ruin the presumed harmony of the USMNT. I argue that such fear-laden critiques are largely rooted in exclusionary nineteenth- and twentieth-century geopolitical conceptions of national identity, ethno-territoriality, and the presumed category of a "real citizen." Additionally, I document the various ways in which the legitimacy and political allegiances of dual national players are questioned publicly. My critical analysis of interviews conducted by media members with current dual national players further challenges xenophobic and nationalist claims that dual national players, due to their supposedly divided loyalties and torn psyches, do not "fight for the shirt" like other "real" American players. Rather, it is my contention that these players' connection to the United States is every bit as real and affective as single nationality players. I begin with a discussion of contemporary scholarship on issues of dual citizenship and hybridized identities.

DUAL CITIZENSHIP, MULTICULTURALISM, AND TRANSNATIONAL IDENTITIES

There is little scholarly consensus regarding the meaning of the term "citizenship," as it is a rather vague category open to many different interpretations.[1] Historically, the Western concept of "the citizen" is of classical origin, dating back to the Greco-Roman era where the [male] citizens of the polis and/or the Empire were supposed to be guaranteed legal protection and political participation.[2] Beginning with these classical European societies, the idea of the citizen as a societal category divided people into binary categories of included and excluded, influenced heavily by racial, class, and gender differences.[3] With the nineteenth-century rise of the state and the advent of European nationalist ideology, citizenship became more than a guarantee of legal and political status. It was now a crucial element of nationalist movements, as "the citizen" became a legal category for tying together disparate members of states into collective community of identity, history, and memory.[4] To be a citizen demanded loyalty to the state, as citizenship became affectively constructed as a deeply rooted and primordial membership of culturally distinct people.[5] Conversely, immigrant and dual national populations were now portrayed as disloyal or potentially disloyal to the nation, as the prevailing construction of citizenship demanded allegiance to one nation-state. As Williams suggests, "the very logic of conceptions of citizenship as identity is inescapably partial and exclusivist...no matter how general or abstract we strive to make the desirable content of identity, our articulation of it will never be perfectly equivalent to the plural and contradictory identities born by actual individuals."[6]

Given these connections between citizenship and purified notions of national identity, it is not surprising that the history surrounding the legal concept of dual or transnational citizenship has been highly contentious. The category of dual citizens was legally rejected by most of the international community as a result of the Bancroft Treaties in the late nineteenth century. The nineteenth-century statesman and former US Ambassador to the German States George Bancroft himself once stated that countries "should as soon tolerate a man with two wives as a man with two countries...as soon bear with polygamy as that state of double allegiance which common sense so repudiates that it has not even coined a word to express it."[7] This fear of the perfidious dual national became a common justification for anti-immigrant actions in the twentieth century, including the forced internship and imprisonment of German, Italian, and Japanese Americans during World War II.

The reflexive and sometimes violent reaction against the idea of dual and multinational citizenship in the United States is, at least in theory, not consistent with tropes of American nationalism that portray America as a welcoming place, the "melting pot" of the world. In practice, American citizenship has always been an exclusionary category requiring new immigrants to fully assimilate by leaving behind their prior cultural traditions in order to adopt new and a presumed homogenous set of American values.[8] This assimilation model of citizenship constructs a narrative of the United States as the greatest nation on Earth, a laboratory of democracy where the old ethnic and class antagonisms of Europe dissolved within a landscape of unlimited opportunity.

By the late 1980s, hundreds of years of cultural and economic interactions facilitated by imperialist actions, geopolitical conflicts, the rise of neoliberalism, the fall of the Soviet Bloc, and the growth of new immigrant-driven countries created a migratory world where plural national identities became increasingly commonplace and people live in states of permanent exile from their homeland.[9] In a world forever changed by the contacts of imperialism and globalization, the category of the transnational or dual national emerged as a counter to essentialist claims of national identity and citizenship.[10] As Hall suggests, "the [idea of a] fully unified, completed, secure, and coherent identity is a fantasy...We are faced with a bewildering, fleeting multiplicity of possible identities—each of which we could identify with."[11] Within academic scholarship, a great deal of research has focused on the construction of transnational identities as hybridized, flexible, and pluralistic.[12] As Portes, Guarnizo, and Landholt suggest, "thick webs" of transnational connection allows dual citizens to "live dual lives, speak two languages, have homes in two countries, and make a living through continuous regular contact across national borders."[13] Beginning in the 1980s, states around the world began to finally recognize the legality of dual citizenship, through either formal declaration of acceptance or "don't ask, don't tell" policies. In the case of the United States, though the official government policy still outlaws dual citizenship, these laws are rarely enforced.[14]

Immigration, Dual Nationals, and FIFA

As a cultural site for understanding politics and identity formation, mass sport offers a great deal for scholars seeking to understanding issues of nationalism and citizenship.[15] As the world's most popular spectator sport, there are few global sports or cultural practices as intertwined with issues of national identity and politics than international football.[16] According to Kellas, national team matches became "the most popular form of nationalistic behavior in many countries...masses of people become highly emotional in support of their national team."[17] By 1904, the explosive growth of the game internationally led to the establishment of a new global body (FIFA) to regulate the game. Following the end of World War I, men's national teams began to play international matches again, culminating in FIFA staging the first World Cup tournament in 1930. National team football matches soon became among the most viewed and followed sporting events in the world.

As is the case with all international sporting competitions, the eligibility of players became a major issue as these events became more lucrative and competitive. As Mercer and Hague suggest, decades of "global migration, geopolitics, refugee status, naturalization, and the increasing complexities of grand-parental antecedents of players under consideration for national teams have rendered players' nationalities pliable."[18] At a very basic level, FIFA struggled to determine if players should be required to be citizens of a particular state, or to allow non-citizen players eligibility for the country where they play their domestic professional football. Due to the multiplicity and differences of citizenship laws among global states, it was easier for foreign players to become naturalized citizens within some countries than others, particularly in states where citizenship can be granted to individuals by royal or government decree.

Not surprisingly, this led some footballing federations to abuse this rule, as national federations worked with federal governments in order to allow prominent footballers to gain eligibility. The Qatari national teams in the 1980s and 1990s featured multiple players of Brazilian heritage who were mysteriously granted citizenship by the ruling royal family. In Spain, players from other countries who suited up for Real Madrid or Barcelona were often granted Spanish citizenship once they had proven themselves worthy. Initially, FIFA also allowed players with multiple citizenships to represent more than one country in senior national team matches. The Argentine-born and Real Madrid striker Alfredo Di Stéfano played for three separate national teams (Spain, Argentina, and Colombia) during his playing career from 1947 to 1961. Similarly Ferenc Puskás led his home nation of Hungary to a World Cup final in 1954 only to later appear four times as an outfield player for the Spanish national team in the early 1960s.[19]

Beginning in 2004 and amended four years later, FIFA began to update their eligibility laws for international soccer to ban many of these practices and loopholes. Non-citizen players could only become eligible for naturalization after spending a period of over "five consecutive years" in the territory of another federation.[20] Additionally, players were eligible for a one-time switch if either the player or one of his/her parents or grandparents were born in the country of the new federation. The new regulations forced players with dual citizenship to make permanent choices regarding the federation they choose to represent. Players who appear in a senior level competitive FIFA match (non-friendlies) became "cap-tied" to federations and no longer have the option to play for another country.[21]

SOCCER IN THE UNITED STATES
AND THE GHOST OF DAVID REGIS

The growth of football (soccer to most Americans) in the United States has been inextricably linked with immigration and dual national communities. While American gridiron football developed as an indigenous mix of rugby with association football, soccer was very popular within the rapidly expanding Eastern and Southern European immigrant communities of the late-nineteenth and early-twentieth century. Emerging amateur and professional clubs, including fabled teams like Bethlehem Steel and the Fall River Marksmen, developed significant popular support within immigrant-heavy Eastern industrial communities.[22]

Due to its popularity among first- and second-generation Americans, soccer was often portrayed by the American sporting media as a game for foreigners.[23] As a result, American soccer in the early to mid-twentieth century rarely received national media attention and was largely relegated to these urban enclaves. The USFA, the United States Football Association, (now USSF, United States Soccer Federation) failed to adequately regulate the professional game, which resulted in a variety of regional professional leagues destroying each other rather than cooperating among leagues.[24] Throughout this same era, the USMNT achieved modest to excellent results at the World Cup, particularly given the relative instability of the game domestically. With teams largely comprising first- or second-generation immigrants, the USMNT finished fourth at the 1930 World Cup and qualified for the final rounds in 1934 and 1950. The most fabled American soccer victory of the twentieth century occurred at the 1950 World Cup, where a Haitian-born resident alien named Joseph Gaetjens scored the only goal in a 1-0 victory against world power England. This would prove to be a false dawn for US soccer, as the national team failed to qualify for the World Cup for another 40 years.

During the American soccer "Dark Ages" from 1950 to 1980, the geographic centers of soccer relocated from urban immigrant neighborhoods to the plush green playing fields of the American suburbs. Soccer in America became a largely middle-class youth sport exploding in popularity among suburban white children. Foer suggests that soccer was "a sport onto which a generation of parents could project their values...it came to represent the values of yuppie parenting, the spirit of Sesame Street, and Dr. Benjamin Spock. It would foster self-esteem and minimize the pain of competition while teaching life lessons."[25] It is important to note, however, that though the game had largely become the providence of suburbanites, the national team player pool continued to have a significant number of players from first- or second-generation immigrant families.[26]

The qualification of the United States into the 1990 World Cup ended 40 years of American soccer isolation. The United States hosted the 1994 World Cup, a mega event that both broke attendance records for the tournament and ushered in a new dynamic era of American support for the game. Two years after hosting the World Cup, the launching of Major League Soccer (MLS) finally brought a stable professional league to the United States. In addition to MLS players, the USMNT in the 1990s began to be supplemented with dual nationals actively recruited by US Soccer from European leagues. Thomas Dooley (Germany) and Ernie Stewart (the Netherlands), both of whom were sons of American servicemen raised in Europe, were starters and major contributors for the 1994 World Cup team. Additionally, naturalized dual nationals David Regis (of French descent) and Roy Wegerle (South Africa) were also named to World Cup teams in the 1990s.

After the USMNT flamed out of the 1998 World Cup with three straight losses, it was David Regis who received a disproportionate share of the public blame from the media and his fellow players and coaches for the failures of the team by prominent voices within the American soccer community. Regis was a surprise choice by USMNT manager Steve Sampson for the 1998 final roster, as he was not involved in any of the matches during the qualifying cycle and was not a player well known to most American soccer fans. At the time of his naturalization, Regis spoke little English and had never played with any members of the US national team pool. Following three straight losses at the tournament, Regis quickly developed a reputation within the American soccer media as a "mercenary" who had presumably not "given blood" for the cause during the often arduous qualifying schedule.[27] As Turner suggests, "The nativist question [if Regis was] 'truly American' perhaps gets hidden by remarks that he didn't do anything in qualification."[28]

In subsequent interviews after the tournament, players and coaches from the 1998 squad continue to publically claim that the Regis selection was a crucial reason for why the United States finished in last place at the tournament. Coach Steve Sampson blamed the losses on poor "team chemistry," claiming that he "made a mistake" in selecting David Regis for the tournament.[29] Though team chemistry is certainly a significant factor in the success or failure of national teams, it is quite telling that a dual national is specifically targeted as the player most responsible for ruining the team spirit. It is worth noting that, prior to the beginning of the tournament, Sampson removed long-serving team captain John Harkes from the World Cup roster after discovering that he had slept with teammate Eric Wynalda's wife. This act was presumably much more damaging to the team chemistry than the presence of a dual national player.

Through the lens of nationalist discourse, Regis was presumed to be like many other immigrants who had come to the United States and ultimately "failed" to assimilate. Former teammate and current Fox announcer Alexi Lalas reflected about Regis that:

> If [Regis] comes in and through his own fault, or through other factors, is *not absorbed* into the squad's culture, either because of an unwillingness on his part, a language barrier, or a personality trait, then that will come into play. Regis came to the team very late. He just seemed to turn up and away we go...He did not speak much English. Jeff Agoos had been with the team; Regis took his place and started immediately. He lacked a personal connection to the team or the other players and his background was so completely different to ours there was little in the way of inter-relatable background.[30]

Despite a career in which he went on to represent the USMNT 27 times and was a member of the highly successful 2002 World Cup Team, Regis' place in American soccer history seems to be as an apparition used to warn to future national team managers of the dangers of selecting dual national players. In the three months prior to the beginning of the 2014 World Cup, *MLSnet.com* ran two feature articles on David Regis that focused on the connections between Regis and the current crop of dual national players. It is worth noting, however, that neither of the these two articles makes any distinction between the new dual nationals, all of whom either were born in the United States or have at least one parent who is an American citizen, and the quickly naturalized Regis. As is common within the American soccer media, all dual national players are framed as homogenous and worthy of the same suspicion Regis faced. Their own personal stories and connections to the United States are collapsed within the universalized category of the dual national. In writing about German-American player Julian Green, columnist Jonah Freedman suggests that:

> Green didn't endure the controversy that surrounded adjusting to an unconventional coach. He wasn't part of an often-contentious locker room

that somehow rallied around adversity. He didn't have the chance to form a bond with his teammates during tense moments...And yet when the final roster for Brazil is named, it's possible that he'll take the place of a player who did all of those things. It has the makings of an uncomfortable flight. And it's almost the exact same scenario the USMNT faced 16 years ago [with Regis]. George Santayana, another dual-national American, once penned the words, "Those who cannot remember the past are condemned to repeat it."[31]

Like Regis, Green became a "job stealer" who had not fully assimilated into the team. To Freedman, choosing such a player risks "dooming" the United States to the same fate it suffered in 1996, presumably due to Regis' selection. Freedman clearly ignores the reality that within international soccer it is hardly uncommon for players not involved in the qualifying cycle to be named to the final World Cup roster. In the case of the USMNT, Bob Bradley named three dual national players to the 2010 roster (Edson Buddle, Herculez Gomez, and Robbie Finley), none of whom played during the qualification cycle. This 2010 team successfully made it out of their World Cup group, leading to no suggestion from the soccer media that these choices ruined team chemistry. At the 2014 World Cup, Julian Green shook off the ghost of David Regis, scoring a vital goal on his first touch in his only appearance at the World Cup in the knockout round against Belgium.

THE 2014 WORLD CUP TEAM

Beginning in the mid-2000s, the USSF began a concerted effort to discover and then recruit dual national players living outside of the United States to play for the senior and junior male national teams. The current USMNT player pool includes a significant number of dual nationals, including German-American players Jermaine Jones, Terrence Boyd, Fabian Johnson, Danny Williams, Timothy Chandler, John-Anthony Brooks, and Julian Green. From this group, all but Williams and Boyd made the roster for the 2014 World Cup. These players are all the sons of ex-American servicemen based in Germany. Additionally, dual nationals with Icelandic (Aron Jóhannsson) and Norwegian (Mix Diskerud) citizenship became regular USMNT selections and made the final roster. All of these players meet current FIFA eligibility requirements, in that they either were born in the United States or have a mother or father who was an American citizen at the time of their birth.

As a German who married an American and has lived in the United States since his retirement from professional football in 1998, manager Jürgen Klinsmann shared many of the hybrid traits of his dual national players. In the excerpt below, Klinsmann supports a postmodern and postcolonial notion of hybrid citizenship situating the players as being situated "between two worlds." Additionally, he articulates a vision of American national identity combining the traditional melting pot metaphor with a more cosmopolitan and globalized view of citizenship.

> Their background is so different, not matter where they were born...they are [players] between two worlds...I don't care if the kid grows up in an American family in Tokyo or in Johannesburg or in Buenos Aires. If he is eligible for us and he has an interest to play for us, we will talk to the kid. The senior national team will look like what America looks like. It's a melting pot. And I think this is wonderful.[32]

Despite Klinsmann's defense of dual national players, many prominent voices in American soccer criticized his presumed overreliance on German-American players. Former Under 20 national team player Preston Zimmerman openly labeled dual nationals to be "fake Americans." Echoing the mercenary and torn psyche tropes, he stated that "the team is calling in guys who are really Germans who know they've got no chance of playing for Germany so they'll settle with the U.S....the U.S. team needs to comprise Real Americans."[33] As part of an extensive interview with Brian Straus, a number of current American internationals spoke off the record about the national team program's reliance on dual national players. The German-Americans are blamed for instilling "poor team chemistry," and for their ambivalence toward the national team cause: "For several U.S. born players, the increasing stature of Jermaine Jones, Danny Williams, Fabian Johnson and Chandler (and to a far lesser extent, Terrence Boyd)...is harming team chemistry." As two of the anonymous players told Straus, "They stay to themselves...It's like they are here, and they enjoy it, but they don't care as much as they should to play for the national team."[34]

Former and current USNMT team manager Bruce Arena publicly criticized Klinsmann for selecting too many dual nationals for the World Cup roster. He told Doug McIntyre of *ESPN* that "players on the national team— and this is my own feeling—they should be Americans. If they're all born in other countries, I don't think we can say we are making progress."[35] In making such a statement, Arena masks his nativism in player development, suggesting that reliance on players who did not grow up in the United States excludes "real Americans." Though the mechanisms of American soccer development are certainly worthy of critique, the idea that choosing dual nationals suggests a failure of the system is hyperbolic and reactionary. For example, players such Argentine Lionel Messi, a graduate of the famed youth academy of FC Barcelona, received their soccer education in countries far away from their place of birth. Arena's comments are also not without major elements of hypocrisy, as one of the key players on his 2002 World Cup team was Ernie Stewart, a player born in the Netherlands whose development was entirely in Europe. Arena also chose David Regis for the 2002 squad even after his selection to the 1998 team caused such an outcry among some in the American soccer media. Ultimately, Arena's criteria for selection would reduce the player pool to only those passing an arbitrary test of American soccer purity. For example, it is unclear if a Mexican-American player who left the United States to play in Mexico as a teenager would still be classified as an American under Arena's definition of eligibility.

In addition to their recruitment of dual nationals from Europe, Bradley and Klinsmann actively recruited dual nationals residing within the borders of the United States. In particular, this involves developing and ultimately recruiting Latinos such as Joe Corona, Ventura Alvarado, Jose Torres, and Michael Orozco, all of whom were born in the United States but are also eligible to play for Mexico, Central American, or Caribbean nations through familial connections. The recruitment of youth players to the American national team program particularly involves cultivating deep connections within the Mexican-American community, something US Soccer has failed to do for decades.[36] Thousands of Latino-organized soccer leagues have traditionally not been actively recruited by USSF regional and national youth coaches, as the technical style of play of many Latino players was often devalued in favor of a more athletic and "Anglo" style.[37] The soccer writer Paul Gardner, who has written about this topic of Latino exclusion from American soccer for decades, argues that "for the U.S. to become a real force then it must begin to tap into the quality of talent available in the Hispanic community which can be nurtured to take the game to the next level."[38]

The failure to incorporate Latinos into the American soccer community mirrors larger national issues of immigration within the United States. Popular political scholar Samuel Huntington once claimed that the massive growth of the Latin American population posed a threat to American identity, suggesting that the true loyalty of these millions of American dual nationals is to Mexico or the countries of Central America.[39] Renshon similarly argues that Hispanics have a "shallow attachment" to the United States because that it is impossible for anyone to truly love more than one country.[40] Media questioning of the "loyalty" of Hispanic Americans manifests itself regularly whenever the US national team plays Mexico in American states with large Mexican-American communities. At the 2011 Gold Cup Final in Los Angeles, many fans in the stands openly rooted for Mexico, some of whom booed the American national anthem, leading to media and message board outrage against these boorish Mexican-American fans. American goalkeeper Tim Howard even expressed concern that the medal ceremony was conducted in Spanish, claiming that this was a "fucking disgrace. You can bet your ass that if we were in Mexico City it wouldn't all be in English."[41]

WHY DO I PLAY FOR THE UNITED STATES?

Though each of the players themselves articulates their transnational identities in different ways, there are consistent themes that emerge from their descriptions of why they chose to represent the United States. A major theme emerging from interviews with dual national players is that of opportunity and comfort level, as an offer to play for the United States offered these professionals a chance to play the game at the highest level, something that may not have been possible if they chose to commit to play for their other national team option. Before the 2010 World Cup, Jose Torres explained his choice for the USMNT over Mexico by noting that "the opportunity came with the [U.S.] national team [first], and I took it."[42] Rather than framing these choices as opportunistic and mercenary, a common argument made against dual players since David Regis, these decisions should be framed instead as sensible professional decisions. The World Cup is a mass-sporting spectacle offering players the chance to showcase their skills at the highest level. Dual nationals are rather fortunate in that they actually choose to play for a national team offering them the best opportunity to perform at the "shopping window" that is the World Cup. Within a globalized world where labor and capital freely flows across borders, perhaps all players deserve to have such choices.

Another consistent theme from the player interviews is that they view their hybridized dual identities as natural and consistent with their upbringing. To a person, they see themselves as being from "two worlds" with strong connections to both of their cultural homelands. According to Corona, "I always grew up with both cultures. I just felt I was part of both. I lived in Mexico; I now live in San Diego. I feel I always identified with both countries."[43] Julian Green's father explained that Green "grew up, as far as day-to-day routine, in Germany. But he was also here [in the U.S.] every year of his life. Julian would say to his brother, Yeah, well I was born in America and you weren't...You're German and I'm an American."[44] Terrance Boyd stated that he chose to play for the United States because "I just love [the United States], so I love to represent the United States...I didn't really feel that German back in the day—it's funny—although I grew up [there] the entire time."[45]

Terrance Boyd's assertion that "he didn't really feel that German" speaks to another reason the dual nationals from Germany chose to represent the United States: their racial identity. Almost all of the German-American players have African-American heritage on their father's side. As young men of color growing up in Germany, these players were racially marked as different from the majority white society. Jermaine Jones explains that "when you see me, first you will say, 'He's American.' I look American. My name is American."[46] Similarly, Danny Williams explained that "when I look around in the States, there are a lot mixed people, so many mixed players on this time that have the same background as me...always in the back of my head, I [knew that] am mixed...people look at me in Germany, they know that I am not 100 % German. Some people you had to fight with them for saying racist words."[47]

The German-American players generally view the USMNT to be a much more comfortable and inclusive professional environment than the German national team, due in large part to the widespread acceptance of people of color within the program. They also note strong personal connections to the United States and what the country represents to them. To these players, the United States is a multicultural society where being a person of color is normalized and commonplace. It is significant that when dual national alarmists in the media express concern regarding whether or not the players truly love playing for the United States, they fail to consider how these issues of racial identity deeply connect these players to the imagined community of a multicultural and racially tolerant United States (Fig. 10.1).

Fig. 10.1 USMNT friendly versus Colombia, November 14, 2014. *Back row*: Jozy Altidore, Mix Diskerud, Brad Guzan, John Brooks, Jermaine Jones. *Bottom*: Rubio Rubin, Fabian Johnson, DeAndre Yedlin, Alejandro Bedoya, Kyle Beckerman, Greg Garza. Of this group, Diskerud, Altidore, Brooks, Jones, Rubin, Johnson, Bedoya, and Garza are all dual nationals (Photo credit: Ben Queenborough/ISIPhotos. com)

THE POST-2014 WORLD CUP FUTURE

In the 2014 World Cup, the USMNT managed to get out of the "group of death" and advanced into the knockout stage, where it was eliminated from the competition by Belgium by 2-1. The tournament received record television ratings in the United States, including massive watching parties at central locations in cities and towns across the country. Contrary to all of the dire and cautionary public predictions of how the dual nationals would fit into the team, this group of players proved to be among the best and most important contributors to the success of the team at the World Cup. Jermaine Jones played every minute of every match, scored a goal against Portugal, and was generally regarded by most media members as the best American field player at the tournament. Fabian Johnson started every match and was generally excellent. The two youngest dual nationals, John Brooks and Julian Green, took advantage of their minimal playing time to score crucial goals in the last minute of matches. Indeed, Mix Diskerud and Timothy Chandler were the only dual national players who failed to enter a match, though both players were seen on television celebrating with the team and relishing their collective success.

The media and public reaction to the stellar performance of the dual nationals resulted in a rather predictable 180-degree turn from the doom and gloom warnings prior to the onset of the competition. Jermaine Jones went from a malcontented leader of the German-American clique to a "tireless American hero"[48] and a "warrior" who bled for the American cause.[49] Post-World Cup, Jones became a free agent and has taken up residence in Los Angeles. Before negotiating a possible multimillion-dollar contract with MLS and being assigned to the New England Revolution, he was photographed by TMZ at various Southern California parties with notorious celebrities including Charlie Sheen, Paris Hilton, and Mike Tyson.[50] Following his game-winning goal against Ghana, John Brooks received the nickname "Johnny Futbol" from a headline in the *Philadelphia Inquirer*.[51] Brooks also had his Wikipedia page altered by US fans to read that he was "the greatest American since Evil Knievel, Bill Clinton, and Abe Lincoln."[52]

What does the success of the dual nationals at the World Cup mean for the future of American soccer? It suggests that these players, just as certain immigrant groups have managed historically, can become accepted as authentic citizens. It is worth noting, however, that it took heroic achievements on the pitch for these players for the issues of disloyalty and team chemistry to disappear from media discourse. The German-American players seemingly had to prove to prominent members of the American soccer community their value as players as well as their loyalty to the collective cause. It is important to note that my analysis in this chapter does not suggest that most of the American soccer communities are against using dual national players. Rather, I have generally found the opposite to be true. One major reason for this is that American soccer fans desperately want the team to succeed, and they are willing to openly accept players to the team as long as they strengthen the roster. The success of the dual nationals at the 2014 World Cup certain suggests that American soccer would be well served by continuing to recruit dual national players.

The impact of the 2014 World Cup on the acceptance of future dual national players will certainly be an interesting trend to watch. As I argue in this chapter, the roots of xenophobia and nativism in the United States certainly extend into American soccer. The comments I analyze in this study largely came from very prominent figures within the American soccer community including active and former national team players and the most successful manager in US National Team history. These are voices with extensive media platforms where their opinions can be heard. It is difficult to determine whether these voices will forget the "Ghost of David Regis" or if future critical losses by the national team will be blamed on the perceived disruptive presence of dual national players. It should be noted, for example, that the off-the-record comments to Brian Straus that questioned the commitment of the German-American players came after the United States lost its first game in the final round of qualifying against Honduras.[53] There is no reason to believe that this could not happen again, even if players like Jermaine Jones, John Brooks, and Julian Green might now be inoculated against it. It is ultimately my hope that the United States continues to expand its player pool through inclusive programs that recognize the shifting landscape of global citizenship and identity politics.

NOTES

1. Nicholas Steiner, *International Migration and Citizenship Today* (New York: Routledge, 2009), 96.
2. Jane F. Gardner, *Being A Roman Citizen* (London: Routledge, 1993).
3. Peter Kivisto and Thomas Faist, *Citizenship: Discourse, Theory, and Transnational Prospects* (Maiden, MA: Blackwell, 2007), 17.
4. Steiner, 97.
5. Jason Dittmer, *Popular Culture, Geopolitics, and Identity* (Latham, MD: Rowman & Littlefield, 2010), 75; David Jacobson, "New Frontiers: Territory, Social Spaces, and the State," *Sociological Forum* 12, no. 1 (1997): 121–133.
6. M. Williams, "Nonterritoral Boundaries of Citizens," in *Identities, Affiliations, and Allegiances*, eds. S. Benhabib, I. Shapiro, and D. Petranovic (Cambridge, UK: Cambridge University Press, 2007), 233–34.
7. Kivisto and Faist, 11.
8. Christian Joppke, "Immigration, Citizenship, and the Need for Integration," in *Citizenship, Borders, and Human Needs*, ed. R. M. Smith (Philadelphia: University of Pennsylvania Press, 2011), 159.

9. T. Alexander Aleinkoff and Douglas Klusmeyer, "Plural Nationality: Facing the Future in a Migratory World," in *Citizenship Today: Global Perspectives and Practices*, eds. T.A. Aleinkoff and D. Klusmeyer (Washington, DC: Carnegie Endowment for International Peace, 2001); Rainer Bauböck, *Transnational Citizenship* (Aldershot, UK: Edward Elgar, 1994).

10. Anthony Ilona, "Hanif Kureishi's *The Buddha of Suburbia*: A New Way of Being British," in *Contemporary British Fiction* eds. R. Lane, R. Mengham and P. Tew (Cambridge: Polity, 2003).

11. Stuart Hall, "The Question of Cultural Identity," in *Modernity: An Introduction to Modern Sciences*, eds. S. Hall, D. Held, D. Hubert and K. Thompson (London: Blackwell, 1996), 598.

12. Homi K. Bhabha, *The Location of Culture* (London: Routledge, 1994); Stuart Hall, "Culture, Community, Nation," *Cultural Studies* 7, no. 3 (1993): 349–363; Paul Gilroy, *The Black Atlantic: Modernity and Double Consciousness* (Cambridge, MA: Harvard University Press, 1993); Doreen Massey, *For Space* (London: Sage, 2005); Nicholas Van Lear, *New Diasporas* (Seattle: University of Washington Press, 1998).

13. Alejandro Portes, Luis E. Guarnizo and Patricia Landolt, "The Study of Transnationalism: Pitfalls and Promise of an Emergent Research Field," *Ethnic and Racial Studies*, 22, no. 2: 217.

14. Kivisto and Faist, 113.

15. Natalie Koch, "Sport and Soft Authoritarian Nation-Building," *Political Geography* 32 (2013): 41–52; J. Mercer and E. Hague, "Op-Ed: The Fixity and Fluidity of National Identities in Men's Professional Soccer," *AAG Newsletter* 8 (2011).

16. John Bale, "Sport and National Identity: A Geographical View," *The International Journal of the History of Sport* 3, no.1 (2007): 18–41.

17. James Kellas, *The Politics of Nationalism and Identity* (New York: Macmillan, 1991), 21.

18. Mercer and Hague, 8.

19. Ibid., 8.

20. Jerome Valcke, *FIFA Circular #1147*, June 18, 2008, http://www.fifa.com/mm/document/affederation/administration/81/10/29/circularno.1147-eligibilitytoplayforrepresentativeteams_55197.pdf.

21. Youth national team matches are exempt from these rules, provided the player is already a dual citizen (or eligible for dual citizenship) at the time of his/her first youth FIFA competitive match. As is the case with senior national teams, friendly matches do not "cap-tie" players to a particular country; only matches designated by FIFA as competitive do so.

22. Roger Allaway, *Rangers, Rovers, and Spindles: Soccer, Immigration, and Textiles in New England and New Jersey* (Haworth, NJ: St. Johann Press, 2005).

23. Andrei Markovits and Steven Hellerman, *Offside: Soccer and American Exceptionalism* (Princeton: Princeton University Press, 2001); Elliott Turner, "Julian Green and the Ongoing Saga of US Soccer's Immigration Policies." *The Guardian,* March 26, 2014. http://www.theguardian.com/football/2014/mar/26/julian-green-ongoing-saga-us-soccers-immigration-policies,

24. Markovits and Hellerman 2001; Allaway 2005.

25. Franklin Foer, *How Soccer Explains the World: An Unlikely Theory of Globalization* (New York: Harper Collins, 2004).

26. Turner, 2014.

27. Quoted in Roger Bennett, "Now He Has Committed, Green Must Prove Himself." *ESPN FC.com,* March 18, 2014. http://www.espnfc.com/blog/_/name/relegationzone/id/1732?cc=5901.

28. Turner, 2014.

29. Greg Lalas, "What Jurgen Klinsmann Can Learn From Steve Sampson & USMNT 1998 World Cup Disaster." *MLSnet.com,* April 1, 2014. http://m.mlssoccer.com/worldcup/2014/news/article/2014/04/01/what-jurgen-klinsmann-can-learn-steve-sampson-usmnts-1998-world-cup-disaster.

30. Quoted in Bennett, 2014.

31. Jonah Freedman, "What the Legacy of David Regis Says About the USMNT's Julian Green." *MLSNet.com,* April 19, 2014. http://www.mlssoccer.com/news/article/2014/04/18/what-legacy-david-regis-says-about-usmnts-julian-green-word.

32. Quoted in Charles Boehm, "The American Identity." *US Soccer Players.com,* July 5, 2013. http://www.ussoccerplayers.com/2013/07/the-american-identity.html.

33. Quoted in Brian Straus, "Journeyman Questions Klinsmann's Inclusion of 'Fake Americans'." *Sporting News.com,* December 29,

2011. http://www.sportingnews.com/soccer/story/2011-12-28/journeyman-preston-zimmerman-questions-jurgen-klinsmanns-inclusion-of-fake-ameri.

34. Quoted in Brian Straus, "Friendly Fire: U.S. Coach Jurgen Klinsmann's Methods, Leadership, Acumen in Question." *Sporting News.com*, March 25, 2013. http://www.sportingnews.com/soccer/story/2013-03-19/jurgen-klinsmann-us-mens-soccer-coach-national-team-usa-american-world-cup-2013.

35. Quoted in Doug McIntyre, "Pitch Imperfect." *ESPN: The Magazine*, March 20, 2013. http://espn.go.com/sports/soccer/story/_/id/9070226/la-galaxy-coach-bruce-arena-ready-lead-team-third-consecutive-title-espn-magazine.

36. Jorge Iber, Samuel Regalado, Jose Alamillo and Arnoldo De Leon. *Latinos in U.S. Sport: A History of Isolation, Cultural Identity, and Acceptance* (Champaign, IL: Human Kinetics Press, 2011).

37. Jesse Zwick, "Latino Immigration and US Soccer." World Cup Blog: *The New Republic*, June 10, 2010. http://www.newrepublic.com/blog/world-cup/75440/latinos-and-us-soccer.

38. Quoted in Timothy Abraham, "US Soccer Needs Hispanic Talent to Succeed." *CNN.com World Sport*, July 1, 2009. www.cnn.com/2009/SPORT/football/06/30/progress.of.us.soccer/index.html?eref=rss_latest.

39. Samuel Huntington, *Who Are We? The Challenges to American Identity* (New York: Simon & Schuster, 2004).

40. Stanley Renshon, *The 50% American: Immigration and National Identity in an Age of Terror.* (Washington, DC: Georgetown University Press, 2005), 74.

41. Quoted in Brian Hickey, "American Patriot Tim Howard Thinks Soccer Ceremonies in America Should Be Conducted in American English." *Deadspin*, June 26, 2011. http://deadspin.com/5815531/american-patriot-tim-howard-thinks-soccer-ceremonies-in-america-should-be-conducted-in-american-english.

42. Quoted in Brent Latham, "Rising Star Torres Faced Tough Decision." *ESPN.com*, March 22, 2010. http://m.espn.go.com/soccer/story?storyId=5017820&wjb.

43. Quoted in Boehm, 2013.

44. Quoted in Nate Scott, "Julian Green's Father Reveals What Drove the Bayern Munich Phenom to Pick the U.S. over Germany." *USA*

Today.com. March 24, 2014. http://ftw.usatoday.com/2014/03/julian-green-jerry-green-usmnt-germany.

45. Quoted in Boehm, 2013.
46. Ibid.
47. Quoted in Soledad O'Brien, "German-Born Soccer Stars Choose to Play for U.S. National Team." *In America: CNN.com*, October 31,2003.http://inamerica.blogs.cnn.com/2012/10/31/german-born-soccer-stars-choose-to-play-for-u-s-national-team/.
48. Andrew Wiebe, "World Cup: Jermaine Jones listens to teammates, "Keeps shooting"—to heroic effect for USMNT." *World Cup Blog: MLSSoccer.com*. June 23, 2014. http://www.mlssoccer.com/worldcup/2014/news/article/2014/06/23/world-cup-jermaine-jones-listens-teammates-and-keeps-shooting-heroic-effect.
49. Joe Prince-Wright, "Second broken nose of World Cup for US, this time it's Jermaine Jones." *Pro Soccer Talk*, June 27, 2014. http://prosoccertalk.nbcsports.com/2014/06/27/second-broken-nose-of-world-cup-for-us-this-time-its-jermaine-jones/.
50. Andy Edwards, "Jermaine Jones is Living a Very SoCal Summer, Hanging Out with Mike Tyson, Paris Hilton." *Sideline: MLSsoccer.com*, June 28, 2014. http://www.mlssoccer.com/sideline/news/article/2014/07/28/jermaine-jones-living-very-socal-summer-hanging-mike-tyson-paris-hilton.
51. Matt Bonesteel, "The Best Newspaper Headlines from U.S. Soccer's Win Against Ghana at the World Cup." *Washington Post*, June 17, 2014. http://www.washingtonpost.com/blogs/soccer-insider/wp/2014/06/17/the-best-newspaper-headlines-from-u-s-soccers-win-over-ghana-at-the-world-cup.
52. Unattributed, *Telegraph Sport*. "John Brooks: World Cup Hero and Greatest American since Abraham Lincoln." *The Telegraph*, June 17, 2014. http://www.telegraph.co.uk/sport/football/teams/usa/10905001/John-Brooks-USA-World-Cup-hero-and-greatest-American-since-Abraham-Lincoln.html.
53. Straus 2012.

WORK CITED

Abraham, Timothy. "US Soccer Needs Hispanic Talent to Succeed." *CNN.com World Sport*. Retrieved from July 1, 2009, www.cnn.com/2009/SPORT/football/06/30/progress.of.us.soccer/index.html?eref=rss_latest.

Aksoy, Asu, and Kevin Robins. "Banal Transnationalism: The Difference That Television Makes." *University of Oxford Transnational Communities Program*. Retrieved from http://www.nabilechchaibi.com/resources/Banal%20Transnationalism.pdf.

Aleinkoff, T. Alexander and Douglas Klusmeyer. "Plural Nationality: Facing the Future in a Migratory World." In *Citizenship Today: Global Perspectives and Practices*, edited by T.A. Aleinkoff and D. Klusmeyer, 36–62. Washington, DC: Carnegie Endowment for International Peace, 2001.

Allaway, Roger. *Rangers, Rovers, and Spindles: Soccer, Immigration, and Textiles in New England and New Jersey*. Haworth: St. Johann Press, 2005.

Bale, John. "Sport and National Identity: A Geographical View." *The International Journal of the History of Sport*. 3, no. 1 (2007): 18–41.

Bauböck, Rainer. *Transnational Citizenship*. Aldershot: Edward Elgar, 1994.

Bennett, Roger. "Now He Has Committed, Green Must Prove Himself." *ESPN FC.com*. Retrieved from March 18, 2014, http://www.espnfc.com/blog/_/name/relegationzone/id/1732?cc=5901.

Bhabha, Homi K. *The Location of Culture*. London: Routledge, 1994.

Boehm, Charles. "The American Identity." *US Soccer Players.com*. Retrieved from July 5, 2013, http://www.ussoccerplayers.com/2013/07/the-american-identity.html.

Bonesteel, Matt. "The Best Newspaper Headlines from U.S. Soccer's Win Against Ghana at the World Cup." *Washington Post* (online). Retrieved from, June 17, 2014, http://www.washingtonpost.com/blogs/soccer-insider/wp/2014/06/17/the-best-newspaper-headlines-from-u-s-soccers-win-over-ghana-at-the-world-cup.

Brown, H. "The Ugly American." *1700AM ESPN.com*. Retrieved from 2011, http://www.espnradio1700.com/pages/landing_page?THE-UGLY AMERICAN=1&blockID=535735&feedID=8549.

Burdsey, Daniel. "If I Ever Play Football, Dad, Can I Play for England or India? British Asians, Sport and Diasporic National Identities." *Sociology*. 40, no. 1 (2006): 11–28.

Danforth, Loring. "Is the World Game and Ethnic Game or an Aussie Game? Narrating the Nation in Australian Soccer." *American Ethnologist*. 28, no. 2 (2001): 363–387.

Dittmer, Jason. *Popular Culture, Geopolitics, and Identity*. Latham: Rowman and Littlefield, 2010.

Edwards, Andy. "Jermaine Jones Is Living a Very SoCal Summer, Hanging Out with Mike Tyson, Paris Hilton." *Sideline: MLSsoccer.com*. Retrieved from July 28, 2014, http://www.mlssoccer.com/sideline/news/article/2014/07/28/jermaine-jones-living-very-socal-summer-hanging-mike-tyson-paris-hilton.

Foer, Franklin. *How Soccer Explains the World: An Unlikely Theory of Globalization*. New York: Harper Collins, 2004.

Freedman, Jonah. "What the Legacy of David Regis Says About the USMNT's Julian Green." *MLSNet.com*. Retrieved from April 19, 2014, http://www.mlssoccer.com/news/article/2014/04/18/what-legacy-david-regis-says-about-usmnts-julian-green-word.

Gagen, Elizabeth. "Making America Flesh: Physicality and Nationhood in Early Twentieth-Century Physical Education Reform." *Cultural Geographies* 11 (2004): 417–442.

Gardner, Jane F. *Being a Roman Citizen*. London: Routledge, 1993.

Gilroy, Paul. *The Black Atlantic: Modernity and Double Consciousness*. Cambridge, MA: Harvard University Press, 1993.

Gilroy, Paul. "Black Cultural Politics: An Interview with Paul Gilroy by Timothy Lott." *Found Object* 4 (1994): 46–81.

Hall, Stuart. "Culture, Community, Nation." *Cultural Studies* 7, no. 3 (1993): 349–363.

———. "The Question of Cultural Identity." In *Modernity: An Introduction to Modern Sciences*, edited by S. Hall, D. Held, D. Hubert, and K. Thompson, 596–635. London: Blackwell, 1996.

Huntington, Samuel. *Who Are We? The Challenges to American Identity*. New York: Simon & Schuster, 2004.

Iber, Jorge, Samuel Regaldo, Jose Alamillo, and Arnoldo De Leon. *Latinos in U.S. Sport: A History of Isolation, Cultural Identity, and Acceptance*. Champaign: Human Kinetics, 2011.

Ilona, Anthony. "Hanif Kureishi's *The Buddha of Suburbia*: 'A New Way of Being British." In *Contemporary British Fiction*, edited by R. Lane, R. Mengham, and P. Tew, 87–105. Cambridge: Polity, 2003.

Jacobson, David. "New Frontiers: Territory, Social Spaces, and the State." *Sociological Forum* 12, no. 1 (1997): 121–133.

Joppke, Christian. "Immigration, Citizenship, and the Need for Integration." In *Citizenship, Borders, and Human Needs*, edited by R. M. Smith, 157–176. Philadelphia: University of Pennsylvania Press, 2011.

Kivisto, Peter, and Thomas Faist. *Citizenship: Discourse, Theory, and Transnational Prospects*. Maiden: Blackwell, 2007.

Koch, Natalie. "Sport and Soft Authoritarian Nation-Building." *Political Geography* 32 (2013): 41–52.

Lalas, Greg. "What Jurgen Klinsmann Can Learn from Steve Sampson & USMNT' 1998 World Cup Disaster." *MLSnet.com*. Retrieved from April 1, 2014, http://m.mlssoccer.com/worldcup/2014/news/article/2014/04/01/ what-jurgen-klinsmann-can-learn-steve-sampson-usmnts-1998-world-cup-disaster.

Latham, Brent. "Rising Star Torres Faced Tough Decision." *ESPN.com*. Retrieved from March 22, 2010, http://m.espn.go.com/soccer/story?storyId=501782 0&wjb.

Levin, Josh. "Julian Green, Age 19, Scores Spectacular Goal in his World Cup Debut." *Slate Magazine*. Retrieved from July 1, 2014, http://www.slate.com/ blogs/the_spot/2014/07/01/julian_green_goal_the_19_year_old_scores_a_ spectacular_goal_in_his_world.html.

Lovatt, Adam. "Changing Nationality in Football: The FIFA Rules That Helped Brazilian Diego Costa Play for Spain." *Law in Sport*. Retrieved from November 4, 2013, http://www.lawinsport.com/blog/adam-lovatt/item/changing-nationality-in-football-the-fifa-rules-that-help-brazilian-diego-costa-play-for-spain.

Markovits, Andrei, and Steven Hellerman. *Offside: Soccer and American Exceptionalism*. Princeton: Princeton University Press, 2001.

Massey, Doreen. *For Space*. London: Sage, 2005.

McIntyre, Doug. "Pitch Imperfect." *ESPN: The Magazine*. Retrieved from March 20, 2013, http://espn.go.com/sports/soccer/story/_/id/9070226/ la-galaxy-coach-bruce-arena-ready-lead-team-third-consecutive-title-espn-magazine.

Mercer, J., and E. Hague. "Op-Ed: The Fixity and Fluidity of National Identities in Men's Professional Soccer." *AAG Newsletter* 8 (2011).

O'Brien, Soledad. "German-Born Soccer Stars Choose to Play for U.S. National Team." *In America: CNN.com*. Retrieved from October 31, 2013, http:// inamerica.blogs.cnn.com/2012/10/31/german-born-soccer-stars-choose-to-play-for-u-s-national-team/.

Prince-Wright, Joe. "Second Broken Nose of World Cup for US, This Time It's Jermaine Jones." *Pro Soccer Talk*. Retrieved from June 27, 2014, http:// prosoccertalk.nbcsports.com/2014/06/27/second-broken-nose-of-world-cup-for-us-this-time-its-jermaine-jones/.

Renshon, Stanley. *The 50% American: Immigration and National Identity in an Age of Terror*. Washington, DC: Georgetown University Press, 2005.

Scott, Nate. "Julian Green's Father Reveals What Drove the Bayern Munich Phenom to Pick the U.S. over Germany." *For the Win: USA Today.com*. Retrieved from March 24, 2014, http://ftw.usatoday.com/2014/03/julian-green-jerry-green-usmnt-germany.

Steiner, Nicholas. *International Migration and Citizenship Today*. New York: Routledge, 2009.

Straus, Brian. "Journeyman Questions Klinsmann's Inclusion of 'Fake Americans'." *Sporting News.com*. Retrieved from December 29, 2011, http://www.sportingnews.com/soccer/story/2011-12-28/journeyman-preston-zimmerman-questions-jurgen-klinsmanns-inclusion-of-fake-ameri.

————. "Friendly fire: U.S. Coach Jurgen Klinsmann's Methods, Leadership, Acumen in Question." *Sporting News.com*. Retrieved from March 25, 2013, http://www.sportingnews.com/soccer/story/2013-03-19/jurgen-klinsmann-us-mens-soccer-coach-national-team-usa-american-world-cup-2013.

Telegraph Sport. "John Brooks: World Cup Hero and Greatest American Since Abraham Lincoln." *The Telegraph* (online). Retrieved from June 17, 2014, http://www.telegraph.co.uk/sport/football/teams/usa/10905001/John-Brooks-USA-World-Cup-hero-and-greatest-American-since-Abraham-Lincoln.html.

Turner, Elliott. "Julian Green and the Ongoing Saga of US Soccer's Immigration Policies." *The Guardian.com*. Retrieved from March 26, 2014, http://www.theguardian.com/football/2014/mar/26/julian-green-ongoing-saga-us-soccers-immigration-policies.

Van Lear, Nicholas. *New Diasporas*. Seattle: University of Washington Press, 1998.

Wiebe, Andrew. "World Cup: Jermaine Jones Listens to Teammates, "Keeps Shooting"–to Heroic Effect for USMNT." *World Cup Blog: MLSSoccer.com*. Retrieved from June 23, 2014, http://www.mlssoccer.com/worldcup/2014/news/article/2014/06/23/world-cup-jermaine-jones-listens-teammates-and-keeps-shooting-heroic-effect.

Williams, M. "Nonterritoral Boundaries of Citizens." In *Identities, Affiliations, and Allegiances*, edited by S. Benhabib, I. Shapiro, and D. Petranovic, 226–256. Cambridge: Cambridge University Press, 2007.

Zwick, Jesse. "Latino Immigration and US Soccer." *World Cup Blog: The New Republic.com*. Retrieved from June 10, 2010, http://www.newrepublic.com/blog/world-cup/75440/latinos-and-us-soccer.

PART V

Sexuality and Gender

CHAPTER 11

Social Climbing, Cultural Experimentation and Trailblazing Metrosexual: Franz Beckenbauer in the 1960s and 1970s

Kay Schiller

Franz Beckenbauer is perhaps the greatest individualist in the history of German football. This character trait combined with a willingness to make necessary decisions and take opportunities when they present themselves ensured that life brought him more than most of his contemporaries: outstanding success as an athlete and coach, great wealth, the adulation of the public and membership in an international elite of sportspeople. This chapter argues that despite his uniquely elevated position, Beckenbauer can serve as an example of broader trends in football and popular culture. His career as a player and football celebrity after the end of his playing days is a good reflection of social and cultural developments from the 1960s onward in Germany and beyond.

In this chapter I advance three main arguments: First, Beckenbauer's rise to national and international stardom is exemplary for football's movement from the margins to the center of modern mass culture and the beginnings of the hyper-commodification of the sport in the second half of the twentieth century. From the 1960s onward top-level professional football started to

K. Schiller (✉)
Department of History, University of Durham, Durham, UK

© Hofstra University 2017   205
B. Elsey, S. Pugliese (eds.), *Football and the Boundaries of History*,
DOI 10.1057/978-1-349-95006-5_11

become part of show business and the entertainment industry in Germany and elsewhere. The influx of increasing amounts of money through advertising, merchandising and television over the following decades led to the emergence of a class of highly paid elite athletes of which Beckenbauer is a good example.[1] Moreover, sport stars like Beckenbauer actively shaped the way football and other sports were sold to the public. Secondly, both as an individual and as a media construct—in the case of public figures like Beckenbauer the two cannot be easily separated—he became an agent and symbol of wider social and cultural trends in the West. Beckenbauer's life and career can serve as a case study for the rise of individualism, consumerism and hedonism. Very much a child of his time, Beckenbauer was also an example of cultural experimentation, as well as of the liberalization of private lives and the democratization of the public sphere in West Germany in the 1960s and 1970s. Third and finally, Beckenbauer, along with other players of his generation, acted as a trailblazer for post-modern stars and the likes of David Beckham, the "metrosexual" footballers of the 1990s. He played an important role in the redefinition of masculinity in German and international sports in the second half of the twentieth century. He did so by challenging the dominant soldierly German masculinity of the first half-century through his appearance and behavior on and off the pitch as well as his elegant and stylish play.[2]

Beckenbauer, the "Kaiser," does not require much in terms of an introduction. As early as the 1970s there was virtually no one in Germany who had not heard of him and arguably he is the most famous German on the globe.[3] He was the first ever world star of football hailing from Germany. Having played in the FIFA World Cups in 1966 and 1970 and advanced with West Germany into the final and semifinal, respectively, Beckenbauer lifted the trophy captaining the national side in 1974. In the same year he won the first of three European Champions Cups with FC Bayern Munich, the club for which he had made his first-team debut ten years earlier. Upon winning the European Championships with West Germany in 1972 he was voted European Footballer of the Year. In May 1977 he joined Giorgio Chinaglia and Pelé at the New York Cosmos where he won the North American Soccer League (NASL) title three times. He retired in 1983 after two more seasons in Germany with Hamburger SV and a further spell at the Cosmos. Famously, Beckenbauer won the World Cup title for a second time as national team coach in 1990, a feat achieved only by one other footballer, the Brazilian Mário Zagallo. The sobriquet "Emperor," invented by the press in 1968 or 1969, is therefore quite fitting.

From 1994 to 2009 he was president of Bayern Munich, and as internationally popular figurehead of German football he was instrumental in bringing the World Cup to Germany in 2006, although, as the public found out at the end of 2015, by not shying away from unfair, perhaps criminal, means in the process. At the time of writing he is still under investigation by FIFA and Swiss prosecutors over irregular payments made in the run-up to 2006 to Mohamed bin Hammam, the disgraced former Qatari member of FIFA's powerful Executive Committee. Beckenbauer also served as the chairman of the local organizing committee of the 2006 tournament. In 2007 he came close to becoming UEFA President but then decided against running for office. From January 2007 to June 2011 Beckenbauer himself sat on FIFA's ExCo. He was temporarily banned from football and fined in 2016 for initially refusing to collaborate with a FIFA investigation into possible ethics code breaches during the time when the 2018 and 2022 World Cups were awarded to Russia and Qatar.

As far as his long and distinguished career is concerned, Beckenbauer is "the man who succeeded in everything" (*der Mann, dem alles gelang*),[4] his life in football making him the 500th richest man in Germany with an estimated wealth of euros 150 million.[5] However, the "shining light" (*Lichtgestalt*) of German football has recently lost much of his luster.

SOCIAL CLIMBING

In socioeconomic terms Beckenbauer's background is best described as aspirational lower-middle class. Born in 1945, a few months after the end of World War II, his beginnings were humble. He grew up in cramped living conditions in Giesing, a working-class neighborhood of Munich. There was always food on the table, as father Franz brought in a regular income as a postal employee and parts of the family in the countryside where willing to occasionally help with eggs, bread and meat.[6] Like all boys of his neighborhood he first learned to play football on the street to then quickly move on to the locally based SC München 1906. Due to an altercation with a player of TSV München 1860 during a youth match, Beckenbauer, an outstanding player from early on, decided to join Bayern Munich in 1958, then only the city's second club, rather than the much more famous and successful "Munich Lions" of 1860.[7]

Beckenbauer's rise to national stardom and, beginning with his international breakthrough at the 1966 World Cup, to the status of world star of football on a par with George Best, Johan Cruyff and Pelé was mirrored in his rising income in the 1960s and 1970s. He was part of the "football of affluence, the football of high industrial Europe"[8] which developed during the economic boom years from the 1950s to the 1970s and saw players grow rich. However, when he became a first-team regular for Bayern in 1964, his official initial club salary was capped at a paltry 160 Deutsche Marks (DM) per month. He got this from Bayern on top of a regular income of DM 450 that he earned as an employee of Allianz Insurance Company. At this time the average monthly gross income in the Federal Republic was DM 714. To put this sum further into perspective, his father earned about the same after a life of service as Beckenbauer Jr. did at the beginning of his career as a player.[9]

But this does not tell the whole story. On top of this Beckenbauer was probably paid handsomely in "backhanders," though it is impossible to know how much he received. This was because at the time the top flight of German football was not yet officially professionalized. But this did not mean that German clubs did not pay their elite footballers well to stop them from changing clubs or moving abroad. Salaries for non-existing side jobs, brown envelopes, rent-free flats and presents in the form of expensive cars were normal practices. They had been for decades. But in order for the clubs to hold on to subsidies from the public purse and tax breaks based on their services for the "common good," the German football association Deutscher Fußball-Bund (DFB) upheld the fiction that all players were essentially amateurs. Historians have shown that sham amateurism at the top level of German football was a constant during the Weimar Republic, National Socialism and the Federal Republic.[10]

Certainly from 1972, when financial caps were officially removed in the Bundesliga and Bayern moved to the 80,000-spectator Olympic Stadium in Munich and turned football crowds into money, Beckenbauer became a big earner, with a salary from football alone in the hundreds of thousands of Deutsch Marks.[11] With West German average per-capita incomes rising fourfold and real incomes and GDP quintupling between 1950 and 1973,[12] his club salary alone increased by more than 50 times in the decade from 1963. Much more came in through advertisement deals. In the 1970s his total yearly income before tax was estimated to be in the region of between one and two million DM.[13] During the World Cup year of 1974 he earned an estimated DM 1.5 million with product endorsements alone. Even though his income was taxed at 56 %, with the West German treasury keeping up to 73 % of any additional revenue from advertisement and sponsorship deals, by normal standards Beckenbauer became a very wealthy man.

In hiring Robert Schwan, Beckenbauer was the first German football player to employ a business manager.[14] With Schwan's assistance the "Kaiser" became the first fully "marketized" German athlete and set the stage for German top athletes and stars in other sports like Boris Becker in tennis and Michael Schumacher in Formula One. Like many of the German players of the time but always on a grander scale Beckenbauer made money from product endorsements, beginning in the mid-1960s with, among others, instant soup (Knorr), sports gear (Adidas) and petrol. He had an exclusive contract with German petrol brand Aral at the 1970 and 1974 World Cups when the other German national team players had less lucrative deals with rivals Esso.[15] Despite clearly not being able to sing, he released a single in 1966 that made it to number 31 in the German charts and grossed him DM 100,000.[16] Over time Beckenbauer became more astute in using his business activities also as instruments of self-promotion and, following the logic of Pierre Bourdieu's social distinction, in order to fashion a more refined and classy image for himself.[17] Not surprisingly, the dull and unsophisticated soup adverts went rather quickly and he gave up singing too.

His public presence through advertisement, his business acumen and his undeniable charisma aside, other qualities were required for Beckenbauer to become a superstar. There were, most importantly, his skills as a player and representative of the "beautiful game": the ease and elegance of his movements on the pitch which looked as if he did not break into sweat and his artist-like agility with the ball, including his ability to turn a match with a long run from defense or to pass accurately across the pitch to an attacker some 50 meters away. Perhaps most important was that unusual for a defensive player he managed to stand out and become identified with a dominant role on the playing field, that of the free-roaming "libero," an attacking sweeper without a direct marker. *Libero* was also the title of a 1973 feature-length semi-documentary on the life of the "Kaiser," another tool for self-promotion and exercise in product placement for the companies whose goods he helped to promote. While Beckenbauer certainly would have felt the downsides of being famous, the film ironically pretended that the "free man" had to constantly defend his freedom and privacy off the pitch from the commercial and other pressures that came with being a superstar footballer.[18]

Not surprisingly, Beckenbauer also made money with a first 1975 installment of memoirs entitled *One Like Me* (*Einer wie ich*).

Ghost-written by a journalist of the magazine *Der Spiegel*, the book came out with publishing giants Bertelsmann and had an initial print-run of 200,000 copies. With a marketing budget of DM 250,000 it was the most professionally advertised football book till then. This account of his career so far was testament to Beckenbauer's individualism and it was no coincidence that neither goals nor balls featured in its title. Other than the memoirs of famous German football icons like Uwe Seeler (*All My Goals*, 1965) and Gerd Müller (*Goals Decide*, 1967), the book claimed to be "the first insider account on the hardest entertainment business of the world"—thus the slogan of Bertelsmann's advertisement campaign. While the basic ingredients of the book did not differ at all from other memoirs, Beckenbauer used the volume to present himself primarily as a figure of pop culture, as a star and businessman rather than as an athlete and footballer. He stressed that professional football had become part of showbiz and the entertainment industry and that economic considerations played an important role for him: "For me a football team is an interest group. It forms to enjoy the game and also to be successful together. Titles are there to be won. For me that is not just an objective in sports but an economic necessity."[19]

This emphasis on the financial gains to be made from the game let Beckenbauer appear greedy and removed from the German football public and did not ingratiate him to many fans, at least outside his native Bavaria. Even though he redeemed himself through his selfless efforts in the 1974 World Cup final against Holland, this was evident, for example, when he was booed alongside Gerd Müller in Hamburg after a weaker performance against Australia in the early stages of the tournament. His reaction to spit out in front of the crowd seemed to confirm the public's negative view of the "Kaiser." While this was a short loss of self-control for which he later apologized, Goldblatt put it fittingly when he writes that Beckenbauer "had an air of ease, aloofness and arrogance, none of which seemed to sit well with the mainstream German football public."[20]

Many saw their prejudices confirmed when Beckenbauer stated in a television interview that West German Chancellor Willy Brandt was a "national misfortune."[21] This seemed to prove that he was rather right wing at a time when in the aftermath of "1968" it was fashionable to be on the political left. The left was where most sports commentators located Beckenbauer's antagonist, the unconventional long-haired blond midfielder Günter Netzer, who before moving to Real Madrid played for Borussia Mönchengladbach, the team that competed with Bayern

Munich for preeminence in German football in the decade from 1969. In reality, neither Netzer nor Beckenbauer did care all that much about politics, although it is fair to assume that as high-earning football stars both might have preferred a conservative government which ideally would not have required them to leave more than half of their income to the taxman. Both Netzer's and Beckenbauer's careers abroad and current status as tax exiles in Switzerland and Austria, respectively, seem to confirm this point.

In *One Like Me* Beckenbauer also emphasized that along with improving his bank balance his career as a professional footballer had helped him to educate himself and develop his personality by acquiring social and cultural capital. He took riding and English lessons, went regularly to the theater and the opera and put in appearances at society events like the Salzburg Festival and the Vienna Opera Ball. This way he demonstrated that he and his wife Brigitte had climbed up the social ladder: "Bayreuth for the first time, Wagner festival. The secretary of the Begum welcomes us. The widow of the Aga Khan had heard that the Beckenbauers would also be present this time. She wanted to use the opportunity to meet me in person. We were introduced to her."[22] While hailing from a petty bourgeois background and remaining conventional in lots of ways Beckenbauer and his wife Brigitte became part of the German fashion-film-and-sports in-crowd through encounters like this and acquired more than just a sprinkle of stardust. In Richard Giulianotti's socio-historical taxonomy of elite footballers Beckenbauer became a typical "star" and "celebrity" who was as well known for his achievements on the pitch as for his off-the-field personality and lifestyle via the media.[23] In the public's attention he replaced "traditional" players and local working-class "heroes" like Uwe Seeler, the striker of Hamburger SV, the best-loved German footballer of the 1960s who, while still playing at the same time as Beckenbauer, in many ways represented an earlier generation.[24]

For players like Beckenbauer and others to advance socially it was necessary that football increasingly lost the stigma attached to it in Germany as a sport of and for the "uneducated" working classes. What had been primarily a proletarian pastime since the days of the Weimar Republic by the 1960s and 1970s moved from the margins to the center of modern mass culture. "Football is no longer a closed milieu. There is no special football 'class.' Football has become a big deal, a sport that has both followers and opponents."[25] This is how Beckenbauer characterized the status of the game in Germany in 1975. It had lost its marginal status through expanding media coverage, especially via the spread of German state television shows like *Sportschau* and *Aktuelles Sportstudio* that covered the Bundesliga every weekend. Players' lives were no longer interesting just for sports fans but provided entertainment for a broad tabloid readership that was regularly treated to interviews and home stories, including by Beckenbauer.[26]

Unsurprisingly, having become a star, Beckenbauer felt quickly at ease with the glitzy Hollywood and Warner Communications jet set crowd at the New York Cosmos. By 1977 he had outgrown the Federal Republic and mixed confidently with the likes of Mohammed Ali, Andy Warhol, Mick Jagger and Henry Kissinger in the dressing room of Giants Stadium and at Ian Schrager's nightclub Studio 54 in Manhattan. Having befriended Soviet-born ballet dancer Rudolf Nureyev, who lived in the same building on Central Park South, he regularly went to the Metropolitan Opera where he mingled with Placido Domingo, Luciano Pavarotti and other stars. Moving to the the Cosmos, he said when interviewed for a documentary, "was one of the best decisions I ever made."[27] Not only did he earn significantly more than in Germany, most importantly, life in New York as a representative of a sport of little importance in the United States also granted him a degree of anonymity and individual freedom which he had not considered possible in Munich.[28]

Cultural Experimentation

My second main argument is that as an individual and media construct Beckenbauer became symbolic of wider social, cultural and political trends in Western Europe. Very much a child of his time, he came to symbolize individualism, consumerism and hedonism. He was both an agent and an example of the cultural experimentation of the 1960s and 1970s, as well as of the liberalization of private lives and the democratization of the public sphere in West Germany.

There are many examples that demonstrate his individualism and interest in new experiences. Beckenbauer was a keen traveler who greatly appreciated the opportunities to see the world life as a professional footballer offered him.[29] Regarding his individualism one need only look at his sideway career move to the Cosmos, which was considered a national catastrophe by some and almost led to a state of collective shock and mourning in West Germany. Sections of the press, including the best-selling tabloid *BILD-Zeitung*, went so far as to brand Beckenbauer a "traitor of the fatherland" (*vaterlandsflüchtig*).[30] Leaving for the United States also did not come cheaply in other ways. It meant that Beckenbauer was forced to give up captaining and playing for the national team, no less than the current World Champion, because the German FA president Hermann Neuberger thought the NASL, the North American Soccer League, was an uncompetitive "operetta league" without any sporting merits.

True, the German tax authorities had knocked on Beckenbauer's door one early morning in 1977; his marriage was on the rocks by then and he was heading for a divorce. Moreover, Bayern were arguably past their peak. There were therefore very good reasons to leave. Still it took courage and a willingness to take risks for Beckenbauer to take this step. While the details are unknown, the Cosmos's offer must have also looked very attractive in financial terms. It proved so difficult to resist for Beckenbauer that he decided to pay out of his own pocket the difference between the sum Warner Communications CEO Steve Ross was willing to pay for him and that which Bayern demanded for his release, some DM 375,000.[31]

Beckenbauer could probably afford it. His petty-bourgeois origins had taught him not to indulge unnecessarily in too much conspicuous consumption, one of the attributes usually associated with rich stars and celebrities. He was not especially keen to display his wealth all that openly. To be fair, at the same time he did not hide it either. So when Netzer famously showed off his Ferrari as a fashion accessory, Beckenbauer was content to buy the latter's Jaguar E-Type secondhand, and, when having problems driving it, to trade it in for a big Mercedes or BMW limousine.[32] Of course, before moving to Manhattan he had lived in an exclusive mansion on the outskirts of Munich with his family and neither he nor his wife shied away from wearing expensive fur coats in public when it was cold in the winter. However, despite these tokens of his success and his eagerness to accumulate cultural capital Beckenbauer appeared to be remarkably normal against the background of ever increasing overall living standards in the Federal Republic in the 1960s and 1970s. There was nothing flashy or especially flamboyant about him. Different from Netzer he kept his hair relatively short and while usually well groomed, he was not especially fashion-conscious, mostly shunned extravagant clothing and had an air of well-to-do normality about him.

Different from Pelé and Chinaglia, Beckenbauer was not exactly a hedonist either and did not participate actively in the alcohol-and-drugs-fuelled sexual shenanigans that feature prominently in Gavin Newsham's book on the New York Cosmos, *Once in a Lifetime*. He preferred to watch from the sideline:

> A real big show for me. In the seventies there was this club, Studio 54. Everybody was there: Hollywood, rock stars and artists. And we of the Cosmos had our own table. Pelé and Carlos Alberto pepped up the Studio, they had never seen anything like it there. All of a sudden, people danced samba in the Studio and everyone was wide-eyed in amazement. You ought to know that Pelé was at least as fantastic at samba dancing as he was a foot-baller. Not me though. I just watched this calmly with a drink.[33]

Cosmos goalkeeper Shep Messing summed up the lives of players in the pre-AIDS days of the 1970s with the following words: "Women, drink-ing, dancing, alcohol and back on the field the next day."[34] Beckenbauer, while having the occasional drink, was a professional athlete from head to toe who believed that alcohol and sport did not mix very well. Though no puritan he represented a manliness based on self-discipline and there-fore was not part of the football macho culture characterized by copious amounts of alcohol, the objectification of women, homophobia and the consumption of expensive objects. George Best, the archetype of British football celebrities who died from alcoholism-related causes in 2005, probably best encapsulated this hedonistic lifestyle.[35]

In other respects, however, Beckenbauer was equally happy to go against bourgeois conventions. Like many successful men of his genera-tion in West Germany he turned into a serial monogamist with his female partners getting younger as he grew older. Beckenbauer, fathering five children in the process, is currently on his third wife. At age 18 in 1963 he fathered an illegitimate son whom he raised with his first wife Brigitte. Then a child out of wedlock was still considered a scandal and meant that he almost was not selected by the traditionally conservative DFB to play for the national youth team.[36] While moral attitudes had become more liberal by 1977, Beckenbauer would have still found it difficult captaining West Germany as a divorcee.

In sexual respects Beckenbauer certainly did not care all that much about traditional morality either. While he fended off sexual advances by Nureyev, he was not a homophobe and remained friends with the Russian dancer: "Well, he gave it a try. Afterwards we never talked about it again, I was not angry with him either. Unrequited love is, of course, a classical motif in opera, therefore I did not want to rub salt in the wound."[37] Statements like this demonstrate that Beckenbauer was a product of West Germany's post-war liberalization that did not stop at football locker rooms.

At the same time as a public figure whose every step was followed by the media he was arguably also an agent of social change. This is how highbrow culture and football authors like Karl-Heinz Bohrer saw him and other stars.[38] In their writings this generation of players was closely associated with the social and cultural upheavals of the 1960s in West Germany and the so-called "second foundation of the Federal Republic" by "1968."[39] Günter Netzer, for example, was elevated from football player to "symbolic figure of a different Germany,"[40] a country in which traditional national values like "fighting spirit and competitive strength" (*kämpferischer Einsatz und Leistungswillen*) had been replaced by individualism and a willingness to speak one's mind both on and off the pitch.[41] Such assessments have since often been repeated. Historian Rudolf Oswald, for example, has emphasized a generation and paradigm change in the governing bodies of the DFB in the 1960s that allowed for the replacement of the German "football soldier" of the 1954 winning World Cup side with the "individual player personality."[42]

It is with this background of the liberalization and democratization of West Germany in mind that one ought to understand the unprecedented financial negotiations that Beckenbauer imposed on the DFB on behalf of the national team on occasion of the 1974 World Cup. A couple of weeks before the tournament began Beckenbauer famously declared that the players were no longer content to simply play for the national honor. For the first time ever they threatened to abandon the tournament altogether, unless they were given a financial reward for their participation. Bonuses had been paid before but never explicitly demanded. The players eventually made the football functionaries agree to pay a premium of 60,000 DM each for winning the title. This was not an especially large sum compared to what the players made from advertising. Its real relevance lay in its symbolism.[43] When asked provocatively by a *BILD* journalist whether the money was really necessary to motivate the team, Beckenbauer replied: "Of course! The player needs to feel that he is worth something. Then he enjoys playing. Whenever I hear this shit that we should play for the honour or for the eagle on our chests, that's a joke and nobody believes in this any longer."[44]

As is obvious from this quotation, Beckenbauer's challenge to traditional authority came with an outspoken disdain for nationalism. This was typical of the Federal Republic at the time. Whereas winning the 1954 World Cup title was remembered as a nationalist revival, the first two major sports events Germany itself hosted after the war, the 1972 Munich Olympics and the 1974 World Cup, stood for the polar opposite. For the Germans these mega-events symbolically marked the country's return to full participation in the international community.[45] Beckenbauer's preference for internationalism and cosmopolitanism over nationalism also comes across well in his comments on the Cosmos:

> In the World Cup there were eleven Germans on the field, in the win of the European Cup there were nine Germans and two foreigners, with the New York Cosmos we had fourteen different nations, so it was like a family. It was fantastic. It was really an experience. I will never forget this.[46]

In the latter stages of the 1974 tournament, captain Beckenbauer also had a much greater than usual say in tactics and team selection. When Coach Helmut Schön, himself a refugee from East Germany, was at the end of his tether after the famous defeat at the hands of the GDR in the preliminary round, a group of key players with Beckenbauer in the lead effectively took over from Schön, though only unofficially and denying the obvious when asked. For a player to be more than the executor of his coach's will on the pitch would have been unthinkable under the 1954 World Cup-winning coach Sepp Herberger. His former assistant Schön, though, had explicitly stated that he preferred a more collegial approach and a team "made of talents, individualists and personalities" rather than a Wehrmacht-style collective of comrades.[47] The middle-of-the-road German broadsheet *Süddeutsche Zeitung* commented approvingly that in the national team, a new, more mature, more universal and outspoken type of player had replaced the previous sportsmen who were without a sense of history, soldierly, apolitical, silent and asexual.[48]

TRAILBLAZER FOR METROSEXUAL FOOTBALLERS

This leads to the final point of this chapter, my argument that Beckenbauer acted as a trailblazer for the European "metrosexual" footballers of the 1990s. According to Mark Simpson who coined the term in 1994, "the typical metrosexual is a young man with money to spend, living in or within easy reach of a metropolis—because that's where all the best shops, clubs, gyms and hairdressers are. He might be officially gay, straight or bisexual, but this is utterly immaterial because he has clearly taken himself as his own love object and pleasure as his sexual preference."[49] For Simpson, David Beckham is "the biggest metrosexual in Britain."[50] Along with others of his generation Beckenbauer arguably paved the way for the likes of Beckham. In the 1960s and 1970s he prepared the "metrosexual turn" of the 1990s by helping to establish a new model of manliness through sports.

Underlying this thesis is Raewyn Connell's theory of "hegemonic masculinity," or, in Arthur Brittan's terminology, "hierarchic heterosexualism."[51] For Connell, the political, social and economic order is created in the image of men and expressed in specific forms of masculinity. It is based upon unequal power relations between men and women, as well as between different categories of men. In drawing on Antonio Gramsci's concept of "hegemony" Connell argues that this "structure is maintained not only by force, but by cultural means such as education and the popular media." [52] And this is where sport and especially football show their relevance. Not only are masculinities culturally constructed, but in the postwar era "sport has come to be the leading definer of masculinity in mass culture."[53] With football moving to the center of European mass culture from the 1960s onward, this sport rather than any other became the leading definer of masculinity in this part of the world (Fig. 11.1).

Historians agree that sports are never purely autotelic and have historically been imbued with other purposes. In the first half of the twentieth century there has been an especially marked tendency to see sporting activities as a preparation for military combat and war. Historians have shown how in the German context football and the military influenced and benefited from each other.[54] As a result players during this period were symbols and agents of a hegemonic military masculinity that had its origins in the *levée en masse* of the French Revolution and the following nineteenth-century militarization of males in European nation-states through mass conscription.[55] While footballers were not required to make the ultimate sacrifice and die on the battlefield, they were, nevertheless, meant to be soldiers on the pitch, tough and robust, prepared for subordination and ready to suffer and overcome their weaker selves. Herberger, for example, was a firm believer in military discipline. His key terms as a coach were "commitment, subordination, comradeship and dedication."[56]

Importantly, hegemonic masculinities are never stable and subject to challenges, for example, by women who assert their rights. Moreover, "not all men identify with hegemonic masculinity, and may indeed subscribe to

Fig. 11.1   Franz Beckenbauer of New York Cosmos holds the North American Soccer League Trophy (Photo credit: Allsport UK/Allsport)

practices and values which are incompatible with it; hence the proscription of homosexual behaviour and the resistance of men identifying as gay or 'queer. '"[57] In this reading Beckenbauer stands for a "new" non-militarist model of man, athlete and player which characteristically emerged during the relatively peaceful economic boom years and challenged the older soldierly hegemonic masculinity. Tellingly, while the intimate connection between sporting prowess and military fitness was loosened during the *trente glorieuse*, professional football became ever more closely linked with the entertainment industry that is constantly on the lookout for new audiences including among women.

Not that the masculinity of aggressive, bellicose and homophobic macho sportsmen was replaced altogether but through Beckenbauer and others it lost its dominance in providing meaning of what it meant to be a man on and off the pitch. It is probably no coincidence that he and many other prominent players of his generation avoided being conscripted into the German army. As opposed to the 1954 World Cup team Beckenbauer was no "football soldier." He and others complemented traditional manifestations of manliness in football and sports with a softer and more empathetic and, dare one say, feminine version of masculinity. Consider what one observer said about the young Beckenbauer:

> There was fresh snow on the pitch and all players had problems with the ball and with keeping their balance. Only one of them was dribbling and gliding on the white surface as if the ball was glued to his foot. He did not even look at the ball but kept his head up looking for his teammates. "That is not a footballer, that is a dancer," I exclaimed. That was the day on which I fell in love with the way of play of my friend Franz Beckenbauer.[58]

In linking the tango and sports like football and polo with aspects of modern Argentine national identity, the anthropologist and football scholar Eduardo Archetti famously claimed that

> [i]mages of men need images of women as well as of "other" men. The technical ability and individualism of the Argentinian football player called for the contrasting image of the disciplined and collectively orientated English player. The physical strength and moral courage of the Argentinian polo player required the conservative and restrained figure of the English rider. The romanticism and fidelity of the man displayed in the tango asked to be accompanied by the image of a free woman.[59]

One may, of course, question whether the Argentine masculinities described here are as dominant and stable as Archetti wants us to believe. German hegemonic masculinities have certainly been subject to successful challenges by football as a definer of manliness. While here like in Argentina images of men require images of women and images of other men against which to assert themselves to reproduce the gender order of society, the battle for hegemony between the harder and softer versions of masculinity has been decided in favor of the former. Philosopher Klaus Theweleit, whose groundbreaking investigation *Male Fantasies* (1977) put the spotlight on the hard, violent and misogynist fantasies of German fascist men, certainly thinks so. For Theweleit football along with feminism and environmentalism in the 1970s "put an official end to the latent soldierly (*das latent Soldatische*)" in German society.[60] Looking at the 2014 German World Cup winning side, it is indeed hard to imagine a team with fewer traces of the old military manliness than this one.

However, older images of manliness, while no longer hegemonic, continue to thrive in Germany as well. Take gayness, the ultimate taboo for the "old" hegemonic masculinity, as "gay sex introduces rivalry and jealousy into ranks of men, and thus weakens their solidarity in defence of patriarchy."[61] Despite the coming out of former international Thomas Hitzlsperger in 2014, not being heterosexual is still marginalized in German football as much as in other, including Latin American, countries and homophobia continues to be rampant among coaches, players and fans. This was an important factor in making "The Hammer" Hitzlsperger wait until the end of his active career before making his sexual orientation public.[62]

But let us return to Beckenbauer. What makes him a trailblazer for Beckham? Clearly there are both similarities and differences between these two stars from Germany and England. The obvious contrasts between Beckenbauer and Beckham in economic terms are due to the fact that they belong to different eras. Beckenbauer's career coincided with the beginnings of the football of affluence whereas Beckham's falls into the period of the sport's hyper-commercialization after the Bosman ruling of 1995, which was also the year of his debut for Manchester United. This allowed Beckham to turn himself into a brand that was unimaginable for Beckenbauer and explains his greater personal wealth at a younger age. In 2013 Beckham was worth an estimated at £165 million easily making him the richest British sports star of all times.[63]

However, both Beckenbauer and Beckham share a similar lower-middle-class social background and owe their social rise to their outstanding abilities on the pitch and their distinctively elegant playing styles. Both have been extremely successful as club footballers, winning national and European titles. Both captained their national teams and played football in Europe and the United States. While before Bosman football players normally could not move from one club to another and control the contracts they entered freely, Beckenbauer and a few others of his generation were willing to take risks and behave as if they could. Beckham also spent the last decade of his career as a "free agent," moving from one country and continent to another on a regular basis until his retirement (Real Madrid, LA Galaxy, AC Milan, LA Galaxy, AC Milan, LA Galaxy, Paris Saint-Germain).

But what about metrosexuality? While not a metrosexual in Mark Simpson's definition, I argue that Beckenbauer helped to establish a softer and more empathetic model of manliness that made the latter possible. His individualist take on life, (limited) penchant for consumerism and responsible pleasure-seeking represented an alternative to football's traditional macho culture and its destructive and violent attitude toward drinking, women and gay men. Homosexuality never bothered Beckenbauer, a trait that he also shares with Beckham. While Beckenbauer was friends with Rudolf Nurejew, Beckham is with Elton John. True, Beckenbauer in many ways exudes an air of normalcy. Beckham in turn possesses the "looks of a gay porn star"[64] and is a fashion icon. However, he also seems comfortable with women's challenges to the gender order of society and is a family man, reportedly carrying a fair share of the burden of bringing up his children.

In fact, media reporting about Beckham is inextricably linked with that about his equally successful pop-star-turned-fashion-designer wife Victoria and their four children. "Brand Beckham" not only includes "Becks" and "Posh" but also Brooklyn, Romeo, Cruz and Harper and presents the family as a closely knit unit, thus demonstrating the success of the model of masculinity that Beckenbauer helped to establish.

NOTES

1. Adrian Walsh and Richard Giulianotti, *Ethics, Money and Sport: This Sporting Mammon* (London: Routledge, 2007), 1.

2. I owe this observation to the great German football historian Markwart Herzog.
3. Torsten Körner, *Franz Beckenbauer: Der freie Mann* (Frankfurt/M.: Fischer, 2006), 213.
4. http://www.kicker.de/news/fussball/bundesliga/startseite/541878/2/slideshow_beckenbauer_der-mann-dem-alles-gelang.html
5. "Die reichsten Deutschen." In *Manager Magazin*, October 9, 2012.
6. Körner, *Beckenbauer*, pp. 21–22.
7. Ibid., pp. 47–48.
8. David Goldblatt, *The Ball Is Round: A Global History of Football* (London: Penguin, 2007), 398.
9. Franz Beckenbauer, *Einer wie ich* (Munich: Bertelsmann, 1975), 14 and 33.
10. Erik Eggers, "Profifußball im Amateurverband. Der deutsche Sonderweg." In *Fußball zwischen den Kriegen. Europa 1918–1939*, ed. Christan Koller and Fabian Brändle, (Münster: Lit Verlag, 2010), 221–243 and idem, "'Berufsspieler sind Schädlinge des Sports, sie sind auszumerzen ...': Crux und Beginn eines deutschen Sonderwegs im europäischen Fußball der Weimarer Republik." In *Der lange Weg zur Bundesliga: Zum Siegeszug des Fußballs in Deutschland*, ed. Wolfram Pyta, (Münster: Lit Verlag, 2004), 91–112; Nils Havemann, *Fußball unterm Hakenkreuz. Der DFB zwischen Sport, Politik und Kommerz*, Frankfurt/Main: Campus, 2005 and idem, *Samstags um halb 4: Die Geschichte der Bundesliga* (Munich: Siedler, 2013).
11. Körner, *Beckenbauer*, p. 211.
12. Hans-Ulrich Wehler, *Deutsche Gesellschaftsgeschichte. Vol. 5: Von der Gründung der beiden deutschen Staaten bis zur Vereinigung 1949–1990*. (Munich: C.H. Beck, 2008), 154.
13. Ulfert Schröder, *Franz Beckenbauer* (Munich: Copress, 1974), 111.
14. Körner, *Beckenbauer*, pp. 104–105.
15. Folke Havekost and Volker Stahl. *Fußballweltmeisterschaft 1974 Deutschland* (Kassel: Agon Sportverlag, 2004), 15.
16. Körner, *Beckenbauer*, p. 105.
17. Pierre Bourdieu, *Distinction: A Social Critique of the Judgement of Taste* (Cambridge, Mass.: Harvard University Press, 1986).

18. Wigbert Wicker, *Libero*. Semi-documentary, Rina Film, 1973.
19. Beckenbauer, *Einer wie ich*, p. 82 [my translation].
20. Goldblatt, *The Ball Is Round*, p. 474.
21. Körner, *Beckenbauer*, p. 131.
22. Beckenbauer. *Einer wie ich*, p. 225.
23. Richard Giulianotti, *Football: A Sociology of the Global Game* (London: Routledge, 1999), 118–20.
24. Kay Schiller, *WM 1974: Als der Fußball modern wurde* (Berlin: Rotbuch, 2014), 163–164.
25. Beckenbauer, *Einer wie ich*, p. 154.
26. Katja Schmitz-Dräger, *Vom "Wunder von Bern" bis "Schwarz-Rot-Geil": Die Berichterstattung der BILD-Zeitung zu den Fußballweltmeisterschaften 1954, 1974 und 2006* (Frankfurt/M.: Peter Lang, 2011), 69–71.
27. Paul Crowder and John Dower, *Once in a Lifetime: The Extraordinary Story of the New York Cosmos*. Documentary, Miramax, 2006.
28. Körner, *Beckenbauer*, p. 111 and "Ich hatte ein perfektes Leben:" Interview with Franz Beckenbauer. In *Süddeutsche Zeitung Magazin*, June 11, 2010.
29. "Ich hatte ein perfektes Leben."
30. "Meine deutsche Zukunft ist abgelaufen." In *Der Spiegel*, April 25, 1977, p. 124.
31. Körner, *Beckenbauer*, p. 216.
32. Helmut Böttiger, *Günter Netzer – Manager und Rebell* (Essen: Klartext, 2006), 88–89.
33. "Ich hatte ein perfektes Leben" [my translation].
34. Gavin Newsham, *Once in a Lifetime: The Extraordinary Story of the New York Cosmos* (London: Atlantic Books, 2006), 129.
35. Gary Whannel, *Media Sport Stars: Masculinities and Moralities* (London: Routledge, 2002), 124.
36. Körner, *Beckenbauer*, pp. 57–58.
37. "Ich hatte ein perfektes Leben."
38. See, most prominently, Bohrer's famous article "Wembley: Nachruf auf die schönen Verlierer," in *Frankfurter Allgemeine Zeitung*, October 27, 1973.
39. See Ulrich Herbert, "Liberalisierung als Lernprozess: Die Bundesrepublik in der deutschen Geschichte – eine Skizze." In *Wandlungsprozesse in Westdeutschland: Belastung, Integration,*

Liberalisierung, ed. Herbert (Göttingen: Wallstein, 2002), 7–49 and Manfred Görtemaker, *Geschichte der Bundesrepublik Deutschland: Von der Gründung bis zur Gegenwart* (Munich: C. H. Beck, 1999).

40. Böttiger, *Günter Netzer*, pp. 93–113.
41. Wolfram Pyta, "German Football: A Cultural History," in *German Football: History, Culture, Society*, ed. Alan Tomlinson and Christopher Young (London: Routledge, 2006), 1–22, 15.
42. Rudolf Oswald, *"Fußball-Volksgemeinschaft": Ideologie, Politik und Fanatismus im deutschen Fußball 1919–1964* (Frankfurt/M.: Campus, 2008), 307.
43. Schiller, *WM 1974*, pp. 159–160.
44. *BILD*, 15 July 1974.
45. Kay Schiller and Christopher Young, *The 1972 Munich Olympics and the Making of Modern Germany* (Berkeley: University of California Press, 2010), 50, 84, 94, 99, 113, 239 and Schiller, *WM 1974*, pp. 13–15, 36, 194–197.
46. Crowder and Dower, *Once in a Lifetime*.
47. Folke Havekost and Volker Stahl. *Helmut Schön: Der Mann mit der Mütze* (Kassel: Agon, 2006), 52.
48. *Süddeutsche Zeitung*, 10 July 1974.
49. Mark Simpson, "Meet the Metrosexual," in *Salon.com*, July 22, 2002.
50. Ibid.
51. R. W. Connell, *Masculinities* (Berkeley: University of California Press, 2nd ed. 2005); Arthur Brittan, *Masculinity and Power* (London: Wiley, 1991).
52. John Tosh, "Hegemonic Masculinity and the History of Gender," in *Masculinities in Politics and War: Gendering Modern History*, ed. Stefan Dudink, Karen Hagemann and Tosh (Manchester: Manchester University Press, 2004), 41–58, 42.
53. Connell, *Masculinities*, p. 54.
54. See, for example, Christiane Eisenberg, *English Sports und deutsche Bürger: Eine Gesellschaftsgeschichte, 1800–1939* (Paderborn: Schöningh, 1999), 191–193, 330–331 and Markwart Herzog, "'Sportliche Soldatenkämpfer im großen Kriege' 1939–1945: Fußball im Militär – Kameradschaftsentwürfe repräsentativer Männlichkeit," in *Fußball zur Zeit des Nationalsozialismus: Alltag – Medien – Künste – Stars*, ed. Herzog (Stuttgart: Kohlhammer, 2008), 67–148.

55. Tosh, "Hegemonic Masculinity", 48; see Joan B. Landes, "Republican Citizenship and Heterosocial Desire: Concepts of Masculinity in Revolutionary France," in *Masculinities in Politics and War: Gendering Modern History*, ed. Stefan Dudink, Karen Hagemann and John Tosh (Manchester: Manchester University Press, 2004), 96–115.

56. Jürgen Leinemann, *Sepp Herberger: Ein Leben, eine Legende* (Berlin: Rowohlt, 1997), 325.

57. Tosh, "Hegemonic Masculinity", p. 43.

58. Körner, *Beckenbauer*, p. 33 [my translation].

59. Eduardo P. Archetti, *Masculinities: Football, Polo and the Tango* (Oxford: Berg, 1999), 190–191.

60. Klaus Theweleit, *Tor zur Welt: Fußball als Realitätsmodell* (Cologne: Kiepenheuer & Witsch, 2004), 219; see also Markwart Herzog "Footballers as Soldiers: Rituals of Masculinity in Twentieth-Century Germany: Physical, Pedagogical, Ethical and Social Aspects," (unpublished manuscript), 13.

61. Tosh, "Hegemonic Masculinity,"46.

62. "Homosexualität wird im Fußball ignoriert." Interview with Thomas Hitzlsperger in *Die Zeit*, January 16, 2014.

63. According to the *Sunday Times Rich List* 2013.

64. Ellis Cashmore, *Beckham* (Cambridge: Polity, 2002), 232.

CHAPTER 12

Standing on Honeyball's Shoulders: A History of Independent Women's Football Clubs in England

Jean Williams

THE LOST GENERATIONS OF BRITISH WOMEN'S FOOTBALL 1921–71

In 1951, the editors of a volume called *Sport for Girls* published the results of a survey of 4238 young female readers in the United Kingdom. Aged between 11 and 18 years, those surveyed were asked which hobbies they preferred.[1] Of the respondents, 96 % said that they were interested in sport, leaving 3.2 % to declare no enthusiasm and the small remainder undecided. Without giving too much significance to the findings therefore, sport generally compared favourably with other hobbies such as reading (50 %) and dancing (36 %).

Cricket was declared to be the "favourite" sport for young women in the *Sport for Girls* poll because of the combination of spectator interest, fandom and participation. Cricket topped the ten games that girls liked to watch in 1951 with 75 % expressing an active support, followed by soccer

J. Williams (✉)
Wolverhampton University, Wolverhampton, UK

© Hofstra University 2017
B. Elsey, S. Pugliese (eds.), *Football and the Boundaries of History*,
DOI 10.1057/978-1-349-95006-5_12

227

(54 %), ice hockey (47 %), rugby (45 %), speedway (35 %) and lawn tennis (28 %). Soccer was in a dismal 22nd place at just 0.5 % participation rate, and less popular even than darts, putting, stoolball and boating.

Fifty years after the *Sport for Girls* survey, football was called "the fastest growing sport in the country" amongst women and girls with 55,000 registered female enthusiasts and "soon to overtake netball as the number one participation team game."[2] How then to contextualise this disparity between the enthusiasm for watching soccer and low rates of female participation in the early 1950s and the more recent rise in popularity?

The longer history of women's participation in football is beyond the scope of this discussion. However, when the young men of the Football Association (FA) formed a set of rules in 1863, this reflected their interest in their own enjoyment rather than in having an eye on posterity. The Fédération Internationale de Football Association (FIFA), the world governing body, was formed in 1904.[3] A Women's World Cup (WWC) was launched in People's Republic of China in 1991. A Women's Football Association (WFA) was eventually formed in England in 1969 and assimilated into the FA structures in 1993. The perception of women in the football industry as a whole remains problematic.[4]

In 1970 FIFA conducted a survey of its 139 constituent affiliated national associations. This produced 90 responses, only 12 of which replied in favour of endorsing the women's game.[5] While Simon Kuper and Stefan Szymanski's generalisations that "big, rich" nations win in women's soccer because no one has much experience are not borne out by the historical evidence it is clear that poorer nations tend not to support their female players at all.[6]

So the word "independent" has several overlapping uses in this chapter. There have been three main kinds of club ownership and practice in women's football since the 1970s. Firstly, sports clubs like Røa in Norway and Umeå IK from Sweden have a much wider remit than football. Here soccer is one of many sporting codes in a community-driven club that is not linked to a professional men's side. Sports clubs with women's football teams have been important at top-level European female competition, nevertheless. Secondly, English club Arsenal, France's Olympique Lyonnaise, FC Bayern Munich in Germany and AZ Alkmaar from the Netherlands are all adjuncts to professional men's football clubs, or were until very recently. Arsenal is a prime example of the extension of football in the community schemes run by Premier League and Football League Clubs since 1992 and place women's football as part of what Redhead has called the "ambient marketing" of these clubs.[7] Thirdly, FFC Turbine Potsdam and FCR 2001 Duisburg in Germany are proudly independent women's clubs as were British club Doncaster Belles at the outset. This degree of affiliation affects the way that the organisations perceive their role in the community and in their own self-image. The chapter explores the ambiguity of those multiple identities. With an estimated 30 million female players globally, the evolution of football as a sport and as an industry over the past 60 years has been dramatic.[8] However, behind narratives of progress historical continuities of a deeply conservative nature continue to abide.

This chapter first looks at the history of women's clubs and teams independent of FA, and then Football League (formed in 1885) control from 1881 to 1921. The main focus is on independent women's teams like Doncaster Belles (informally known as the Donny Belles, now formally called the Doncaster Rovers Belles). The chapter illustrates that much of women's football in the United Kingdom relies upon autonomous women's teams for the majority of female participation but that increasingly at the elite level teams are obliged to combine with men's Football League and Premiership organisations.[9] This not only condescends to those who have pioneered football for women as self-determining and self-regulating, but also attempts to erase memories of how archaic football governance in the United Kingdom has been, and still remains. Women are not a minority population, but, worldwide today, even by FIFA's own exaggerated and unverified figures, the proportion of female football players is no more than 10 % of the total number *at best*.

THE GIRLS OF THE PERIOD PLAYING BALL: WOMEN'S FOOTBALL PIONEERS 1869–1921

The first home international women's association football match took place on May 9, 1881, when a team calling themselves England played a side named Scotland at Easter Road, Edinburgh. Scotland won 3-0, and although the teams played at least seven matches, information remains patchy. More intriguingly, the collector and popular historian of football, Chris Unger, has an image from *Harper's Bazaar* on his website dated August 1869 showing young women in fashionable dress playing what appears to be soccer, although it is unclear whether this was an organised match or evidence of a "kick-about" or "pick-up" game.[10]

Edinburgh versus Grimsby scheduled a match in 1887, leading the English port to claim the first women's football club side, though working women in Sunderland also played. A London-based team, the British Ladies Football Club (BLFC), was founded in 1895 with Secretary Nettie Honeyball, although it is generally accepted that this was a poetic pseudonym. They began with a London-based match in front of 10,000 spectators and also played in Scotland and the North-East. Aristocrat and explorer Lady Florence Dixie agreed to act as President and promoted the club in newspaper interviews. The club continued for over 100 matches with over 20 more as Mrs. Graham's Eleven.

The paying crowds for women's football grew rapidly between 1917 and 1921 in Britain, although the economic conditions were not favourable to spectator sport. This was largely as a result of the changing nature of female work but also because of a larger sense of social collective action on behalf of a paying public.[11] One of the most well-known female British football teams had begun to play seriously in October 1917 based at the Strand Road tram building and light railway works in Preston, Lancashire, originally founded by W.B. Dick and John Kerr of Kilmarnock. Dick, Kerr's Ladies were formed in 1917 and continued to play in various guises until 1965. Dick, Kerr's Ladies considered fostering a league but instead concentrated on wider networks in order to facilitate competition and raise funds for charity, more after World War I had concluded than during the conflict. What distinguished the estimated 150 British women's football teams during World War I from previous industrial welfare was the degree of commercial success with sustained large crowds raising significant sums of money for charity. This remains a research agenda in need of more detailed analysis.

There were other work-based women's teams such as Horrockses' Ladies, of the mill owned by the family known as the Cotton Kings of Preston, and Atalanta, an affiliation of professional women, such as teachers and nurses.[12] Lyons tearooms had several women's football teams too, for instance, and the company had a national network of outlets.

In 1920 and 1921 the crowds grew, in spite of difficult economic conditions across Britain. The coal disputes of 1921 and 1926 in Britain saw more sides develop in response to localised deprivation: teams included the Soup Canteen Ladies, Blaydon Ladies FC and the Marley Hill Spankers.[13] In early March 1921 *The Lancashire Daily Post* announced an international 9-0 win against a Scotland side at Celtic Park. Many of the England team were Dick, Kerr players and the Preston team had played again in an

8-1 win the previous Saturday at Coventry City in front of 27,000 with gate receipts £1622.[14]

Rather suddenly, the FA "banned" women's teams from playing football on League and Association-affiliated grounds from December 5, 1921. The FA ruled that too much money had been absorbed in expenses and the game was "unsuitable" for women. Following the ban, some medical opinion held that football was too vigorous a game and affected women "internally," contrary to the evidence no serious injury had been sustained.[15] Dick, Kerr Ladies toured in 1922 to Canada and the United States; they played against male professional and semi-professional teams. On their return to Britain in 1923 the impetus to form a coherent, nationwide response to the FA ban had been lost. The FA ban remained and was enforced periodically (especially in 1946 and 1949) until informally rescinded following the intervention of FIFA in the late 1960s and formally withdrawn when the first FA international England women's team was formed in 1972. A young British woman growing up during World War I may well have had more opportunities to play football than a young woman in the 1950s therefore, although female teams and clubs continued to be founded.

THE DONNY BELLES AND BRITISH INDEPENDENT WOMEN'S FOOTBALL TEAMS 1969–2014

England's World Cup victory of 1966 has been constantly reinterpreted, reappraised and revised as a historical moment in the history of Association football, particularly in Britain.[16] There is some evidence that it did inspire a new generation of women to play football.[17] Shortly after, for example, the WFA was formed in 1969 with 44 constituent clubs. For some important international players and coaches in England, such as Sue Lopez, 1966 did seem to be some sort of catalyst;[18] The Deal international women's football tournament was first held in Kent in 1967 and overseen by Arthur Hobbs. An awareness of European football was also helped by the attendance at Deal of Sparta Praha and Slavia Kaplice from Czechoslovakia and a side from Vienna. Cambuslang Hooverettes, the Scottish champions from Glasgow, also participated. The Deal tournament grew to a 32-team event in 1968 and had 52 entries the following year.

Also frequently described as corresponding with "second wave" feminism of the 1970s playing football seemed to combine the invasion of traditionally "male spaces" such as the pitch and the locker room with signs of an assertive female physicality. However, my research in this area found that most of the women playing in the 1970s did not define themselves as feminists or as politically active. They simply had been introduced to football, enjoyed playing and continued. In the 1970 Deal tournament, an unprecedented degree of international interest developed, and this had parallels with what was happening in Italy. Combined with the Butlins Cup (which was jointly organised by the holiday camp chain, the commercial television channel ITV and the newspaper *The Daily Mirror*) the Deal tournament encouraged unprecedented degrees of connectivity. The first WFA Cup began in 1970–71 as the Mitre Challenge Trophy, sponsored by the sporting goods manufacturer. There were 71 entrants, including teams from across Britain. For the first three years Southampton beat Scottish teams (Stewarton and Thistle, Lee's Ladies and Westhorn United, respectively) to take the title. As there was no official England women's team, many women also travelled to Italy to the Fédération Internationale Européenne de Football Féminine (FIEFF) tournament between 1969 and 1972 to discover how advanced women's football was in Europe. But amidst this wider and increasing connectivity, how did individual clubs form?

Doncaster Belle Vue Belles were formed in 1969 by a group of women who sold "Golden Girl" tickets, a fundraising promotion, for the Doncaster Rovers men's team at Belle Vue in South Yorkshire. Shortened to the Doncaster or "Donny Belles" in 1971, founder members included captain Sheila Stocks. A trained teacher and physiotherapist, Sheila later married the ex-professional player and coach who was to become manager of the Belles, Paul Edmunds, who worked at the same school. [19] An ex-Leicester City player whose career was cut short through injury, Paul Edmunds pioneered the professional attitude of coaching men's football at Belles and they have had a tradition of bringing through talented young players as a result. Retiring as a player for the team after 24 years, in her early 40s, Sheila Edmunds is still President of the club today.

In 1972 the team joined the Sheffield League, before moving to the Nottingham Regional League in 1975. As well as playing 11-a-side matches, small-sided games developed the skills of the players and the team retained the National Market Traders Association 5-a-side Trophy from 1972 to 1976. However, after winning the Red Cross Cup in the 1975/76 season, the Belles concentrated on the 11-a-side game and became one of the most significant women's teams for the next 20 years.

This included winning the Nottingham Regional League 11 times between the 1976/77 and 1988/89 seasons. The team won the Women's Football Association Cup six times from 1983 onwards and were beaten Finalists on seven occasions.[20]

In 1983 the WFA affiliated to the FA on the same basis as the County Football Associations and it was by no means an easy transition. A 24-club National League was not to be established by the WFA until 1991 and further neglect by the FA caused resentment. Participation levels between 1976 and 1991 stagnated and the FA policy of holding the WFA at a distance from its male-focused development programmes was shown to be actively inhibiting female involvement. At the start of this gradual and painful process of assimilation, the 1983 WFA Cup-winning Donny Belles team featured stars such as Jackie Sherrard, Julie Sutcliffe, Tracey Davidson, Lorraine Hanson, Wendy Hardistry, Donna Young, Sue Coddrington, Sheila Stocks, Tracey Hunt, Doreen Jones, Carol Carr, Ruth Derrick, Catherine Derrick and Jill Hanson. Many would go on to representative honours in the 1980s and 1990s. For well over a decade, this core team and new signings continued to provide key members of the England national squad and they twice won the Women's FA Cup and the Women's Premier League National title, in 1991–92 and 1993–94. The Belles were also part of European tournaments, including a Women's European Cup in Holland in August 1983, against the Dutch champions RKTVC, Belgian, Danish, German and Norwegian and counterparts.[21]

By 1988 England Women's national team had been named Team of the Year in the *Sunday Times* Annual Women's Sports awards after winning an unofficial World Cup (the Mundialito or Little World Cup) in Arco, Northern Italy. [22] Playing against France, Italy, Germany and the United States, former and current Belles players involved in the squad included Jackie Sherrard (a production clerk); Tracey Davidson (an office clerk), Karen Walker (student), Gill Coulthard (factory worker) and Joanne Broadhurst (forklift driver). Even so, respected journalist and popular historian Brian Glanville neglected the Mundialito or any other versions of women's world cups in his supposedly "definitive" account.[23] Old prejudices die hard, apparently. Were there any doubt about the amateur nature of women's football in this period, the Belles squad at this time numbered a chef (Toni Evans), two schoolgirls (Samatha Eyre and Suzanne Otley), a shop assistant (Karen Skillcorn), a storekeeper (Carol Carr), a machinist (Jill Hanson), a bank clerk (Lorraine Hunt) and a housewife and mother (Jackie Mayes).[24] Most Belles players managed a regime of four training sessions plus at least one match for the average week during a season, plus off-season tours and regional or international fixtures.

As with the 1984 Mundialito squad for England, the Belles provided key young players and more experienced internationals. After joining Doncaster Belles as a 13-year-old, Gill Coultard would win her first England cap at 18 against the Republic of Ireland in 1981 while still a sixth former at Throne Hill Grammar School in the town. Later to become captain of the national women's side, Coultard went on to obtain 119 caps, scoring 30 goals. This made her the first woman and only amateur to have reached over 100 caps for England by the time of her international retirement in 2000. It remains a shocking oversight that Coultard is the most prominent female England captain since the national team began in 1972 not to have been acknowledged in the honours system, when others who have not led their country or had such a distinguished career have been recognised. Similarly, Karen Walker, who had begun as a 16-year-old centre forward, had a career spanning 20 years with the club and scored 40 goals for England.

Few fans of football, however obsessive, will have heard of Harry and Doreen Stocks and this is another whole research agenda. Although volunteers facilitate the majority of football participation in Britain, most academic research has been drawn towards the more glamorous, elite elements of the industry. After being part of the founding team for Belles, Doreen and Harry continued in multiple volunteer roles including making the half-time tea and cutting the oranges, washing the kit, acting as club secretary and treasurer and supporting the team during matches. However, when Donny Belles received an invitation to play in the FA Women's National League in 1991, "Mr. and Mrs. S" stood down from their various commitments with the club because the travel interfered with their family commitments.[25] The club hosted a farewell party to celebrate 23 years of loyal voluntary service. This is unlikely to be an isolated case in the independent tradition of women's clubs (or for that matter male and junior teams).

The so-called "demise" of the Belles once the FA took more control of the women's game in England has been much exaggerated, as this section has shown. It is perhaps more fair to say that their domination became increasingly challenged by a London-centric Football Association, particularly a public relations emphasis on female clubs affiliated to men's teams such as Fulham, Croydon, Charlton and Arsenal. Vick Akers at Arsenal brought in many of the methods that had been pioneered by Paul

Edmunds, such as regular and specific training, in addition to a youth policy. Partly because the same players tended to move en masse to Croydon, Friends of Fulham and so on, claims for professionalisation in the 1990s can be overstated. Examples of where this ostensible professional Football League support ultimately failed included Fulham, which has often (mistakenly) been called the first fully professional women's club in English history.[26] Funding for the Fulham women's team was announced in June 2000 and withdrawn in 2006 in order to allow the club to focus on its (male) Premiership aspirations, as it faced relegation. This left friends, family and volunteers to step into the breach but the volunteers could not stop Fulham's Women's Football Club from closing in 2010. This was not an isolated case. Charlton took over the successful Croydon women's club in 2000 before withdrawing its funding three seasons later. Even those current teams that superficially share the name of a male professional team in the Women's Super League, such as Birmingham City LFC, often train and play on inferior grounds (in this case in Stratford Upon Avon in Warwickshire 50 miles away) with little access to facilities or support. Ambient marketing is indeed to the fore in these community-based initiatives.

It cannot be disputed that by the 1990s there were more British women players, achieving higher standards of technical ability than ever before. As a result of the 1992 and 1994 title doubles, Belles passed into popular culture in ways that were to have a far-reaching impact for the team and individual players. Journalist and author Pete Davies spent the 1994/95 season with the team and his sympathetic experiences became the popular book *I Lost My Heart To The Belles* (1996). [27] However, Davies patronised the players as living in a godforsaken northern outpost with little in the way of prospects, education or culture and this later inspired Kay Mellor to write a television series based on the same melodramatic principles called *Playing the Field*. Worse, a controversial BBC TV programme "The Belles," broadcast in January 1995, dramatised the documentary elements of Davies' research. There were scenes showing some of the Belles fighting and intoxicated after a night out at a club. This was cause enough for the Football Association to suspend Gill Coultard as England captain and appoint Debbie Bampton instead. Bampton was an experienced player who went on to 95 caps herself but the blow in the approach to the 1995 WWC in Sweden for Gill Coultard and the Yorkshire team was severe. Belles understandably became wary of the media from then on.

More fundamentally, preferential FA funding was being given to establish Centres of Excellence. At that point in 1998, the Belles were trying to obtain planning permission for their own ground. When this was unsuccessful, a merger with Doncaster Rovers was mooted in 2002 and, though it was not without problems, it took place in 2003. The most recognisable name in the British women's game began to sell their merchandise in the Rover's shop. More recently, in 2009 the Belles launched a social enterprise initiative, to promote community, social, health and educational services, with female sport as a focal point.

The Belles were one of the eight founder members of the FA Women's Super League in 2011 but in 2013 it was announced that they would be relegated to the newly created second tier of the franchise, as a result of their lack of facilities and commercial acumen. The decision by the selection panel not to offer the club an FA WSL1 licence was due primarily to them being unable to satisfactorily meet minimum facility requirements, alongside further concerns on their commercial and marketing strategies.[28]

No football reasons were given for this decision, though Belles finished the 2012/13 season at the bottom of the Women's Super League with just six points, deflated by the decision which had been taken midpoint in the fixture list. The FA decision-making process regards Doncaster remains available online but the transparency and independence remain in doubt for those of us who have seen the Belles undermined repeatedly over time. It looks like a case of an aristocracy of wealth in women's football, supported by the FA. What then is the future for independent clubs in the elite of women's football in England? This larger research question remains.

CONCLUSION: THE AMBIGUOUS FUTURE OF WOMEN IN FOOTBALL

When Karen Espelund, a respected Norwegian player and former General Secretary of the Norwegian Football Association, was "co-opted" on to the executive board of the European Football Confederation (UEFA) in 2011 it was heralded an important first by the governing bodies and the media.[29] But what kind of first was it? We know that women had pioneered important aspects of football back as far as 1881 and had sought to administer the sport in high-profile leagues since at least 1895. Espelund's appointment is symptomatic of football's governing bodies' more recent policy of integrating the women's game in part to appear more inclusive. In 2012 Lydia Nsekera, the President of the Burundi Football Association and a member of the Committee for Women's Football and the FIFA WWC and of the Organising Committee for the Olympic Football Tournaments, became the first woman co-opted member of the FIFA Executive Committee.

In the framework of the FIFA reform process, Nsekera holds little power as the 25th member of the FIFA Executive Committee. Four confederations proposed a candidate for the election in May 2013: Moya Dodd (Australia), Lydia Nsekera, Sonia Bien-Aime (Turks and Caicos Islands) and Paula Kearns (New Zealand). Europe therefore became the only confederation not to have nominated a candidate for the role. Dodd and Bien-Aime were co-opted onto the ExCo but their post is reliant upon not upsetting the members who could just as easily reverse their appointment. None of the countries represented by women on the ExCo are in the top ten nations for men's or women's soccer.

The supposed "newness" factor is an invented tradition relating to women players. The first official Women's World Championship (later to be called a World Cup) took place in the People's Republic of China in 1991, backed by FIFA and sponsored by confectionary company M&Ms. China also hosted the 2007 WWC. The United States has held two such competitions in 1999 and 2003 and Sweden one in 1995. Arguably, it was not until the success of WWC 1999 in the United States (where 34 UEFA member associations expressed a wish to participate in the tournament) that the commercial prospects for women's football became a priority for FIFA. There are now also two youth versions: the Under-20 and Under-17 WWC tournaments were held in Germany and Trinidad and Tobago, respectively, in 2010. The 2011 WWC, hosted by Germany in 2011, was intended as a record-breaking female-only sports tournament on the continent. It certainly created a new high for Twitter social networking traffic with over 7100 messages a second for the final: more than for the Royal Wedding, the death of Osama Bin Laden or the Japanese tsunami the same year.[30]

This use of social media does not wholly counteract the historical tabloidisation of the sports media since Australian businessman Rupert Murdoch took over the *News of The World* in 1969, and then *The Sun*, before developing interests in New York in 1974.[31] Many print and broadcast journalists, like Glanville, Merritt and others referenced in this chapter, have adopted a form of tabloid-speak in relation to women and sport since then.

This tabloidisation and "trial by media" has nowhere been more evident than in the recent treatment of US Women's National Team goalkeeper Hope Solo, who pleaded not guilty to two charges of misdemeanour and domestic violence in an alleged assault of her half-sister and 17-year-old nephew in June 2014. Solo's previous anger-management issues had seen her removed from the US Women's National Team in 2007 and then return a leaner, more focused athlete in the 2008 and 2012 Olympic Games: cemented with successive US Women's National Team Olympic gold medals. After appearing on "Dancing with the Stars," more recent alcohol issues have, however, called her judgement and ability to act as a role model into question.

The court dismissed all four aspects of the claim against Hope Solo for domestic violence in January 2015. Solo's sponsors, including Nike, and the Seattle Reign and US Women's National Team appeared to be vindicated by supporting their star player in a case where the facts were in dispute. This did not stop journalists from making tenuous links with several National Football League (NFL) controversies involving players admitting to various kinds of domestic violence (such as Ray Rice, Greg Hardy, Jonathan Dwyer and Adrian Petersen). Cindy Boren of *The Washington Post* claimed that there are clear parallels and Solo should not have been allowed to play in the winning US team in 2015 while awaiting trial.[32]

Within two weeks of the acquittal, Hope Solo and her husband, former NFL player Jerramy Stevens, were stopped in one of the official US Soccer minivans while out in LA and he was charged with Drinking under the Influence (DUI) on the way back to the US team hotel. This was during a training camp to begin the US WWC campaign for Canada. Solo then failed to inform team officials about the incident and did not contest a 30-day ban in January and February 2015 in which her recovery appeared to be a significant aspect. As Grant Wahl shrewdly analysed in response to these episodes, Solo may not be popular with her teammates, or the poster girl for US Soccer, but she remains the best goalkeeper in the Women's National Team Squad.[33]

As the Hope Solo case indicates, issues of mental health can be just as challenging for female athletes who achieve a degree of public recognition as for male sports stars. Solo won her place on the team because of her professional athletic ability, not for her impeccable moral conduct, and this is in some ways more like men's sport. Gendered sporting moral codes mean that the optimism for the future of women's sport has to be tempered by the continuities of the past.

This chapter focused on one of the many independent clubs in British women's football, so necessary to the female game because of the condescension and neglect of the sports authorities. There was a lack of consultation and respect for the Doncaster Belles in their demotion to level two of the Women's Super League in the 2013/14 season and this trend looks set to continue. Supposedly, the FA wanted to build the local fan base of such teams but has continually caused a dislocation between its high-handed treatment of the club and supporters. This has done little for claims that the FA is acting for the wider good of the women's game and, by extension, grass-roots football.[34] Leaving the Women's Super League and choosing to play in alternative competitions would make it highly unlikely that players would get picked for national teams. Like it or not, unless the FA withdraw funding for the Women's Super League in the near future, its conservative assumption that the structures of male football are the practices that an infantilised women's game needs to emulate will continue to shape access for English female players in the twenty-first century.

NOTES

1. William John Hicks, "What Games Do Girls Like Best?," in *News Chronicle Sport For Girls,* ed. Carolyn Dingle (London: News Chronicle Publications Department, 1951), 20.
2. Vivek Chaudrey, "Women Players Get Football Fever," *The Guardian,* July 28, 2001 http://www.theguardian.com/uk/2001/jul/28/football.vivekchaudhary. Accessed 6 Oct 2014.
3. Christiane Eisenberg et al., *100 Years of Football: The FIFA Centennial Book* (London: Weidenfeld and Nicholson, 2004), 20–2.
4. Jean Williams, *A Game for Rough Girls: A History of Women's Football in England.* (Oxford: Routledge, 2003), 10–2.
5. FIFA, *Minutes of the First UEFA Women's Football Conference,* March 22, 1972 (Zurich: FIFA Archive), 22.
6. Jean Williams and Megan Chawansky, "Namibia's Brave Gladiators: Gendering the Sport and Development Nexus From the 1998 2nd

World Women and Sport Conference to the 2011 Women's World Cup," in *Women's Sport in Africa, a Special Edition of Sport in Society: Cultures, Commerce, Media, Politics,* eds. Michelle Sykes and John Bale, 17, no. 4 (December 2013): 550–562.

7. Steve Redhead, *Post-Fandom and the Millennial Blues: The Transformation of Soccer Culture* (London/New York: Routledge, 1997), 12–14.

8. FIFA, "FIFA Big Count 2006: 270 Million People Active," FIFA. com, May 31, 2007 http://www.fifa.com/mm/document/fifa-facts/bcoffsurv/bigcount.statspackage_7024.pdf. Accessed 3 Oct 2014.

9. Jayne Caudwell, "Women's Football in the United Kingdom: Theorising Gender and Unpacking the Butch Lesbian Image," *Journal of Sport and Social Issues* 23, no. 4 (December 1999): 390–403 and Jayne Caudwell, "Women's Experiences of Sexuality within Football Contexts: A Particular and Located Footballing Epistemology," *Football Studies* 5, no. 1 (January 2002): 24–45.

10. Anonymous, "The Girls of The Period, Playing at Ball," *Harper's Bazaar,* August 1869, in Chris Unger *The History of Women's Football* http://thehistoryofwomensfootball.com/1800s.html. Accessed 6 Feb 2015.

11. Alethea Melling, "'Ray of the Rovers': The Working Class Heroine in Popular Football Fiction 1915–25," *The International Journal of The History of Sport* 15, no. 1 (April 1998): 97–122; Alethea Melling, "Cultural Differentiation, Shared Aspiration: The Entente Cordiale of International Ladies' Football 1920–45," *The European Sports History Review* 1, no. 1 (August 1999): 27–53.

12. Margaret Burscough, *The Horrockses: Cotton Kings of Preston* (Preston: Carnegie Publishing, 2004).

13. Patrick Brennan, "Soup Kitchen Soccer: Women's Football in North-East England During the 1921 and 1926 Coal Disputes" *Women's Football* http://www.donmouth.co.uk/. Accessed 3 Oct 2014.

14. Anon. "Dick, Kerr's Still Winning," *The Lancashire Daily Post,* March 2, 1921, p. 4.

15. Anon. "Health Giving Kicks–Girl Footballer Who Scored 368 Goals Saw Doctor Only Once," *The Daily Mirror,* December 9, 1921 p. 7.

16. Jean Williams, *A Beautiful Game: International Perspectives on Women's Football* (Oxford: Berg, 2007), 25.
17. Harold Mayes, ed. *The Football Association World Cup Report 1966* (London: William Heinemann Ltd and The Football Association, 1967), 41–7.
18. Jean Williams, *A Game for Rough Girls*, 55.
19. Anonymous *Doncaster Belles Information Sheet* unpublished circa 1993: 7–8 (Personal Collection of the Author).
20. Mike Sinclair, "Bonnie Belles," *The Doncaster Star*, March 17, 1983, p. 32.
21. John De Pater, "When They Win the English Smile; and When They Lose, They Also Smile," *Yorkshire Post*, August 31, 1983, p. 6.
22. Linda Whitehead, "England Team of The Year," in *Women's Football Association Newsletter* (Cradely Heath, Birmingham: Women's Football Association, 1988), 41.
23. Brian Glanville, *The Story of the World Cup* (London and Boston: Faber and Faber, 1997).
24. Women's Football Association, *WFA Cup Final Souvenir Programme: Norwich Ladies FC and Doncaster Belles LFC 4 May 1986* (Cradely Heath Birmingham: Women's Football Association, 1988), 4–8.
25. Brian Mentz, " Belles Say Thanks With A Surprise," *The* Star, September 14, 1991, p. 5.
26. Stephjanie Merritt, "Something for the Ladies," *The Guardian*, April 8, 2001. http://www.theguardian.com/football/2001/apr/08/newsstory.sport7. Accessed 3 Oct 2014.
27. Pete Davies, *I Lost My Heart to The Belles* (London: Random House, 1996).
28. The Football Association, "Statement Doncaster Belles," The FA.Com June 28, 2013 http://www.thefa.com/News/governance/2013/jun/doncaster-belles-appeal-statement.aspx. Accessed 28 Sept 2014.
29. "UEFA Executive Committee Concludes June Meeting," *UEFA. com the official website for European football*, June 17, 2011 www.uefa.com/uefa/abouttuefa/organisation/executivecommittee. Accessed 27 Sept 2014.
30. Evan Fanning, "Women's World Cup Final Between USA and Japan Sets Twitter Record," *The Guardian*, July 18, 2011 www.

guardian.co.uk/football/2011/jul/18/womens-world-cup-twit-ter-record. Accessed 15 Sept 2014.

31. David Rowe, *Sport, Culture and Media* (Buckinghamshire: Open University Press, 2003), 34–6.

32. Cindy Boren, "Hope Solo and The Domestic Violence Case No One Is Talking About," *The Washington Post*, September 19, 2014 http://www.washingtonpost.com/blogs/early-lead/wp/2014/09/19/hope-solo-and-the-domestic-violence-case-no-one-is-talking-about/. Accessed 24 Sept 2014.

33. Grant Wahl, "Circumstances Have Yet to Threaten Hope Solo's Career, Unlikely to Now," *Sports Illustrated*, January 26, 2015 http://www.si.com/planet-futbol/2015/01/26/hope-solo-jill-ellis-sunil-gulati-uswnt. Accessed 6 Feb 2015.

34. David Bond, "Sport England Cuts FA funding by £1.6m After Grassroots Decline," *BBC Sport*, March 27, 2014 http://www.bbc.co.uk/sport/0/football/26760067. Accessed 3 Oct 2014.

Work Cited

Anonymous. "The Girls of the Period, Playing at Ball, *Harper's Bazaar*, August 1869." Chris Unger *The History of Women's Football*. http://thehistoryofwo-mensfootball.com/1800s.html. Accessed 6 Feb 2015.

———. "Dick, Kerr's Still Winning." *The Lancashire Daily Post*. March 2, 1921.

———. "Health Giving Kicks–Girl Footballer Who Scored 368 Goals Saw Doctor Only Once." *The Daily Mirror*, December 9, 1921.

———. *Doncaster Belles Information Sheet* unpublished circa 1993 (Personal Collection of the Author).

Blatter, Josep. "President's Corner." *FIFA World: For the Game, for the World*. Zurich: FIFA, May 28, 2010: 27.

Bond, David. "Sport England Cuts FA funding by £1.6 m After Grassroots Decline." *BBC Sport*, March 27, 2014. http://www.bbc.co.uk/sport/0/foot-ball/26760067. Accessed 3 Oct 2014.

Boren, Cindy. "Hope Solo and the Domestic Violence Case No One Is Talking About." *The Washington Post*, September 19, 2014. http://www.washington-post.com/blogs/early-lead/wp/2014/09/19/hope-solo-and-the-domestic-violence-case-no-one-is-talking-about/. Accessed 24 Sept 2014.

Brennan, Patrick. "Soup Kitchen Soccer: Women's Football in North-East England During the 1921 and 1926 Coal Disputes." *Women's Football*. http://www.donmouth.co.uk/. Accessed 3 Oct 2014.

Burke, Peter. *A social history of workplace Australian football 1860–1939.* Unpublished PhD Royal Melbourne Institute of Technology, University Melbourne, 2008.

Burscough, Margaret. *The Horrockses: Cotton Kings of Preston.* Preston: Carnegie Publishing, 2004.

Caudwell, Jayne. "Women's Football in the United Kingdom: Theorising Gender and Unpacking the Butch Lesbian Image." *Journal of Sport and Social Issues* 23E, no. 4 (December, 1999): 390–403.

———. "Women's Experiences of Sexuality Within Football Contexts: A Particular and Located Footballing Epistemology." *Football Studies* 5, no. 1 (January, 2002): 24–45.

Chaudrey, Vivek. "Women Players Get Football Fever." *The Guardian*, July 28, 2001. http://www.theguardian.com/uk/2001/jul/28/football.vivekchaudhary. Accessed 6 Oct 2014.

Davies, Pete. *I Lost my Heart to the Belles.* London: Random House, 1996.

De Pater, John. "When They Win the English Smile; and When They Lose, They Also Smile." *Yorkshire Post*, August 31, 1983: 6.

Dietschy, Paul. *Histoire du Football.* Paris: Librairie Académique Perrin, 2010.

Eisenberg, Christiane et al. *100 Years of Football: The FIFA Centennial Book.* London: Weidenfeld and Nicholson, 2004.

Fanning, Evan. "Women's World Cup Final Between USA and Japan Sets Twitter Record." *The Guardian*, July 18, 2011. www.guardian.co.uk/football/2011/jul/18/womens-world-cup-twitter-record. Accessed 15 Sept 2014.

FIFA. *Minutes of the First UEFA Women's Football Conference.* March 22, 1972. Zurich: FIFA Archive.

FIFA. "FIFA Big Count 2006: 270 Million People Active." *FIFA.Com* May 31, 2007. http://www.fifa.com/mm/document/fifafacts/bcoffsurv/bigcount.statspackage_7024.pdf. Accessed 3 Oct 2014.

Glanville, Brian. *The Story of the World Cup.* London/Boston: Faber and Faber, 1997.

Goldblatt, David. *Futebol Nation: A Footballing History of Brazil.* London: Penguin Books, 2014.

Goldblatt, David, and Jean Williams *A History of the World Cup in 24 Objects.* International Centre for Sports History and Culture, De Montfort University and the National Football Museum, Manchester, 2014.

Hicks, William John. "What Games Do Girls Like Best?" In *News Chronicle Sport for Girls*, edited by Carolyn Dingle. London: News Chronicle Publications Department, 1951.

Kunz, Mattias. "*The Female Figure: Vital Statistics from the Women's Game.*" *FIFA World* Zurich: FIFA, 2010, March.

Kuper, Simon, and Stefan Szymanski. *Soccernomics: Why Transfers Fail, Why Spain Rule the World and Other Curious Football Phenomena Explained.* London: HarperCollins, 2012.

Lopez, Sue. *Women on the Ball: A Guide to Women's Football.* London: Scarlet Press, 1997.

Mayes, Harold ed. *The Football Association World Cup Report 1966.* London: William Heinemann Ltd and The Football Association, 1967.

Melling, Alethea. "'Ray of the Rovers:' The Working Class Heroine in Popular Football Fiction 1915–25." *The International Journal of The History of Sport* 15, no. 1 (April 1998): 97–122.

———. "Cultural Differentiation, Shared Aspiration: The Entente Cordiale of International Ladies' Football 1920–45." *The European Sports History Review* 1, no. 1 (August, 1999): 27–53.

Merritt, Stephanie. "Something for the Ladies." *The Guardian*, April 8, 2001. http://www.theguardian.com/football/2001/apr/08/newsstory.sport7. Accessed 3 Oct 2014.

Mentz, Brian. "Belles Say Thanks with a Surprise." *The Star*, September 14, 1991.

Redhead, Steve. *Post-Fandom and the Millennial Blues: The Transformation of Soccer Culture.* Routledge, London/New York, 1997.

Rowe David. *Sport, Culture and Media.* Buckinghamshire: Open University Press, 2003.

Sinclair, Mike. "Bonnie Belles." *The Doncaster Star*, March 17, 1983.

Taylor, Matthew. *The Leaguers: The Making of Professional Football in England, 1900–1939.* Liverpool: Liverpool University Press, 2005.

The Football Association. Statement Doncaster Belles. The FA.Com, June 28, 2013. http://www.thefa.com/News/governance/2013/jun/doncaster-belles-appeal-statement.aspx. Accessed 28 Sept 2014.

UEFA. "UEFA Executive Committee Concludes June Meeting." *UEFA.com the official website for European football,* June 17, 2011. www.uefa.com/uefa/aboutuefa/organisation/executivecommittee. Accessed 27 Sept 2014.

Vertinsky, Patricia. *The Eternally Wounded Woman: Women, Doctors and Exercise in the Late Nineteenth Century.* Manchester/New York: Manchester University Press, 1990.

Wahl, Grant. "Circumstances Have Yet to Threaten Hope Solo's Career, Unlikely to Now." *Sports Illustrated,* January 26, 2015. http://www.si.com/planet-futbol/2015/01/26/hope-solo-jill-ellis-sunil-gulati-uswnt. Accessed 6 Feb 2015.

Whitehead, Linda. "England Team of the Year." *Women's Football Association Newsletter.* Birmingham: Women's Football Association, 1988.

Williams, Jean. *A Game for Rough Girls: A History of Women's Football in England.* Oxford: Routledge, 2003.

———. *A Beautiful Game: International Perspectives on Women's Football.* Oxford: Berg, 2007.

———. "Women's Football During World War One." In *The Greater Game: A History of Football in World War One*, edited by Alex Jackson. Oxford: Shire Publications and National Football Museum, 2014.

Williams, Jean, and Megan Chawansky. "Namibia's Brave Gladiators: Gendering the Sport and Development Nexus From the 1998 2nd World Women and Sport Conference to the 2011 Women's World Cup." In *Women's Sport in Africa, a Special Edition of Sport in Society: Cultures, Commerce, Media, Politics*, edited by Michelle Sykes and John Bale. 17, no. 4 (December, 2013): 550–562.

Women's Football Association. *WFA Cup Final Souvenir Programme: Norwich Ladies FC and Doncaster Belles LFC 4 May 1986*. Birmingham: Women's Football Association, 1988.

PART VI

The State and Civil Society

Politics, Power and Soccer in Postwar Italy: The Case of Naples

Rosario Forlenza

Fittingly, for a nation that has given the world the Renaissance, grand opera and Machiavelli, a history of Italian soccer reveals a beguiling mixture of the artistic, the overblown and the scheming. Unlike football played in Spain, Germany or France, say, Italian soccer possesses a uniquely seductive quality that often amounts to more than the sum of its parts. This is because soccer in Italy is not as it is in other countries: this is a nation where the largest selling daily newspaper (*Gazzetta della Sport*) is dedicated almost entirely to soccer, and where two other popular daily newspapers focus on sport (mainly soccer), where one of its much discussed and controversial prime ministers, Silvio Berlusconi (1994–1995, 2001–2006, 2008–2011), owned and still owns one of the league's most famous clubs (AC Milan), and where the political organization he founded in 1994 was named after the chant to encourage the national team (*Forza Italia*, i.e., Let's Go, Italy!). Soccer, it seems, is Italy, and Italy is soccer, and so, inevitably, a narrative about the game cannot help but be a narrative about the country as a whole—its dynamics, its preoccupations, its outlook and its problems—and about its politics, its history and its identity.

R. Forlenza (✉)
Center for European and Mediterranean Studies, New York University,
New York, NY, USA

© Hofstra University 2017
B. Elsey, S. Pugliese (eds.), *Football and the Boundaries of History*,
DOI 10.1057/978-1-349-95006-5_13

To be sure, the relationship between politics and soccer has been a central aspect of twentieth-century Italian history, well before the advent of Berlusconi in the political arena.[1] Benito Mussolini, the Duce of Fascism, was always attuned to the use of popular culture in his desire to hold power and transform Italian society. Soccer was a key part of this strategy.[2] Fascists took control of the world of soccer in the mid-1920s, built stadia all over the peninsula and created a national team which dominated the international game for four years, winning two world cups (1934 and 1938) and an Olympic gold medal (1936). In short, Mussolini was not the first leader to recognize the political potential of sports, but the Fascist regime was the first to use sports as an integral part of government, and only later many of the techniques that Mussolini originated were imitated by Hitler in Nazi Germany.[3]

However, soccer and politics remained indivisible also in post-Fascist Italy. The story of Silvio Berlusconi is now paradigmatic. In 1994, Berlusconi, a businessman worth an estimated 10 billion euros who controlled a business empire that spanned insurance, banking, film, real estate and Italy's three biggest commercial TV channels, launched his political campaign on the back of his ownership of AC Milan. Berlusconi announced his candidacy for Prime Minister of Italy stating that he had "chosen to *take the field* and involve myself in public life." Having chosen to "take the field," a phrase appropriated directly from the soccer lexicon, Berlusconi succeeded in eventually blurring the distinction between soccer, media and politics. Scholars, observers and opinion-makers have considered Berlusconi and his political adventure as the most blatant and perhaps best-orchestrated example of "soccer politics"—meaning the wholesale transfer into the political sphere of the language, iconography, symbolism, and metaphor of soccer—since the interwar period.

Yet Berlusconi was certainly not the first big businessman and power freak of postwar Italy to control a major football club and to use the team, along with his mass-media system and his economic power, to serve his political ambitions. In the 1950s, the shipping magnate Achille Lauro developed populist politics through investment and the appropriation of another football team: S.S. Napoli.[4] Coinciding almost entirely with his term as the city's mayor in the 1950s, his slogan throughout was "A great Napoli for a great Naples." While he was clearly a sincere and devoted fan of his club, his interest had a socioeconomic and political dimension to it, linked to a creation of a broad consensus among voters. In short, it was Lauro who was the creator of "soccer politics," Italian style, anticipating

Berlusconi in his populist, anti-establishment message, irreverent public persona and pugnacious rhetorical style.

The aim of this essay is to highlight some crucial aspects of Lauro's story. This specific focus will shed light on the challenges post-World War II Italy struggled to deal with: the Southern Question, reconstruction, the advent of democracy, the economic miracle, the identity of the nation after Fascism and military defeats. The story of Lauro will elucidate the vicissitudes of Italy's history, its political system and its society.

ACHILLE LAURO, THE KING OF NAPLES[5]

Lauro had made his first millions from the arms trade linked to Fascism's colonial adventures, after he won the navy contracts for the African campaign of the 1930s, which culminated in the conquest of Ethiopia. From 1912, when he inherited his first small coastal vessel, until the outbreak of World War I, he had gradually built up a fleet of ships only to have it requisitioned for the war effort. At war's end, he started again from scratch, and by 1933, with the help of influential members of the Fascist Party that he had joined, his fleet grew to 21 ships. After the African campaign and by the time World War II broke out, he had increased the number to 57, yet only 5 remained at the end of hostilities. As partial compensation for the ships he lost, Mussolini allowed him to acquire an interest in several important Neapolitan newspapers and in the influential Banco di Napoli. In 1936 he took control of the Napoli team for the first time, but he left the club in 1940, disillusioned by his lack of success.

The war changed everything. In 1943, on the arrival of the Allies, he was charged with aiding and abetting Fascism. After 22 months in a prison camp, he was acquitted of all charges and released.

After the war Lauro began, for the third time, to reconstruct his company. This time, along with a merchant marine, he moved into the round-the-world-passenger-liner market, carrying Italian emigrants to Australia and New Zealand and bringing tourists back to Europe. Now a multimillionaire, he decided to branch directly and without intermediation into politics. As representative democracy was being established in Italy in the mid-to-late 1940s, Lauro had the pragmatic intuition that to get into serious and successful businesses, he needed to find a political space within the new regime. Christian Democracy refused him membership, as major Christian Democrats feared he was uncontrollable.[6] He joined the Fronte dell'Uomo Qualunque (Everyman's Front), a populist movement which competed with the Christian Democrats for the moderate and anti-Communist vote in 1946–1947. The movement benefited from the lack of trust in the postwar political class and from the legacy of populist formulae of the Fascist regime, from the uncertainty of the political–institutional transition and from the fear of revolution deeply felt in a country where one-third of the voters cast their vote with the Communist and Socialist parties.[7]

With the disappearance of the Everyman's Front he joined the Partito Nazionale Monarchico (National Monarchic Party, PNM), giving it a new dynamic identity and well-needed funds. In a way, this was an act of pragmatic flexibility, and the obvious choice for him in the circumstances. Naples had shown that it was the most monarchical big city in the 1946 institutional referendum transforming Italy into a Republic. More than three quarters of Neapolitans had voted in favor of the monarchy, and Lauro was already attuned to the beliefs and political views of his fellow Neapolitans.

In 1952, he led a maverick monarchist coalition that romped to power in local elections, winning an astonishing 117,000 preference votes. In 1956 this figure was almost tripled. He was mayor for most of the 1950s, governing with massive majorities and with the support of ample sectors of Neapolitan society. The result of this remarkable consensus was immense power and a system known as *Laurismo*, at the center of which was this populist businessman, the self-made man *par excellence*, or simply, as he was called, "O' Comandante" [the Commander].

Intent on revitalizing the city and developing local tourism, Lauro talked about "the taste of money, of wealth, of full wallets, of living a better life at whatever cost." He also talked of canceling images of "Neapolitan hunger, of the resignation to that total misery that marked the south, which the liberal bourgeoisie looked at little or never."[8] His pharaonic electoral campaign reinforced his immense popularity. Before elections, he handed out free packets of pasta or offered voters a new left shoe, giving them the right one once they could prove they had made the "right" choice.

He wanted to make Naples the new *Cinecittà*, the most important port of the Mediterranean, a modern and industrial city. He completed the construction of the railway station at Piazza Garibaldi, and embarked on a massive program of building, road construction and real estate development. He warmly encouraged northern industrials, such as the Agnelli or the Piaggio family, to establish factories in Naples or extract oil from the South.[9] He also set a schedule of festivals ranging from April to October, mixing San Gennaro with the singing tradition of Piedigrotta, literary awards with social parties, beauty contests with fireworks. At times he offered Neapolitans (voters and soccer fans) free entry to theaters, cinemas and operas. He constantly looked after his voters' clientele, no matter which social class they were from, both personally and through his staff. He found jobs for the unemployed and homes for the homeless, spent on social care for poor people, demanded bribes from builders in order to replenish the relief fund; he multiplied recruitments, assignments, repayments, contracts; he systematically combined public and private affairs, upsetting financial balances and bureaucratic procedures in supreme contempt of any law.

One of his official activities as mayor was to promote and defend Naples and its traditions, taking the title of "vice-King" of the South and fighting for the monarchical cause with emphatic rhetoric. He missed no opportunity to express his contempt for the political class and parties, considered as parasites and enemies of the collective interest. After all, he governed using his own riches, not wasting or stealing public money, as his voters claimed. He also missed no opportunity to attack central government, to claim Naples' *diritti negati* ("denied rights") and to request a special law (with financial provisions) to meet the demand and needs of Naples and other neglected Southern cities. When in 1953 Naples was granted the Special Law—a weird bill administered by Naples and not by the central government—his promises seemed to come true. He amplified the anarchical anti-centralistic and anti-Roman feelings of many Neapolitans.

This was understood by a variety of observers as one of the reasons for his popularity.[10] Between the end of the war and the beginning of the 1950s the socioeconomic conditions of the city were indeed bleak, as a parliamentary inquiry (first published in 1953) revealed.[11] Writers such as Curzio Malaparte (with his 1949 novel *The Skin*) and Anna Maria Ortese (with her short stories collected in the 1953 volume *The Bay is Not Naples*) as well as journalists such as Michele Tito (in a 1953 report published in the city's daily newspaper *Il Mondo*) depicted the abject and inhuman conditions of Naples, subjugated in an atmosphere of "stagnant paralysis,"[12] where "reason" was enslaved by "nature."[13] To many Neapolitans, Lauro seemed to overturn the state of biological or historical immobility in which the city appeared frozen and atrophied. After the 1956 elections, the radical–liberal intellectual Francesco Compagna—a fierce opponent of Lauro—explained that the mayor nurtured "the meanest instincts of masses," at the same enticing "the old inferiority complex engrained in the souls of Naples' common people and bourgeoisie." "What has been said by the rhetoricians of *napoletanità*, such as Scarfoglio, Porzi, Labriola?" He continued "that Naples was humiliated, that Naples was sacrificed, that Naples was the object and victim of a sinister conspiracy organized by all other Italian cities."[14]

Naples in those years was much more dynamic than it had been. Lauro was supported not only by the illiterate inhabitants of the poor areas, but also by a vast range of political and economic forces, and by the most advanced bourgeoisie that the city could offer. This was well understood by the Communist Abdon Alinovi who, commenting on the plebiscite of 1956, wrote: "Lauro and his group have offered to the Neapolitan bourgeoisie a limited yet substantial perspective of capitalist growth."[15] Moreover, Lauro enjoyed approval from comedians such as Totò and from writers such as Malaparte and Giuseppe Marotta (the author of the very popular short stories titled *The Gold of Naples*, 1954).[16]

Christian Democracy (DC) did not interfere with the administration of Naples. There was a deal, in the end. In 1954 Lauro split with the PNM, and established his own party, the Partito Monarchico Popolare (PMP, Popular Monarchy Party). The votes of Lauro's MPs ensured DC-led national governments a stable majority in the national parliament. Likewise, in many Southern towns and cities, the votes of Lauro's followers supported DC-led local councils. His reign came to an end when the Christian Democrats lost patience with him. After the 1956 plebiscite in his favor, and after the success of his party in the 1957 Sardinian regional elections, Lauro tried to leverage his power at the national level, creating a new party. But the DC had finally organized at a local level, imposing its hegemony and weaving itself into the patterns of Southern interests— through agrarian reform and other special investments.[17] The government decided to intervene in the administration of Naples, ditching Lauro through an anti-corruption drive, which led to the dissolution of the local council in 1958, just before the new local elections. He became mayor again in 1961, for a few months, but his golden age had vanished.

SOCCER POLITICS, NEAPOLITAN STYLE

Soccer was a founding and critical feature of *Laurismo*. While appealing to local traditions and developing his charismatic cult as a sort of demigod, Lauro consistently handled soccer and the Napoli team to establish support and a sense of belonging. In 1952, when he became mayor, Lauro again took control of Napoli. The team became a supplement to his persona and political movement. It conveyed his political intentions and consolidated his power base.

In the autumn of 1952, a few months after his successful electoral campaign, Lauro led a long line of donkeys (symbol of the Napoli team) dressed in blue through the historical quarters of Naples, to publicize the 105 million lire—an astronomical sum of money—spent on Bergamo Atalanta's Hasse Jeppson. Like the national economy, *calcio* was equally top-heavy with the majority of big clubs based within Italy's northern economic triangle of Milan, Turin, and Genoa. Constricted by the minimal number of southern footballers, ambitious team owners began importing expensive foreign players and managers. Jeppson's purchase indicated Lauro's ambitions both for the team and for Naples, translating the South's battle against the North into an understandable language for citizens, while simultaneously restoring hope to Napoli fans. All this money was not enough and the much-awaited *scudetto*, the national championship, never materialized. In Jeppson's four seasons with the club, Napoli finished 4th, 5th, 6th and 14th. The team went down to *Serie B* twice, in 1961 and in 1963. Napoli's failure to break the North's grip on the *scudetto* only further confirmed the financial gulf between the peninsula's haves and have-not. Lauro handed over the reins of power, remaining Honorary Life President. His legacy was a team full of stars who gave the fans innumerable memories, but whose victories amounted to little. The trophy cabinet remained empty (apart from two Italian Cups) until the arrival of a small Argentinian genius in 1984.

Lauro transferred into the political sphere the language and symbolism of soccer, which became an obsessive feature of his speeches, discourses and political performances. The "soccerization of politics" as developed by Lauro contained a vision of society and the role of the representation within that society which resorted systematically to Carl Schmitt's friend–enemy opposition—the content of politics defined as opposition to the "other," the "enemy," the "stranger."[18] To be sure, the soccer match is the quintessential, perfect allegory and epitome of "us versus them" antagonism, stylizing and miniaturizing human and political conflict (Fig. 13.1).

In the 1950s the most dangerous stadium for referees was that of Napoli, first in the old Vomero ground and later at the new San Paolo. In a few cases, there were mass pitch invasions, and referees were forced to flee for their lives. In November 1955, Napoli's opponent was Bologna. The referee was Mario Maurelli, and Napoli was cruising to victory at 3–0 with

Fig. 13.1   Achille Lauro enters Napoli's stadium, 1950s (Photo credit: Archivio Riccardo Carbone, Naples)

15 minutes left. Bologna made a great comeback, however, and snatched a draw with a last-minute penalty. Immediately after the penalty was taken, Maurelli blew the final whistle. At that point, the crowd invaded, chasing the referee, who locked himself in the dressing room. Later, the Bologna players were also besieged inside their hotel.

Napoli's punishment was a four-game home ban. Lauro backed his own supporters, transferring the battle on the pitch into a political battle between "us and them," the North and the South. He sent the team to Bari—their next opponent—for a political demonstration as well as for a match. "The walls of the city [Bari]," a journalist wrote, "were covered by posters invoking the unity of all Southerners against the arrogance and the oppression of Northerners." Meanwhile, Lauro went to Milan, to face the governing board of the FICG (Italian Soccer Federation). In a dramatic press conference, he complained about Bologna's penalty and waxed lyrical about his city, justifying the riot. After a brief survey of Neapolitan history, Lauro called for professional and/or foreign referees. It later turned out that the Mayor had seen little of this with his own eyes, as he had left 15 minutes from the end, with Napoli 3-0 up.

Neapolitans very much liked Lauro's protest and requests. Nobody else had been so enthusiastic and dedicated in defending "the interests and the honor" of Naples. His prestige grew. The FIGC confirmed the ban. At Napoli's home game, following the end of the ban, similar incidents exploded, which led to yet another ban. Lauro and his followers put the blame on not well-identified "agents" paid by "enemies." Who were the enemies?

> Lauro does not explain [who are the enemies]; it is enough to throw this around those quarters where his faithful live. His appeal to Neapolitans to get the Vomero stadium open...conjured up the atmosphere of the 1940–43 war. He invited Neapolitans to be on the lookout for and to unmask the agents of the Enemy.[19]

To bolster his image as an outsider, distanced from the men and mindset of old-style Italian politics, Lauro very carefully gauged the different layers that were to make up his public image. Emphasis was given in turn to his qualities as a self-made man, as a successful businessman, as the head of a journal (*Roma*) able to break the "Northern" monopoly in both journalism and soccer and as an entertainment impresario. In this narrative, a hybrid of political and sporting (soccer) language was developed. Emphasizing his role as chairman of Napoli and the publicity this afforded, Lauro adopted a communication register comprising a wide mix of symbolic signifiers taken from the most diverse sources. Sports stylemes were constantly reiterated as part of a two-pronged strategy: first, the need to keep ever-present in the public mind the most effective image of a leader who won every contest he entered, and, second, the plan to remodel the symbolic forms of political consensus, introducing new forms of electorate motivation and loyalty based on the model of soccer competition whose matrix was that of opposing sides confronting one another.

Other forms of contamination between soccer and politics were subsequently to appear, such as the element of the challenge. The element of *challenge* is a first ingredient of the hybridization of politics and sport, to a certain extent recalling the "political athleticism"[20] and the transfer of the sports competition matrix to the domain of politics. Lauro's electoral campaigns made reference to political athleticism directly, as a metaphor for the *topos* of the titanic *challenge* he had tackled. This construction was couched in the appropriate mythical narrative context such as the voyage of the Argonauts, David and Goliath, the labors of Hercules and even the *chanson de geste*, and it became part of a state-of-the-art manipulative strategy.[21] His autobiography published in 1958 titled *La mia vita, la mia battaglia* [My Life, My Battle] intentionally, and clumsily, mimicked Hitler's *Mein Kampf.*[22]

The classical rhetoric of athleticism was also part of this communication strategy. He was careful to release pictures of himself engaged in keeping physically fit and leading a healthy lifestyle. The light in his office was constantly on—as Mussolini—as a sign of his tireless, almost superhuman will to work, act, watch over and secure the fate of Neapolitans while they were sleeping. His sexual appetite was proverbial. A blue-eyed man of medium height, always well dressed and perfumed, Lauro was an unrepentant ladies' man. He successfully juggled two parallel families. His long-suffering first wife, Angelina, gave him three children, while Jolanda, his "official" mistress, gave him a son. He broke up with Jolanda to date Eliana Merolla, a beautiful young actress 50 years his junior, whom he married when he was 83, after Angelina's death.

In many ways, Lauro can be considered as an example of one of the *innovative leadership* categories described by the social psychologist Howard Gardner, a leader able to *tell an innovative and clear story.*[23] With Lauro, the *story* narrated by the man himself and by the imposing media and propaganda machine he owned told of a successful businessman, not part of the close-knit, family dynasties that made up Italian capitalism, who, to avert the possibility of "communism" from coming to power and the menace coming from "Rome" (the epitome of the oppressive, centralizing nation-state and national politics), had decided to sacrifice his own economic livelihood and enter the political arena by forming a *rassemblement,* to the supreme benefit of citizens, the "every-man." The narration emphasized several key features: the self-made man; the person who started from nothing and yet achieved the highest prizes in whatever endeavor he took on; the personal sacrifice made for the common good of Neapolitans and Southerners; the threat to community from Communist forces, from the disorder of republican parties, from Rome and the North; the wholly new type of political venture; and, especially, the equation made between the Christian Democratic party (the dominant party) and the impersonal Power (the system of intrigue, corruption, and exploitation of the old politics to the detriment of the "every-man").

A well-established tradition in philosophy and sociology, from Blaise Pascal to Umberto Eco, summons us to treat sporting events and mass gatherings (generally speaking) with great caution, and to define their primary function as something which deflects attention away from essential matters, rather than expressing them. We are told we are dealing with the opium of the people, popular entertainment which helps blur people's perception of their place in society and of their everyday problems, both as individuals and as a group, a fleeting and illusory sense of unanimity which mask tensions and conflicts of everyday life, the manipulation of the masses, compensatory fantasies. This reading seems quite appropriate to define Lauro and his system of power. The argument is that soccer is a valuable political tool. The related argument is that the mobilization of football for social and political purpose is the exclusive preserve of powerful individuals, or states.

Yet this narrative risks considering soccer fans only as ignorant fools, or easily manipulated dupes. To be sure, Lauro used soccer to achieve political power; however, the popularity of the sport affected the extent to which his message was perceived by the public and, indeed, shaped his political adventures. In short, the story of Lauro cannot be confined to a top-down process, and to a reductive reading of soccer as a political weapon. Is it possible to advance the hypothesis that if Neapolitans loved these events and loved Lauro first as chairman of Napoli and later as mayor of Naples, this was not only because they wanted to win a (futile) game, but because a profoundly significant game was being played out on the field, which intensified and enacted fundamental values of a historical period. Soccer became a worldview.[24] Can we deal with a football match as Clifford Geertz does with cockfighting in Bali, considering it as "deep play," a sort of meta-social comment, a philosophical dramatic tale, producing emotions with cognitive purpose?[25] And what were the values and emotions at the stake in those years?

If soccer fascinated Neapolitans, it was due first and foremost to its capacity to represent their uncertainty in years of great transformation. World War II had left a legacy of civil war and bitter contrasts. The political transition from monarchy to republic had not undermined the symbolism and prestige of the House of Savoy in the Italian South. The roots of monarchism in Naples, after all, relied on a centuries-old belief, founded on an earlier historical reality, that the monarchy meant work, subsidies, public assistance and public spectacles. The Neapolitans were not prepared to exchange monarchist beneficence for the abstract ideal of the Republic. In addition, the economic miracle of the 1950s entailed deep transformation in society and in the beliefs and behavior of individuals. To this uncertainty, Neapolitans opposed the "us versus them" mentality epitomized by a soccer match and emphasized by Lauro. "Them" stood for the enemy, for the Northerners and—with the Cold War at its peak—for Communists. To this uncertainty, combined with the feeling of being oppressed from Rome and the North, Neapolitans opposed the reassertion of their local identity. They perceived Napoli (the team) as a symbol of a specific mode of collective existence, and not as a simple arbitrary sign of a common identity. Jeppson and all the other Neapolitan players in the Lauro years became soccer freedom fighters for the downtrodden, rebellious Neapolitans, embodying their desire for revenge, symbolizing a South that did want not to be exploited politically, culturally, economically subjugated by the North, forgotten by Rome and by the new Republic.

Underlining their status as forgotten, national outcasts, the support for Naples meant questioning whether it was really worth supporting republican Italy. Neapolitans did not abandon their nation; and yet their support of Napoli clashed with national identity underlying a, at times, conflicting idea of national identity. In a nation-state built upon diversity, such as language, region, geography, history—and in a city left after World War II by the central government and by the dominant party to its fate, as a body incurable, supposedly genetically unable to change its historical trajectories—soccer became a way to express an alternative identity, and otherwise unspeakable values and political views.

Hands Over the City

Lauro and his administrations have frequently been criticized for the building speculation in Naples during the boom years of the 1950s and for the corruption this led to, famously depicted in the 1963 cinematic masterpiece *Le mani sulla città* [Hands Over the City] by director Francesco Rosi. The movie overlooked the complicity of Christian Democrats, as well as the complicated legislation of postwar Italy in the field of town planning.

It also overlooked that only in the years *after* the reign of Lauro did speculation and devastation take off. Quite likely, these were conscious choices. A close look at historical fact reveals the inaccuracy of Rosi's indictment.

In 1952, Lauro decided on the withdrawal of the 1946 master plan inspired by the town-planning assessor Luigi Cosenza (an architect and a member of the Communist Party), as "not corresponding" with the new administration's programs. Lauro announced the need for a new plan that would transform Naples into "the garden of Europe on the sea."[26] Despite the injunction of the Minister of Public Works to adopt a new plan in 1954, Lauro let three years pass before appointing the committee responsible for drafting it. The activity in the building sector rose well above that authorized in earlier plans, and, in less than 20 years, the city became a mass of concrete and was effectively disfigured.

Laurismo rested on the development of the "housing bloc" (*blocco edilizio*), a socioeconomic alliance across classes formed as a result of the postwar economic growth that fulfilled the particular pressing social need for the reconstruction of the city. The political success of *Laurismo* was due to the fact that city building speculation furnished a sufficiently large domain to benefit all strata of Neapolitan society, which were also supporters of Naples soccer: profits for builders and developers—and in particular for those bricklayers who became *palazzinari* (shady property developers), fees for professionals (lawyers, architects and engineers), bribes for local government officials, wages for skilled and unskilled workers. The mirage of a home also mobilized large sectors of the middle classes, and even larger sectors of the working classes and poor people.

The speculation was also a result of the complicity of the administrative courts, as well as of central government. In 1953 two decisions of the Council of State allowed the Lauro administration to ignore the 1939 master plan then in force. The 1958 plan drafted by Lauro—later defined "an hallucinatory program of exploitation"[27]—was approved by his successor (the prefectorial commissioner appointed by the DC in 1958). It was only in April 1962 that the Higher Council of Public Works finally rejected the 1958 plan. These combined events opened the way to real and more devastating estate speculation. But here we are in a post-Lauro era of the prefectorial commissioners (1958–1962), followed by the period of DC mayors' (five succeeded each other in 12 years), who conceived the administration as an intermediary organism for distributing public funds.[28] In the period 1951–1960, 11,500 planning permissions were granted while the real estate patrimony increased by some 300,000 rooms. The *lottizzazioni*[29] granted in the period 1951–1960 amounted to 1,989,144 cubic meters. In the following post-Lauro period *lottizzazione* amounted to 10,905,510 cubic meters.[30]

Where were the Communists? In the narrative of *Hands Over the City*, Communists were the fiercest opponents of the building speculation. Indeed, it was only in the post-Lauro period that Communists engaged in a harsh and uncompromising anti-speculation campaign. In the 1950s Communists were not environmentalists. Their major concerns were agrarian reform, the battle against clericalism and NATO, and the movement called "Rinascita del Sud," a call for public works and investments in the South. In 1957 Communists voted in favor of the budget prepared by Lauro and Gerardo Chiaromonte attacked the central government that had stopped the funding of the Special Law and sent two inspectors to investigate how Naples was administrated without defining the timeline of the inspection.[31] Perhaps as a consequence of the symbolic impact of *Hands Over the City*, the Neapolitan left has constantly claimed an important role in the end of the reign of Lauro. Yet, *Laurismo* ended when Christian Democracy changed its strategy.

CONCLUSION: LAURO AND "MODERNITY"

Percy Allum's classic study on Naples has used Tönnies's *Gemeinschaft-Gesellschaft* formulation to account for Naples's apparently anomalous relationship with modernity.[32] He argues that the residual hallmarks of a feudal–monarchical social system and the persistence of familist relations had stifled the emergence of a modern society based around collective (working-class) interests and organized action. The economy, social practices and ideals of the inhabitants of the "casbah" in the old city reflected a static, pre-modern world. Here the boundary between the public and private was blurred and collective, impersonal ties were practically non-existent. Instead, life was dominated by the closed, communal structure of the "slum economy" in which everyday survival revolved around minor remunerations, favors and social allegiances. In this narrative, Lauro and its political style are the epitome of a pre-modern world, and of the typical and traditional patron–client relationship. The most colorful and undisputed example of slum economy were the now notorious incidents of the elections when voters for Lauro candidates received one shoe before the voting and the other afterwards.

Yet, Allum's narrow model, which has been followed ever since almost uncritically, does not capture the contradictions and complexity of *Laurismo* and therefore obscures a fuller and more complex comprehension.[33] To be sure, ignoring reason over spectacle and speculation, *Laurismo* had limits and tragic consequences. Yet, as this essay has attempted to show, it was the highest moment of the Right in power. Likewise, it was a political populist experiment mixing residuals of the past, as well as features of an open, full-fledged—although controversial, and sometimes devastating—modernity, including a relationship between mass and leader based on the symbolic power embedded in soccer, and the overwhelming significance of visibility and communication.

NOTES

1. John Foot, *Calcio: A History of Italian Football* (London: First Estate, 2006).
2. On this see Simon Martin, *Football and Fascism: The National Game under Mussolini* (Oxford/New York: Berg, 2004).
3. Bill Murray, *The World's Game: A History of Soccer* (Chicago: University of Illinois Press, 1996), 65.
4. In the following, sections, "Napoli" will indicate the soccer team, "Naples" the city.
5. When not otherwise specified, the following sections are based on Rosario Forlenza, *Le elezioni amministrative della Prima repubblica: Politica e propaganda locale nell'Italia del secondo dopoguerra, 1946–1956* (Rome: Donzelli, 2007), 143–156.
6. On this see Percy Allum, *Politics and Society in Postwar Naples* (Cambridge: Cambridge University Press, 1973), 307–308.
7. Sandro Setta, *L'Uomo Qualunque, 1944–1948* (Rome-Bari: Laterza, 2005).
8. Quoted in Simon Martin, *Sport Italia: The Italian Love Affair with Sport* (London/New York: IB Tauris, 2011), 145–146.
9. On this see his speech to the town council (August 11, 1956) in Archivio di Stato di Napoli, Prefettura di Napoli, Gabinetto, III versamento, b. 1916.
10. For example, see the police report of June 9, 1952, in Archivio Centrale dello Stato, Ministero dell'Interno, Atti di Gabinetto, Relazioni, b. 217, f. 13096.

11. See Paolo Braghin, ed. *Inchiesta sulla miseria in Italia 1951–52. Materiali della Commissione Parlamentare* (Turin: Einaudi, 1978).

12. Michele Tito, "I misteri di Napoli," *Il Mondo* 5, no. 4 (January, 24, 1953): 4.

13. Anna Maria Ortese, *Il mare non bagna Napoli* (Milan: Adelphi, [1953] 1994), 67.

14. Francesco Compagna, "Le amministrative del 1956." *Nord e Sud* (June 1956), now in idem, *Lauro e la Democrazia Cristiana* (Naples: Opere Nuove, 1960), 15–19: here 15–16.

15. Abdon Alinovi, "Il voto di Napoli." *Cronache meridionali*, 3, no. 6 (June 1956): 395–404: here 395–96.

16. See "Marotta risponde a Marco Ramperi," *Roma*, (September 29, 1955); see also a series of articles by Malaparte published in *Il Tempo* in 1955 quoted in Enrico Falqui, ed. *Battibecco 1953–1957* (Florence: Vallecchi, 1967), 403, 406, 412.

17. Rosario Forlenza, "A Party for the Mezzogiorno: the Christian Democratic Party, Agrarian Reform and the Government of Italy." *Contemporary European History* 19, no. 4 (2010): 331–349.

18. Carl Schmitt, *Begriff des Politischen* (Munich: Denker & Humboldt, 1932).

19. Emilio Speroni, "Pochi goal, pochi voti," *L'Espresso* 2, no. 9 (February 26, 1956) 15.

20. John M. Hoberman, *Sport and Political Ideology* (Austin: University of Texas Press, 1984).

21. Murray Edelman, *The Symbolic Uses of Politics* (Urbana: University of Illinois Press, 1964).

22. Achille Lauro, *La mia vita, la mia battaglia* (Naples: Editrice Sud, 1958).

23. Howard Gardner, *Leading Minds* (New York: Basic Books, 1995), 42.

24. Christian Bromberger, "Football as World-View and as a Ritual." *French Cultural Studies* 6 (1995): 293–311.

25. Clifford Geertz, "Deep Play: Notes On the Balinese Cockfight," in *The Interpretation of Cultures* (New York: Basic Books, 1973), 412–453.

26. See Lauro's speech for the 1952 elections as reported by *Il Mattino*, February 2, 1952.

27. Vezio De Lucia, *Se questa è una città* (Rome: Editori Riuniti, 1992), 14.

28. On the continuity in the town-planning policies between Lauro and the DC see Percy Allum, "The Politics of Town Planning in Post-War Naples." *Journal of Modern Italian Studies* 8, no. 4 (2010): 500–527 (esp. 507–508).
29. *Lottizzazione* is an intensive urban development where vast tracts of land are parceled out and all the parcels are used only for buildings.
30. Vezio De Lucia, *Napoli. Cronache urbanistiche 1994–1997.* (Milan: Bastaldi & Castoldi, 1998), 59.
31. Quoted in Pierluigi Totaro, *Il potere di Lauro: Potere e amministrazione a Napoli, 1952–1958* (Salerno: Laveglia Editore, 1990), 96.
32. Allum, *Power and Society.*
33. See, for example, John Foot, *Winning at All Costs: A Scandalous History of Italian Soccer* (New York: Nation Books, 2007), 362–64.

WORK CITED

"Achille Lauro a L'Aquila auspica una grande destra nazionale," *Roma*, (October 14, 1956).
"Lauro a Piaggio," *Roma*, (April 22, 1957).
"Travolgente discorso di Lauro a Bari. Sotto i segni di 'Leone e Corona' per le maggiori fortune della Patria," *Roma*, (April 9, 1956).
Alinovi, Abdon. "Il voto di Napoli". *Cronache meridionali* 3, no. 6 (1956, June): 395–404.
Allum, Percy A. *Politics and Society in Postwar Naples.* Cambridge: Cambridge University Press, 1973.
———. "The Politics of Town Planning in Post-war Naples". *Journal of Modern Italian Studies* 8, no. 4 (2010): 500–527.
Braghin, Paolo, ed. *Inchiesta sulla miseria in Italia 1951–52. Materiali della Commissione Parlamentare.* Turin: Einaudi, 1978.
Bromberger, Christian. "Football as World-View and as a Ritual". *French Cultural Studies* 6 (1995): 293–311.
Compagna, Francesco. *Lauro e la Democrazia Cristiana.* Naples: Opere Nuove, 1960.
De Lucia, Vezio. *Se questa è una città.* Rome: Editori Riuniti, 1992.
———. *Napoli. Cronache urbanistiche 1994–1997.* Milan: Baldini & Castoldi, 1998.
Edelman, Murray. *The Symbolic Uses of Politics.* Urbana: University of Illinois Press, 1964.

Falqui, Enrico, ed. *Battibecco 1953–1957*. Florence: Vallecchi, 1967.

Foot, John. *Calcio: A History of Italian Football*. London: First Estate, 2006.

———. *Winning at All Costs: A Scandalous History of Italian Soccer*. New York: Nation Books, 2007.

Forlenza, Rosario. *Le elezioni amministrative della Prima repubblica: Politica e propaganda locale nell'Italia del secondo dopoguerra, 1946–1956*. Rome: Donzelli, 2007.

———. "A Party for the Mezzogiorno: The Christian Democratic Party, Agrarian Reform and the Government of Italy". *Contemporary European History* 19, no. 4 (2010): 331–349.

Gardner, Howard. *Leading Minds*. New York: Bask Books, 1995.

Geertz, Clifford. "Deep Play: Notes on the Balinese Cockfight. In *The Interpretation of Cultures*, 412–453. New York: Basic Books, 1973.

Hoberman, John M. *Sport and Political Ideology*. Austin: University of Texas Press, 1984.

Lauro, Achille. *La mia vita, la mia battaglia*. Naples: Editrice Sud, 1958.

Le dichiarazioni programmatiche del Sindaco Achille Lauro: Napoli 26 gennaio 1953. Naples: Francesco Giannini e Figli, 1953.

Martin, Simon. *Football and Fascism: The National Game Under Mussolini*. Oxford/New York: Berg, 2004.

———. *Sport Italia, the Italian Love Affair with Sport*. London/New York: IB Tauris, 2011.

Murray, Bill. *The World's Game: A History of Soccer*. Chicago: University of Illinois Press, 1996.

Ortese, Anna Maria. *Il mare non bagna Napoli (1953)*. Milan: Adelphi, 1994.

Schmitt, Carl. *Begriff des Politischen*. Munich: Denker & Humboldt, 1932.

Setta, Sandro. *L'Uomo Qualunque, 1944–1948*. Rome-Bari: Laterza, 2005.

Speroni, Emilio. "Pochi goal, pochi voti". *L'Espresso* 2, no. 9 (1956, February 26): 15.

Tito, Michele. "I misteri di Napoli". *Il Mondo* 5, no. 4 (1953, January 24): 4.

Totaro, Pierluigi. *Il potere di Lauro: Potere e amministrazione a Napoli, 1952–1958*. Salerno: Laveglia Editore, 1990.

CHAPTER 14

The Politics of Football in Post-colonial Sierra Leone

Tamba E. M'bayo

I would like to stress that without the commitment and the money of governments, African football would be unable to accomplish its very congested schedule. Football and politics can and should work together. This has been prove[n] in 2011. Issa Hayatou, President of CAF (Issa Hayatou, "Editorial: Football and Politics can Work Together," *CAFOOT* 95 [January 2012], 1).

Sierra Leone, like Ghana, was one of several British West African colonies where British seamen and colonial officials introduced football (soccer) in the late nineteenth and early twentieth centuries. By the first half of the twentieth century, football was gaining popularity in Freetown, the capital city, where British and Sierra Leonean civil servants, company officials, and soldiers played matches to foster good relations and camaraderie. Likewise, students, faculty, and staff of institutions such as Fourah Bay College (later the University of Sierra Leone) and the Church Missionary Society Grammar School (later Sierra Leone Grammar School) in Freetown played football regularly as part of their sports program. Today, however, unlike Ghana that has represented Africa in the FIFA Football World Cup competitions at both senior and junior levels, Sierra Leone's "soccerscape" has been dysfunctional for

T.E. M'bayo (✉)
Department of History, West Virginia University, Morgantown, WV, USA

© Hofstra University 2017
B. Elsey, S. Pugliese (eds.), *Football and the Boundaries of History*,
DOI 10.1057/978-1-349-95006-5_14

the best part of its postcolonial existence since independence in 1961.[1] Paradoxically, even with the myriad problems associated with "professional" football in contemporary Sierra Leone, it is by far the country's most popular sport and an important facet of the cultural and socioeconomic lives of the people.

This chapter argues that despite producing gifted football players such as Ismael Dyfan (1956–2001), Brima "Mazolla" Kamara, and Mohammed Kallon, among others, Sierra Leone's progress in football has been mired by political wrangles, financial mismanagement, myopic leadership, and conflicting personal agendas among officials of the Sierra Leone Football Association (SLFA) and politicians. Since appearing at the Confederation of African Football (CAF) Africa Cup of Nations tournaments in Tunisia in 1994 and South Africa in 1996, Sierra Leone's development in football has stagnated, if not receded. Although its civil war (1991–2002) disrupted the growth of football in the country, Sierra Leone's regression in the sport has been due mainly to the misplaced priorities of government officials rather than structural damages resulting from the war.

Against this backdrop, this chapter investigates Sierra Leone's football malaise in the postcolonial period using the intersection of sports and politics as a frame of reference. It first provides a brief background about the introduction of football in Sierra Leone and its growth during the colonial period. The chapter then moves forward into the postcolonial period to explore the state of football in the country, highlighting the paradox that typifies its stature as a national pastime with socioeconomic import for ordinary Sierra Leoneans and its politicization as officials of SLFA and politicians jockey for institutional control over the sport. The final section of the chapter juxtaposes the country's football misadventure with Ghana's progress as a football powerhouse.[2] Through this comparative approach the chapter aims to locate the case of Sierra Leone in both a wider West African and a global context. In so doing it brings the literature on the politicization of football in Africa into conversation with the literature on Africa and global football through two intertwined questions: (1) How do we account for the paradox football in Sierra Leone embodies: its stature as a national pastime and unifier yet afflicted with a chronic leadership crisis, corruption, and stunted development? (2) With more Sierra Leonean footballers playing in Europe and other parts of the world than ever before, how do we assess the impact of globalization on the country's "soccerscape"?

The empirical evidence on which this chapter relies is drawn mainly from the historical literature on football in Africa, Sierra Leonean and international newspapers, information from FIFA and CAF accessed online, and interviews and informal conversations with ex-players and fans of Sierra Leone's national football team, the Leone Stars. Archival holdings on football in Sierra Leone during the colonial period are few and far between, while those covering the postcolonial period are mostly official records, minute books, and correspondences FIFA and CAF have stored intermittently since SLFA became an affiliate of both organizations in 1967.

Even so, the dearth of archival records does not explain why historians and other scholars who study Sierra Leone have yet to recognize the cultural and socioeconomic importance of sports, particularly football, in the country. Indeed, it is ironic that while "scholarly articles, books, and postgraduate theses on the socioeconomic, cultural, historical, and political significance of sport in African societies"[3] have been increasing during the last three decades, Sierra Leone has hardly received any serious attention from scholars about its sporting culture. By contrast, the country's civil war and related issues have dominated recent academic studies and literary and popular works.[4]

This chapter therefore sets the tone for redressing the lacuna on sports culture in Sierra Leone's historiography. For this purpose the chapter takes its cue from studies on the politicization of football in Africa, particularly the works of Wiebe Boer, Paul Darby, Laura Fair, and Hamad Ndee (on Nigeria, Ghana, Zanzibar, and Tanzania, respectively), to name but a few, which have employed sports to elucidate wider political, social and cultural currents that shape African societies.[5] Together, these studies reveal the complex relations between sports and sports organizations on the one hand and formal political structures and the state apparatus on the other. Likewise, the cultural and social history of organized sports in Africa underscores football's significance as a platform for players, fans, and elites to manifest their identities, challenge and negotiate between various actors, and facilitate better understanding of themselves and others.[6] This chapter, then, draws attention to yet another sports ground of contestation, that is, postcolonial Sierra Leone, where football and politics have intersected with far-reaching outcomes.

THE BIRTH OF A PASTIME:
FOOTBALL IN COLONIAL SIERRA LEONE

Africanist football historian Peter Alegi has attributed the introduction of modern sports, especially football, in sub-Saharan Africa to the British after the late-nineteenth-century conquest of the continent by European powers.[7] In major port cities such as Freetown (in Sierra Leone) and Cape Coast (in Ghana or Gold Coast, as it was known), British nationals and West Africans played football during the early colonial period. In Sierra Leone, Freetown's natural harbor, which could berth large oceangoing vessels, was a regular port of call for British and other European seamen, whose pastime included football, gambling, drinking, and courting local prostitutes in bars and hotels on the waterfront of Freetown.[8] In Ghana, British seamen introduced the sport in Cape Coast, which soon became a springboard for spreading football to other cities such as Accra and Sekondi on the coast and Kumasi in the interior.[9] A common sight in these colonial settlements was British sailors and officials and other European nationals playing football whenever they were free from official duty. Even with the racist ideology that underpinned colonial relations, football matches occasionally involved teams with Europeans and Africans playing together or against each other. Likewise, spectatorship at such matches, largely comprising indigenous people, belied the racial divide that typified colonial societies in Africa. In this context, football victories for Africans against Europeans, as Fair observes in her study on colonial Zanzibar, meant much more than simply a sporting issue; it symbolized their future aspiration and determination to continue their struggle for liberation.[10] Darby amplifies this point by suggesting that whereas it would have taken time for Africans to rectify the economic and political inequities European colonialism thrived on, football provided an immediate outlet for demystifying the presumed racial superiority of Europeans.[11]

With the construction of railways in Sierra Leone in the early twentieth century, football spread into the interior and gradually became a popular leisure activity among boys and young men. Railway towns soon emerged as sites of both commercial exchanges and cultural dissemination, with football as a core component. Such towns attracted players interested in the game as well as spectators from nearby villages and other towns where football had yet to gain popularity. This meant players and spectators often had to travel several miles by foot to play or watch football matches in the mushrooming railway towns. Two such towns that began to attract football enthusiasts in their respective districts were Bo in southern Sierra Leone and Kenema in the eastern part of the country. With the construction of more roads in rural areas, a similar growth continued in other provincial towns like Makeni (in the north) and Koidu (in the east), the center of diamond mining in the country.[12]

Football was also popular among colonial military and police forces as well as administrative officials. With time, army championships and "national" competitions spread steadily throughout West Africa, with colonies like Nigeria and Ghana competing at a level that ignited intense "nationalistic" fervor among spectators. After World War II, returning Sierra Leonean soldiers who had served the British army in Southeast Asia, particularly Burma, took up football as their favored sport while "sitting in limbo" awaiting their pensions and demobilization.[13] The teams selected to play often represented the different battalions the ex-servicemen had served in during the war. Within the police force, the teams were drawn from various units such as the Criminal Investigation Department (CID), the traffic unit, and the legal and justice department. Other government departments arranged football matches on public holidays, on a special day in honor of a visiting dignitary and for pick-up teams among employees.

Meanwhile boys in both Christian missionary and government schools engaged in competitive football competitions featuring different teams. As Alegi observes, "Mission schools and government schools made sport into an important meeting ground for Western and indigenous cultures."[14] In Sierra Leone, as in other British West African colonies, sports and physical education were an important element of the curriculum in schools such as the CMS Grammar School, Albert Academy, Saint Edward's Secondary School, and Prince of Wales Secondary School, all in Freetown. Alongside football, cricket and athletics featured prominently in the sports programs of the schools. For students of these schools, as James Mangan recollects from a former student, "games were compulsory...we played cricket in the dry season, and football in the rainy season....[And] there were competitions for the house shields in cricket, football, and athletics, including cross-country training."[15]

In colonial Sierra Leone, then, the situation Ossie Stuart describes about football in Africa during the colonial period is only partially correct. According to Stuart, "Soccer remained an activity of the privileged throughout the colonial period. First, it was found in the elite African schools and later in the towns. Soccer never became a universal sport in colonial Africa. Those who played the game were always the fortunate few in societies where the vast majority of people could afford neither to feed their children, nor educate them."[16] Contrary to Stuart's view, however, the popularity of football in Sierra Leone during the colonial period (and in the postcolonial period) was due mainly to its non-elitist appeal insofar as both the urban and rural poor could play the game without spending too much money on footballs, footwear, and jerseys.[17] In fact, playing football barefooted was more or less the norm in most towns and villages at the time. This trend continued into the postcolonial era when football grew immensely popular among underprivileged youth and school drop-outs in urban areas, especially Freetown, in sharp contrast to cricket that most Sierra Leoneans considered (and still do to some extent) an elite sport.

In this context, Paul Richards' description of the state of football in postwar Sierra Leone could well have been that of the 1950s: "The interest of Sierra Leonean youth in soccer crosses most social divisions in the country. Rich and poor, Muslims and Christians, women as well as men, all enjoy the game. Soccer pitches are found in the remotest villages as well as in urban areas. The game can be (and is) played by barefoot enthusiasts on the roughest of pitches, with a minimum of facilities (rag balls if need be, and bamboo sticks for goals)."[18] Although it took time for football to spread across Sierra Leone during the colonial period, its popularity had much to do with the fact that very little to no money was needed for young boys and men to participate in it. In addition, even as women's football was uncommon at that time football matches for boys and young men attracted their fair share of enthusiastic female spectators who competed with opposing camps in cheering for their respective teams.

Indeed, "professional" football did not exist in Sierra Leone during the colonial period; however, a number of teams in Freetown played competitive football in a league format.[19] Some teams such as the Ports Authority Football Club, the Railway Games Club, and the Prisons Football Club represented government departments. Other clubs formed by a small group of people or an individual from a particular neighborhood or section of town identified with the locality where the bulk of their fans resided. Football clubs such as Kingtom Rovers and East End Lions, for example, had the core of their fan base from Kingtom in the northwestern and eastern neighborhoods of Freetown, respectively. Still, other clubs like Mighty Blackpool and Arsenal borrowed their names from English football clubs, possibly convinced that such familiar names from abroad would garner support for the local clubs. Blackpool, the earliest football club in the country, started as Saco FC founded in 1923.[20] This was followed by East End Lions FC, which came into existence five years later in 1928. The two oldest football clubs would develop a rivalry that is still unlike any other in Sierra Leone. More football clubs emerged in the post-World War II period as the sport continued to attract more players and spectators, especially in Freetown and regional centers such as Bo, Kenema, and Makeni.

During this period a number of Lebanese/Syrian businesspersons and their families began to get involved in football by providing financial support for the struggling clubs, a trend that would continue well into the postcolonial period.[21] A Lebanese merchant, Billy Bamin, founded Arsenal FC of Freetown in 1958.[22] He, like others of the Lebanese community, had a long history of involvement in trade in Sierra Leone since the beginning of the twentieth century. The earliest Lebanese in the country were mostly petty traders who sold trinkets, tobacco, candies, and similar merchandise. By the 1930s, when diamonds were discovered in Kono, in eastern Sierra Leone, some Lebanese had accumulated enough capital to get involved in the diamond trade. Others managed wholesale and retail stores that dealt with assorted goods ranging from foodstuff to clothing and automobile spare parts. Involvement in commerce allowed some successful Lebanese to bankroll football teams of their choice. Among prominent Lebanese families were the Ahmed, Bahsoon, Basma, Hassaniyeh, Khadi, and Sasso families, who were not only keen football patrons and fans, but they also had children (at times with indigenous women) who played for school football and club teams. In Bo, the Mattar family, another family of Lebanese descent, was well known for promoting football in the southern part of the country.[23] And in the diamond-mining district of Kono, Lebanese families like the Hejazi and Fawaz played a prominent role in sponsoring football clubs.

The increasing economic disparity between the affluent Lebanese and the rest of the population caused resentment among Sierra Leoneans toward the wider Lebanese merchant community from time to time. Some of the richest Lebanese in Kono such as Henneh Shamel, for example, would use their wealth to gain favors from the political elite. Shamel hailed from the Shi'ite Shamel family in South Lebanon. As early as 1936 the family had slightly over 1000 men employed in the diamond and gold mines of Sierra Leone, where illicit mining was (and still is) the order of the day. The close ties between Lebanese merchants/traders and politicians provided a reason for Sierra Leoneans to believe that there was a conspiracy between their leaders and the Lebanese to fleece the nation.[24] In any case, with the introduction of full-blown party politics and general elections in the postcolonial period, the patron–clientele relationship in football would mutate into a politicized and more virulent variety. Lansana Gberie remarks: "Siaka Stevens, who became prime minister (later president) in 1967, became the embodiment of this elite, making the country's large Lebanese merchant community part of his charmed circle and his partners in criminalizing the diamond industry."[25] Even with concerns about the dubious role of the Lebanese merchant community in the country's political economy, however, football fans generally welcomed money their Lebanese patrons provided for football clubs and players.

Earlier, in the late colonial period, meanwhile, a footballing tradition involving schools grew as teams from various institutions competed with each other in inter-school football competitions. Other than schools in Freetown those in the interior of the country organized similar competitions, most times comprising schools in the same administrative district. Some schools like the Bo Government Secondary School (Bo School) and Christ the King College (CKC), both in southern Sierra Leone, produced outstanding football players, who were coveted by schools in Freetown in order to reinforce their teams. In some instances even when such players lacked competitive academic records they were admitted just because of their "football intellect." Such discretionary accommodation had the unintended effect of reinforcing the idea that football and excellent academic performance were incompatible, a perception parents often invoked to discourage their sons from taking football too seriously as a potential profession. Even so, several school teams were feeders for football clubs like Old Edwardians, Regent Olympic, and Saint Anthony's FC playing in the first division league in Freetown. Fans of these clubs were typically students of the schools (Saint Edward's Secondary, CMS Grammar School, and Saint Anthony's Primary School, respectively), their parents, alumni, and/or those affiliated with the institutions one way or another (teachers, staff, auxiliary personnel, and so on). With a bigger fan base and wealthier patrons, clubs like Blackpool and East End Lions often recruited players whose formative years started with school teams in Freetown, Bo, Kenema, Koidu, and Makeni. Across the country, then, well before the end of the colonial period in 1961, football had become the foremost sport even as cricket attracted a cross section of spectators in Freetown and other urban areas, where school cricket teams competed with each other for trophies donated by an alumnus or a similar patron.

THE PARADOXES OF SIERRA LEONE'S POSTCOLONIAL FOOTBALL MISADVENTURE

It was not until Sierra Leone's independence from Britain was looming that SLFA, the country's football governing body, came into being in 1960. Yet it would take another seven years before the association joined FIFA and CAF in 1967. At a time most newly independent African countries were eager to validate their autonomy and promote nationalism, Sierra Leone joined the founding members of CAF, namely, Egypt, Ethiopia, South Africa, and Sudan, as well as other countries, among them Ghana, which was already cultivating a reputation as a competitive footballing nation.[26] But if Sierra Leone was aspiring to emulate the early success of the Black Stars of Ghana, its record in international football during the next two decades after joining CAF was far from impressive. In fact, the country's northern neighbor, Guinea, far less accomplished than Ghana in footballing terms, produced a competitive national football team *Syli Nationale* (National Elephant) and clubs such as Hafia and Horoya that were more successful than the Leone Stars and clubs from Sierra Leone during the 1970s. *Syli Nationale* reached the final of the African Nations Cup tournament in 1976 and afterward advanced to the quarterfinal stage in three successive tournaments (2004, 2006, and 2008).[27] By contrast, the Leone Stars only qualified for the continental tournament for the first time in 1994 (in Tunisia) and reappeared two years later in South Africa for the 1996 tournament. In both competitions, however, Sierra Leone was eliminated after the first round. Still, it was during this period that the country achieved its highest FIFA ranking ever—51st.[28]

Back in the 1970s, victory for the Leone Stars against teams from Guinea, Ghana, Nigeria, and Liberia was not guaranteed even when playing international football matches on home turf at the Brookfield's Stadium (later renamed Siaka Stevens Stadium and then National Stadium) in the west end of Freetown. Occasional victories against these teams, however, were enough for Sierra Leoneans to erupt in frantic celebrations, encouraging many to believe that the country was ready to compete with the best teams continent-wide. Such optimism notwithstanding, however, qualification for the African Cup of Nations would continue to elude the Leone Stars until the 1990s, as indicated above. In his tribute to the late Edward Keister (1940–2014), who played for Sierra Leone and End End Lions in Freetown, Sierra Leonean journalist Leeroy Kabs Kanu lamented the country's plight in football: "The only reason that Sierra Leone did not win laurels in those days [1970s] was that soccer was not financed or supported and we did not have world-class coaches to train these stars to give their maximum input."[29] Kabs Kanu's comment resonates with public discourse in Sierra Leone about the dysfunctional state of football in the country.

Always cash-strapped and unable to build a healthy financial base to take care of its responsibilities, SLFA could not invest money in the development of football at any level in Freetown, the capital city, let alone towns in the interior of the country. Nor could the government, which never ranked sports high enough in its list of priorities to allocate money for football's improvement, do any better. Most teams competing in domestic leagues across the country, even when representing a government department, had to depend on the patronage of individuals or families, usually Lebanese businesspersons and/or their Sierra Leonean descendants, for financial support. Mighty Blackpool, Santos (later named Bolton, then Freetown United), Old Edwardians, Diamond Stars of Kono, and Kamboi Eagles of Kenema were all beneficiaries of financial backing from such families. When Mighty Blackpool emerged as successive league and FA Cup champions in the 1960s and early 1970s, a Lebanese merchant, Adib Basma, was the club's financial provider. In 1978, the most prominent Lebanese business tycoon, the late Jamil Sahid Mohamed, a close confidant of the then President of Sierra Leone, Siaka Stevens, took over a newly promoted team from the second division (Republicans) and formed Sierra Fisheries Football Club, named after his (Mohamed's) fishing company. About the same period, another team, Real Republicans, an offshoot of Kingtom Rovers, benefitted from the financial support of an indigenous Sierra Leonean Police Commissioner, the late Bambay Kamara.[30]

Since most football clubs operated on a tight budget, their priority was to remain afloat rather than to invest money in long-term youth development programs. The absence of well-organized and sponsored youth football programs meant those aspiring to become football players had to learn their craft playing "street football" and/or in "neighborhood leagues," often bankrolled by private individuals. Among the most popular neighborhood leagues in Freetown were "Parade" in central Freetown, Fourah Bay and Cline Town, both in the east end of the city, where a number of would-be national football players honed their skills during their teens. Similar leagues existed in major towns in the interior of the country. At best, then, youth development in football was nothing more than a number of privately sponsored teams in a neighborhood competing against each other.

It is hardly any surprise therefore that Sierra Leone had its first football academy only in 2007, when the Welsh international footballer, Craig Bellamy (played for Manchester City, Liverpool and Cardiff), founded the Craig Bellamy Foundation in Freetown as his contribution to the country's post-civil war reconstruction effort.[31] In an interview with Sierra Leonean journalist, Edward Kargbo, in 2011, Bellamy affirmed: "This [the academy] has solely been my money. It is not for me, it is about giving kids the same opportunity I had."[32] He added that the project cost him close to a million British pounds ($1.6 million). Many Sierra Leonean football fans believe Bellamy's initiative is the kind their government, in consultation with SLFA, should have taken decades ago to nurture the country's young and talented footballers.

Sierra Leone's standout football players during the 1970s included Kama Dumbuya, Amadu Kargbo, Kawuta Dumbuya, Christian Cole, Bai Kabia, Edward Keister, Patrick Kemokai, and Chico Cole. Most of these players, however, did not play football on a full-time basis. If at all employed, they were often government employees in low-ranking positions with their meager monthly salary as their main source of income. Due to their limited education and lack of any marketable skills besides football, they were employed mostly as drivers, security personnel, police officers, soldiers, and so on. At a time footballers in the country seldom earned enough from their full-time jobs to look after their financial responsibilities, it was the norm for them to depend on money from Lebanese and other patrons before and/or after football matches (an incentive for the teams). Players of a victorious club often embarked on a "collection tour," a day after defeating a rival football club in a match. Lebanese and local merchants/traders received the players at their stores in the central and eastern parts of Freetown and presented cash gifts not considered part of the official budget of the clubs. Many players used such cash handouts to cover their monthly rents for housing, transportation, and meals for their families. Patrons who owned bars and restaurants often obliged with drinks and food to celebrate a victory.

By the early 1980s another cohort of younger and even more talented players had emerged. Among them were Kolleh Dumbuya, Obi Metzger, Ismael Dyfan, Sento Johnson, Joseph Toby, Brima "Mazolla" Kamara, and John Agina Sesay. Besides Dyfan who played for foreign clubs in Côte d'Ivoire and Egypt, a few of this new crop of players also plied their trade outside Sierra Leone. Mazolla preceded Dyfan in playing for Africa Sports d'Abidjan in Côte d'Ivoire, John Agina Sesay had a short stint in Gabon, and Leslie Allen played for Dragons of Benin. Musa Kallon, the elder brother of Sierra Leone's most famous player, Mohamed Kallon, also played for Union de Douala and Racing de Bafoussam in Cameroon. Yet the only player among this group who played professional football in Europe was an East End Lions striker, Gbassay Sesay, whose career reached its peak when he signed a contract with Vitória Setúbal of Portugal from 1992 to 1994.[33]

By the late 1980s and early 1990s, football scouts from Europe were visiting West Africa (and other parts of the continent) to hunt for talented young players for recruitment by European clubs. This would initiate an exodus of players from Sierra Leone, most notably Ahmed Kanu, Mohamed Kallon, Lamin Conteh (Junior Tumbu), and Junior Parade, who headed to Belgium and later other countries in Europe (the Netherlands, France, Italy, and Sweden) in pursuit of professional football careers.[34] Intriguingly, even though Sierra Leone was a former British colony, most of the players heading to Europe at that time went elsewhere, unlike the situation in France, which was (and still is) home for a large number of football players from former French colonies, as Laurent Dubois' *Soccer Empire* reveals.[35]

Conversely, Sierra Leone had a long history of hosting "football mercenaries," most notably from Ghana, Guinea, and Liberia, who came to earn a living from playing football in Freetown and other parts of the country, especially Kono, Kenema, and Port Loko. Among the most prominent of these players were Thomas Ampomah, Ben Mortey, Atto Mensah, and Simon Awuah from Ghana; Musa Suma and Kollev Kamara from Guinea; Sie Vava George from Liberia; and Wasiu Summunu from Nigeria. It was also common for some Sierra Leonean players, such as Manneh Peters and Augustus Lawson, who had Liberian family ties, to play in Sierra Leone during a football season and then travel to Liberia at the end of the season to play for teams such as Barolle, Invincible Eleven, and Bame during the same year. At the end of the football season in Liberia, they returned to Sierra Leone and resumed playing for their previous clubs. At the time, official transfers between football clubs were not stringent, the football associations of both countries accepted the practice.

Fig. 14.1 Ready for the game to begin in Makeni, Sierra Leone, Craig Bellamy Foundation (Photo credit: Laura Cook)

In more recent years, with the injection of money from Europe for players recruited from domestic clubs in Sierra Leone, football has received much more attention than ever before from both officials of SLFA and politicians. The financial reward of the sport is now evident as players who have traveled abroad have been able to remit money back home for luxurious houses to be constructed for them. Among the trademark of success for many of these players are either a high-end four-wheel drive SUV or a sleek custom-built Mercedes Benz car equipped with the latest navigation and audiovisual gadgets available on the market. The accumulation of material wealth by this generation of footballers marks a departure in mindset from those of the 1970s, who maintained that they were playing football "for the love of the game." Significantly, playing football in Europe has allowed several Sierra Leonean footballers to break free from the vicious circle of poverty that had characterized their playing days back home. They can now afford to provide decent homes for their families, meet their financial responsibilities, and improve their quality of life. At the same time, the flaunting of newfound wealth by foreign-based players, football officials, and politicians in Sierra Leone has intensified their struggle in a desperate bid to control the sport at all levels. In their view, this would increase their stake in the financial benefit that accrues to local clubs and players when one of them signs a contract with a European club.

Although the growing interest of European clubs in players from Sierra Leone and other countries in Africa has had a debilitating effect on most domestic leagues on the continent, it has also motivated individual football players to work harder with the hope that European scouts might spot them.[36] For most of these players who come from poverty-stricken families with no proper educational background, they see football as their only hope for the future even as the grim reality is that only a few among the very best will ever become successful professional footballers abroad.

While the national league in Sierra Leone nowadays attracts far less spectators than the English Premier League, La Liga in Spain, and the Bundesliga in Germany available via satellite TV, football is a thriving business in the country with local firms and wealthy entrepreneurs taking advantage of its popularity to promote their businesses. Sponsorship of football clubs, billboards, advertising in stadiums, TV and radio commercials are all outlets for bringing more visibility to privately owned and corporate enterprises in the country. It is indeed ironic that while SLFA and past and present governments in Sierra Leone have done little to invest money in the development of football over the years, the sport is now generating revenue on an unprecedented scale in the history of the country. Little wonder then that officials of SLFA and politicians have been vying with each other to assert more control over the administration of football with a view to benefitting more directly from its financial inducement. This desire to micromanage the financial feeders, especially from abroad, has been the bane of politicizing football in Sierra Leone.

SIERRA LEONE'S FOOTBALL UNDERDEVELOPMENT AND GHANA'S FOOTBALL DEVELOPMENT

In March 2004, the then Minister of Sports in Sierra Leone, Dr. Dennis Bright, expressed frustration over the state of football in the country. He voiced his anger in a blunt manner: "The people of Sierra Leone and the footballers have been deprived of their favorite sport for too long and it is now time for me to take action."[37] The problem the minister referred to was the long-standing impasse between football club officials and executive officers of SLFA over when to convene the association's annual August congress for 2003. SLFA called for a postponement while football clubs demanded that the meeting go ahead immediately, as there were pressing issues and key decisions pending. Still, SLFA refused to budge and insisted that it would not meet until early in 2004. To compound the problem, in February 2004, a high court judge in Freetown ruled that the congress be delayed further.[38]

The crux of the matter was that the retiring president of SLFA, Justice Tholla Thompson, who had been head of the association since 1996, favored his vice president, Joseph S. Kelfala, to succeed him. Meanwhile, the relationship between football clubs in Freetown and those in the interior of the country (Bo, Kenema, Koidu, and Makeni) was far from being amicable. The latter felt that their Freetown counterparts had always sought to marginalize them when it came to decision making about football in the country. As such, representatives of the provincial clubs rejected the suggestion by Freetown clubs that the executive led by Tholla Thompson be dissolved and an interim body formed to oversee the congress. As the secretary-general of the Freetown-based clubs (Council of Clubs), Foday Turay, emphasized: "We do not recognize the Justice Tholla Thompson-led executive because they can't function constitutionally and we'll never kick football again under them."[39] But Brima Jalloh, the public relations officer of one of the district football clubs, Wusum Stars, pointed out that the Freetown clubs had often acted in bad faith, believing that they were better than clubs from the interior of the country (not only in football terms, he insinuated). While denying this accusation, representatives of the Freetown clubs retorted that the provincial clubs were only supporting the current executive because they wished Mr. Kelfala to become the first official from the provinces to head SLFA.

With the national football league in Sierra Leone suspended for about eight months because none of the feuding parties was willing to give in, the Minister of Sports attempted on several occasions to resolve the problem, but failed. Dr. Bright himself was aware that FIFA did not entertain the idea of politicians interfering in football matters: "FIFA may say politicians are not allowed to interfere in football but I think the point has come for me to act because the game has been paralyzed due to infighting."[40] Still, the minister, like most football-loving Sierra Leoneans, had become disillusioned about SLFA's perennial problems, which over the years had been manifested in incompetent leadership, personal vendettas, and financial mismanagement, all to the detriment of football in the country. While Dr. Bright himself may not have had a ready solution to all SLFA's problems, it was clear from his words that something drastic needed to be done, and immediately, to restore at least a semblance of order in the country's football administration.

The problem described above is symptomatic of the state of football in contemporary Sierra Leone. Not surprisingly, the country's national team has failed to qualify for all major competitions since 1996. One problem after another has hampered the development of football in Sierra Leone. Although the country's civil war disrupted and almost paralyzed most activities in the country, the regression in football has been due mainly to the misplaced priorities of government officials rather than structural damages resulting from the war. The catalog of problems with football administration in Sierra Leone has not only preceded the civil war, but it has also outlived it.

Undeniably, a few Sierra Leoneans have invested money in football clubs in the country in recent years in an effort to improve the quality of the domestic leagues. Mohamed Kallon, the ex-Inter Milan and Monaco player, for example, now owns FC Kallon (previously Sierra Fisheries FC), which plays in the national league and has produced a number of players for the country's national team, the Leone Stars. Likewise, the current President of SLFA, Mrs. Isha Johansen, who is married to a wealthy Norwegian entrepreneur and owner of a cement factory and other businesses in Sierra Leone, is proprietor of another football club FC Johansen.

Even as both Kallon and Mrs. Johansen have contributed significantly to developing football in postwar Sierra Leone, however, their personal ambitions also motivated them to run for the presidency of SLFA in 2013. Kallon was disqualified from the election on account of his failure to meet "residency requirements," while Mrs. Johansen received public support from the Minister of Sports, Paul Kamara, who got embroiled in a war of words with supporters of Kallon and two other disqualified candidates. The minister's involvement in the SLFA election debacle only fueled speculation about bribery and favoritism, especially as Mrs. Johansen's wealthy husband was behind her candidacy. Kallon minced no words in expressing his disappointment: "I'm very disappointed about the decision and I believe it was politically motivated because the Sports Minister Paul Kamara has publicly backed Isha. I know I'm qualified. I have given over 19 years of my life playing for Sierra Leone, spent a lot of cash on Kallon FC and helped to develop kids—more than 15 boys now have a career professional football abroad—and produced 80 % of the players now playing for Leone Stars, this is how they are paying me back."[41] In the end,

Isha Johansen was elected President of SLFA in an election in which she was the sole candidate.[42]

As one might expect, the Vice President of SLFA, former Sierra Leonean international footballer, Brima "Mazolla" Kamara, explained why he teamed up with Mrs. Johansen: "I believe in the leadership of Madam Johansen and I'm optimistic, she is a resilient woman with a vision that I admire so much. She is a visionary leader, passionate and above all patriotic; that's why we are giving her our utmost support in the drive to change the face of football in Sierra Leone."[43] Although it is too early to judge the new administration, recent events in Sierra Leone and results of the Leone Stars do not reflect the optimism and visionary leadership Mazolla alluded to in praise of Madam Johansen.

Among other issues, the country lost two games in a row in the qualifying campaign for the 2015 Africa Cup of Nations tournament in Equatorial Guinea. Following defeats by Côte d'Ivoire and the Democratic Republic of the Congo, the coach of the Leone Stars, Johnny McKnistry, from Northern Ireland, was dismissed. More perplexing for Sierra Leoneans, however, was the appointment of an ex-Leone Stars player, Ghanaian-born Atto Mensah, who has never before managed a club or a national team. According to Mohamed Fajah Barrie, a Sierra Leonean reporter for the BBC, "Mensah's appointment comes four months after sports minister Paul Kamara attempted to install him as coach of the national U-20 side, a move that was rejected by the Sierra Leone Football Association who favoured another coach."[44] Thus the obvious question is, Why did SLFA accept Atto Mensah's appointment as national team coach after it had rejected his appointment as coach of the national U-20 team? For most Sierra Leonean football fans and observers, in spite of Mensah's pedigree as a football player whose brilliance led to two championships for East End Lions FC in the 1980s, this is a step in the wrong direction. And it just confirms that no matter what vision sports officials and politicians might profess they have for the country they continue to take the populace for a ride, believing that once in office people are powerless to remove them. For all the talk about encouraging African coaches to head African national teams, the above-mentioned appointment in Sierra Leone hardly makes any sense, a situation very much unlike that in Ghana.[45]

Ghana's long history as a competitive football nation is well known among football fans in Africa. The Black Stars, the country's national football team, won the African Cup of Nations trophy at two consecutive tournaments in 1963 and 1965. In the 1963 final in Accra, the Ghanaians defeated their Sudanese counterparts 3-0. Then in the 1965 final in Tunis the Black Stars beat the Tunisian national team 3-2. Although the Ghanaians did not win the 1968 tournament held in the Ethiopian capital of Addis Ababa, they reached the final and lost narrowly to the Democratic Republic of the Congo (Congo Kinshasa at the time), 1-0. Thereafter, after winning the African Cup of Nations trophy in 1978 and 1982, the Black Stars went through a dry spell without winning any major trophies, while the Indomitable Lions of Cameroon emerged as the main flag bearers of Africa at the 1990 World Cup in Italy.

At the time, the Ghanaian sports commentator, Ben Dotsei Malor, remarked that Ghana's past successes were now mere "memories," because other African nations had eclipsed the West African nation.[46] Among the various reasons provided to explain Ghana's decline in football during the late 1980s and 1990s was "government complacency," referring to the failure of successive administrations to invest money in football, which only compounded the deteriorating sporting facilities in the country, a situation that bears some similarities to the scenario in present-day Sierra Leone.

When the government of President John Jerry Rawlings launched its "Soccer Recovery Program" in an attempt to rescue Ghanaian football from sinking further into an abyss, it did not yield immediate results. Despite parading illustrious footballers like Abede Pele Ayew, Anthony Yeboah, and Nii Odartey Lamptey, Ghana could not qualify for the 1990 World Cup Finals. Two years later, the Black Stars lost the final of the 1992 African Cup of Nations to Cote d'Ivoire, a defeat Ghanaian football fans found particularly difficult to swallow as it came from a neighbor. Ghana also failed to qualify for the 1994 World Cup Finals in the United States, while another archrival, Nigeria, enjoyed the honor of being one of Africa's representatives. Meanwhile, however, Ghana's youth teams were making tremendous strides as they excelled in the Scotland Under-16 competition in 1989, then at the 1992 Olympics in Barcelona with an Under-23 team that won a bronze medal, and then the 1993 Under-17 Championship in Australia, where the team was runners-up. By all indications it was becoming clear that Ghana's investment would pay off in the long term.

Today, Ghana's football fortune at both the junior and senior levels has changed for the better. (Fig. 14.1) Since 2006 the Black Stars have qualified for every World Cup competition, with the 2010 tournament in South Africa their best ever performance, when they reached the quarterfinal stage. Although Ghana was eliminated in the group stage of the 2014 World Cup, FIFA's most recent ranking puts the country at 33rd in the World Ranking list and 3rd in Africa.[47] Moreover, the Ghanaian Under-20 team won the 2009 FIFA Under-20 Championship, defeating Brazil 4-3 in a penalty shootout.

It is safe to conclude that such impressive results were not achieved by merely paying lip service to sports and youth development in Ghana. Rather, the evidence indicates that deliberate planning focused on long-term goals should be the way forward for any African country serious about developing football and other sports. The case of Ghana demonstrates that Sierra Leone, especially sports officials and politicians, could learn from thinking beyond selfish ends and clamp down on financial misappropriation and vindictive boardroom power struggles, as evidenced by the recent SLFA presidential election. Football then should be a unifier rather than a political weapon used against those who dare to challenge the status quo.

CONCLUSION

Despite the optimism expressed by the President of CAF, Issa Hayatou, in 2012 that football and politics can work together,[48] the case of Sierra Leone (and several other countries in Africa) reveals quite the contrary. Football and politics have been strange bedfellows in the West African nation, where Sierra Leoneans' love of the game has remained steadfast even as sports officials and politicians have shown little interest in developing football in the name of national interest. Today, despite experiencing one of Africa's most gruesome civil wars, the love of football continues to bind Sierra Leoneans together regardless of ethnic differences, political orientation, gender, and socioeconomic status. Ironically, however, the Leone Stars and football clubs in the country have never won any major continental trophy in Africa. And it has never qualified for the FIFA World Cup tournament. For youth competitions, the country's best achievement was a runner-up position in the 2003 African Under-17 Championship in Swaziland. The team thus qualified for the FIFA Under-17 Championship in Finland, only to finish last in a group comprising Spain, the United States, and South Korea.

All this then suggests that the country's postcolonial developmental path in football has been erratic at best. Of course, it would be unfair to suggest that Sierra Leone should pour a huge chunk of its limited resources into the development of football in the country, especially considering that it is "already burdened by the demands of reconstruction and rebuilding the lives of [its] citizens."[49] Still, football's significance for Sierra Leoneans extends beyond the merely sporting; it plays a pivotal role in the socioeconomic and cultural lives of its inhabitants. For millions, it is a symbol of hope for poor people, whose interests successive governments in the postcolonial era have not taken seriously. Yet with more and more young footballers getting the chance to play abroad, a lifeline has been handed to the "wretched of the earth" living in the slums of Freetown and impoverished communities in the interior of the country, who see the game as a means of transforming their lives from abject poverty to unexpected riches. But with sports officials and politicians often embroiled in bitter vendettas in order to assert more control over football governance in the country, corruption and its related vices—nepotism, embezzlement, grafting, and smear campaigns—now have a guaranteed place in contemporary Sierra Leonean sports discourse. This, obviously, trumps any spirit of national reconstruction that might have emerged in the aftermath of the country's brutal civil war. Ossie Stuart summed it up best when he stated: "Success on the sports field and national progress are inseparable, which means that soccer failure can very quickly be perceived as political failure. The reverse may also be true."[50]

NOTES

1. "Soccerscape" is a term borrowed from the title of Peter Alegi's book on Africa's role in the globalization of soccer. See Alegi, *African Soccerscapes: How a Continent Changed the World's Game* (Athens: Ohio University Press, 2010).
2. Ghana participated in the 2014 World Cup tournament in Brazil and was eliminated after the first round of the competition. In the previous 2010 World Cup tournament held in South Africa, Ghana progressed to the quarterfinal stage before being eliminated by Uruguay in a penalty shootout.
3. Paul Darby, "'Let us Rally around the Flag': Football, Nation-Building, and Pan-Africanism in Kwame Nkrumah's Ghana," *The Journal of African History* 54, no. 2 (July 2013): 223.
4. See, for example, Ibrahim Abdullah, "Bush Path to Destruction: The Origin and Character of the Revolutionary United Front (RUF/SL)," *African Development* 22, no. 3/4 (1997): 45–76;

Jimmy D. Kandeh, "Ransoming the State: Elite Origins of Subaltern Terror in Sierra Leone," *Review of African Political Economy* 81 (1999): 349–66; Paul Richards, "West-African Warscapes: War as Smoke and Mirrors: Sierra Leone 1991-2, 1994-5, 1995-6," *Anthropological Quarterly* 78, no. 2 (Spring 2005): 377–402; Ernest Cole, *Theorizing the Disfigured Body: Mutilation, Amputation, and Disability Culture in Post-Conflict Sierra Leone* (Trenton: Africa World Press, 2014); Aminatta Forna, *The Devil That Danced on the Water: A Daughter's Quest* (New York: Grove Press, 2003).

5. Darby, "Let us Rally around the Flag"; Wiebe Boer, "Football, Mobilization and Protest: Nnamdi Azikiwe and the Goodwill Tours of World War II," *Lagos Historical Review* 6 (2006): 39–61; Laura Fair, "Kickin' It: Leisure, Politics and Football in Colonial Zanzibar, 1900s-1950s," *Africa* 76, no. 2 (1997): 224–51; Hamad Ndee, "Sport, Culture and Society from an African Perspective: A Study in Historical Revisionism," *International Journal of the History of Sport* 13, no. 2 (1996): 192–202.

6. Ibid.

7. Alegi, African Soccerscape, 1–13.

8. Graham Greene's fascinating novel, *The Heart of the Matter*, set in Freetown during World War II, provides a glimpse of the seedy lives of European expatriates in West Africa. See Greene, *The Heart of the Matter* (London: Heinemann, 1948).

9. Alegi, African Soccerscape, 1–13.

10. Fair, "Kickin' It."

11. Darby, *Africa, Football, and FIFA: Politics, Colonialism, and Resistance* (Portland: Frank Cass, 2002).

12. Diamonds featured prominently as one of the root causes of the conflict, attracting both scholarly and general public attention. See Ian Smillie, Lansana Gberie, and Ralph Hazleton, *The Heart of the Matter: Sierra Leone, Diamonds and Human Security* (Ottawa: Partnership of Africa, 2000); John L. Hirsch, *Sierra Leone: Diamonds and the Struggle for Democracy* (Boulder: Lynne Rienner Publishers, Inc., 2001); William P. Murphy, "Military Patrimonialism and Clientalism in the Liberian and Sierra Leonean Civil Wars," *African Studies Review* 46, no. 2 (December 2003): 61–87.

13. David Killingray, *Fighting for Britain: African Soldiers in the Second World War* (Suffolk: James Currey, 2010); Adrienne M. Israel,

"Measuring the War Experience: Ghanaian Soldiers in World War II," *The Journal of Modern African Studies* 25, no. 1 (March 1987): 159–68.

14. Alegi, African Soccerscapes, 9.
15. James A. Mangan, "Ethics and Ethnocentricity: Imperial Education in British Tropical Africa," in *Sport in Africa: Essays in Social History,* eds. William J. Baker and James A. Mangan (New York: Africana, 1987), 148, cited in Alegi, *African Soccerscapes,* 10.
16. Ossie Stuart, "The Lions Stir: Football in African Society," in *Giving the Game Away: Football, Politics and Culture on Five Continents,* ed. Stephen Wagg (London: Leicester University Press, 1995), 24–51, here 28.
17. Informal interviews with four Sierra Leonean football fans including octogenarian Edward Swarray, living in Lansing, MI. Swarray reminisced about his boyhood playing days while growing up in Pujehun, a town in southern Sierra Leone, close to the Liberian border. The other three interviewees, Patrick Boyenneh, Sahr Jusu, and Sahid Sesay, range in age from 36 to 45 (March 2014).
18. Paul Richards, "Soccer and Violence in War-Torn Africa: Soccer and Social Rehabilitation in Sierra Leone," in *Entering the Field: New Perspectives on World Football,* eds. Gary Armstrong and Richard Giulianotti (Oxford: Berg, 1997), 141–158, here 150.
19. Today, the country has a national league that comprises teams from not only Freetown, but also Bo, Kenema, Koidu, and Makeni.
20. The change of name by Saco FC to Blackpool FC was in part due to the immense popularity of the Blackpool and England player Sir Stanley Matthews (1915–2000), who helped his club win the English FA Cup in 1953. In 1954, Blackpool of Freetown became Mighty Blackpool.
21. For more on the Lebanese in Sierra Leone, see Martin H. Y. Kaniki, "Attitudes and Reactions Towards the Lebanese in Sierra Leone During the Colonial Period," *Canadian Journal of African Studies* 7, no. 1 (1973): 97–113; H. L. van der Laan, *The Lebanese Traders in Sierra Leone* (The Hague: Mouton, 1976).
22. Leeroy Kabs Kanu, "Yes, Sierra Leone too had Arsenal 'The Gunners' Before, and They Were One of the Giants of Our Soccer," *Cocorioko Newspaper,* June 23, 2013.
23. Ibid.

24. As Gberie explains, "Shamel became involved in diamond smuggling in the 1950s, and was a supporter of Siaka Stevens, an up-and-coming political leader. By the time Stevens became Prime Minister of the country in 1967, however, he had fallen out with Shamel, and in 1969, after armed robbers purloined $3 million worth of diamonds at Hastings Airport, Shamel was arrested and charged with the theft. In January 1970, a judge dropped the charges against Shamel, but Stevens had him deported anyway." Lansana Gberie, "War and Peace in Sierra Leone: Diamonds, Corruption and the Lebanese Connection," *The Diamond and Human Security Project, Occasional Paper #6,* November 2002, 12.

25. Ibid, 6.

26. Founded in 1957, CAF rescinded South Africa's membership in 1958 and banned the country from participating in all CAF-organized competitions due to the country's apartheid policy. With apartheid starting to crumble in the early 1990s, however, CAF readmitted South Africa in 1991. Five years later, in 1996, South Africa hosted and won the Africans Nations Cup for the first time in its history. In the case of Sierra Leone, by the time it became a member of CAF Ghana had already won the Africa Cup of Nations trophy twice, in 1963 and 1965. The Black Stars would go on to win the competition again in 1978 and 1982.

27. In September 2014, Guinea was 48th in FIFA's World Ranking list and 9th in Africa. http://www.fifa.com/worldranking/ranking-table/. Accessed 1 Sept 2014.

28. Ibid. FIFA ranked Sierra Leone 75th in the world and 17th in Africa.

29. Leeroy Kabs Kanu, "Obituary: The Death of a Soccer Legend, Edward Keister," *Cocorioko International Newspaper,* March 26, 2014. http://cocorioko.info/?p=7967, Accessed 23 June 2014.

30. Kabs Kanu, "Sierra Leone's Leone Star, " *Sierra Leone Football,* September 10, 2014: 1. http://sierraleonefootball.com/index.php?option=com_content&view=article&id=145:leone&catid=1:latest-news. Accessed 15 Aug 2014.

31. Edward Kargbo, "Craig Bellamy: The Man in Love with Sierra Leone," *New African* August/September 2011, 102–103.

32. Ibid.

33. Gbassay Sesay featured for the Leone Stars at the 1994 and 1996 African Nations Cup tournament in Tunisia and South Africa, respectively.

34. After playing with Reggina and Inter Milan in Italy and Monaco in France, Mohamed Kallon had a short stint in the United Arab Emirates before returning to Sierra Leone in 2009. He is now proprietor of a football club, FC Kallon, which plays in the national league in Sierra Leone.

35. Laurent Dubois, *Soccer Empire: The World Cup and the Future of France* (Berkeley: University of California Press, 2010).

36. Stephen Wagg, *Giving the Game Away: Football, Politics and Culture on Five Continents* (London and New York: Leicester University Press, 1995); Darby, Africa, Football and FIFA.

37. Mohamed Fajah Barrie, "Sierra Leone Crisis Continues," *BBC Sport: African Football*, March 16, 2004, http://news.bbc.co.uk/sport2/hi/football/africa/3517536.stm. Accessed 2 August 2014.

38. Ibid.

39. Ibid.

40. Ibid.

41. Mohamed Fajah Barrie, "Mohamed Kallon Disqualified from Sierra Leone FA Elections," *BBC Sport: African Football*, July 29, 2013, http://www.bbc.com/sport/0/football/23490525. Accessed 2 Aug 2014.

42. Mohamed Fajah Barrie, "Johansen Confirmed as SLFA President," *BBC Sport: African Football*, August 3, 2013, http://www.bbc.com/sport/0/football/23560252. Accessed 2 Aug 2014.

43. Abu Bakarr Kamara, "Brima Mazolla Kamara: A Veteran International with a Difference," *Sierra Leone Football Association*, August 30, 2014, http://www.slfa.sl/news-article/brima-mazolla-kamara-veteran-international-difference. Accessed 11 Sept 2014.

44. Mohamed Fajah Barrie, "Atto Mensah appointed Sierra Leone Coach," *BBC Sport: African Football*, September 18, 2014, http://www.bbc.com/sport/0/football/29257379. Accessed 19 Sept 2014.

45. At the time of writing, a press release from SLFA on September 29, 2014, rejected Atto Mensah's appointment as national coach of the Leone Stars. According to SLFA, "despite several reminders to

both Mr. Mensah and the Ministry of Sports, SLFA has not received any evidence of Mr. Atto Mensah's coaching credentials (B-Coaching License). http://www.slfa.sl/news-article/press-release-slfas-decision-new-appointments. Accessed 16 Nov 2014.
46. Ben Dotsei Malor, "Focus on Africa 2.3," *BBC Magazines*, July/ September, 1991.
47. See http://www.fifa.com/associations/association=gha/. Accessed 19 Sept 2014.
48. See note 1 above.
49. Kabs Kanu, "Sierra Leone's Leone Star."
50. Stuart, "The Lions Stir," 38.

WORK CITED

Abdullah, Ibrahim. "Bush Path to Destruction: The Origin and Character of the Revolutionary United Front (RUF/SL)." *African Development* 22, no. 3/4 (1997): 45–76.

Alegi, Peter. *African Soccerscapes: How a Continent Changed the World's* Game. Athens: Ohio University Press, 2010.

Barrie, Mohamed Fajah. "Sierra Leone Crisis Continues." *BBC Sport: African Football*, March 16, 2004. http://news.bbc.co.uk/sport2/hi/football/africa/3517536.stm. Accessed 2 Aug 2014.

———. "Mohamed Kallon Disqualified from Sierra Leone FA Elections." *BBC Sport: African Football*, July 29, 2013. http://www.bbc.com/sport/0/football/23490525 Accessed 2 Aug 2014.

———. "Johansen Confirmed as SLFA President." *BBC Sport: African Football*, August 3, 2013. http://www.bbc.com/sport/0/football/23560252. Accessed 2 Aug 2014.

———. "Atto Mensah Appointed Sierra Leone Coach." *BBC Sport: African Football*, September 18, 2017. http://www.bbc.com/sport/0/football/29257379. Accessed 19 Sept 2014.

Boer, Wiebe. "Football, Mobilization and Protest: Nnamdi Azikiwe and the Goodwill Tours of World War II." *Lagos Historical Review* 6 (2006): 39–61.

Cole, Ernest. *Theorizing the Disfigured Body: Mutilation, Amputation, and Disability Culture in Post-Conflict Sierra Leone.* Trenton: Africa World Press, 2014.

Confederation of African Football (CAF). http://www.cafonline.com/association/sierra-leone/information. Accessed 24 May 2014.

Darby, Paul. *Africa, Football, and FIFA: Politics, Colonialism, and Resistance.* Portland: Frank Cass, 2002.

————. "Let Us Rally Around the Flag': Football, Nation-Building, and Pan-Africanism in Kwame Nkrumah's Ghana." *The Journal of African History* 54, no. 2 (July, 2013): 221–246.

Dubois, Laurent. *Soccer Empire: The World Cup and the Future of France.* Berkeley: University of California Press, 2010.

Fair, Laura. "Kickin' It: Leisure, Politics and Football in Colonial Zanzibar, 1900s–1950s." *Africa* 76, no.2 (1997): 224–251.

Fédération Internationale de Football Association (FIFA). http://www.fifa.com/associations/association=sle/index.html. Accessed 24 May 2014.

Forna, Aminatta. *The Devil That Danced on the Water: A Daughter's Quest.* New York: Grove Press, 2003.

Gberie, Lansana. *War and Peace in Sierra Leone: Diamonds, Corruption and the Lebanese Connection. The Diamond and Human Security Project, Occasional Paper #6*, 2002, November.

————. *War and Peace in Sierra Leone: Diamonds, Corruption and the Lebanese Connection.* Ottawa: Partnership Africa Canada, 2002.

Greene, Graham. *The Heart of the Matter.* London: Heinemann, 1948.

Hayatou, Issa. Editorial: Football and Politics Can Work Together. *CAFOOT* 95, 2012, January.

Hirsch, John L. *Sierra Leone: Diamonds and the Struggle for Democracy.* Boulder: Lynne Rienner Publishers, Inc., 2001.

Israel, Adrienne M. "Measuring the War Experience: Ghanaian Soldiers in World War II." *The Journal of Modern African Studies* 25, no. 1 (March, 1987): 159–168.

Kabs Kanu, Leeroy. "Yes, Sierra Leone Too Had Arsenal 'The Gunners' Before, and They were One of the Giants of Our Soccer." *Cocorioko Newspaper*, June 23, 2013.

————. "Obituary: The Death of a Soccer Legend, Edward Keister." *Cocorioko International Newspaper,* March 26, 2014. http://cocorioko.info/?p=7967. Accessed 23 June 2014.

————. "Sierra Leone's Leone Star." *Sierra Leone Football*, September 10, 2014. http://sierraleonefootball.com/index.php?option=com_content&view=articl e&id=145:leone&catid=1:latest-news. Accessed 15 Aug 2014.

Kamara, Abu Bakarr. "Brima Mazolla Kamara: A Veteran International with a Difference." *Sierra Leone Football Association*, August 30, 2014. http://www.slfa.sl/news-article/brima-mazolla-kamara-veteran-international-difference. Accessed 11 Sept 2014.

Kandeh, Jimmy D. "Ransoming the State: Elite Origins of Subaltern Terror in Sierra Leone." *Review of African Political Economy* 81 (1999): 349–366.

Kaniki, Martin H. Y. "Attitudes and Reactions Towards the Lebanese in Sierra Leone During the Colonial Period." *Canadian Journal of African Studies* 7, no. 1 (1973): 97–113.

Kargbo, Edward. "Craig Bellamy: The Man in Love with Sierra Leone." *New African* (August/September 2011): 102–103.

Killingray, David. *Fighting for Britain: African Soldiers in the Second World War.* Suffolk: James Currey, 2010.

Malor, Ben Dotsei. "Focus on Africa 2.3." *BBC Magazines,* July/September, 1991.

Mangan, James A. "Ethics and Ethnocentricity: Imperial Education in British Tropical Africa." In *Sport in Africa: Essays in Social History,* edited by William J. Baker and James A. Mangan, 172–195. New York: Africana, 1987.

Murphy, William P. "Military Patrimonialism and Clientalism in the Liberian and Sierra Leonean Civil Wars." *African Studies Review* 46, no. 2 (December, 2003): 61–87.

Ndee, Hamad. "Sport, Culture and Society from an African Perspective: A Study in Historical Revisionism." *International Journal of the History of Sport* 13, no. 2 (1996): 192–202.

O'Flaherty, Michael. "Sierra Leone's Peace Process: The Role of the Human Rights Community." *Human Rights Quarterly* 26 (2004): 29–62.

Richards, Paul. "Soccer and Violence in War-Torn Africa: Soccer and Social Rehabilitation in Sierra Leone." In *Entering the Field: New Perspectives on World Football,* edited by Gary Armstrong and Richard Giulianotti, 141–158. Oxford: Berg, 1997.

———. West-African Warscapes: War as Smoke and Mirrors: Sierra Leone 1991–2, 1994–5, 1995–6. *Anthropological Quarterly* 78, no. 2 (Spring, 2005): 377–402.

Sierra Leone Football Association (SLFA). http://www.slfa.1hwy.com/. Accessed 24 May 2014.

Smillie, Ian, Lansana Gberie, and Ralph Hazleton. *The Heart of the Matter: Sierra Leone, Diamonds and Human Security.* Ottawa: Partnership of Africa, 2000.

Stuart, Ossie. "The Lions Stir: Football in African Society." In *Giving the Game Away: Football, Politics and Culture on Five Continents,* edited by Stephen Wagg, 24–51. London: Leicester University Press, 1995.

van der Laan, H.L. *The Lebanese Traders in Sierra Leone.* The Hague: Mouton, 1976.

Wagg, Stephen. *Giving the Game Away: Football, Politics and Culture on Five Continents.* London/New York: Leicester University Press, 1995.

CHAPTER 15

The Competitive Party: The Formation and Crisis of Organized Fan Groups in Brazil, 1950–1980

Bernardo Buarque de Hollanda

A Character

Throughout the past century, many fans stood out in their clubs and gained notoriety in the eyes of their respective supporters. Since at least the 1930s, even before the founding of the official organized fans, there were supporters who were given nicknames such as "ambassadors" or "fan leaders." They were responsible for representing the whole crowd base at the stadium or even when traveling abroad. It was they who enthusiastically demonstrated the support for their teams, evidenced through proving their selflessness and self-sacrifice.

In Rio de Janeiro, some of them became known outside the stadiums, propelled by public opinion to be regarded as the most dedicated fans in the support of their clubs. They were recognized in the streets and often found frequenting common public sporting gathering areas, such as cafes, pubs and bars in Lapa, Flamengo, in the North Zone. Some of them have been forgotten over time, but many became a subject of journalistic record that now allows their names to be remembered. Here

B.B. de Hollanda (✉)
School of Social Sciences, Fundação Getúlio Vargas, São Paulo, Brazil

© Hofstra University 2017   295
B. Elsey, S. Pugliese (eds.), *Football and the Boundaries of History*,
DOI 10.1057/978-1-349-95006-5_15

are some of the notable names, with their nicknames from the stands: Domingos Ramalho, João de Luca and Tia Aida, from Vasco da Gama; Salvador Peixoto and Tolito, from Botafogo; Peitão and Guimarães, from Fluminense; Alfredo Pinto and Tia Helena, from Flamengo.

In the following decades after the construction of the Maracanã, there were six known fan leaders in the city; they were identified as legitimate leaders by their supporters: Jaime, from Flamengo; Dulce Rosalina, from Vasco; Paulista, from Fluminense; Tarzã, from Botafogo; Juarez, from Bangu; and Elias Bauman, from América. The biographical profile and social origins of the six leaders are expressive by the way in which the fan leaders represented the popular Brazilian classes of the time. They were leaders who had modest professional occupations and their social standing meant they often performed the most menial tasks. However, they managed to achieve certain fame through football, something similar to what happened with players from black and working-class backgrounds at the turn of the century.

This chapter examines one of these fan leaders, Jaime de Carvalho, founder of the Charanga, in 1942. This character's path can be considered paradigmatic, because it properly embodies those two dimensions associated with the origins of the organized supporter groups: the disciplinary and the festive sphere. Being a traditional reveler from dances in Largo do Machado, Jaime would not allow the use of swear words or fire in his group of fans. It was a personal characteristic, but it was shown through his charismatic leadership over the years in which he was in charge of the Charanga, imprinting upon the crowd a mark of order and family.

Jaime's importance was also concerned with his own projection, which he acquired between the 1930s and 1970s in Rio de Janeiro, during which time he was seen as a symbolic Flamengo supporter. He was a fairly prominent personality in town, appearing in newspaper photos and even in society columns. One final reason for choosing Jaime is because he was a fan leader to not only Flamengo fans. For years, he was the fan leader for the Brazilian National Team, a position that was recommended for him by the press and the authorities. The prominence of this job required him to travel abroad and represent Brazilian fans in countries in Europe and South America.

Due to the status that he acquired over time—that earned him special sympathy from columnists—it is possible to compile a larger amount of information about him, which is useful for reconstituting his biography. He was born on December 9, 1911, in the city of Vitória da Conquista,

South Bahia, Jaime's case was typical of a Northeastern emigrant who arrived in Rio de Janeiro, capital of the Republic, even in the 1920s. Over 35 years, Jaime de Carvalho divided his time between appointments with the federal civil service—he was a concierge agent of the Ministry of Justice since 1932—and his activities with the supporters' organization.

Journalists tell an anecdote about how he chose to become a Flamengo supporter and suggest a degree of randomness that would seal his destiny as a Flamengo supporter. In 1927, as newcomer to the Rio, he was a resident of the Catete neighborhood, where he lived in a room in a boarding house. When he was still without a team, but with a soft spot for Fluminense, he went to watch a training session at the Laranjeiras stadium. The club's gates were closed and Jaime decided to cross the street and head to the Flamengo pitch, which was on the corner of Rua Paissandu at that time. Since then, according to people from the time, he leaned toward Flamengo and became a fervent admirer of the club.

The narrative of his conversion, a typical description of a "origin myth," continued in accounts that describe the official founding date of his fan organization, ironically dubbed "Charanga" by Ary Barroso, on radio Tupi. During the1930s, Jaime had already become close to Flamengo, becoming a member and even oarsman of the club; it was because of this that he moved from the Flamengo neighborhood to the new headquarters in Gávea, in the vicinity of Lagoa Rodrigo de Freitas. While watching the training sessions and team games, in 1936, Jaime had already been recognized as one of the Flamengo fan "leaders," if newspaper reports at the *Fan's duel* during the Flamengo versus Fluminense game are to be believed.

However, for journalists, the founding dates to 1942, at the final of the Carioca championship that was also played at the traditional Fluminense stadium. The importance of the decision caused Jaime to mobilize his friend Manoel da Silva Jesuino in making a supporting banner for the team. In his house, already a Laranjeira resident, on vila da Rua Ipiranga (No. 44, house 9), Jaime and his friend painted the banner on a piece of mori fabric. With the cloth ready and painted, they took it into the Laranjeiras and put it in a position overhanging the railing, with the following inscription: "Onward, Flamengo!"

The idea spread relatively quickly, at least if we consider what unfolded for the club following the victorious campaign for the Championship on October 11, 1942. The title paved the way for the team to achieve its first triple-championship status in its history (1942–1943–1944) and for Jaime to consolidate the Charanga as the supporting band in the stadiums and for the post-match victory celebrations during marches in the streets, in parades on trams (1940s), or on buses (1950s and 1960s).

The crowd was composed of a group of percussionists who, while in possession of other instruments, particularly the trumpet, would support the team on the pitch with music from the stands. In addition to the musical orchestra, Jaime took the initiative to take the flag, one of the few existing at that time in the city. The stadiums, up until the Charanga existed, were used to waving handkerchiefs taken from the lapel. Another *charengueiro* innovation was to wear shirts that were identical to those being worn by the players on the pitch. This type of clothing was unusual for the more usual formal style of fans' clothing at the time and was a novelty.

The Charanga was therefore composed of a small orchestra, banner, flag and shirt. In the wake of the victories, a handful of fans not exceeding two or three dozen began to regularly attend Flamengo Carioca Championship football games in the 1940s. Its creation would inspire the other bands into existence, such as the one from Botafogo, between 1944 and 1949, led by Tolito. Some of them would be recognized through organized or uniformed fans, as was the case with Vasco fans. These, on March 7, 1944, would found the TUV, (Torcida Uniformizada Vasco) which would subsequently be called the TOV (Torcida Organizada Vasco) this being known by a banner with the altruistic inscription: "With Vasco wherever Vasco is."

Jaime's popularity expanded exponentially from the 1950s onward, with the creation of the Maracanã and with the World Cup being in Brazil. It is worth saying that since 1945 he went on to support the Brazilian national team in their games in Rio de Janeiro, the Charanga having regularly been invited to support the national squad. In 1950, such was the concern in projecting an image of a sensible country, the authorities delegated a good part of the responsibility for controlling the fans' behavior to Jaime de Carvalho. The organizers recognized the importance of a fan leader who would help the police chief to maintain good behavior on the part of the fans. One press campaign looked to highlight the inappropriate nature of throwing objects on the pitch and using profanities and recommended that fans arrive at the stadiums early so as to avoid problems in the entrances to the stands. With these aims in mind, the media gave a full endorsement to the Charanga, under the sponsorship of a clothing store, to advertise their activities, their preparations and their surprises for game days.

The public's peaceful reaction at the competition's final, after the unexpected defeat by Uruguay, earned the fans numerous praise, including from FIFA President Jules Rimet. At "home" the Brazilians had given a sporting lesson, showing how to lose like men and with patriotism.[1] Prior to this, the fans' creativity had already been emphasized in the match against Spain when, in the face of being embarrassingly routed by Spain with a six to one score line, there was a spontaneous outcry by the crowd who were chanting the carnival song "Bullfights in Madrid," composed by João de Barros in 1936, an ironic allusion to the debacle from the *fúria espanhola* (Spanish fury) that afternoon. Journalistic legend has it that, at the game, Braguinha became emotional and cried when he heard his song being sung by a crowd estimated to be around 200,000 people.

Jaime de Carvalho's success in terms of the fans' conduct would prove to be fruitful thereafter, with the inauguration of a cycle of international trips that started with the subsequent World Cup, in Switzerland, in 1954. After putting themselves in front of the crowd during the knockout stage of the World Cup, Didi and other members of the delegation, such as Flamengo players, Índio and Rubens, spoke in favor of the Charanga leader being present in Europe. With the request having been accepted, a campaign promoted by *Jornal dos Sports* and by a commercial establishment raised funds for the trip and granted Jaime not only the trip, but also the status of Brazilian supporter Ambassador.

Jaime left for the capital of Switzerland in June 1954, equipped with various pieces of paraphernalia, including 10 leather hides to produce Brazilian bass drums, 300 harmonicas, 2 sirens and a pair of musical symbols. The Brazilian squad's first game was marked by their entry in the pitch along with the Brazilian radio broadcasters. Jaime spread over the fence a green and yellow sign with "Forward, Brazil!" embroidered in white, an innovation in the international footballing environment.

In the same year of 1954, Jaime, then hailed as "the King of Fans," would participate in the South American Championship in Argentina. His wife, Laura de Carvalho, a Portuguese woman from Trás os Montes, whom he had met during a Carnival dance in Largo do Machado and married in 1936, would be responsible for making the biggest Brazil flag that had ever been made up to that time. The huge flag was eight meters in width and ten meters in length and was unfurled when the players came onto the pitch. The flag was completely homemade, dyed in old tin cans on a wood stove; using this immense flag would make it easy for the fans to identify themselves as being united from one country, a truly unusual showing for the time.

This traveling experience would become a reoccurring theme for Jaime over the decades and would continue until his death. His participation would extend to the knockout stages against Paraguay in Asuncion, one of the classification games for the Mexican World Cup in 1970, when Brazil was victorious for the third time. Two years before his death, Jaime went to the 1974 World Cup in Germany, under the auspices of the *Jornal dos Sports*, Ponto Frio and Chanteclair. After boarding with 1000 harmonicas, similar to Ary Barroso's, with dozens of flags and reco-recos, (Brazilian percussion instruments) he would go on to watch the players train in Frankfurt and also organize several rallies through the German cities.

Jaime de Carvalho would remain in charge of the Charanga until his death, which happened as a result of cancer, on May 4, 1976. While sick in a state hospital in Rio de Janeiro (*Hospital dos Servidores*), he would send letters to the readers' section of the city's newspapers, where he would continue to instruct fans and propagate their pedagogical–nationalist ideals, expressed in slogans such as "Flamengo teaches you how to love Brazil above all things" and "When you find a Flamengo fan, you find a friend." Before his death Jaime would pass the baton of responsibility to his wife, Laura, who would assume the leadership of the fans' organization and did so until the 1980s.

JUVENILE SCHISMS

Upon the death of Jaime de Carvalho, his influence on the footballing world continued, but there was no longer had unanimity within the Flamengo fan group. His longevity at the forefront of the fans' organization gave him even more respect, with journalistic appreciation for his "stoicism." This characteristic even earned him tributes from opposing supporters, such as Corinthians Paulista fans. In 1972, at the 30th anniversary of the Charanga, São Paulo fans awarded Jaime a plaque, reading "leader of leaders" for supporters in Rio.

However, in the early 1970s, such leadership was no longer an uncontested matter and the "King of fans" ceased to be an absolute monarch. The view from stands will be reasonably modified when compared with previous decades. In practical terms, it is worth saying that the Charanga, despite the "official" airs, no longer existed as being an exclusive group of supporters, the only representative of the club among the fans. New fan organizations, along with their own bases, now also followed Flamengo.

It is true that during the 1950s, 1960s and up until the mid-1970s it was Jaime who continued to lead the successive *Fan's duels*. He was the main spokesman and organizer who had the greatest experience that allowed him to prepare the Flamengo fan strategies against the fans of Vasco, Fluminense and Botafogo. Incidentally, the Supporters' Competition remained active throughout this time and was repeated over the years, in an interspersed or sequential way, in 1960, 1961, 1962, 1965 and 1973. With the purpose of "transcending the spirit of rivalry between the fans and increasing the spectacle's beauty," while attracting a larger crowd, the regulations became more sophisticated and the prizes more significant.

From this point onward, prizes were divided into two categories: one collective; the other individual. When added together, they made a total of ten trophies, for example, before a Fla X Flu game in October 1965: (1st) "Best Charanga"; (2nd) "Loudest Cheering"; (3rd) "Best goal celebration by fans"; (4th) "Crowd with the largest number of flags"; (5th) "Largest crowd"; (6th) "Most expressive crowd"; (7th) "Most original male Flamengo supporter"; (8th) "Most original female Flamengo supporter"; (9th) "Most original Fluminense supporter"; (10th) "Most original female Fluminense supporter."

At each contest, Jaime planned the celebration and was named to receive the trophies at the headquarters of the *Jornal dos Sports*, where he was photographed and made his speeches. During the game, he never failed to perform his duties in assisting match-day policing, which he did through special requests. This was done by means of a megaphone, which was imported from the United States by club chairman George Helal. Jaime instructed the crowd using the megaphone, saying: "do not burn paper," "do not throw bottles," "let us hear it for our team," "no fires." On game days for the Brazilian national team, such as during the 1965 game against the Soviet Union at a full Maracanã, Jaime recommended that fans not wear clubs shirt, this in order to avoid unnecessary animosity. Thanks to this collaboration, Captain Nelson de Mello, who was responsible for monitoring the Maracanã, provided him, from as early as 1958, with a military police diploma and the title "Number 1 Fan" at the Municipal Stadium.

All this legitimacy came from his position of leader that tradition had bestowed upon him. However, in the new situation, parallel competition began to influence proceedings, this having been non-existent before the 1960s. The leadership unity of the organized fans would become disrupted in the second half of the 1960s, not only at Flamengo, but at all the major teams in Rio de Janeiro. At the end of the troubled decade of 1960, dissent began to brew in the stands within the fan associations.

There were explicit justifications that came on the surface in the speeches of the disgruntled supporters. The alleged reasons were understood to be apparently simple, caused by the illness of older leaders and by common observance that these leaders needed to be replaced. Other explanations were of a harsher and more accusatory tone. They were motivated by restrictions that were placed on the fans, which would hamper the fans' free expression. Allegations circled the argument, finally, around the right to "boo" and more scathing criticism toward the team, be it against their leaders, their coaches and/or their players, during crisis situations in team performance.

The swirl of facts subsequently generated a wave of successive crises that put the figure of the leader and his "charisma" in check. The materialization of such discord began with Fluminense fans, when, in May 1967, a banner appeared with the following inscription: "Dissident Fan." This was extended by Bolinha, the Number 2 representative of the Fluminense fans in the stands, known for ringing his bell at the stadium. It is worth noting that, as was the case with Jaime de Carvalho, Paulista, head of the Fluminense Organized Fans (TOF), had health problems and needed to get away for a few months. Bolinha substituted him and took over charge of the group. When Paulista recovered, he returned to the games, where he encountered resistance from his former assistant, who then decided to create a fan group that separated the Fluminense fans.

Aside from this case, in which the dispute for power became more visible between two characters, all remaining disagreements had a higher rhetorical tone, which little by little were being read as a dramatization of a "generation gap," which occurred both in society and in the stands. In the "microphysics of fan power," the stadiums were equally fields of conflict, arenas of dispute by space and modes and representations of domination. Ultimately, this was a power struggle.

The time, marked by international student rebellion, saw youth movements such as in France in May 1968, which echoed around the world. In parallel, the newest members of the fan organizations reflected such issues, in a way that was clearly somewhat diluted, diffuse and indirect. There was a homology in slogans of revolt and insurgent symbols, although brief and episodic: funeral coffins, demonstrations, graffiti, verbal intimidation, telephone threats, assaults, stone attacks, protests and demands of more or less peaceful resignation.

The demand for new participatory methods at the stadiums thus manifested itself. In protagonizing this generational conflict in their own way, these young people were claiming the right to protest and to offer contestation during critical phases for the team. To this end, they inverted the normative principles of organized fans between the 1940s and 1960s, which prescribed unconditional support for the club. A veto to the authority of the older leaders resulted in repercussions on the modifications being given to the fans' actions. This would achieve new meanings and take other directions, generated by the split in the unity of the fan organizations and in its constitutive unit principle: *one* club, *one* crowd, *one* leader.

The difficulty became even more emphasized in the 1960s, when the Maracanã saw its average crowd numbers increase significantly. The *Fla-Flu* game on December 15, 1963, for example, set a record of 177,656 paying attendees, with a total audience of 194,603 people. It was in this decade that the stadium recorded the largest ever number of paying fans: in 1969, the turnstiles revolved 183,341 times at the Mario Filho stadium, setting a public record. That afternoon, Brazil secured their qualification for the 1970 World Cup with a one-nil win over Paraguay.

In this sense, the growing crowds at Maracanã Stadium may have been a contributing factor for fermenting the disagreements within fan organizations, in addition to the structural changes in the world of football: the second movement for players moving toward professionalism, the creation of a national club tournament and the consolidation of television broadcasts, which made the network of Brazil's teams even more broad.

Returning to Flamengo's case, what happened to them would be similar to that which was experienced by Fluminense, with a movement away from having a routine leader, compromised at the end of the 1960s, when Jaime de Carvalho became sick and had to face the medical reality of high blood pressure and diabetes. This temporary removal of leadership from the stadiums created a vacuum in the crowd, which created a crisis in his wake, made more extensive by the team's poor performance in the second half of 1968.

In 1967, Flamengo fan Pedro Paulo Bebiano, originally from a family of Botafogo leaders, was an engineering student at Gama Filho

University. At the age of 18, it was he who had a bone of contention with Jaime. It was known that the veteran supporter turned a blind eye to swearing, booing and fireworks; this was a source of dissatisfaction among young people. Pedro Paulo, among other boys in the youth wing of the Charanga, left the fan organization and was the founder of *Young Power*.

Their first act was symbolic. In the stands of the Maracanã Stadium, they decided to leave the left sector of the radio boxes and go to the high stands behind the goal. In a somewhat spontaneous manner, they created a movement of fans to the side, safe from alleged restrictions of the old leader. The group, which had not yet properly configured a fan organization, would be known as *Young Power*—this was the inscription on their banner in 1967 and 1968. Only by the end of 1969, after a meeting in the *estádio da Gávea* stands, would the group come to institutionalize themselves with the name "Young Flamengo Fans."

Just as what happens in a chain reaction, supporters were constantly having internal disagreements. The problems were always associated with the figures responsible for leading the groups. Botafogo is a perfect example, since the club's performance was excellent, then the two-time state champion (1967–68), there was no reason for dissent and segmentation, which might otherwise be justified by poor results on the pitch. Even so, Tarzã, who had been leader of Botafogo fans since the 1950s, came to be criticized more often at that time.

Due to work commitments, the Botafogo leader had to travel with some regularity to Belo Horizonte. Born in Minas Gerais, blessed with an excellent physique—having worked in construction before entering the clothing trade in the city center—he began to attend the Mineirão, where he supported the Charanga of Júlio, a legendary character from Atlético Mineiro fans. He was accused of being negligent, due to his travels from Rio to Minas Gerais and his constant absences from the Maracanã Stadium, and the younger fans became increasingly critical of him. Many of them did not even join the Botafogo Organized Fans (TOB). As was the case with Flamengo, they created a parallel movement namesake, titled *Young Power*. This group, in 1969, went on to be named "Young Botafogo Fans."

The series of dismemberments would culminate in 1970. At Vasco, the "Young Force" emerged, whose official founding date was in February of that year. This splinter group was led by Eli Mendes, who left the Vasco Organized Fan group, commanded by Dulce Rosalina. This female supporter, in a less common case of an organized fan group being led by a woman, seemed even more vulnerable to criticism, despite her good reputation with the press and Vasco fans. Although not the direct cause, the break coincided with the fact that Dulce had a car accident in a caravan of Vasco fans going to São Paulo, in 1968, the reason for her temporary departure from TOV.

At Fluminense, the second half of 1970 would lead to fractures in its supporter representation, with the emergence of two organized fan groups: The *Força Flu*, in November, and the Young Flu, in December, of the same year. After those ephemeral experiences such as Bolinha's "Dissident Fan" and the *Young Flu* movement in 1967, the two other fan groups would have a more stable presence in the Fluminense stands during the 1970s.

IN THE DOCK

The factual description that has been listed up to this point aims to provide an insight into the cyclical transformations that the organized fans went through at that time. These changes paved the way to further the understanding of the directions that these groups took during the course of the 1980s. The climate at the end of the 1960s constitutes an inflection regarding the participation of football devotees. In expressing their dissatisfaction and arguing for the creation of dissident supporter groups, the fans were gunning for not just one specific target—one leader—but the dissolution fissure of a model.

The direct attack's underlying argument was with the adjunctive role of the organized fans. They were seen as passive or subordinate by the club management, by the press and by their own leaders. It was not therefore about mere name changes or petty dislikes of a personal nature. It was a desire for greater freedom and autonomy from the club and less reverence to the individuals in authority. New fans were driven by a social agenda with political connotations.

It was not important if these were conscious or unconscious, the question of power, in its broad and strict sense, permeated passion and the football club experience. From the carnivalization (1930s, 1940s and 1950s) to the juvenization (1960s, 1970s and 1980s) of organized fans,

Toledo points to the historical consonance of the need for new youth and popular associative forms in the sport within the autocratic institutional context:

> This model of support, which has been instituted and incremented by these uniformed fans lasted until the 70s, when participation model, clearly more popular, and the contender, from a certain perspective, won significant support and appeal among fans from the popular classes. (...) It is relevant to correlate the emergence of these supporter institutions in a broader value context of popular institutions at a time in which political and citizenship rights were curtailed by the then military regime. When following an authoritarian model regarding football management, fan groups mobilize themselves around alternative institutions for participating on the fringes of professional football.[2]

The events of the 1970s created a precedent for fragmentation and the profusion of countless self-titled organized fan associations, brought now in the absence of former leaders, within a club. Three identifying dimensions were attributed to the nomenclature of the fans of that decade: youth identity (Young Fans), community identity (fans from the street, neighborhood or city) and gender identity (female supporters). Besides the fans being given a stamp of recreation and socialization, Elisabeth Silva Murilho notes, quite correctly, that the neighborhood belonging is more accentuated from that decade:

> Most of these fans begin with groups of friends and neighbors who already go to the stadiums together. The fan has links with his own supporting section. It is not that he does not have a strong attachment to his chosen club, but to go to the stadiums, pick a team, support the team and celebrate the victory is, above all, something that the fan enjoys with the greatest intensity.[3]

Professional football's new structure also enhanced the scale of fan organizations in the 1970s. They were less personalized and more bureaucratized, with their own cards, shirts and symbols. An incipient internal distribution of power is performed, with duties being assigned and responsibilities being divided. From a few dozen adherents, the fans become numbered in the hundreds. For example, in 1971, the Young Flamengo Fans had 291 members. A self-referenced universe, in parallel with the club, is created, with all the inherent gregarious potential therein.

Traveling to matches in other Brazilian states demanded a high degree of preparation and greater integration among its members. The caravans go beyond the scope of stadiums and supporter sociability becomes entrenched throughout the week in ads written for the newspapers, in the strategies for chartering and selling the bus tickets and the disclosures focused on promoting the fans. At weekends, they often spend hours and even days together, with the nightlong trips to and away from the games.

The wonder of the senses–community, youth, associative, recreational–for the fans during the 1970s would also have their less festive and more hostile counterparts. Simultaneously, with the development of such groups, another historical significance would be given to fans during the interval that marked the military regime in Brazil (1964–1985). Only with the fall of the dictatorship, in the early 1980s, would this significance appear sharper in journalistic accounts and sociological analyses. The incorporation of a "spirit of time" would point to a transition in the phenomenon of the fans, whose meaning was going to be from carnivalization to militarization.

Sociologist Mauricio Murad, pioneering academic researcher of football in Brazil, coordinator between 1991 and 1996 of the first systematic research on the phenomenon of organized fans at the Football Sociology Department at the State University of Rio de Janeiro (UERJ), summarized the coordinates of that process well. The configuration only proved to be clearer in the late 1970s and at the beginning of the 1980s, around the "time of openings," when some supporters began to systematize their forms of struggle and confrontation within and outside the stadiums.

The moment when fan violence was systematized in football can be pinpointed to the 1970s, when Brazil was under dictatorial control, in the words of Murad:

Historically, the violent organized fans arose in the 70s, at the height of the military dictatorship. In particular between 1969 and 1973, when the "organized fans" ("uniformed" in São Paulo) were born, who, today, terrorize the country. Founded at the height of a neo-fascist state of Brazil, implanted in Brazil from 1964, its genesis was demarcated by the ideology of political violence, defining the period "AI-5-Medici" (Institutional Act n. 5, by President Medici). Fed by a view of the world that was intolerant, exclusionary and anti-democratic, its practice could not be any another, this accumulated in its contemporary experience: "wild competitiveness, an antagonism oppressor, territorial invasion and settling differences by force."[4]

Changes in the behavior of "organized fans" did not happen until 10 to 15 years after their conception, until they began to appear in police reports. From being carnavalized they began to be militarized, following the doctrines and standards of militarism in force, which sunk into all sectors of society. These fans, as a result, were structured in "platoons," "detachments," "squads," "shock troops," "commandos," "armies," "families"—yes, family, but in the same way that the mafia is a family. Furthermore, their leaders are called "captains," "lieutenants" and "sergeants." Its symbols are military in nature, as are their relationships of power, internal hierarchy and group cohesion.

Militarization, hierarchization and bureaucratization were therefore the grim legacy of Brazil's political regime on many civilian institutions within Brazilian society and, in this case, on some of the organized fans. These, in particular the Young Fans in Rio de Janeiro, would draw the media's attention; they would highlight themselves away from the others and absorb smaller groups—mini-groups in truth—from ephemeral life in most cases. Little by little they would become a part of the collective imagination of common sense, which accentuated the deformity and one-dimensional stigma of violent fans. In the vocabulary of the press from early 1980s, the rebelliousness that signaled the end of 1960s would be transformed into violence.

Consequently, there was, in accordance with the scheme proposed by Murad, a homology between the arbitrary use of physical force and the creation of a corporative force, organically linked to violence, in the football world.

This process came into being in 1983, when the *Mancha Verde do Palmeiras* (Green Patch of Palmeiras) was born in São Paulo. The crowd, made up as a result of a merger between three small, organized fan groups of the club, the Green Empire, the Green Hell and the *Alviverde* Guild, had the explicit purpose of self-defense and coping with fans from the opposing team. According to testimony by Paulo Rogério Serdan, its founder and former president: "We usually say that it was a necessary evil, because Palmeiras fans, before the *Mancha* was created, was a shunned group of fans. It was a crowd that was beaten by everyone. It was a discredited crowd."

While 1983 was marked by the founding of a fan group that was directly linked to an image of violence, it is also the year that the Rio de Janeiro Association of Organized Fans (ASTORJ) appeared, which was the result of an attempt to increase integration and to open dialogue between representatives of the rival teams' fans. Idealized by Armando Giesta, from Young-Flu, the movement was triggered by the leaders of the main organized fan groups in Rio de Janeiro at the time, which sought to alleviate shocks between the members of the groups, in addition to being a corporative force to the football authorities, such as the Sport Secretary in the State of Rio, who made 23 rooms available for their members at the Maracanã Stadium in the early 1980s.

Attempts to create friendly relationships among the organized fans would be repeated throughout that decade. In 1985, a "Symposium for Peace" would be promoted, headed by Niltinho, President of Young Flamengo Fans. Then in 1987 there was the first Congress of Major Clubs' Organized Fans, held in the city of Porto Alegre, which saw the formation of *the Clube dos 13* (an organization responsible for representing the interests of the most powerful football clubs of Brazil), which would put forward a new agenda for administering and managing Brazilian football. In the same year, the leaders involved wanted to found a Brazilian Association of Organized Fans.

In spite of such timely efforts, these fan assemblies would not be successful in the following years. A new upsurge of feuds and intolerance between the factions would aggravate the belligerent tone of their inter-fan group relationships. In 1988, Cléo, leader of the *Mancha Verde*, was murdered. The crime was never solved nor the obscure circumstances involved ever clarified by the police. There was provocation, in stadiums in Rio de Janeiro, when Palmeiras played, with the exception of São Januário and Caio Martins, where Palmeiras had its allies and faithful friends; you could hear the chant in the vengeful chorus: "Cleo is dead, the Mancha is fucked!"

The fans became more commonly mentioned in police reports, thereby progressively distancing themselves from sports pages. In recurring trials and surveys, which intensified along with an escalation of riots, vandalism and deaths in the course of the following years, the organized fans have not since left "the dock."[5]

CONCLUSION: FAREWELL, SAMBA PLOT?

In the late 1980s, there was a musical hit in the Maracanã Stadium stands. It was a version of "Rap do Pirão," by DJ Malboro, sung in popular funk music clubs in the city. The message, with the original lyrics being peaceful, was, however, entirely undermined in the fans' voices. It was sung thusly, with momentum that accentuated the strong beating of the bass drum, interspersed with explosive clapping from the chorus, along with the new lyrics as adapted by one group of organized Flamengo fans. For example, fans changed the verse, "Come to the dance my friend/Come with love in your heart" to "I am of the Flamengo race/The terror of this nation."[6]

In powerful unison, emulated by that beat that seemed to make the stadium shake, the musical hit would dictate the latest rhythmic preference in the stands and the dances, which corresponded with the growing problems that were triggered in the Rio slums and other regions. There was a greater willingness to have fights between groups; a binary logic of side A against side B, a pulsating gestural–visual dynamic along with a more aggressive body posture was adopted. Supporters abandoned the rhythm of samba songs that had been hegemonic since the late 1960s, and thinned their repertoire with the genre of choice for young people from the slums and the emerging juvenile groups.

They increasingly saw themselves seduced by the symbols of strength and power of Young Supporters from Rio, with their armies, platoons, squadrons and commandos, expressed in words inscribed on their banners: "the most feared in Brazil," "the terror of you all," "above everything, below nothing."

At the beginning of the 1980s and 1990s, there was not only a new beat or a distinct musical style that began to be heard. There was the opening of a new page in the history of the football fans. No matter what differences they had with other issues, other morphologies and other dilemmas, the fans would continue expressing that which a remarkable historian called "the crude, brilliant, brutal, sublime world of the football fan."[7]

NOTES

1. The term shows the universe of family metaphors in football terminology and designates the way in which fans see their own stadium, giving rise to the expression, "playing at home" and "playing away."
2. Luiz Henrique de Toledo. "A invenção do torcedor de futebol: disputas simbólicas pelos significados do torcer," in *Futebol, espetáculo do século*, ed. Márcia Regina da Costa, et al. (São Paulo: Editora Musa, 2000), 149.
3. Elisabeth Murillo Silva, "A violência no futebol e a imprensa esportiva," in Costa, *Futebol, espetáculo do século*, 175.

4. Mauricio Murad, "Futebol e violência no Brasil," in *Futebol: síntese da vida brasileira*, ed. Mauricio Murad, et al. (Rio de Janeiro: UERJ, Departamento Cultural/ SR-3, 1996), 22.

5. The expression is inspired by the Portuguese translation of the book *Football on Trial* by Eric Dunning, John Williams and Patrick Murphy. *O futebol no banco dos réus*. (Oeiras: Celta Editora, 1994).

6. https://www.youtube.com/watch?v=XuxI06MijIw Accessed 4 May 2016.

7. Boris Fausto, "De alma lavada e coração pulsante," in *Revista de História da USP* (São Paulo, 163, July–December 2010), 148.

Work Cited

Da Costa, Márcia Regina, et al. *Futebol, espetáculo do século*. São Paulo: Editora Musa, 2000.

Fausto, Boris. "De alma lavada e coração pulsante". *Revista de História*. São Paulo: n. 163, July/December 2010.

Frank, Sybille, and Silke Steets. *Stadium Worlds: Football, Space and the Built Environment*. New York: Routledge, 2010.

Leite Lopes, José Sérgio. "Le Maracanã, coeur du Brésil". *Sociétés et représentations*. Paris: no publisher. no. 7 (1998).

Lyra Filho, João. *Cachimbo, pijama e chinelos*. São Paulo: no publisher, 1963.

Moura, Clóvis, and Roberto Assaf. *História dos campeonatos cariocas de futebol – 1906–2010*. Rio de Janeiro: Maquinaria Editora, 2010.

Moura, Gisela de Araújo. *O Rio corre para o Maracanã*. Rio de Janeiro: Editora FGV, 1998.

Murad, Mauricio, et al. *Futebol: síntese da vida brasileira*. Rio de Janeiro: UERJ, Departamento Cultural/SR-3, 1996.

Negreiros, José Plínio Labriola de C. "Construindo a nação: futebol nos anos 30 e 40". In *Futebol, espetáculo do século*, edited by M. R. da Costa, et al. São Paulo: Editora Musa, 2000.

Rodrigues Filho, Mario. *Histórias do Flamengo*. Rio de Janeiro: Record, 1966.

Sander, Roberto. *Anos 40: viagem à década sem Copa*. Rio de Janeiro: Bom Texto, 2004.

———. *Lógicas no futebol*. São Paulo: HUCITEC/FAPESP, 2002.

———. "Torcer: A metafísica do homem comum". *Revista de História*. São Paulo: no. 163, July/December 2010.

Touguinhó, Oldemário. *Maracanã, onde todos são iguais*. Rio de Janeiro: Relume Dumará, 1998.

Viveiros de Castro, Maria Laura. *Carnaval carioca: dos bastidores aos desfiles*. Rio de Janeiro: Ed. UFRJ; FUNARTE, 1994.

PART VII

Philosophy and Critical Theory

"Another World (Cup) Is Possible!": Twenty Theses About Modern Football

Tim Walters

The motivation for this analysis is twofold. First, it is my contention that the governance of the top tier of elite men's professional football is today in an unprecedented state of disrepair, moral bankruptcy and public disrepute such that hitherto unimaginable transformations have become possible. Second, this chapter is interested in addressing what I take to be a significant lack in the growing body of critical writing about football. In his "Introduction" to *Capital in the Twenty-First Century*, French economist Thomas Piketty explains that the genesis of his sweeping analysis of inequality is a belief that historical debates among economists were a "dialogue of the deaf"[1] by virtue of the fact that "research on the distribution

Earlier versions of parts of this essay were presented on the "Philosophy of Football" panel at the *Soccer as the Beautiful Game Conference* ("What Is Football For? A Modest Proposal," Hofstra University, Long Island, NY, April 10, 2014) and as a keynote address at Manchester Metropolitan University's *Football and Communities of Resistance Conference* ["'Another World (Cup) is Possible!': Brazil 2014 and the Birth of Occupy Football," Manchester, UK. June 12, 2014]. I would like to acknowledge the many positive contributions of the participants at these events for their valuable feedback, which has changed the shape of this work.

T. Walters (✉)
Department of English, Okanagan College, Kelowna, BC, Canada

© Hofstra University 2017
B. Elsey, S. Pugliese (eds.), *Football and the Boundaries of History*,
DOI 10.1057/978-1-349-95006-5_16

of wealth was for a long time based on a relatively limited set of firmly established facts together with a wide variety of purely theoretical speculations."[2] He explains how his discipline has been historically blighted by an excess of deeply held theoretical views, all of which were based on very little or no hard evidence or concrete analysis grounded in data. More so than his conclusions or diagnoses, Piketty's primary contribution to our thinking around inequality has been the creation of, and engagement with, massive data sets within which he looks for larger patterns and the theories to account for them.

Critical thinking about football has precisely the opposite problem. It is a field overflowing with up-to-the-minute data, awash with micro-analyses and carefully researched histories (of players, clubs, leagues, nations, contests, eras), but a paucity of theory, of broad, unifying claims. As a growing and resolutely interdisciplinary discipline, it has yet to produce its own theoretical apparatus. And while football has been written about fleetingly by various critical theorists from outside the field—Theodor Adorno, Roland Barthes, Jean Baudrillard, Terry Eagleton, Antonio Gramsci and so forth—thinking about football has remained largely non-dialectical, episodic and unsystematic, which is to say "football needs theory." Here, and elsewhere, I advocate for the particular suitability of the work of Slovenian theorist Slavoj Žižek for this purpose.[3] My attempt is to transpose Žižek's idiosyncratic fusion of a Marxist critique of political economy with Lacanian psychoanalysis and Hegelian philosophy to the world of football. It's time that we start thinking about football more theoretically, and I believe Žižek's approach, with its emphasis on the "good old-fashioned art" of critique of ideology, insistence upon viewing phenomena in their totality and conception of the various registers of violence, provides a model with which to map out and begin to develop this analysis. The 20 theses that follow are an attempt to begin this theoretical work, to unify the analyses done elsewhere into a broader set of shared conclusions about the state of the game today.

THE RELATIONSHIP BETWEEN FOOTBALL AND CAPITAL HAS CHANGED

It has become commonplace to say it, but it bears repeating, as it has become broadly determinative of the entire orientation of the game today: modern football has become, and is becoming, more and more intertwined with modern (transnational, corporate) Capital in ways we do and do not understand, some, but not all of which, are new. While business has been involved with football almost since its formation as an organized endeavor, there is more money coursing through more parts of the elite game today from, and to, a greater variety of stakeholders than at any other point in the history of football or indeed of any other sport, and this quickly growing influence is an escalating concern, as it should be. All analyses of the game today ought to take as their starting point the many effects and implications of this unprecedented influence.

This Changed Relationship Has Generated More Negative Than Positive Effects

Football has, and we as its supporters have, reaped certain spectacular benefits from this ongoing drawing together and tangling up of Capital and football. As a result of its huge commercial appeal, for instance, its international accessibility has improved enormously, so that now anyone with a high-speed Internet connection or a cellphone signal can watch just about any live game they choose regardless of how far away from the field of play they might physically be. I can watch my hometown team—Middlesbrough FC—play every week, despite living more than 7000 kilometers from the Riverside Stadium, which would have been unimaginable even 20 years ago. There are many other benefits that have also been well documented. Attending a match is for the most part a safer and more welcoming experience than was the case a few decades ago. More attention is generally paid to the physical well-being of players than has historically been the case. The racism, homophobia and misogyny that were once endemic to football are no longer as prevalent or as pervasive as they once were, although much remains to be done in each of these areas.

However, regardless of its benefits, those elements of modern football that are most offensive to most people are most often direct or indirect functions of its specific relationship(s) with Capital. The list is too long and too familiar to fully enumerate here, but we might begin with obscene player salaries; outrageous ticket prices; the myriad encroachments of commercialization into the game through omnipresent branding, merchandising, synergistic ventures and so on, and the attendant shift from the football fan to the football consumer; the subordination of the game and its cheapening in countless ways to the spectacular demands of television and other media; the delocalizing effects on the game in the post-Bosman era; the use of football as a greenwashing tool for energy giants (Gazprom, Azerbaijan, Qatar, etc.); the growing chasm between the game's rich and poor (within and between leagues and countries) and related diminishment of competitive balance; the remarkable financial precariousness and unsustainability of the modern game; the use of billions in public funds to build private stadia and subsidize mega-events that are too expensive for many of the general public to attend and which appear to primarily benefit global corporations and international footballing authorities; the growing influence of agents and third-party owners; the upscaling and making generic of football stadia and surrounding areas, including forced relocations; and so on.

Most People Who Are Interested in Football Believe the Effects of Capital Are Corrosive

Which is to say that, on balance, a good many people now think that the enterprise of football has been made comprehensively worse by Capital, and those people are right to think this. There is now, somewhat surprisingly, a widespread shared understanding that recent increases in the rate and breadth of the capitalization of football have come at a real cost, and the prevalence and intensity of this attitude is a new development in the popular discourse about football. The prevailing public attitude toward the increasing monetization of the game is now characterized by weariness, disgust and bewilderment, which now underscores most media engagement with the football business. This is a hugely important perceptual shift.

In Myriad Ways, Modern Football Is a Symptom of Modern Capitalism, and Should Be Treated as Such

Those theoretical and critical apparatus that can help us better understand the political economy of the world at large can and ought to be used to help us understand the crises besetting modern football; or, the diagnoses and solutions to the problems of the one are inextricably related to the other, and often revealingly so. If modern football is symptomatic of modern capitalism, ways of addressing the one might also be used to address the other. Obviously, this is not meant to minimize the important ways in which football is unlike other sectors of the economy or culture, nor is it to suggest that all of the myriad ways of arranging football are uniform. However, while acknowledging the particular internal logics of different systems, my analysis operates from the position that since the problems of football are primarily functions of the core features of its current political economy, then the solutions to its problems might be the same as those which address those problems in similarly blighted spheres.

Modern Football Is Useful, and Maybe Even Necessary, to Modern Capitalism

Indeed, as our most popular source of shared pleasure as a species, as a privileged cultural field within which ideas of the acceptability of vast economic inequality, the determinative capacities of wealth and the omnipresence of commerce are normalized, it may be not far from indispensable to it lately, but this seems to be changing. Much has been written about this relationship, from Juvenal's "bread and circuses" to Marcuse's "repressive desublimation" and beyond. As Marxist critic and World Cup abolitionist Terry Eagleton argued on the eve of the 2010 tournament in South Africa:

> The World Cup is another setback to any radical change…If every rightwing think-tank came up with a scheme to distract the populace from political injustice and to compensate them for lives of hard labour, the solution in each case would be the same: football. No finer way of resolving the problems of capitalism has been dreamed up, bar socialism. And in the tussle between them, football is several light years ahead.[4]

I dare say his position would be at least a little different today, when football has been made by many activists and concerned citizens into a tool to bring the world's attention to political and economic injustices in Brazil, Russia and Qatar in the wake of the tournament in South Africa, where these issues began to be broadly considered in mainstream media for the first time. The World Cup and football more generally might still be bread and circuses, a useful distraction to the masses, but the notion of football's utility to capitalism is becoming considerably less straightforward.

Public Feeling About the Political Economy of Football Has Changed

Even before the latest FIFA scandal, popular thinking around the World Cup in particular had fundamentally changed in the years since the Confederation's Cup protests in Brazil in 2013, so that the mainstream media discourse surrounding the tournament now routinely focuses on corruption, exploitation, FIFA's internecine shenanigans and other alarming symptoms of our current system. In the lead-ups to these tournaments, coverage routinely spotlights stories about FIFA corruption, often-sympathetic coverage of protestors in Brazil and elsewhere, articles about Qatari labor standards and so forth. The months before the 2014 finals in Brazil were marked by countless articles in the popular international press calling for the dismantling of FIFA, and while the ostensible motivation for them was the contemporaneous discovery of evidence of vote buying for the Qatari World Cup, the reason for their appearance in plain view is the massive public interest in the tournament in Brazil, and the work of the protestors in that country in the wake of the Confederation Cup a year prior. The events of the summer of 2013 have helped to familiarize people with the idea of thinking about the politics and socioeconomics of football tournaments, something that had barely registered in the public consciousness up to this point. While the currently unprecedented degree of media interest will wane once the FIFA scandal is resolved, in important ways these crises have led to the creation of a new normal in terms of coverage of the game and have permanently reoriented the popular discourse surrounding it.

FIFA and The(ir) World Cups Have Made This Inevitable

In part, this shift is an indirect consequence of FIFA's since-abandoned continental hosting rotation system that led to their decision to host the 2010 finals in South Africa, which was exacerbated by the awarding of the 2022 tournament to Qatar, but which really took off in the wake of the 2013 protests in Brazil. To most people, there is something recognizably obscene, indeed murderous, about the taxpayers of developing nations spending billions of their citizen's money building white elephants and erecting a massive security infrastructure while a Swiss non-profit and a select group of multinational corporations walks away with the profits

(£3–5 billion per tournament, tax free). This is not British footballing racism, as has regularly been suggested by President Blatter to deflect ongoing criticism on this front, nor is it nostalgic, imperialist Eurocentrism. Obviously, an argument can be made for giving developing countries in overlooked regions a chance to host the finals, as it is the World Cup after all.[5] However, no argument can be made for continuing to finance and run World Cups in these regions according to the same formulas used for Germany, France, Japan/South Korea and the USA, whose infrastructure (sporting and otherwise) is such that they didn't really need to build much of anything. In such a context, FIFA walking away from host nations with billions in broadcasting, marketing and ticketing revenue makes a certain kind of sense, or at least doesn't offend. Unfortunately, but in no way surprisingly, it seems that this is a conversation FIFA's Executive Committee never really had when they adopted this policy, to the massive detriment of bidding nations.[6] Accordingly, in 2010, South Africa spent around $4.7 billion to host, and received an estimated $500 million in economic benefits. Brazil spent $17 billion. Russia is currently predicting that it will invest $19 billion in spending related to the 2018 tournament, although only two years ago they were predicting a $9 billion spend, so it's very difficult to estimate what the final costs will be. In 2022, the Qatari government will shatter all records related to public spending on a mega-event with its proposed $120 billion World Cup, which is an outlay of approximately one million dollars for every citizen. Russia can arguably afford this kind of profligacy, and Qatar can, if anyone can, but the decision to grant these nations the opportunity to host was broadly recognized as being self-evidently problematic for a variety of other reasons: both countries lack a well-developed footballing culture and both have appalling human rights records and practices that directly contravene FIFA's own mission statement[7] and both appear to have absolutely nothing other than crude financial claims to make as regards their being best suited to host an event of this sort.

2013–2022: An Opportunity for Us to Get Back to Basics: *What Is Football for?*

Accordingly, a rare window of opportunity has opened within which to offer a new answer to the most fundamental question about the beautiful game as a growing economic and cultural force in the world: *what is football for?* Obviously, for most people it is played and watched and debated largely for its own sake, for the pleasure it affords, for the thrill of play and the community and excitement it can bring into being. However, what is considerably less clear is what it is and will be for at the very highest levels of play. In only a few decades, contests like the World Cup, UEFA Champion's League and the British Premier League have been transformed into multibillion dollar enterprises that capitalize on the attention of billions of viewers, and we need to decide what best to do about this development. The aforementioned recent hosting decisions, and FIFA's farcical and corrupt business practices more generally, have inadvertently generated the displays of resistance we have seen in Brazil for at least a few more years, which will no doubt be followed by similar actions ahead of the next two tournaments. Accordingly, FIFA and its critics have opened up a window of opportunity—roughly between 2013 and the 2022 tournament in Qatar—a rupture in the sleek edifice of the big money game, within which the near and long-term future of football will largely be determined and shaped. This is the era in which it will be decided *what football will be for* in the twenty-first century, which ought to be the most important and foundational question regarding the game today, and the one we don't spend nearly enough time thinking and talking about, possibly because it has long seemed a settled issue. It isn't.

FIFA HAVE BUILT THE STAGE FOR OCCUPY FOOTBALL

Largely as a result of FIFA's policies, their choice of hosting locales and the various injustices associated with bringing World Cups into being, the unseemly inequities of the big money game have become foregrounded in public thinking about football. Mega-events provide a massive microphone to the world through which otherwise ignored critical voices, social movements and activist groups can get their message out globally, and the international media now routinely latch on to these protests despite FIFA and the host government's best attempts to stifle and marginalize this dissent. It is the reason for the huge media interest in Brazilian social issues in the summers of 2013 and 2014, as well as the reason why many people around the world know anything about the conditions faced daily by migrant workers in the Middle East. The monstrous Qatari *kafala* system might not yet be a household term, but it will be by 2022 unless something dramatically changes, which all indications suggest it will not.

It's Critical That We Make the Most of This Opportunity (For a Change)

For those of us who care about transforming football or (its relationship to) Capital, this window is an exceptionally rare opportunity that must be seized, and seized properly, because it is only because of a combination of the grossest managerial incompetence and absolute ethical bankruptcy (primarily but not exclusively) on the part of FIFA that it has appeared in the first place. Unlike the Right, who do their best work in moments like these, the Left has a grand tradition of completely failing to take advantage of rare and unexpected opportunities for revolutionary systemic transformation (consider, for instance, our largely unchanged global financial system in the wake of the 2008 crash) and we need to get it just right this time.[8] How might this happen? What could and should world football be for if not this?

Occupy Football Must Be "Infinitely Demanding"

Those of us who believe football requires not just minor reforms or changes in personnel but sweeping revolutionary transformation should look to the streets, and to what Simon Critchley calls the "infinite demands"[9] of the protestors in Brazil. The activism we saw there is most akin to that of the Occupy movement, with which it shares a broad-based distrust/rejection of Capital and those charged with administering it, a linking of specific, local issues with broader, ethical commitments, a willingness to form provisional coalitions with often unlikely allies in order to demonstrate solidarity against an oppressive system and an insistence on a wholesale transition from whatever this strange neoliberal beast we have now is to a political economy based on fairness, dignity and equality.

We Should Refocus Our Analysis/Critique to Emphasize Economic Institutions and Systems. Or: It's the Economy, Stupid!

Collectively, we need to stop focusing on individuals rather than systems, stop focusing primarily on structures of governance rather than economic ones, and not let our obsession with covert corruption blind us to those overt forms of corruption which are both much more ubiquitous and more corrosive than their shadowy counterpart. None of this is to say that FIFA is not a staggeringly corrupt organization, or that Sepp Blatter or Jack Warner or Mohamed Bin Hammam or Chuck Blazer or whomever the next FIFA Executive Committee member to be found guilty of stealing the wealth of the game is not a ruinously corrupt and self-serving individual. It is and they are. Although there is value in this work—it is the attention given to these spectacular moments that allows more disruptive questions to be foregrounded—as with the political economy of the world in general, the focus on it to the exclusion of broader and more uncomfortable analyses is functionally diversionary and ultimately conservative (Fig. 16.1).

Then what? In both the world at large and the world of football, the problem is ultimately economic/capitalist rather than political/democratic. Žižek is one of a growing group of influential radical contemporary theorists (Alain Badiou, Antonio Negri, Frederic Jameson, etc.) for whom modern global Capitalism is fundamentally unable to alleviate the inequities, shocks, and crises it generates any longer. The ur-problem of modern football is not a problem of governance, or of accountability, or of Asian

Fig. 16.1 FIFA President Sepp Blatter showered with American dollars by British comedian Lee Nelson at a press conference in Zurich, July 2015 (Photo credit: Arnd Weigmann/Reuters)

gambling syndicates or doping or FIFA or the Premier League or Sky (although all of these things are symptoms): it is modern capitalism, and this is what needs changing if we are to change the game for good. We have a tendency to focus on criminality, covert corruption and theft, rather than analyzing a system that is overtly corrupt. The Bin Hammam scandal is emblematic of this: while it is now clear that he distributed bribes in order to secure the tournament, Qatar's only real argument to make for its suitability to host the tournament in the first place was precisely its willingness to spend the most money to do so. The "corruption" was simply the obscene informal extension of the logic of the formal bidding process itself.

Examples of this useful misdirection abound in writing about the game. An analogous misplacing of emphasis, of not seeing the forest for the trees, is found, for instance, in those who argue[10] that the greatest threat to the very future of professional football comes from Asian gambling syndicates, whose crime is trying to use money to unduly influence the outcome of games. While this is a problem, to be sure, the idea that black market gambling is the primary way in which money is inappropriately determinative of the outcome of games is rather to miss that point. Legal money has a much greater influence than illegal money ever will. As Simon Kuper and Stefan Szymanski demonstrate in *Soccernomics*[11], in the top leagues, how much a team spends on players "explained a massive 92 percent of variation of their league position."[12] If the concern is that money is tilting the playing field such that it determines the outcome of individual games and entire seasons, illegal match fixing ought to be among the very least of our worries. Financial doping is considerably more influential than actual doping or match fixing. If you want the inside scoop on how your team will do this weekend or this year, the most reliable indicator is the size of its wage bill, which is predictive of league position more than nine times out of ten.[13] That this is deemed more or less acceptable and illegal gambling is deemed an existential crisis to the idea of fair competition that is prerequisite to the appeal of the sport is an indication of the extent to which we have accepted the wholesale submission of football to the logic of free markets. Again, the problems besetting football have to do with its economic structure and the belief among its allegedly "apolitical" administrators that it should be bent in every way to align it more smoothly with the demands and logic of Capital.

DEMOCRACY CANNOT SAVE THE WORLD
(OF FOOTBALL) FROM CAPITAL

Given some of the characters who presently run the game, we who take football seriously spend a lot of time and energy talking critically about governance reform and the politics of the sport. However, and perhaps troubling to our liberal sensibilities, the idea of democracy being the mechanism by which the worst excesses of Capital are restrained seems less convincing than ever, and compelling arguments can be made that both the world of football and the world at large are in some ways blighted by a surplus of a certain kind of democracy, rather than by a paucity of it. Greater democracy cannot revolutionize or even meaningfully reform FIFA or football any more than it can the political economy at large, since lots of people either don't care about or actually quite *like* systems that produce inequality, even when they're on the business end of them.

FIFA is a particularly instructive organization here, since it is precisely its democratic structure—with each confederation and national association possessing equal representation and voting rights, regardless of its population size or footballing power—that is largely responsible for the majority of the problems that beset it. The idea of "one nation, one vote" seems fundamentally admirable in theory, but in practice it has directly enabled some of the organization's most enduring problems. Among the many reasons why this is the case is the lengthy recent record of smaller nations' greater susceptibility to offers of bribes and other forms of corruption than larger and better-resourced nations. While most people who follow the sport would agree that Russia and Qatar are not the two best countries in the world to host the World Cup Finals, the decision to allow them to do so was a democratic one, and if the voting were done again today, the outcome would likely be the same: Blatter's lengthy reign and many of the most contentious decisions made during his tenure were the result of FIFA's democratic governance model, not perversions of it.

Democracy isn't, nor can it be, the solution to these problems. Rather, our collective faith in the necessary fiction that liberal democracy will serve as the mechanism that restrains the excesses of Capital is part of the reason these problems exist in the first place. The problems that beset football are ultimately not about who is running the show, or how: the problems are caused by what it's being run *for*, and changing that is where we ought to be directing our critical energies.

(Football) Capitalism Isn't Broken: *It's Working*

For Žižek, this is one of the grand narratives that sustains our present socioeconomic order: the notion that current crises generated by capitalism are flaws of the system, or breakdowns in its smooth functioning, that can be fixed by better management.[14] As regards world football, I will follow his lead and suggest that they aren't, and it can't. Neither Capitalism nor Football Capitalism is broken–*they're working*. Viewed from a certain angle, world football is in great health. Each World Cup is more popular and profitable (for some) than the one that came before, and if the audiences and television and commercial sponsorship deals all keep increasing in size, then what really is the problem? From this perspective, the present onslaught of sporadically bad press is just a consequence of some transparency and governance issues that can be sorted with some managerial reforms and personnel changes. This was the position assumed by Sepp Blatter, for instance, who seemed constantly in a state of genuine bewilderment that people could be so fiercely opposed to the changes we have seen to the game during his tenure, and to a lesser extent it is the position of the mainstream media also, who typically conclude even scathing critiques with advocacy for rather superficial changes to football governance since so much about it seems to be going very well indeed.

If the criteria by which we evaluate the game are financial in nature, then all is well. Its value is increasing at impressive rates. The final match between Argentina and Germany will be the first sporting event in history to be watched by more than 1 billion people, besting the 909.6 million who tuned in for the 2010 final.[15] During the month of the entire 2014 finals, fans generated 3 billion World Cup-related Facebook interactions and 672 million Twitter messages.[16] However, these apparent successes would not have been possible without the equally unprecedented presence of many of the less savory features of this tournament, which have been well-documented elsewhere.[17] Mass evictions, the deaths of construction workers, the forced relocation of indigenous peoples, the suppression or gentrification of the *favelas*, the routinely brutal suppression of expressions of dissent by an expanded and increasingly militarized Brazilian security apparatus, the forced privatization of public areas to create FIFA's corporatized "zones of exclusion," the overturning of Brazilian law by a Swiss not-for-profit organization walking away from the tournament with between $3 and $5 billion in profits while the Brazilian taxpayers were left with a bill for around $11.63 billion: this is the price of running the most successful World Cup in history, and for those in charge of running football today, it's obviously a price worth paying. This is what business as usual looks like, and it's booming. FIFA's official self-evaluation of the tournament was an impressive 9.25/10.[18] Their revenues were the most money they've ever made from a single event, until the next one.

Forget Utopia: Capitalism Cannot Save Us or Football from the Excesses Caused by Capitalism

Even Marx was in awe of Capitalism's resilience, its fluid adaptability—what he called its "self-revolutionizing" character—but it cannot resolve every problem, and it seems less and less well equipped to solve the most significant ones it is causing today. I claim, then, following Žižek, that changing the bidding process and hosting arrangements, or replacing Blatter as President, or even outright replacing FIFA[19] as the body charged with organizing world football are attractive but ultimately short-termist solutions whose impact might be to inadvertently sustain the system by temporarily improving or making it superficially more palatably democratic or transparent while it continues to rot from within. Contemporary capitalist football cannot ultimately be saved by more democracy or better governance processes or the adoption of some quasi-socialist European model. And, crucially, it cannot keep going as it is today. For Žižek, *this* is the true utopian fantasy as regards our present economic system—the delusional idea is not that Capital cannot be replaced, but rather *that it can keep on going as it is forever*. The modern football economy is nothing if not unsustainable. Despite astonishing flows of capital into the game in the past generation, more than half of the teams in Europe are losing money as this incredible wealth has been used primarily to inflate player salaries and transfer fees to levels that are obscene by any measure. Ticket prices and television subscription fees continue to increase at rates hugely out of step with working people's wages, so the game is becoming increasingly expensive to those audiences upon whom it absolutely depends. Even the most avowedly capitalist, pro-free-market observers of the game today have little choice but to acknowledge that it is currently dependent on unsustainable financial bubbles and not built to endure. Capitalist football has no long-term future—the game cannot continue to be run the way it has been run of late. Then what? What should an Occupy football movement be aspiring to from beyond the matrix of Capital? How might it be made to be *for* something else?

THE FUTURE (OF FOOTBALL) SHOULD BE COMMUNIST

Football does not need reforming; it needs revolutionizing. Football needs to remove itself from the commodifying structures and profit motives of Capital or, to put it another way, it needs to become *for* something else besides money. Until this is the case, it will always be subject to the same kinds of crises, compromises, misrule and clientelism that beset it today. With Žižek,[20] and with all the usual caveats about not wishing to repeat the same errors of the past, I will call this alternative vision of the future *communist football*, a name chosen both because it signals the strongest possible rejection of the current capitalist model and because it makes absolutely central the idea of the commons, to which football must belong, if anything does. Modern capitalism is ill equipped to deal with those phenomena that belong to the commons and so the system with which we replace it must be one fit to purpose, one fit to manage a globally shared resource. We need a fundamentally different system if we aim to stop treating the collective resources of football as private property and the commanding heights of the game itself as an opportunity for actively recreating as entertainment the same kinds of inequalities that beset the world beyond the pitch.

This kind of a shift may seem as inconceivable or naïve in the world of football as it does in the world at large, an imaginative obstacle that is boundlessly useful to those who would perpetuate the rule of Capital indefinitely. As Fredric Jameson famously asserted, "[i]t seems to be easier for us today to imagine the thoroughgoing deterioration of the earth and of nature than the breakdown of late capitalism; perhaps that is due to some weakness of our imaginations."[21] However, it is worth pointing out that this incapacity to envision a path to a radically different political economy is a relatively recent development, as is the flooding of money into the game in the past three decades. Football's relationship with Capital can be radically transformed once more. This could happen easily and quickly, but most importantly: *it can happen.* There are many different ways in which football could undergo a process of decapitalization or communization, so I will end with a brief outline of at least two possible paths by which this kind of a sweeping transformation might happen.

A third option, of course, would simply be to do away with the World Cup, although I see little value in the abolitionist perspective. Aside from depriving the people of the world of one of the things that makes our time together here most pleasurable, it also presupposes an "either/or" dichotomy that seems to me both unimaginative and theoretically unhelpful. Instead, football can be transformed from a symbol of much that is contemptible in the modern world to something potentially liberatory and revolutionary, which is more in keeping with the creative nature of the game itself.

Pulling the Plug on Modern Football?

The first of the two potential general directions in which the game could move involves a regression to a bygone era: a concerted effort could be made to deflate the precarious financial bubble that has inflated in and around the game. World Cups used to be organized quite cheaply, and could be again. Most of the astronomical spending is new and utterly unnecessary. In order to sufficiently appreciate these spectacles, do we need to watch tournaments played in newly erected stadia, many of which will never be full again and many of which are paid for with public funds? Do we need the surface-to-air missile installations, drones and small armies of militarized police forces that have become ubiquitous features of recent sporting mega-events?

This move is one that could extend across the entire elite game. Efforts could easily be made to move backward toward a decapitalized game, which would provide no less pleasure to most people than it does today, only without the obscene, alienating excesses that seems to many to diminish its charm. We could gradually reduce player salaries, allow branding arrangements and corporate partnerships to whither, deflate the television bubble, move toward the nationalization of football leagues and teams and so forth.

Football "For the World"?

While the previous proposal has the advantage of simplicity on its side, and will obviously appeal to nostalgic sentiments about the gradual corruption of the game—the reversal of which might help purify it—another set of possibilities exists. Rather than draining the money, and thus its pernicious influence(s) from the game, efforts could be made to redirect an increasing percentage of the remarkable surplus value the game now generates to alleviate the kinds of suffering it presently exacerbates. FIFA could be replaced by a body with minimal organizational responsibilities and a very narrow mandate, whose raison d'être is to redistribute the income generated by the world's love of football to those that need it most, wherever they might be. This may seem far-fetched,[22] but if we do not need a garish FIFA style World Cup spectacle, then very little is required to organize a tournament that is as good (or better) and as profitable as the ones we have now. Obviously, FIFA does already redistribute some of its income to local associations (a minimum of $250,000 annually) and the federations (each of which get $2.5 million), but in spite of its flowery self-aggrandizing statements about doing so much good for the world, it currently gives only $27 million to development projects, which is slim compared to the $102 million it gives to its staff and the $36.3 million it gave out last year in executive bonuses, not to mention its current $1.4 billion in reserves; $27 million is also almost exactly the amount FIFA recently spent on the production of *United Passions*, an utterly delusional "autobiographical" feature film about the rise to power of Sepp Blatter and his band of "passionate mavericks" to their current position of dominance over the world's game—a truly embarrassing public relations exercise.[23]

For reasons that have not very much to do with football itself, the upper economic tier of the game has become awash with money. Football has found itself the spectacular beneficiary of broader economic shifts related to remarkable advances in communications technology, changes to corporate models of advertising and branding and, most recently, the influx of billions of dollars from petro-states into the higher echelons of the game each year. While one can certainly understand the impulse to return to a time before money became such a distorting, centrifugal force in the game, to do so is to miss a chance to permanently reorient the game in ways that do it credit and which might actually meet FIFA's current lofty mandate of existing "For the Game. For the World."

Contra the previously discussed strategy of aspiring to the recreation of a less capitalized time, approaches to revolutionizing football in this particular way would utilize and redirect its newfound wealth rather than attempting to back away from it. By imposing sensible limits on how the wealth of football is presently deployed that just about everyone would agree with, those charged with running the sport would have massive surpluses that could be made available for redistribution. The money that could be diverted to international aid agencies, for instance, from even one World Cup would be enough to save the lives of tens of millions of people globally, as well as to vastly improve the lives of millions of people in host nations. If used for this purpose, FIFA's current cash reserves could save the lives of a million people before the 2018 World Cup finals begin.[24]

As strange as this proposal may seem given the current hyper-capitalist state of world football, nothing about this would be particularly difficult from a practical perspective. It could easily be implemented in a few years were the will there to make it happen. Indeed, it would be a tremendously popular idea with many of the key stakeholders in the game. Fans would presumably—rather their spending on tickets and replica shirts and television subscriptions—contribute something positive and meaningful. Advertisers and corporate sponsors would appreciate the chance to be associated with good charitable works rather than endless stories of graft, greed and corruption. Many of those individuals who are most financially invested in the sport have done so with a knowledge that doing so will cost them a small fortune but will benefit their business in other less apparent ways (free advertising, good publicity, greenwashing and so forth), so a shift of this sort would benefit them even more than does the current arrangement. This is what communist football might look like: a mechanism for the eradication of economic inequality.

FOOTBALL AS A WEAPON OF THE REVOLUTION (AGAIN!)

Only a move of this type—one fully away from the acquisitive drives of global capitalism—can save football in the long term. If there are fortunes to be made from Capital, if it is organized around generating profit as the locus of winning, around competition off the field (in the spheres of retail, branding, global marketing, synergies, player speculation and so on) for the product that is on it, then it will always exhibit the same tendencies it does at present. And so it goes with the rest of the world as well. An ancillary benefit of this approach is that football is a powerful teaching tool, and a radical economic shift in its basic orientation may make similar national and international shifts more comprehensible and attractive to its billions of fans. If football can help teach us how to be subjects in a capitalist world—and it has been doing that for quite some time, among other things—it can and must be reshaped to help us create a better one.

THESE ARE THE BEST OF TIMES;
THESE ARE THE WORST OF TIMES...

As a result of the situation of the game today, we are entering a tremendously exciting time whether we like it or not. The dismal depths to which elite football has been dragged of late have made even the most radical, exciting, egalitarian possibilities widely imaginable, in some ways perhaps even inevitable. There is a huge groundswell of revolutionary, critical energy emanating around the world which began in South Africa and really kicked off on the streets of Brazil, where the rallying cry of the Popular Committees of the World Cup was "World Cup for Who?" Žižek says that "[i]n football we win if we obey the rules. In politics we win if we have the audacity to change the rules."[25] A window of opportunity has appeared within which we can be audacious. We have the chance for a short while to fundamentally change the rules by which world football has come to be governed, to reshape the ideological framework within which football has come to be defined and understood and to work toward a game that does much good in the world. All of this can be done, and it can be done, in the words of the peerless footballing philosopher Socrates, while "struggling for freedom, for respect for human beings, for equality, for ample and unrestricted discussions, for a professional democratization of unforeseen limits, and all of this while preserving the ludic, and the joyous, and the pleasurable nature of this activity."[26]

NOTES

1. See Piketty's, *Capital in the Twenty-First Century*, 4.
2. Ibid, 3.
3. See Walters, "White Elephants and Dark Matter(s): Watching the World Cup with Slavoj Žižek," "What's the Matter with English Football Fans? Watching the Match with Slavoj Žižek," and "Football's 'Dark Matter'(s): Differing Registers of Violence at the FIFA World Cup Finals."
4. See Terry Eagleton's, "Football: A Dear Friend to Capitalism."
5. Although it is not an argument I agree with.
6. I have argued at length elsewhere that this spending ought to be understood as an act of violence against the people of South Africa and Brazil by those in charge of ruling them. See my "White

Elephants and Dark Matter(s): Watching the World Cup with Slavoj Žižek."

7. See FIFA's "Mission and Statutes."

8. See Naomi Klein's *The Shock Doctrine: The Rise of Disaster Capitalism.*

9. See *Infinitely Demanding: Ethics of Commitment, Politics of Resistance* by Simon Critchley.

10. See in particular Declan Hill's, *The Fix: Soccer and Organized Crime.*

11. See Simon Kuper and Stefan Szymanksi, *Soccernomics.* 11–46.

12. Ibid, 12.

13. See Nick Harris's characteristically excellent analysis "It's the economy, stupid! How money fuels glory in the Premier League" on the *Sporting Intelligence* website.

14. See Slavoj Žižek, *The Year of Dreaming Dangerously.*

15. See Dion Dassanayake's "One billion people set to tune in to watch Germany and Argentina battle for the World Cup"

16. Reported by ESPN FC in "World Cup final sets US TV record."

17. For the best analysis of the tournament in Brazil, see David Goldblatt's *Futebol Nation: A Footballing History of Brazil,* Dave Zirin's *Brazil's Dance With the Devil: The World Cup, the Olympics, and the Fight For Democracy* and Christopher Gaffney's excellent *Hunting White Elephants* blog.

18. See "Global Parties, Galactic Hangovers: Brazil's Mega Event Dystopia" by Christopher Gaffney.

19. Quite who would best fill the void left by FIFA is difficult to say, as none of football's major governing bodies appear notably interested in operating in a fundamentally different way than does the sport's present administrators.

20. See Žižek, *Living in the End Times, The Year of Dreaming Dangerously, The Idea of Communism* and *The Idea of Communism 2.*

21. See Jameson's "Introduction" to *The Seeds of Time.*

22. And it is, but what about the political economy of modern football, which doesn't seem far-fetched these days?

23. See James Riach, "FIFA film *United Passions* is PR exercise that rankles even with its stars."

24. The amount of charitable giving required to save a human life in the world today is based on the analysis of Canadian activist and author Steven Lewis (*Big Ideas*) and Australian ethicist Peter Singer

25. (*The Life You Can Save*).
26. See Žižek on *philosophyfootball.com*
27. Cited in Goldblatt, *Futebol Nation* (151).

WORK CITED AND CONSULTED

Auclair, Philippe. "Qatar Hero". *The Blizzard* 5 (June 2012): 41–47.

Calvert, Jonathan, and Heidi Blake. "Plot to Buy the World Cup". *The Sunday Times*. Web, Last accessed 13 June 2014, http://www.thesundaytimes.co.uk/sto/news/uk_news/fifa/article1417325.ece.

Corbett, James. "The Fall Out". *The Blizzard* 5 (June 2012): 7–41.

Critchley, Simon. *Infinitely Demanding: Ethics of Commitment, Politics of Resistance*. London: Verso, 2007.

Dassanayake, Dion. "One Billion People Set to Tune in to Watch Germany and Argentina Battle for the World Cup". *The Sunday Express*. Web, Last accessed 20 July 2014, http://www.express.co.uk/news/world/488521/World-Cup-2014-Fans-gear-up-for-Germany-v-Argentina-final.

Eagleton, Terry. "Football: A Dear Friend to Capitalism". *The Guardian*. Web, Last accessed 3 Dec 2010, http://www.theguardian.com/commentisfree/2010/jun/15/football-socialism-crack-cocaine-people.

ESPN FC. *World Cup Final Sets U.S. TV Record*. Web, Last accessed 3 Sept 2014, http://www.espnfc.com/fifa-world-cup/story/1950567/world-cup-final-most-watched-soccer-game-in-us-historymore-than-26-million-viewers.

FIFA. *Mission and Statutes*. Last accessed 16 Oct 2014, Web, http://www.fifa.com/aboutfifa/organisation/mission.html.

Gaffney, Christopher. "Global Parties, Galactic Hangovers: Brazil's Mega Event Dystopia". *Los Angeles Review of Books*. Web, Last accessed 2 Oct 2014, http://lareviewofbooks.org/essay/global-parties-galactic-hangoversbrazils-mega-event-dystopia#.

———. *Hunting White Elephants*. Blog. Last accessed 7 Oct 2014, Web, http://www.geostadia.com/.

Goldblatt, David. *The Ball Is Round: A Global History of Football*. London: Penguin, 2007.

———. *Futebol Nation: A Footballing History of Brazil*. London: Penguin, 2014.

Harris, Nick. "It's the Economy, Stupid! How Money Fuels Glory in the Premier League". *Sporting Intelligence*. Web, Last accessed 20 June 2013, http://www.sportingintelligence.com/2012/05/14/its-the-economy-stupid-how-wages-aid-success-in-the-premier-league-140502/.

Hill, Declan. *The Fix: Soccer and Organized Crime*. Toronto: McLelland & Stewart, 2009.

Jameson, Frederic. *The Seeds of Time*. New York: Columbia University Press, 1996.

Jennings, Andrew. *Foul!: The Secret World of FIFA: Bribes, Vote Rigging and Ticket Scandals.* London: HarperSport, 2006.

Klein, Naomi. *The Shock Doctrine: The Rise of Disaster Capitalism.* Toronto: Vintage Canada, 2008.

Kuper, Simon, and Stefan Szymanksi. *Soccernomics.* Philadelphia: Nation Books, 2012.

Lewis, Stephen. *Big Ideas.* Podcast. Last modified 22 December 2012, Web, http://bigideas.tvo.org/episode/180746/grandest-challengept-3--samantha-nutt-and-stephen-lewis.

Panja, Tariq. "Sochi Olympics $51 Billion Price Tag Deters Host Cities". *Bloomberg News,* Web, Last accessed 1 Nov 2014. http://www.bloomberg.com/news/2014-10-30/sochi-olympics-51-billion-price-tag-deters-host-cities.html.

Piketty, Thomas. *Capital in the Twenty-First Century.* Translated by Arthur Goldhammer. Cambridge: The Belknap Press of the Harvard University Press, 2014.

Riach, James. "FIFA Film *United Passions* is PR Exercise that Rankles Even with Its Stars". *The Guardian.* Web, Last accessed 25 Oct 2014, http://www.theguardian.com/football/2014/oct/25/fifa-united-passions-pr-exercise-sepp-blatter.

Singer, Peter. *The Life You Can Save: Acting Now to End World Poverty.* New York: Random House, 2009.

Walters, Tim. "Football's 'Dark Matter'(s): Differing Registers of Violence at the FIFA World Cup Finals". In *Football and Communities Across Codes,* edited by Deirdre Hynes, Annabel Kiernan, and Keith D. Parry, 161–173. Oxford: Inter-Disciplinary Press, 2013a.

———. "What's the Matter with English Football Fans? Watching the Match with Slavoj Žižek". In *Football and Communities Across Codes,* edited by Deirdre Hynes, Annabel Kiernan, Keith D. Parry, 107–122. Oxford: Inter-Disciplinary Press, 2013b.

———. White Elephants and Dark Matter(s): Watching the World Cup with Slavoj Žižek. In *Žižek and Media Studies: A Reader,* edited by Matthew Flisfeder, and Louis-Paul Willis, 115–130. New York: Palgrave Macmillan, 2014.

Yallop, David. *How They Stole the Game.* London: Constable, 2011.

Zirin, Dave. *Brazil's Dance with the Devil: The World Cup, The Olympics, and the Fight for Democracy.* Chicago: Haymarket Books, 2014.

———. "Brazil: Yes, Blame the Damn World Cup". *Dissident Voice.* Web, http://dissidentvoice.org/2013/06/brazil-yes-blame-the-damn-world-cup/. Accessed 25 June 2013.

———. "FIFA Denies Women's World Cup Players an Equal Playing Field—Literally". *The Nation.* http://www.thenation.com/blog/187129/fifa-denies-womens-world-cup-players-equal-playing-field-literally#. Accessed 3 Nov 2014.

————."Why Are Brazilians Protesting the World Cup?". *The Nation*. Web, http://www.thenation.com/blog/174999/eduardo-galeano-speaks-outbra-zils-world-cup-protests#. Accessed 26 June 2013.

Žižek, Slavoj. *Violence*. New York: Picador, 2008.

————. *In Defense of Lost Causes*. London: Verso, 2009.

————. "How To Begin from the Beginning". In *The Idea of Communism*, edited by Costas Douzinas and Slavoj Žižek. London: Verso, 2010a.

————. *Living in the End Times*. London: Verso, 2010b.

————. *The Year of Dreaming Dangerously*. London: Verso, 2012.

————. *The Idea of Communism 2*. Edited by Slavoj Žižek. London: Verso, 2013.

————. "Philosophyfootball.com". Web, Last accessed 7 Apr 2013, https://www.philosophyfootball.com/view_item.php?pid=467.

CHAPTER 17

On Virtue, Irony, and Glory: The Pitch and the People

Jason Burke Murphy

Soccer matches and soccer teams are interpreted as representing something other than players competing to win. In a match, events are displayed, representations are posed, and narratives are developed by interpreters. First, I'll give some examples of this representative power. I do not have a complete explanation for it but I will offer two reasons—character and glory. In the section "Virtue", I say more about character, vice, and virtue, and how we refer to it when we explain matches and players. This extends even to discussions of national character. In section "The stage, the canvas, the pitch", I give some explanation for the evocative power that enables soccer to play this role. To do so, I compare the game to art and to dance. In "A short praise of fan irony", I argue that the game presents character traits but not the actual character of players or their communities. For this reason, fans should have an ironic relationship with the narratives they use to interpret the game and the world around it. In "Glory", I try to say something about the glory of the game. I list some different types of glory. Finally, "The creative fan", calls for creative fans to embrace virtue, irony, and glory and insist the game be organized with these three ideas in mind.

J.B. Murphy (✉)
Department of Philosophy, Elms College, Chicopee, MA, USA

© Hofstra University 2017
B. Elsey, S. Pugliese (eds.), *Football and the Boundaries of History*,
DOI 10.1057/978-1-349-95006-5_17

EXAMPLES OF SOCCER'S REPRESENTATIVE POWER

People say "It's the USA versus Mexico tonight." Some match-ups are exciting for strictly footballing reasons, when advancing in a tournament is at stake or if past games make a match interesting. But other matches are backed by off-pitch history.

Let's take West Germany's 1954 World Cup victory in Berne. Called "Das Wunder von Bern" Germany now reenters the world stage. There is a way to participate in the international community again. The defeat and corruption of the Nazis will only haunt the country for so long. This final was the first time the German National Anthem was played at an international event since World War II.

German characteristics are often cited in explaining the victory. Adidas had invented a new boot with screw-in studs so you could keep the same boot on in muddy weather. Teamwork, diligence, and technology will get Germany out of its troubles. Das Wunder von Bern is part of the story of the *Wirtschaftswunder*. The Cold War also comes into play as Germany beat a Hungarian team widely considered one of the most skillful ever.[1] A cold rain is sometimes still called "Fritz Walter weather" after the captain of this team.

Zidane's head-butt in the 2006 World Cup final is another example of the need to invest representative force onto large-scale sporting events. Instead of Zidane just head-butting Materazzi because he was stressed out and exhausted, Materazzi must have said *something* that makes sense of Zidane's massive sporting mistake. There are always multiple details that explain why a moment has become big. In the case of the head-butt, the visual was incredible. Zidane is always well-poised and Materazzi sold the hit. Before we heard the truth, newspapers argued that Zidane was expressing the frustration of the banlieues.

Newspapers claimed that they had hired lip readers and produced different projections onto the moment. "Son of a terrorist whore" was one lip read. (I remember verbally passing that one on. I believed it.) Another claimed Materazzi wished an ugly death on Zidane's family. Another claimed that Materazzi called Zidane a "harkis," which refers to Arab supporters of the French regime in Algeria. (Materazzi would not know this, by the way.) Zidane has apologized to everyone but Materazzi, "To him I cannot. Never, never. It would be to dishonor me. I'd rather die. There are evil people, and I don't even want to hear those guys speak."[2] This statement came four years after the head-butt. Good versus Evil instead of two millionaire athletes losing the plot.[3]

There are hundreds of examples of soccer matches invested with narrative implications. Polish fans remember a match on 3 July 1974 that they call "Der Wasserschlacht," the "Water Slaughter." It had rained all day creating conditions that were widely said to give Germans an advantage. Germany did win the match, knocking Poland out of the tournament. I was very struck to find out that Polish television replayed this entire match right before a live broadcast of these two teams in the 2008 European Championship. How could anyone invest themselves in such grief?

France's World Cup 1998 winning side is celebrated as a triumph for the multicultural vision of France. (The story of Zidane became the stuff of obsession because a multicolored France won in France.) It would be hard now to win with a racist understanding of any national team. Jean-Marie Le Pen stated that he would rather have a team composed of "actual" Frenchman. The team signed a statement that they would not play for France if Le Pen won the French presidential election. The team represents the country and its composition forces a debate. Debating the national team gets people talking to each other who otherwise do not meet. Similarly, many Americans have recently learned of the existence of Black Germans as the US national team has recruited among the children and grandchildren of Americans.

I was struck by an article by Ogo Sylla on *Howler* magazine's website that argues that the 2014 Men's World Cup is the first German victory that "means nothing."[4] It is hard to argue that this victory meant more than the one in 1954 but stories will be told. Right before the World Cup Final, David Goldblatt places the German team in the "real-world" context that informs the sporting narrative:

> Germany, finally emerging as what it has been for decades, the pre-eminent European power, has a football team to match its ambitions and its character: brilliantly organized but instantly flexible, individually accomplished but telepathically networked, technically superior to the Brazilians in touch, positioning and anticipation. Yet they carry other German traits too: a collective solidarity that disdains the egotistical, and a realistic conservatism about an uncertain world, for no one feels victory is assured.[5]

Ogo Sylla is arguing that this German victory does not do what earlier finals did. Sylla argues that Germany will not change its self-assessment or its international reputation. There is no Zero Hour in the recent past nor is there a Cold War in the present. But Goldblatt shows it otherwise; the idea that Germany has it figured out in a world of chaos is a strong one. Links will be made between its soccer success and its continued negotiation of economic and political challenges. This is just one reason why Angela Merkel made a point of being seen with the team.

All of my examples have been national team matches and I have exerted tunnel vision by only looking at geopolitical implications. When club matches are analyzed, a story is told and this story always makes reference to character. Squads doing well have "belief," "leadership," and "quality" while struggling squads are "fragile," "fearful," or "weak." Almost every halftime, announcers speculate about which manager is the "happier" of the two. Players need to "commit themselves." The skills needed to play soccer well are peculiar to sport. Even the emotional stances taken by players do not translate well into family, business, or culture. Why, then has this game taken hold of us? Why do we ever, as in the examples earlier, turn to this game to figure the world out?

Umberto Eco lays it hard on the fans, attributing most of their energy to compulsions linked to psycho-sexual and socio-political frustrations. He argues that sports talk is "chatter." There is no way to test the claims that are being put out. Those who are defeated by an inability to organize their world or even talk about it now answer their drives with an almost unending talk that cannot be countered by unrepeatable games.[6] But the very thing that makes a match an *event* is this unrepeatability. Nick Hornby talked about it. Live theater and dance can come close but even they follow a script. A soccer match has a rulebook but two teams enact something that cannot be repeated.[7] This is abstract art that taps into the very idea of an event. This is why watching a game later in the day just doesn't cut the mustard.

Eco has a point. We seek something separate from a world that worries us when we turn to sporting drama. Sporting worry just isn't like world worry. In reference to sport, I've heard people say that "It matters and it doesn't matter." Eco's diagnosis does not counter my belief that soccer is particularly well suited to project what I will call "ideas of virtue." The pitch and the game have a "glory" to them and I will say something about that term as well as it is sometimes used in soccer discussion. Glory is beautiful but not necessarily good. There are multiple types of glory. We want the game to be good precisely because we find it glorious. This is one reason why fans are told that leagues and tournaments and the FIFA are developing a better world. Fans are disappointed to find out it is not true to the extent it should be. We should think about the consequences of the denial of glory to many parts of the soccer-playing world. Women were once denied venues for play. Now they are denied glory. Some fans of the women's game prefer the more earthly scale. What to do with glory is a question that creative fans face in the future.

VIRTUE

We attribute virtues to players and teams and nations. "Guile," "courage," and "football intelligence" come to mind. Virtue ethics might give us a handle on this. This is an ancient approach to ethics that seeks to explain ethics in terms of character revealed in action as opposed to the mere application of rules. This ethical approach was not developed for sports discussion but one does run into athletic metaphors throughout. Adherents think that the mere application of moral rules is insufficient. One needs to witness people living well and acquire their habits. We have a rich vocabulary of virtue and vice. We can reflect on it through philosophy and literature and we can work hard to present excellence to each other.[8]

Aristotle argued that we cannot know if someone has developed their virtues until they are tested over the course of a life. Sporting events may be too few and too subject to chance to provide a reliable indicator of the sporting virtues that are really in play. But we try. If a player scores a lot, we will want to explain why. If a country has surprised us with an unusually good national team, we will want to tell a story.

To be truthful, we would likely want to separate kinetic virtues, like speed, passing, and shooting, from understanding virtues, like anticipation, positioning, and vision, from ethical virtues, like patience, drive, and team spirit. But we often blend them together.

We depend on diagnoses of character (or at least habit) in order to understand a game. A game is very different when we believe that a team keeps passing backward for its own reasons instead of due to defensive pressure. A team holding out for a zero–zero draw is given credit for its determination if we know that it is outmatched. We denounce a team that plays this way if we think the team can win the match.

Of course, all sports present bodies in motion and people in competition. Historians give reasons for soccer's global dominance. These include global British business enterprise, the movement from the elite to the working class, and investment in the game among many national regimes. I just want to put in a word about the game itself. Soccer is an unusually good presentation of virtue, even if not the most accurate presentation of the virtues of a player or team. Soccer renders the players very visible. The bodies are not covered by equipment. There is often space between the players. Player's faces are visible if you are close enough or watching on television.

The size of the pitch makes for a very dramatic stage. Twenty-two players seem just enough to make scoring a goal difficult without losing track of the teams. Players compete and cooperate, which place different sorts of virtues and vices on display. The game tests patience. Even the best teams are rebuffed more often than they get through the other teams' defenses. Players must deal with risk throughout the match. A far superior team will let in a goal if they lapse in attention. I am going to compare soccer to dance and to painting in order to testify still more to its evocative power.

The Stage, the Canvas, the Pitch

Imagine a stage. A dance.

What do dancers show us? We see bodies capable of difficult performances. If we know a little bit we will be impressed when they make it look easy. The choreography that guides the dancers aims to create drama, to portray bodies at work, to pay homage to past performances and choreographic ideas.

When I watch dance I am always a little envious and I always wonder what it must be like. Ballet can frustrate me because it defines beauty in rather strict ways. I tend to enjoy watching dance that disrupts norms (where it can) while still making use of the ideas and images that come to mind when you hear the word "dance." I am always confronted by a personality that is performed in the work. One can be very surprised to find out that this personality is different off the stage and when no longer dancing. (Yet, how could one be like that all the time?)

Sometimes dance is attached to story and sometimes it is abstracted from that. In all cases, attention is brought to bear on the body and on personality. Dance often just refers to dance, something we see kids do just to liven things up.

It is a funny thing that I can say "imagine a dance" and it means something. After all, there are an infinite number of images you can turn to. But that is just it. When we communicate, we turn to a common life-world and we can anticipate the sorts of images you would conjure.

My bet is that you would imagine a man and woman at some point working together while working with the word "dance." Unless I steer you, you probably imagined people who are good at dancing. If you danced often, you likely remembered that.

Now, imagine a canvas. A painting.

There are ideas behind a painting that guide our interpretation of it. The artist knows that the viewer will bring her own ideas to the work. Often an art critic will let a viewer know which ideas are being implemented by a work or at least the critic will throw out proposals or situate the work alongside other projects that are interestingly distinct or similar.

A painting could have a very direct message. There is political and religious propaganda but there are also paintings that draw your attention to a very general theme without a particular conclusion in play. A very abstract painting seeks to move away from that. All paintings bring attention to bear on color, vision, and shape. Paint also often refers to paint. We see kids paint just to liven things up.

When I say "painting" you form an image. You might remember a painting you saw in a museum. You might have imagined someone by herself moving a brush on a canvas. There are so many possible meanings at work in the word but we draw from a similar enough set of images to be able to communicate.

Now, finally, make the stage much bigger. Instead of a choreography, two sets of 11 dancers will be given some rules to keep in mind. Imagine the canvas is now a green field. Two metaphors are being mixed but that's the happy accident that is soccer.

The pitch is simple. The rules are simple (sort of). Scoring is simple to understand. One could see this whole game as an abstract work of art. The founders of football took a kid's game, combined it with a league that promotes and relegates, and then watched what happened.

I have a lot of the same emotional reactions to art, dance, and sport. Competition is one of the differences that sport poses for the viewer. Artists and performers are in competition for positions and funding but that is not what drives the action and the drama for the viewer. With sport, competition changes the situation. It is why we don't know what is going to happen. There are plans but there are opponents with other plans.

Now and then a player or a team changes our understanding of how the game works. We read that the Scots developed heading and passing. Brazil transforms tricks into successful tactics. Wider pools of recruits continue to pose the question of what strategy best accounts for increased endurance and speed.

Because there is no script, we are often not sure what has happened. Was the offense too aggressive? Is someone in defense injured? Sport generates drama and portrays beauty and virtue in ways analogous to art and stage. In fact, when we learn how athletes are in the rest of their lives, we are a little disappointed to see the drama lapse.

Art, Dance, and Sport have included a tension between their purposes (and there is more to debate there) and markets, social prejudice, and normative expectations. They often defy these pressures and call them into question. They often bolster the strength of these forces. More people visit a museum than a top-level professional sports event in the USA. But most Americans would not believe that.[9] No one has figured how to put a museum on television outside of a travelogue urging you to go see it. What a strange situation. Most people who go to museums think less people go than do.

I am glad that museums do not have artists paint on stage with a winner declared on the spot. (Surely that has happened on television somewhere.) Artists are organizing a different sort of attention for the viewer.

In *Fever Pitch* Nick Hornsby points out the event character of a soccer match. In most theater plays, you would have failed to conduct a play if something entirely different happened the second time. A daunting amount of skill and resources are put into preserving art over long periods of time. But the same rules (and sometimes the same 22 players) are implemented and, even if the score turns out the same, the game would be very different.

My goal here is to "sell" this game as an arena in which humanity is presented. Features of humanity are made a theme. The game provokes images that we draw from within and from outside the game. We try to explain what we see and refer to ideas about skill and virtue like "Strength," "Bravery," "Guile," or "Fortitude."

Soccer has done a good job visually countering stereotypes about countries. The best Swedish player is named "Ibrahimovic." Many Americans now know that there are Black Germans and Black Italians. Hollywood would never cast a Black German actor to play a German or Italian. It is precisely because the team is trying to win that it is willing to ask the public to recognize players as representative, even if the public has to learn something.

It is precisely the evocative force of soccer that makes me worry about it. When I say "soccer" (or the word from your first language) you formed a mental image, just like you did with "dance" or "painting". If you played, you may remember a game you were in. You are also likely to imagine a male player running and kicking. I remember while in Germany (before the Women's World Cup there) discussing how many women play in the USA and in Germany. A woman at my table said she cannot imagine a woman playing. The rest of the table (all cosmopolitical feminists) agreed. Americans may be surprised to hear that. Soccer in Europe is often the sport used to make working class boys into working class men. We have a different set of images associated with the word "soccer." Earlier, we saw how important men's soccer has been in the development of German self-understanding. I would hate to leave this sort of power to a bastion of sexual exclusion.

Too much sports writing is about why this team wins or that team loses. There is also too much written about the celebrity lives of athletes or how happy or unhappy they are with this or that team. This material seems to lapse into cliché very quickly. For instance, I really don't believe the winning team usually wanted to win more than the losing team.

There may be a need to distinguish different types of fandom. A pick-up player watches his friends while playing. A fan watches the player he admired as a child decline. One billion people watch the World Cup.

There are a lot of wasted opportunities when it comes to discussion about soccer. Most mainstream pundits assume that all fans are men affiliated with a single team. They assume the fans only care about winning. At least they seem to believe that fans want players to set it all aside in order to win. The facts hedge against that. There is nothing inconsistent or foolish about wanting a team to win *and* wanting it to represent something good. Creative fans must testify against the reigning model of fan as passive brand loyalist.

A SHORT PRAISE OF FAN IRONY

Umberto Eco has a point and I sympathize with non-fans who must endure contact with fans. But his attack on the sports fan doesn't take the game's presentation of character into account. A story about character is told in every explanation of a match or a season. It must be said, though, that this presentation is deceptive. For one thing, details sometimes get lost in the narrative. The story of the 1954 German World Cup victory often does not include the fact that Ferenc Puskás suffered a hairline fracture from a German tackle in an earlier match. (I have heard a couple of Hungarians include this detail.)

Soccer is a team sport in which luck plays a very real factor. Luck is usually the strongest explanation for the difference between two teams next to each other in the season's standings. Luck will be acknowledged by pundits quickly and then quickly set aside whenever the winner is praised and their strengths are held up for all to see.

All explanations are underdetermined by the facts at hand. One cannot replay a game to determine if the keeper suffered due to weak defenders, or too much offensive strategy, or an injury.

Every narrative you embrace confronts outliers. Even the most energetic player will have a slow game. A team known for its coordination will have breakdowns. Historians struggle with the interaction between larger narratives and instances that do not fit those narratives. How many unruly events do we need before the narrative ought to be questioned? The greatest goal threat will not score in every game. The best goalkeeper will let in goals.

I remember talking with someone about FC Barcelona who argued that they "lump the ball in long" as often as any English team. Barca simply has better public relations. I was a little flummoxed. What if I have been counting Stoke's long balls (and making negative character charges) when they played Tottenham but not Barca's when they played Chelsea? There are enough counterexamples to make selection bias very powerful. (I still think this person is wrong, it should be said.)

The game is complex enough to make the stories of character highly suspect. There are many a player who are promoted to a more competitive team and not played often. That player might be extremely ambitious but it will be hard to tell. Another player seems to lack wit but that is because she is played out of position. My wonderful attitude and character have never led to any presentation of skill on the pitch. Well, there was one time but I'll talk about that later.

Fans who know that other narratives can be derived from the same sets of events they've seen can be called "ironic." Richard Rorty gives an account of irony in one of his most famous works. The ironist "has radical and continuing doubts about the final vocabulary she currently uses because she has been impressed by other vocabularies."[10] Rorty extended this sense of irony to every single belief that is not required for us here. Irony seems important to any truthful relationship with a sporting narrative. As fans of the game, we get to enjoy the stories we tell, without getting lost in the lessons they project.[11]

GLORY

Danny Blanchflower said: "The game is about glory." Blanchflower is making an ethical claim that the game works when players aim for excellence. David Goldblatt depicts glory as arising in soccer due to floodlights, which make the pitch and players look more dramatic, and television, which increased the size of the audience exponentially.[12]

Glory seems hard to grasp.[13] The Greek word for glory, *Kleos* (κλέος), implies "others hear of you." We have had 2,000 years of theological rendition of glory, often with recourse to metaphors of light. Many theologians want to make it clear that glory should only be attributed to God. I will try to give some examples of very different kinds of glory at a human scale. The list is not complete.

Achievement glory. This displays the players in such a way that a low-level game can still take a hold of the viewer. I would draw an analogy with seeing a band play in a garage or at a hole-in-the-wall club. The stage lifts the band up for attention. I often envy an artist just because she can draw, paint, or sculpt at all. This seems distant from others hearing of someone or shining like the sun. Yet, we are impressed when we watch people create.

Testimonial glory. This is the sort the Greeks spoke of. We cannot watch every match or even every important match. We hear people tell the story of great players in the past. Even if we have seen a player a few times, a lot of our attitude toward the player will be based on testimony. When we reach back to the past and hear the list of great names, we depend on testimony—the Old Etonians, Matthias Sindelar, Leonidas, and many, many others.

Even the players who are documented on film and video are usually given a reputation based on testimony. We just can't (and shouldn't) see it all. I've seen television matches in pubs and joined in groans or gulps of fear as a glorified opposing player warms up or suits up to substitute. Most of us in the pub are crazy but not so crazy that we've actually scouted the player. The pub is testifying to the player's abilities. The pub is basing its testimony on that of others.

To make another musical analogy, I think about the legends that surround early blues artists with no recordings or just a few. Art is preserved so you might think testimony is less important but we often look at art a second time if we are convinced of its influence or that it has been assessed by a curator. Testimony is often wrought by the very fact that something is in a museum or on stage. Without it, we would not do the work needed to interpret difficult events or works.[14]

Performative glory. Here one not only can play but one can play well. We watch someone move well and it has an effect on us. We move alongside them. I have never watched artists or dancers without wishing I could do what they do. (Some masochistic or politically vicious works are the only exceptions.) The same goes for soccer players, almost all of who work at a level I wish I could emulate. (Some masochistic, diving, and damaging players as well as politically vicious club cultures provide the only exceptions. I have some questions about wanting to face the pain inflicted by high-stakes competitions.) Again, seeing a musician deliver on a tune or an artist produce something you now know you wanted to see has its own glorious dimension.

Spectacular glory. This is the glory instilled by an event. The crowd plays a role here, as does a television-viewing audience. The crowd turns a game into an event. They set a standard and the tone. Even a relatively small crowd can do this. I have almost fainted a couple of times in packed bars when my club scored. Part of the drama of the World Cup is knowing how many watch it. These first three sorts of glory can be enjoyed in a calm way or a crazy way. Spectacle is harder to resist. Adorno and Horkheimer worried about the new mass cultural technologies they saw. They worried film, radio, and mass rallies overwhelmed the viewer and made a critical, ironic attitude toward the event difficult.[15] Soccer and the Olympics are organized with none of these worries. Of course, lots of things are lit up and put on television. The ironic fan has to admit that many of the joys of the game are analogous to the joys experienced by arena rock fans, movie lovers, and romantic serial viewers.

Apotheosis. Throughout every World Cup, advertisers and commentators speculate about which player will ascend to another level. Zidane's head-butt, and red card, interrupted the narrative in which Zidane moved into the pantheon of greats alongside Pelé and Maradona. Soccer and the Olympics draw from an array of neoclassical presentation of the divine in order to promote the idea that you may get to see a player cross over from great to a-whole-other-level. The international careers of Lionel Messi and Cristiano Ronaldo are often spoken of in a tragic light, which is odd given the glory they have known. It only makes sense if you see another level denied.

Spectacular glory and apotheosis are particularly divorced from the actual character of the players. Glory entails the sort of "willing suspension of disbelief" that Coleridge describes.[16] Glory is portrayed and perceived but it is, again, deceptive. Achievements are often one-shots and not indicative of an ability to achieve. When walking past the practice pitch at my college, a ball went out of bounds and landed in front of me. Still holding all my books, I kicked it hard and was pleased to see it land at the feet of the player. I left quickly before another test showed the truth—I am one of the worst players I have ever seen. Of course, testimony opens up space for exaggeration and distortion. Performances attain glory based precisely on how events are pitched. A friendly pre-season match is accorded less importance than a cup final. Given that all of it matters and doesn't matter—there is no solid reason for the current division of glory.[17] As for spectacle, those matches that are accorded mass attention are usually the product of mass steering by large-scale media enterprises. The actual event is similar to other matches at other times. Lastly, apotheosis seems to be a product of these other forms of glory coalescing at a particular time. All people are mortal. Apotheosis is always a deceit.

Even though the anti-climactic truth about the head-butt was revealed, a 16-foot statue of the moment was unveiled at the Centre Pompidou in September 2012. The drive to glory is hard to stop. The statue was put on public display in Qatar in October of 2013. It was removed to a museum because local leaders denounced it as idolatrous.[18] They have a point.

Talking about image earlier, I noted that women are often excluded from soccer. This was the explicit policy of most countries until surprisingly late. They are certainly excluded from glory. FIFA continues to describe the women's game as "developing" and soccer media seldom builds on the game's past.[19] The fact that Azteca Stadium was filled to see the Women's World Cup final in 1971 and the level of excitement that surrounded the last few cups show that there is plenty of material here for the sort of storytelling that could lend women at play every level of glory mentioned here.[20] There are some players who are accorded attention, often because they are both models and quality players. Other writers are more equipped to lay out the extent of the obstacles women players face. To only speak of denying glory and a lack of images is, of course, to understate the problem. In all discussions of soccer, women are eventually treated as intruders and are often threatened. When we think about women's football, we are thinking about recognizing women as capable of glory. We also have to think about the problematic features of glory.

David Goldblatt's well-loved *The Ball is Round* acknowledges the game was and is organized by sexists, and he never attributes or blames "femininity" for the way the women's game has struggled. Goldblatt also describes some important moments in the women's game. This makes him better than most soccer writers. But he does not go into the many sorts of exclusions and aggressions that mark the game. Had there been as much detail here as there was for—say—stadia design, it would be hard to stick with the tone and the narrative arc of the book. Goldblatt's book is about the movement of the game from boy's schools, to a fixture in several public spheres, to the largest spectacle the world has ever known. It is simply harder to celebrate this ascent to glory as we see what it has meant for others.[21] Deceived by the beauty of the game, we often end up letting the stories of nations be told through events where women are only allowed as decorations.

As Goldblatt notes, the Men's World Cup also sets up Africa and Asia to lose by not giving them sufficient positions in the tournament. This lowers the amount of funding that the continent receives and the tendency for European national teams to beat African and Asian teams perpetuates itself. There should be a maximum allocation for each continent based on population, and a maximum number set by the current method, and then run-offs to determine who finally enters the tournament. Greece should have to play Egypt. Slovenia should have to play Iraq. If European and South American teams win, they can maintain their current number of positions, instead of doing so now by fiat. The majority of the world should have a chance to play for glory.

THE CREATIVE FAN

We might need to wait a long time before FIFA or your national Football Association gets its act together.[22] Until then, we are capable of being creative fans who express a love of the game that explicitly resists imperialism and sexism.[23] In the USA, soccer fans went around mainstream sports media until that media no longer ignored or openly despised the game. With blogs and feeds and all of the other tools of fandom, we can again defy vicious cultures and sexist organizations. The game is beautiful; we also want it to be good.

The new creative fan reports the game as they see it but they also seek to tell the narratives that ought to be told. We care about the game independently of its money and power. Fans do not profit from their investment in their club. They pay to witness events. This is one reason fans turn on mercenary players. Many fans have given up quite a chunk of their money and time. Often that percentage rivals the percentage gain sought by a player who wants a transfer. (I do not object to players seeking big wages but the fans' perspectives on the club and the game are more interesting almost all of the time.) Even fans of the wealthiest clubs are not content to announce their clubs' budget. Fans of smaller clubs have other reasons besides winning. Fans have done well to prevent the game from being more disrupted by commercial forces than it has been. In the USA, televised games of US sports take much longer than they used to in order to work in more commercials. Yet, US sports channels are showing soccer because of the audience. US fans built ways to state their expectations and that has changed the environment. But fans can go much further than this. Creative fans can build fora that insist on a game that promotes the general welfare and opposes classism, homophobia, imperialism, and sexism, instead of shoring them up.[24]

The creative fan has a sense of irony and can love the sport while knowing that it is not good in and of itself. Developing soccer will promote events that display character and glory but that is not by itself good. Why do we keep hearing about the contrast between the beautiful event and the world's poverty? Because when something is that captivating, it should also be beneficial. The game is so interesting, dramatic, and impressive that we knock ourselves back and forth. We forget and then we realize the need to steer all this attention and all this goodwill and all this money toward good ends. Anything else is a wasted opportunity. Creative fans who are citizens of reality are everywhere. The game should belong to them.

Fig. 17.1 Virtue and the people. US Attorney General Loretta Lynch as "FIFA Slayer" (Credit: Kate Niemczyk/Marvel Comics/ESPNw)

Notes

1. See Deutsche Welle 2003. Like many people I also would refer to Goldblatt 2008, in this instance to pg. 346–356. The title of his book quotes Sepp Herberger, the manager of this German team.
2. *The Guardian*, 2010.
3. I treat Zidane in my blog "The Game and the World". Entry "Two: From Head-butt to Worldview The Match Must Represent SOMETHING" at http://thegameandtheworld.blogspot.com/2014/06/two-from-headbutt-to-worldview-match.html
4. Sylla 2014.
5. "The World Cup is Political Theater of the Highest Order", *The Guardian*, July 11, 2014.
6. See "Sports Chatter" and "The World Cup and Its Pomps" in Eco 1986. Eco's essays are synopsized very well in Trifonas 2001.
7. "Maybe you've got a hot ticket for the first night of an Andrew Lloyd Webber show, but you know that the show is going to run for years and years, so you'd actually have to tell people afterwards that you saw it before they did, which is kind of uncool and in any case completely ruins the effect...It's not news in the same way that an Arsenal v Everton semi-final is news: when you look at your newspaper the next day, whichever one you read, there will be extensive space given over to an account of your evening, the evening to which you contributed simply by turning up and shouting." Hornby 2000; pg. 192.
8. My favorite single-essay introduction to virtue ethics is Hirsthouse 2006.
9. Mondello 2008.
10. Rorty 1989; pg. 73.
11. Simon Kuper and Stefan Szymanski point out there is comparably little research on fans and fan behavior. They point to evidence that not all fans are "Hornbies," by which they refer to Nick Hornby description of being "chained" to Arsenal. Many fans, unheralded, follow different clubs. Most change clubs to seek the latest champion but many try different size clubs and different fan cultures. To wander as a fan seems like a great idea. See Kuper and Szymanski 2014 pg. 242ff. We need to hear from these fans.
12. Goldblatt 2008.
13. The parallels I made earlier with art and dance come to mind again. I have not heard the word "glorious" or any similar adjectives in

art criticism or art promotion, though I have with dance. I simply offer that as a witness. I don't want to make very many claims about art and dance and their criticism because I would rather yield to others.

14. See Doyle 2013. Doyle doesn't mention "testimony" the way I have here but she does argue that mainstream art criticism "rejects work once it detects the presence of an identity and a discernible politics" (21). Such work will be denied the testimony needed to convince hearers and viewers to keep listening and seeing. The creative fans I describe will face similar problems.

15. Theodor Adorno and Max Horkheimer, *Dialectics of Enlightenment* (Palo Alto: Stanford University Press, 2007).

16. An important lesson in Kuper and Szymanski 2014 is how little money soccer enterprises actually take in. Whether it's a big club like Real Madrid or FIFA itself, they pale in revenue compared to their sponsors and even compared to most companies. "This is partly a problem of 'appropriability': soccer clubs can't make money out of (can't appropriate) more than a tiny share of our love of soccer" (pg. 51). See Chap. 3 "The Worst Business in the World" pp. 49–71. We don't believe this because we are struck by the glory.

17. I have always wondered why England's Community Shield is not a "bigger deal." It will be listed among important victories but the event just doesn't have that same sense of performative import. It could be that this just isn't the way seasons begin.

18. Al Jazeera. 2013. http://www.aljazeera.com/news/middleeast/2013/10/qatar-removes-zidane-statue-after-outcry-201310302338612974.html

19. See Doyle 2011.

20. See Williams 2003 and 2008.

21. Elsey 2011 shows, in her history of Chilean soccer, that you can include the acts of exclusion and the struggle women footballers wage and still have a compelling sense of a game with something at stake.

22. If you are angry with FIFA, you really should look at the rest of capitalism. FIFA is about as corrupt as your average country or corporation. Of course, it should not at all resemble either. As far as corruption goes, Transparency International's recommendations for independent review and good government provide some

crucial steps. See Transparency International 2011, 2012, and 2013. "Disappointed That FIFA Gives No Strong Signal for Change" posted 30 March 2012.

23. Some existing models for this are the anti-bigotry fan movements, the supporters' trusts, and the German Bund der Aktiven Fußballfans as well as the Football Action Network in England. We should not say that all is well in soccer fan culture. The beauty of the game is one of the things that make people crazy. There is also a frequent focus in soccer fan culture on the base and the ugly. I have emphasized the way that players are made to seem bigger than life. Is there any connection between what I am calling glory and the ugly aesthetic that marks vicious chants, homophobia, sexism, racism, and violence? At times, we cannot get a handle on the amount of emotions the game generates. I can't get a handle on how much of the game culture is ugly.

24. This seems a tall order given the relative lack of resources that FIFA actually acquires—compounded by the amount spent on fancy buildings and cars for executives. However, FIFA, and many National FAs have incredible bargaining powers which are not being used for good. Future hosts' bids will need to account for debt, and bidders should be competing to show grassroots sports and non-sports development. Creative fans need to make it clear that it is not all about first-world hotels when they travel. FIFA owes countries that have hosted world cups and are now burdened with stadia. In order to prepare for the World Cup, Brazil spent an amount equal to nearly 61% of its education budget. (Raposa 2014) FIFA could alternate with Cups where the winning bid is precisely that one that does not impoverish a country. FIFA also needs to repair the damage they have done to these countries.

WORK CITED

Al-Jazeera.com. *Qatar Removes Zidane Statue After Outcry*. Posted 31 October 2013. http://www.aljazeera.com/news/middleeast/2013/10/qatar-removes-zidane-statue-after-outcry-201310302338612974.html.

Deutsche Welle. *Mourning the Miracle of Berne*. 2003. http://www.dw.de/mourning-the-miracle-of-bern/a-948399-1.

Doyle, Jennifer. "Recovering from Soccer's Divorce" at foxsports.com. Last updated on May 21st, 2014, 2011. http://www.foxsports.com/foxsoccer/

womensworldcup/story/history-of-womens-game-wwc-germany-2011-recovering-from-soccer-divorce-070711.

———. *Hold it Against Me: Difficulty and Emotion in Contemporary Art.* Durham/London: Duke University Press, 2013.

Eco, Umberto. *Travels in Hyperreality.* Translated by William Weaver. New York/London: Harcourt, Brace and Company, 1986.

Elsey, Brenda. *Citizens and Sportsmen: Fútbol and Politics in Twentieth-Century Chile.* Austin: University of Texas Press, 2011.

Goldblatt, David. *The Ball is Round: A Global History of Soccer.* New York: Riverhead Books, 2008.

———. "The World Cup is Political Theater of the Highest Order", at the *Guardian,* 11 July 2014. http://www.theguardian.com/books/2014/jul/12/world-cup-football-politcal-theatre-highest-order.

Hirsthouse, Rosalind. "Virtue Theory". In *Ethics in Practice,* edited by Hugh LaFollette. Malden: Blackwell, 2006.

Hornby, Nick. *Fever Pitch.* London: Penguin, 2000. (Originally 1992).

Kuper, Simon, and Stefan Szymanski. *Soccernomics.* Nation Books: New York, 2014.

Mondello, Bob. "A History of Museums. 'The Memory of Mankind'". At *NPR: All Things Considered,* (November 24th 2008). http://www.npr.org/templates/story/story.php?storyId=97377145.

Raposa, Kenneth. "Bringing FIFA to Brazil Equal to Roughly 61% of the Education Budget". At *Forbes,* (6/11/2014). http://www.forbes.com/sites/kenrapoza/2014/06/11/bringing-fifa-to-brazil-equal-to-roughly-61-of-educationbudget/.

Rorty, Richard. *Contingency, Irony, and Solidarity.* Cambridge: Cambridge University Press, 1989.

Sylla, Ogo. "For Germany, for Once, It Means Nothing: Previous Triumphs Were Fraught with Political Overtones But the 2014 Champions Will Be Remembered Solely for Their Soccer" *Howler Magazine* On-line, 2014. http://www.howlermagazine.com/germany-means-nothing.

The *Guardian.* "Zinedine Zidane 'Would Rather Die' than Apologize to Materazzi". (March 1st 2010). http://www.theguardian.com/football/2010/mar/01/zinedine-zidane-marco-materazzi-headbutt.

Transparency International. "Safe Hands: Building Integrity and Transparency at FIFA." Posted August 2011. http://www.transparency.org/whatwedo/pub/safe_hands_building_integrity_and_transparency_at_fifa.

———. "Transparency International Disappointed that FIFA Gives No Strong Signal for Change". Posted March 30th 2012). http://www.transparency.org/news/pressrelease/20120330_FIFA_no_strong_signal.

———. "Saving Football = Good Governance + Anti-corruption". Posted February 27th 2013. http://www.transparency.org/news/feature/saving_football_good_governance_anti_corruption.

Trifonas, Peter Pericles. *Umberto Eco and football.* Cambridge: Icon Books, 2001.
Williams, Jean. *A Game for Rough Girls?: A History of Women's Football in Britain.*
London/New York: Routledge, 2003.
———. *A Beautiful Game: International Perspectives on Women's Football.*
London/New York: Bloomsbury Academic Press, 2008.

INDEX

A

ABCS Cup (2010), 121
Abdessemed, Adel, 45, 46
academic disciplines
  professionalization of, 3
  traditional, 1
achievement glory, 349
AC Milan, 249, 250
Adidas, 340
Adorno, Theodor, 316, 350
Aeskulap, 63
aestheticization, 17
Africa
  European clubs' interest in players
    from, 280
  football during colonial period in,
    271
  introduction of modern sports to,
    270
  and Men's World Cup, 352
  politicization of football in, 269
Africa Cup of Nations
  1963, 283

1965, 283
1976, 275
1978, 284
1982, 284
1992, 284
1994, 268
1996, 268
2004, 275
2006, 275
2015, 283
Ahmed family, 273
Aida, Tia, 296
Aivazian, Haig, 42
Akers, Vick, 234
Aktualita (newsreel company), 61
Alberto, Carlos, 167
Alegi, Peter, 270, 271
Algeria, 47
Alinovi, Abdon, 254
Allen, Graham, 26
Allum, Percy, 262
Altidore, Jozy, 192
Alvarado, Ventura, 189

© Hofstra University 2017
B. Elsey, S. Pugliese (eds.), *Football and the Boundaries of History*,
DOI 10.1057/978-1-349-95006-5

Amancio, 82
amateur status of players
 in Germany, 208
 in Soviet Union, 102
 on Vasco da Gama, 164
American Samoa, 132
Ampomah, Thomas, 278
An Choi-hyok, 147
Angloma, Jocelyn, 123
Anguilla Football Association (AFA),
 128
Answer, Ahmer Nadeem, 35
anti-racism campaigns, 69
antisemitism, 69
Antonioni, Michelangelo, 39
An Yong-hak, 150
apotheosis, 350
Aragones, Luis, 87
Arana, Sabino, 77
Aranycsapat, 112
Ararat Yerevan, 113
Archer, E.G., 130
Archer's Bow, 23
Archetti, Eduardo, 219
Arconada, 84
Arena, Bruce, 188
Aristotle, 343
Arsenal (England), 69, 228, 234
Arsenal (Sierra Leone), 273
Arsenal FC of Freetown, 273
Arshavin, Andrei, 114
art
 commemorative statuary in, 44
 created by children of Terezín, 63
 fetishism of Zidane, 35–9
 museums, 346
 traditional exploration of visual
  material, 15
artforms, football compared to, 344–7
Artforum, 37
Aruba, 121, 128
Arubaanse Voetbal Bond, 121

Ascension Island, 130
Asia
 emergence of soccer in, 140
 and Men's World Cup, 352
Asian Football Confederation (AFC),
 126, 142
Atalanta, 230
Athletic Bilboa, 80, 82
athleticism, political, 257
Atlético Aviación (Atlético Madrid),
 80
Audax Italiano, 109
autonomy of players, 166
autopoiesis, 21, 26, 27
Awuah, Simon, 278
Ayew, Abde Pele, 284
AZ Alkmaar, 228

B
Badiou, Alain, 324
Bahsoon family, 273
Bairner, Robin, 148
Ball is Round, The (David Goldblatt),
 2, 352
Ball, Philip, 74
Bamin, Billy, 273
Bampton, Debbie, 235
Bancroft, George, 181
Bancroft Treaties, 181
Bangu, 163
Barbados, 129
Barnes, Simon, 14
Barrie, Mohamed Fajah, 283
Barroso, Ary, 297
Barthes, Roland, 316
Basma, Adib, 276
Basma family, 273
Baudrillard, Jean, 37, 41, 316
Bauman, Elias, 296
Baumann, Zygmunt, 133
Bayern Munich, 13, 207, 208, 228

Bay is Not Naples, The (Anna Maria
 Ortese), 253
Beas, Chris, 43, 44
beautiful game, the, 170
Bebiano, Pedro Paulo, 303
Beckenbauer, Brigitte, 211
Beckenbauer, Franz (the Kaiser),
 205–21
 background of, 206
 and concepts/images of masculinity,
  211–12
 and movement of football to center
  of mass culture, 211–12
 rise to stardom, 206
 skills as a player, 209
 as symbolic of wider social, cultural,
  and political trends, 212–16
Beckerman, Kyle, 192
Beckham, David, 38, 220, 221
Beckham, Victoria, 221
Bedoya, Alejandro, 192
Belauste, 77, 78
Bellamy, Craig, 277
Belles, The (TV program), 235
Bergamo Atalanta, 255
Berger, John, 24
Berlusconi, Silvio, 249, 250
Bermuda, 129, 131
Bermuda Football Association (BFA),
 129
Bermuda Hogges, 129
Best, George, 40, 43, 214
Bien-Aime, Sonia, 237
Bin Hammam scandal, 324
Birmingham City LFC, 235
Birtwistle, Andy, 41
black-blanc-beur (Black-White-Arab),
 42–5
Black Man in Brazilian Soccer, The
 (Mário Filho), 170
Blackpool, 274, 276
Black Stars, 283, 284

Blanchflower, Danny, 349
Blatter, Sepp, 9, 324, 326, 327, 331, v
Blaydon Ladies FC, 230
Blokhin, Oleg, 104, 114
Blow Up (Lyle Ashton Harris), 37, 38
Boer, Wiebe, 269
Bo Government Secondary School,
 274
Bolinha, 302
Bologna, 255
Bonaire, 121, 126
Bonner, Nick, 139
Bordeaux, 32
Boren, Cindy, 238
Borussia Mönchengladbach, 210
Bo, Sierra Leone, 270, 281
Bosman Ruling of 1995, 14, 86
Bosnia-Herzegovina, 89
Botafogo, 107, 296, 298, 304
Bourdieu, Pierre, 3
boxing, 17
Boyd, Terrence, 187, 188, 191
Bradley, Bob, 187, 189
Braguinha, 299
Brandt, Willy, 210
Brazil
 fan groups in (*see* (fan groups in
  Brazil))
 national identity in, 163
Brazilian Association of Organized
 Fans, 309
Breda, Pavel, 68
Bredekamp, Horst, 16
Bright, Dennis, 280, 281
Britain, Arthur, 217
British Caribbean Football Association
 (BCFA), 129
British Empire
 cricket teams, 129
 and diffusion of football, 2, 267,
  270
 national identity in, 127–31

British Guiana, 129
British Ladies Football Club (BLFC), 230
British Virgin Islands, 128
British women's football
  Donny Belles and independent teams, 1969-2014, 231–6
  FA ban on, 231
  first FA international team, 231
  paying crowds for, 230
  pioneers in, 1869-1921, 229–31
  Sport for Girls survey on, 227–8
Broadhurst, Joanne, 233
Brooks, Gideon, 26
Brooks, John-Anthony, 187, 192, 193
brown professionalism, 164
Bru, Paco, 77
Buddle, Edson, 187
Buenos Aires Western Railway, 109
Burka, Honza, 62
Burns, Jimmy, 74
Butlins Cup, 232
bystander effect, 70

C
Calvin Klein, 38
Cambuslang Hooverettes, 231
Capa, Robert, 24
capital
  benefits of tangling football and, 317
  corrosive effects on football, 318
  democracy as restraint on, 326
  effectiveness of, 327
  offensive elements of relationship with football, 317
  relationship between football and, 316
  sustainability of, 328
Capital in the Twenty-First Century (Thomas Piketty), 315

capitalism
  excesses caused by, 328
  football as symptom of, 318
  football as useful/necessary to, 319
  as foundation of problems, 324
Caribbean Cup
  1993, 126
  2013, 126
Caribbean Football Union (CFU), 122, 124
Carioca Championship (1942), 297, 298
Carr, Carol, 233
Carvalho, Jaime de, 296–301
Carvalho, Laura de, 299, 300
Central Uruguay Railway Cricket Club, 109
Centre Pompidou (Paris), 45
challenge, 257
Chandler, Timothy, 187, 188, 193
character, 347, 348
Charanga, 296–301
Chatriwala, Omar, 47
Chelsea, vi, 69
Chernomorets Odessa, 113
Chiaromonte, Gerard, 262
Chinaglia, Giorgio, 206
Chivadze, Aleksandr, 113
Choi Hyun-duk, 147
Chollima. See North Korean football team
Chongryon players, 145–6
Christian Democracy (Italy), 251, 254
Christ the King College (CKC), 274
Church Missionary Society Grammar School (Sierra Leone), 267
cinematic experience, 41
citizenship
  American, 181
  assimilation model of, 181
  and eligibility of players, 183
  hybrid, 188

meaning of, 180
and national identity, 180 (see also (dual nationals))
in nationalist movements, 180
class, displays of masculinity, power, and, 37
Cleanest Race, The (B.R. Myers), 138, 147
Cléo, 309
Cline Town, 276
Club Atlético Atlanta, 109
Clube dos 13, the, 309
Cobreloa, 109
Cobresal, 109
Coddrington, Sue, 233
Cohen, Roger, 34
Cold War, 103
Cole, Chico, 277
Cole, Christian, 277
colonialism
and Zidane as postcolonial hero, 45–9
Zidane emblematic of issues of, 35
Combeau-Mari, Evelyn, 122, 125
commodity fetishism, 35–40
Commonwealth Games (Britain), 123
communication, 5
Communism, 329
Communists, in Naples, 261
community identity, 306
Comoros, 123
Compagna, Francesco, 253
competition, 345
concentration camp. See Terezín Nazi ghetto-camp
Confederation of African Football (CAF), 268, 275
Confederation of North, Central American and Caribbean Association Football (CONCACAF), 121, 126, 127
Confederations Cup for Brazil, 120

Congress of Major Clubs' Organized Fans, 309
Conmebol, v
Connell, Raewyn, 217
consumerism, 213
Conteh, Lamin (Junior Tumbu), 278
Cooper, Scott, 128
Copa Libertadores, 105
Corona, Joe, 189, 191
corruption
covert and overt forms of, 323
in FIFA, v, 9, 320
misdirection and, 325
in World War II era, 57
Cosenza, Luigi, 260
Costa, Flávio, 168
Costard, Hellmuth, 40
Cotter, Holland, 42
Coultard, Gill, 233–5
Coumoundouros, Antonis, 35
Coup de tête (Adel Abdessemed), 45, 46
Coupe de France, 126
Coupe de l'Outre-Mer (Overseas Cup), 120, 123–6, 131
Courte, Rene, 16, 24, 27
Craig Bellamy Foundation, 277
creative fans, 353–4
Critchley, Simon, 40, 323
critical literature on football, 1, 2, 315–35
theoretical apparatus for critical thinking, 316
theses for analysis of, 316–35
Croatia, 89
Crolley, Liz, 81
Cruyff, Johan, 31, 89
Cruzeiro, 109
CSKA Moscow, 110, 112
cultural historians, 3
cultural trends, football as symbolic of, 212–16

culture
  football as global cultural practice,
    5–9
  movement of football to center of
    mass culture, 211–12
  in reproducing power relations, 3
  in social sciences, 4
  and Spanish national team's
    relationship to regional
    identities, 74 (*see also* (Spanish
    national team *(La Selección)*)))
  symbolic meanings of, 3
Cumings, Bruce, 140
Curaçao, 120
Curaçao Voetbalbond (CVB), 120
Czechoslovakia, pre-World War II
    soccer in, 63

D
Daily Times (Lagos), 107
dance, 344
Darby, Paul, 269, 270
Darnell, Simon C., 133
Davidson, Tracey, 233
Davies, Pete, 235
Deal international women's football
    tournament
  1967, 231
  1970, 232
Deep Play (Harun Farocki), 41
de Florencia, Rodolfo, 35, 36
Del Bosque, Vicente, 88
democracy, as restraint on Capital, 326
Democratic People's Republic of
    Korea (DPRK). *See* North Korea
Derrick, Catherine, 233
Derrick, Ruth, 233
Deutscher Fubball-Bund (DFB), 208,
    215
Diamond Stars of Kono, 276
Dick, Kerr's Ladies, 230, 231

Dick, W. B., 230
diffusion of football, 2
Diskerud, Mix, 187, 192, 193
Di Stefano, Alfredo, 31, 79, 80, 183
diving, 13–30
  bodily violence in, 24–5
  as degeneracy, 27–8
  by English footballers, 15
  as ethics issue, 16
  by German footballers, 302
  standout images of, 23–4
  taxonomy of, 23
  as unmanly, 27
Dixie, Lady Florence, 230
Dnipro Dnipropetrovsk, 112, 113
Dodalova, Irene, 62
Dodd, Moya, 237
Domingos da Guia, 165, 168
Dominica, 129
Doncaster Belles (Donny Belles;
    Doncaster Rovers Belles), 229,
    231–6
Doncaster Belle Vue Belles, 232
Doncaster Rovers, 236
Dooley, Thomas, 185
DPRK. *See* North Korea
Drogba, Didier, 19, 26
dual identity, 73
dual national players, 179–94
  eligibility of, 183
  reasons for playing for USMNT,
    190–1
  unfair characterization of, 179
dual nationals, 181
  fear of, 181
  suspect loyalty of, 181
Dubois, Laurent, 33, 278
Dumbuya, Kama, 277
Dumbuya, Kawuta, 277
Dumbuya, Kolleh, 277
Dutch Antilles, 121
Dutch East Indies, 121

Dutch territories, national identity in, 120–2
Dyfan, Ismael, 268, 277
Dynamo Kiev, 110–13
Dynamo Moscow, 101, 103, 106–8, 112
Dynamo Tbilisi, 106, 107, 110, 112, 113
Dynamo Yerevan, 113
Dynamo Zagreb, 110

E
Eagleton, Terry, 316, 319
East End Lions, 272–4, 283
economic inequality, 5
Eco, Umberto, 258, 342, 347
Edelman, Robert, 102
Edinburgh (team name), 230
Edmunds, Paul, 232
Edmunds, Sheila, 232
El Cid, 44
11Freunde, 13–15, 21, 26
El Fatalismo, 75, 78, 85
Elizabeth II, Queen, 130
Elliot, Michael, 139
Elsey, Brenda, v
Empire Games (Britain), 123
England (team name), 229
England C, 131
England, women's football in. *See* British women's football
England Women's national team, 233
English Football Association (FA), 127, 130, 131
    ban on women's teams by, 231
    and demise of Belles, 236
    original rules set by, 228
    and Women's Football Association, 233
English footballers, diving by, 15
English Premier League, 14, 25
Espelund, Karen, 236

ethical issues
    diving as, 16
    virtue ethics, 343
ethnicities, in Spain
    and football in immigrant communities, 109
    in Korean culture, 147
    in Spain, 74, 82 (*see also* (Spanish national team *(La Selección)*)))
Europe
    foreign players in domestic leagues in, 69
    post-World War II demographic revolutions in, 68
European Champions' Club Cup (Champions' League), 105
European Champions Cup (1974), 206
European Championship
    1960, 101, 103
    1964, 103
    1988, 105
    2000, 33
European Community, Spain in, 84
European Football Confederation (UEFA)
    Espelunds' appointment to board of, 236
    Gibraltar in, 120
European Footballer of the Year (Ballon d'Or), 103, 104, 206
European Nations Cup, 85, 105
    1964, 81
    1972, 104
    1984, 85
    2008, 87
    2012, 87
European Player of the Year, 33
European Union, restrictions on number of E.U.-raised players on teams in. *See* Bosman Ruling of 1995
Evans, Toni, 233

Everyman's Front, 251
excessive demonstrative attitude, 18, 27
Eyre, Samantha, 233

F
Fair, Laura, 269, 270
Falkland Islands, 130–2
Falkland Islands Football League, 131
fan allegiances, 112
fan groups in Brazil, 295
  changes underlying groups'
    directions during 1980s, 305–9
  Charanga, 296–301
  dissent within, 300–5
  and Jaime de Carvalho, 296–301
  in Rio de Janeiro, 295
fans
  creative, 353–4
  information given to, 343
  source of energy of, 342
  types of, 347
fan violence
  Blow Up (Lyle Ashton Harris), 37, 38
  in organized Brazilian fan groups, 305–9
  in 2006 World Cup Finals, 141
Farocki, Harun, 41
Faroe Islands, 132
fascism, 250
Fausto Dos Santos (Maravilha Negra, Black Wonder), 161–70
  character of, 162, 167
  early life of, 163
  health of, 161, 167, 169
  and mixed-race national football
    style, 162–6
  playing style of, 166–7
  political implications of death of, 162

as star, 166
  war with directors of Flamengo, 168
Fawaz family, 273
FC Barcelona, 80, 82, 85, 87, 88, 90, 109, 165, 183, 348
FC Johansen, 282
FC Kallon, 282
FCR 2001 Duisburg, 229
Fédération Française de Football
  (FFF), 120, 123, 125, 126, 131
Fédération Internationale Européenne
  de Football Féminine (FIEFF), 232
Fédération Tahitienne de Football
  (FTF), 123
female football players, number of, 229. *See also* women's football
feminist scholarship, on gender
  hierarchies within sport, 3
Ferguson, Sir Alex, 15
Fernando, 164
Ferrocarril Oeste, 109
fetish-beauty, 37. *See also* commodity
  fetishism
Fever Pitch (Nick Hornby), 346
FFC Turbine Potsdam, 229
FIFA (Fédération Internationale de
  Football Association)
  Arubaanse Voetbal Bond
    membership in, 121
  and Beckenbauer's possible ethics
    code breaches, 207
  corruption scandal, v, 9, 320
  and costs of/returns on hosting of
    World Cup, 320
  CVB full membership in, 121
  democratic structure of, 326
  English/British football associations
    in, 128
  establishment of, 182
  financial assistance from, 128

foreign journalist requirements of, 145
formation of, 228
and inequities of the game, 322
investigation of punishment of North Korean team, 150
Law 12 on simulation, 13
Nsekera on Executive Committee, 237
overseas territory organizations admitted to, 123, 126, 128, 129, 131, 132
and player eligibility, 182
and politicians interfering in football matters, 281
priority for membership in, 133
recognition of diving by, 14
replacement of, 331
requirements for flags and national anthems, 143
Sierra Leone in, 275
sovereign states admitted to, 119
1970 survey on women in football, 228
on women's soccer, 351
World Cup portfolio, 47
Yashin testimonial match, 104
FIFA News, 16
FIFA Under-17 Championship (2003), 285
FIFA Under-20 Championship (2009), 285
Filho, Mário, 170
financial doping, 325
Finley, Robbie, 187
Finn, Gerry P.T., 119
5-a-side Trophy, 232
Flamengo, 166, 168, 295–7, 303
Fluminense, 164, 296, 302, 305
football (soccer)
    artforms compared to, 344–7
    benefits of tangling Capital and, 317

as cauldron of different aspects of life, 43
as communist, 329
corrosive effects of Capital on, 318
corruption in World War II era, 57
critical literature on, 1, 2
deflation of financial bubble around, 330
diffusion of, 2
evaluating, 327
evocative force of, 347
future of, 329
as global cultural practice, 5–9
as greenwashing tool, 318
inequities of, 322
and issues of national identity and politics, 182
as mode of communication, 5
need for revolutionary transformation of, 323
offensive elements of relationship with Capital, 317
opportunity for change in, 323
passions aroused by, 57
political manipulation with, 57 (*see also* (Terezín Nazi ghetto-camp))
post-World War II internationalization in, 105
public feeling about political economy of, 320
reasons for global dominance of, 344
re-identifying purpose of, 321
relationship between Capital and, 316
representative power of, 340–3
social significance of, 4
as spectacle *vs.* as competition, 26
standardized nature of, 2
as symptom of modern capitalism, 318
unifying potential of, 70, 73
as useful/necessary to capitalism, 319

as weapon of the revolution, 332
women in (*see* (women's football))
during World War II, 63
football histories, 3
Football League Clubs, 228
Football League Division One, 14
Football Like Never Before (Hellmuth
    Costard), 40
Força Flu, 305
Ford, Glynn, 147
foreign players, in European domestic
    leagues, 69
Forza Italia, 249
Fourah Bay, 277
Fourah Bay College, 267
Fox, Ruel, 128
France
    egalitarian meritocracy and cultural
        goodwill toward former
        colonies, 35
    football players from former French
        colonies in, 278
    multicultural vision of, 341
    national identity of, 33
    racial integration of, 31, 32
    World Cup 1998, 32
France Football, 104
Franco, Francisco, 74, 79–82
Freedman, Jonah, 184–7
Freetown, Sierra Leone, 267, 270,
    273, 276, 281
French Guiana, 123–6
French Polynesia, 123
French Somaliland, 123
French territories, national identity in,
    122–7
Freyre, Gilberto, 170
Friedenreich, Arthur, 167
Fried, Michael, 39
friend-enemy opposition, 255
Fulham Women's Football Club, 235
Fuste, 82

G
Gadhvi, Aashish, 146
Gaetjens, Joseph, 184
Galeano, Eduardo, vi, 2, 49
Game of Their Lives, The
    (documentary), 139
Gardner, Howard, 258
Gardner, Paul, 189
Garza, Greg, 192
Gazzetta della Sport, 249
Gberie, Lansana, 274
Geertz, Clifford, 259
gender codes in soccer, 37
gender hierarchies within sport, 3
gender identity, 306
gender inequality, 5
George, Sie Vava, 278
German footballers
    Beckenbauer, 205–21
    diving by, 14
Germany, 341
Gerron, Kurt, 61
Ghanian football, 267, 270, 271, 275,
    284–5
Gibraltar, 119–20, 130–3
Gibraltar Football Association (GFA),
    130
Giesta, Armando, 309
Ginola, David, 24
Giulianotti, Richard, 119, 211
Glanville, Brian, 233
globalization
    of popular culture, 201
    of traditional game constructs, 87
    and understanding of *Zidane* film,
        41
    Zidane emblematic of, 32
glory, 342, 349–52
goal celebrations, 16
Goethe, Johann Wolfgang von, 18
Goldblatt, David, vi, 2, 210, 341, 349,
    352

Gold Cup
  2007, 126
  2011, 190
Golden Ball, 33
Gold of Naples, The (Giuseppe
  Marotta), 254
Gomez, Herculez, 187
González, Felipe, 84
Gordon, Daniel, 139
Gordon, Douglas, 37, 39
governance of football, 326
governance of men's football, 315
Gradim, 165
Gramsci, Antonio, 217, 316
graphic unconscious, 41
Great Britain
  Commonwealth Games, 123
  English sporting identity and
    political status of, 127
Green, Julian, 184–7, 191, 193
Greenland, 132
Green Patch of Palmeiras, 308
Grenada, 129
Griffin, Tim, 40
Grimsby (team name), 230
Guadeloupe, 122–6
Guam, 132
Guarnizo, Luis E., 182
Guénif-Souilamas, Nacira, 35
Guimarães, 296
Guinea, 275
Guishard, Raymond, 128
Guzan, Brad, 192

H
Hafia, 275
Hague, E., 183
Hall, Stuart, 182
Hamburger SV, 206
Hand, David, 81
Hands Over the City (cinema), 260–2
Hanson, Jill, 233

Hanson, Lorraine, 233
Hardistry, Wendy, 233
Hare, Geoff, 33
Harkes, John, 186
Harris, Lyle Ashton, 37, 38
Hartley, Tim, 145
Hassaniyeh family, 273
Hayatou, Issa, 267, 285
Hayhurst, Lindsay M. C., 133
Headbutt (Adel Abdessemed), 45, 46
head-butts
  and immigration issues, 42
  by Zidane, 32, 33, 45, 340
Hecker, David, 20
hedonism, 213
hegemonic masculinity, 217
Hejazi family, 273
Helal, George, 301
7Helal, George, 301
Helena, Tia, 296
Herberger, Sepp, vi, 216, 217
hierarchic heterosexualism, 217
history, 4, and Spanish national team's
  relationship to regional identities
  football histories, 3
  political history, 43
  power of propaganda, 61
  research tools for, 4
  social histories, 204
  and Spanish national team's
    relationship to regional
    identities, 74 (*see also* (Spanish
    national team *(La Selección)*)))
  sport histories, 3, 4
  universities' institutionalization of, 3
Hitler, Adolf, 250
Hitzlsperger, Thomas, 220
Hobbs, Arthur, 231
Holocaust denial, 63, 68
homosexuality, 26, 38, 219–21. *See
  also* masculinity
Honeyball, Nettie, 230
Hong Kong, 131

Hong Kong Football Association, 131
Hoolihan, Barrie, 133
Horkheimer, Max, 350
Hornby, Nick, 342, 346
Horoya, 275
Horrockses' Ladies, 230
Howard, Tim, 190
How Great You Are, O Son of the Desert! (film), 42
Huntington, Samuel, 189
Hunt, Lorraine, 233
Hunt, Tracey, 233
hybrid citizenship, 188

I
identity, 109
  of clubs, 109, 110
  dual, 73
  and fan allegiances, 112
  and mass sport, 182
  of Neapolitans, 260
  in organized fan groups of 1970s, 306
  racial, 191
  shared, 73
I Lost My Heart To The Belles (Pete Davies), 235
images/imagemaking
  bodily violence in, 24–5
  boxing photography, 17
  of diving, 14, 23–4 (*see also* (diving))
  harmony and communicability of images, 21
  Laocoön and his Sons, 15, 18
  military-themed, 21
  questions over status of, 16
  transitory and anonymous images, 20
immigrants
  American citizenship for, 181
  suspect loyalty of, 181

immigration
  in post-World War II Europe, 68
  Zidane and, 42–5
individualism, 212
Indomitable Lions of Cameroon, 284
inequality
  economic, 5
  gender, 5
  Piketty's analysis of, 315
Infantino, Gianni, v
innovative leadership, 258
interdisciplinary initiatives, 1
International Football Association Board (IFAB), 14
internationalization of football, post-World War II, 105–8
International Red Cross (IRC), 59
Iran national team, 138, 141
irony, 347–9
Island Games, 120
  1985, 130
  2011, 120
Island Games Association (IGA), 130
Italian soccer
  as fundamental in Italian life, 249
  politics and, 249–51, 254–60
  racism in, 69
Italy
  building speculation in Naples, 260–2
  and Lauro as King of Naples, 251–4
  soccer and politics in, 249–51, 254–60
  "the ball is round" expression in, vii
Ivory Coast team, 19

J
Jackson, Michael, 38
Jacob Wrestling the Angel (Hassan Musa), 47, 48
Jaguaré, 165

Jalloh, Brima, 281
Jamaica, 129
Jameson, Frederic, 324, 329
Japan, *Chongryon* from, 145–6
Jeppson, Hasse, 255, 260
Jeux de la Communauté (Community Games), 122
Jeux de la Francophonie (Francophone Games), 123
Jews
    antisemitism in European leagues, 69
    European prejudices against, 69
    held at Terezín, 59 (*see also* (Terezín Nazi ghetto-camp))
    and Holocaust denial, 63, 68
    in Terezín league, 63
Jiwani, Yasmin, 47, 49
Ji Yun-nam, 148
Johansen, Isha, 282
Jóhansson, Aron, 187
John, Elton, 221
Johnson, Fabian, 187, 188, 192
Johnson, Sento, 277
Jones, Doreen, 233
Jones, Jermaine, 187, 188, 191, 192
Jong Tae-se, 144–8, 150
journalistic literature on football, 2
Juan Carlos, King of Spain, 84
Juarez, 296
Judenrat (at Terrezín), 65
Juventus of Italy, 32, 33

K
Kabia, Bai, 277
Kabs Kanu, Leeroy, 275
Kallon, Mohamed, 268, 278, 282
Kallon, Musa, 278
Kamara, Bambay, 276
Kamara, Brima (Mazolla), 268, 277, 282
Kamara, Kollev, 278

Kamara, Paul, 282, 283
Kamboi Eagles of Kenema, 276
Kanu, Ahmed, 278
Kanyan, Marc, 122
Kaplice, Slavia, 231
Karembeu, Christian, 122, 125
Kargbo, Amadu, 277
Kargbo, Edward, 277
Kearns, Paula, 237
Keff, Michel, 45
Keister, Edward, 275, 277
Kelfala, Joseph S., 281
Kellas, James, 182
Kelly, Des, 24, 26
Kemokai, Patrick, 277
Kenema, Sierra Leone, 271, 281
Kerr, John, 230
Kewell, Harry, 21
Khadi family, 273
Khousa, Mohammed, 141
Khurtsilava, Murtsi, 113
Kim Dae-jung, 140, 143
Kim Il-sung, 137, 141
Kim Jong-hun, 149, 150
Kim Jong-il, 138, 149
Kim Jong-un, 138
Kim Kyong-il, 147
Kim Myong-won, 147
Kingtom Rovers, 272
Klinsmann, Jürgen, 14, 188, 189, vi
Kohler, Jürgen, 14
Koidu, Sierra Leone, 271, 281
Koninklijke Nederlandse Voetbalbond (KNVB), 120–2
Kopa, 79
Korean Central News Agency (KCNA), 142, 144–6, 148–50
Kosovo, 133
Krasnoff, Lindsay, Sarah, 122
Krug, Matthias, 148
Kruschner, Dori, 168, 169
Kuper, Simon, 325

L

La Cantera, 88
La Furia Española, 75–9, 81, 85, 86
Lalas, Alexi, 186
La Masia, 87, 88
Lamptey, Nii Odartey, 284
Landolt, Patricia, 182
Laocoön and his Sons, 15, 18
La Roja
  contemporary branding and
    representation of, 75
  and national and regional ethnicities,
    74
  recent successes of, 75
  success of, against failure for La
    Selecci, 74, 75
  transformation to, 86–91
laurismo, 252, 254–62
Lauro, Achille, 251–4
  building speculation in Naples,
    260–2
  as King of Naples, 251–4
  reasons for popularity of, 253
  and soccer politics in laurismo,
    254–60
Lauro, Angelina, 258
Laws of the Game (FIFA), 13, 16
Lawson, Augustus, 278
Lebanese
  Sierra Leoneans' resentment toward,
    273
  and Sierra Leone football, 273
Lee Myung-bak, 144
Lee's Ladies and Westhorn United,
  232
Leone Stars, 269, 275, 285
Leônidas da Silva, 165, 168, 170
Le Pen, Jean-Marie, 32, 341
Les Bleus, 123, 126, 127
Lessing, Gotthold Ephraim, 18, 21
Lewis, David, 23, 27

Libero (semi-documentary), 209
Liga Terezín, 57–71
  legacy of, 68–70
  in propaganda film, 61
Ligue de Football de Mayotte, 120
Lins do Rego, José, 170
Little World Cup, 233
Ljungberg, Freddie, 38
Lobanovsky, Valery, 112
Lokomotiv, 106, 107, 110, 112
Lopez, Sue, 231
"Loyalist Militiaman at the Moment of
  Death" (Robert Capa), 24
Luca, João, 296
luck, 348
Lynch, Loretta, 354, v
Lyons tearoom women's football
  teams, 230

M

Macau, 132
Major League Soccer (MLS), 185
Makeni, Sierra Leone, 271, 281
Malaparte, Curzio, 253, 254
Male Fantasies (Klaus Theweleit), 220
Malor, Ben Dotsei, 284
Malouda, Florent, 125
Malouda, Lesly, 125
Manchester United, 13, 40, 43
Mandela, Nelson, 68
Manet, Edouard, 37
Mangan, James, 271
Maradona, Diego, 31, 351
Margry, Karel, 61
Marlet, Steve, 125
Marley Hill Spankers, 230
Marotta, Giuseppe, 254
Martinique, 123–6, 809
Marx, Karl, 3, 328
masculinity

aggressive, in sports, 45
codes of, 42
conceptions/images of, 211–12
displays of class, power, and, 37
and diving as unmanly, 27
and excessive demonstrative
    attitude, 18
and Harris' *Blow Up*, 38
metrosexual footballers, 221
mass culture, movement of football to
    center of, 211–12
Materazzi, Marco, 31, 33, 35, 42, 47,
    340
Mattar family, 273
Maurelli, Mario, 255
Mayes, Jackie, 233
Mayotte, 120, 123, 124
McIntyre, Doug, 188
McKnistry, Johnny, 283
media
    American, early portrayal of soccer
        in, 184
    Donny Belles in, 235
    11Freunde, 13–15, 21, 26
    FIFA foreign journalist
        requirements, 145
    information on dual nationals from,
        179
    North Korea's use of, 139
    questions of loyalty of Hispanic
        Americans in, 190
    and women's football, 227–8
Mello, Nelson de, 301
Mellor, Kay, 235
Mendes, Eli, 305
Mendonça, Marcos de, 164
Mensah, Atto, 278, 283
Mercer, J., 183
Merkel, Angela, 342
Merolla, Eliana, 258
Meskhi, Mikhail, 113
Messi, Lionel, 189, 351

Messing, Shep, 214
Metalist Kharkiv, 110, 113
Metreveli, Slava, 113
metrosexual footballers, 221
Metzger, Obi, 277
Mexican Work Cup (1970), 300
Mighty Blackpool, 272, 276
Milla, Roger, 43
Miracle of Bern (1954), 340, vi
Mitre Challenge Trophy, 232
mixed-race national football style,
    162–6
MLSnet.com, 186
Mohamed, Jamil Sahid, 276
Monserrate, 128
Montalban, Manuel Vazquez, 84
Moore, Malcom, 148
Morbo (Philip Ball), 74
Morris, Paul H., 23, 27
Mortey, Ben, 278
Mourinho, Jose, vi
Mrs. Graham's Eleven, 230
mulatto football, 162–6
Müller, Gerd, 210
Mundialito, 233
Muñoz, Miguel, 85
Murad, Mauricio, 307
Murdoch, Rupert, 237
Murilho, Elisabeth Silva, 306
Musa, Hassan, 47, 48
museums, 346
Mussolini, Benito, 250, 251, 258
Myers, B.R., 138, 147, 149
Myerscough, Paul, 40
My Life, My Battle (Achille Lauro),
    258

N

Nacional, 165
Nam Song Chol, 141

Naples, Italy, 251–4, 260–2. *See also* Lauro, Achille
Napoli team, 250, 254, 255
National Association of French Football Districts, 45
National Elephant team, 275
national identity
  American, 188, 189
  in Brazil, 163
  in British Empire, 127–31
  and citizenship, 180
  dual identity, 73
  and dual national players, 179–94
  in Dutch territories, 120–2
  of France, 33
  in French territories, 122–7
  in Gibraltar and Tahiti, 119–20
  and Korean culture, 147
  of non-self-governing territories identified by UN, 132
  in overseas territories, 120
  and politics of sports and fandom, 43
  in Soviet society, 109–13
  in Spain, 73, 89 (*see also* (Spanish national team *(La Selección)*)))
  and U.S. national teams, 132
nationalism(s)
  American, 181
  Beckenbauer's disdain for, 215–16
  Soviet, 110
  in Spain, 76, 89
nationalist movements, citizenship in, 180
National Market Traders Association, 232
National Monarchic Party (PNM), 252
nativism, 189
Nazi concentration camp. *See* Terezín Nazi ghetto-camp
Ndee, Hamad, 269
Nead, Lynda, 17, 18, 23

Neftchi Baku, 110, 113
Negri, Antonio, 324
Nelson, Lee, 324
Netherlands Antilles, 121
Netto, Igor, 103
Netzer, Günter, 210, 213, 215
Neuberger, Hermann, 213
New Caledonia, 123–6
Newsham, Gavin, 213
New Spain, 82
New York Cosmos, 206, 212
Nigerian football, 271
Nilo, 164
Niltinho, 309
North American Soccer League (NASL), 206
North Korea, 137–55
  domestic league matches in, 145
  economic conditions in, 140
  emigration from, 148
  famine in, 141
  isolationism of, 137
  national circumstances in, 151
  recent history of, 137–8
  Russian trade with/aid to, 140
North Korean football team *(Chollima)*
  alleged attempted defection by players, 147
  Chongryon on, 145–6
  punishment for losing Finals, 150
  in 2010 World Cup, 137–51, 138
  in World Cup Finals, 139–42
No That Really is El Cid, He Only Thinks He's Zizou (Chris Beas), 44
Nottingham Regional League, 232
Nsekera, Lydia, 237
Nureyev, Rudolf, 212, 214, 221

O
Oceania Nations Cup (2012), 120
Oh Kyu-wook, 146

Old Edwardians, 274, 276
Olympia (Edouard Manet), 37
Olympic Games, 105, 138
  1920, 76
  1936, 250
  1948, 105
  1950, 121
  1952, 102, 103
  1956, 101, 103, 110
  1968, 129
  1988, 105
  1992, 284
Olympique Lyonnaise, 228
Once in a Lifetime (Gavin Newsham),
  213–14
One Like Me (Franz Beckenbauer),
  209, 211
Orozco, Michael, 189
Ortese, Anna Maria, 253
Oswald, Rudolf, 215
Otley, Suzanne, 233
Overseas Cup. *See* Coupe de l'Outre-
  Mer (Overseas Cup)
overseas territories
  British Empire, 127–31
  Dutch, 120–2
  French, 122–7
  national identity in, 120
  non-self-governing territories
    identified by UN, 132

P
Padilha, José Bastos, 168
paintings, 345
Pak Sung-hyok, 147
Palestino, 109
Palmeiras, 109, 309
Parade (team), 278
Parade, Junior, 278
Park Ji-sung, 147
Parreno, Philippe, 37, 39
Pascal, Blaise, 258

passports, 128
Paulista, 296, 302
Peitão, 296
Peixoto, Salvador, 296
Pelé, v, 206, 351
Peñarol, 109
Pereda, 82
performative glory, 350
Peters, Manneh, 278
philosophy, sporting events and mass
  gatherings in, 258
Piketty, Thomas, 315
Pinkas Synagogue, Prague, 68
Pinto, Alfredo, 296
Piquionne, Frédéric, 125
Pitch Invasions (Chris Beas), 43
Platini, Michele, v
Platoon (film), 21
Playing the Field (television series), 235
Polish premier league, antisemitism in, 69
political action/activism, soccer as
  platform for, 47
political athleticism, 257
political history, 43
political manipulation, with football, 57
political trends, football as symbolic of,
  212–16
politics
  friend-enemy opposition in, 255
  and Italian soccer, 249–51, 254–60
  in Italy, Lauro's contempt for, 253
  and mass sport, 182
  and plight of footballers in 1920s
    30s, 162
  and Sierra Leonean soccer, 273 (*see
    also* (Sierra Leone))
  in Spain, 1898, 76
  and Spanish national team's
    relationship to regional
    identities, 74 (*see also* (Spanish
    national team (*La Selección*)))
  of sports and fandom, 43
  and West African football, 285

popular culture
  Belles in, 235
  globalization of, 2
Popular Monarchy Party (PMP), 254
Portes, Alejandro, 182
Ports Authority Football Club, 272
power
  displays of masculinity, class, and, 37
  of propaganda, 61
  representative, of football, 340–3
power relations
  role of culture in reproducing, 3
  in sport, 3
Praha, Sparta, 231
Premier League Clubs, 228
Primo de Riviera, Miguel, 76
Prisons Football Club, 272
professionalism, 164
propaganda films
  Nazi use of, 58
  from Terezín Nazi ghetto-camp,
    61–3
propaganda, power of, 61
psychology, power of propaganda and,
  61
Puerto Rico, 132
Pugliese, Stanislao, v
Puskás, Ferenc, 79, 80, 183

Q
Qatar, 326
Qatari national teams, 183
Qatar Museums Authority, 45
Quiroga, Alejandro, 73, 74

R
race
  mixed-race national football style,
    162–6
  racial integration of France, 31, 32

racial identity, 191
racial profiling, 42
racism, 69
Railway Games Club, 272
Ramalho, Domingos, 296
Ranke, Leopold von, 3
"Rap do Pirão" (DJ Malboro), 309
Rapinoe, Megan, vi
Rawlings, John Jerry, 284
Real Madrid, 33, 39, 79, 80, 82, 88,
  183
Real Sociedad, 84
Red Army (Soviet Union), 60
Red Cross Cup (1975-76), 232
Red Star Belgrade, 110
Regent Olympic, 274
regional ethnicities, in Spain, 74. See
  also Spanish national team (La
  Selección)
regionalism, in Spain, 75, 76, 84
Regis, David, 186–7, 189
Rein, Raanan, 109
Renshon, Stanley, 189
representative power of football,
  340–3
research tools, 4
"Resurgence and Fall of Zinedine
  Zidane" (Ahmer Nadeem
  Anwer), 35
Réunion, 123–5
Rey, 165
Richards, Paul, 272
Rinet, Jules, 299
Rio de Janeiro Association of
  Organized Fans (ASTORJ), 308
Røa, 228
Roja, La (Jimmy Burns), 74
role models, players as, 16
Roma, European prejudices against,
  69
Ronaldo, Cristiano, 351
Rooney, Wayne, 13–15, 26

Rorty, Richard, 348
Rosalina, Dulce, 296, 305
Rosi, Francesco, 260
Ross, Steve, 213
Rous, Stanley, 82
Rubin, Rubio, 192
Russia, 326
Russinho, 165

S
Saco FC, 273
Saint Anthony's FC, 274
Saint Martin, 124, 126
Saint Pierre and Miquelon, 123, 124
Samitier, 77
Sampson, Steve, 185, 186
Santamaria, 79, 80
Santayana, George, 187
Santos, 276
Sao Tome et Principe, 128
Sapotille, Jocelyne, 128
Sasso family, 273
Schmitt, Carl, 255
Schoeller, Martin, 34
Schön, Helmut, 216
Schwan, Robert, 209
Schweinsteiger, Bastian, 13
Scotland (team name), 229, 230
Scotland Under-16 competition
    (1989), 284
Sebes, Guzstav, 112
Seeler, Uwe, 210, 211
Serdan, Paulo Rogério, 308
Sesay, Gbassay, 278
Sesay, John Agina, 278
Sewell, William, 4
sexism, in European leagues, 69
sexual objects, players as, 37
Shaktar Donetsk, 110, 113
Shamel, Henneh, 273
shared identity, 73

Sheffield League, 232
Sherrard, Jackie, 233
Sierra Fisheries Football Club, 276
Sierra Leone, 267–86
    civil war in, 285
    colonial football in, 270–4
    contemporary state of football in,
        280–3
    cultural and socioeconomic
        importance of sports in, 269
    football mercenaries in, 278
    politicization of football in, 269
    post-colonial football in, 275–80
    school sports and physical education
        in, 271, 274
Sierra Leone Football Association
    (SLFA), 268, 269, 275, 276,
    279–83
Silee, Etienne, 121
Silva Jesuino, Manoel da, 297
Simonian, Nikita, 103, 113
Simpson, Mark, 216
Simpson, Neal, 21
simulation, 13. *See also* diving
Sint Maarten (Dutch), 121, 126
Skillcorn, Karen, 233
Skin, The (Curzio Malaparte), 253
Slovenia, 89
Smith, Tom, 127
Soccer As the Beautiful Game
    conference (2014), v
Soccer in Sun and Shadows (Eduardo
    Galeano), 2
Soccernomics (Simon Kuper and
    Stefan Szymanski), 325
social disorder, 42
social histories, 3
social psychology, 57
social sciences, culture in, 4
social significance of football, 4
social trends, football as symbolic of,
    212–16

sociology, sporting events and mass gatherings in, 258
Socrates, 333
Solo, Hope, 238–9
Soreze, Alain, 126
Soup Canteen Ladies, 230
South Korea, 142–6
Soviet international football (soccer), 101–13
  amateur status of players, 102
  competitive disadvantage for, 102
  Dynamo tour 1945, 103
  golden era in, 103
  and national identity in Soviet society, 109–13
  and post-World War II internationalization of football, 105–8
  Russian and non-Russian teams in, 112
  in 1970s, 104
  in 1980s, 104
  unfulfilled promise of, 101
Soviet Union
  cultural relations with Third World countries, 107
  foreign trips for football, 106
  liberation of Theresienstadt, 60
  national identity in, 109–13
  nationalisms of, 110
  sports bureaucracy in, 107
Spain, 75
  autonomous communities in, 84
  core values of, 79
  national identity in, 73 (*see also* (Spanish national team))
  nationalisms in, 76, 89
  notion of unitary Spanish state, 78
  political landscape at 1898, 76
  regionalism in, 75, 76, 84
  sports policy in, 90
  1982 World Cup in, 85

Spanish football (soccer), 73–6
  club football, 74, 76, 82, 86
  club rivalry, 80
  and dual identity, 73
  and Gibraltar teams, 130
  racism in, 69
  at time of Antwerp Olympics, 76
Spanish national team *(La Selección)*, 73–96
  and Antwerp Olympics, 76–8
  and constructs of nationalism, 80–3
  and contested nationalisms within Spain, 83–5
  future of, 89
  La Furia, 76–8
  in projecting wider cultural values, 76–8
  and rival constructions of ethnicity/identity, 78–80
  and shared national identity, 73
  and transformation to La Roja, 86–91
Spartak Moscow, 106, 108, 112
Spartak Yerevan, 113
spectacular glory, 350
sponsors, transnational, 40
sport(s)
  cultural and socioeconomic importance of, 269
  for development and peace, 132, 133
  educational value of, 74
  gender hierarchies within, 3
  historic views of purpose of, 217
  Mandela on, 68
  as part of visual culture, 17
  prominence of science and technology in, 42
  as seeking something separate from the world, 342
  as surrogate for superpower competition, 102

Sport for Girls, 227
sport histories, 3, 4
sporting independence, 120
sporting press, 2
sport scholarship, 2
Stalin, Joseph, 101
Star Player # 1 (Rodrigo de Florencia), 36
Star Players series (Rodrigo de Florencia), 35
stereotypes, countering, 346
Stevens, Siaka, 274
Stewart, Ernie, 185, 189
Stewarton and Thistle, 232
St Helena, 130
"Stilling the Punch" (Lynda Nead), 17
Stocks, Doreen, 234
Stocks, Harry, 234
Stocks, Sheila, 232, 233
Straus, Brian, 189
Strel'tsov, Eduard, 103
Stuart, Ossie, 271, 286
St Vincent, 129
Suarez, 82
Suma, Musa, 278
Summunu, Wasiu, 278
Supporters' Competition, 301
Sutcliffe, Julie, 233
Sylla, Ogo, 341
symbolic meanings of culture, 4
Symposium for Peace (Rio), 309
Syngman Rhee, 137
Syrians, Sierra Leone football and, 273
Szymanski, Stefan, 325

T
"Tackling Diving" (Paul H. Morris and David Lewis), 23
Tahiti, 119–20, 124
Tarză, 296, 304

Taussig, Jirka, 67
Taylor, Louise, 140
T&C Football Association (TCIFA), 127, 128
television
 cinematic experience in age of, 41
 length of televised games in the United States, 353
 telecracy, 39–42
Terezín Nazi ghetto-camp, 57–71
 background on life in, 58–60
 legacy of Liga Terezín, 68–70
 Liga Terezín, 507–11
 propaganda films, 61–3
territories. *See* overseas territories
Terry, John, 15
testimonial glory, 349
Theresienstadt, 57
Theresienstadt (film), 61
Theweleit, Klaus, 220
Thompson, Tholla, 281
Thuram, Lilian, 122, 125
tiki-taka, 87, 90
Tito, Michele, 253
Toby, Joseph, 277
Toledo, Luiz Henrique de, 306
Tolito, 296, 298
Torpedo, 106, 110, 112
Torres, Jose, 189, 190
Totò, 254
Tottenham Hotspur, 14, 24
Toussaint, Jean-Philippe, 33
"Toward a Sociology of Sport", 3
transitory images, 20
transnationalism, 43, 182
 of sponsor labels, 40
Trinidad, 129
Truss, Lynne, 2
TsSKA, 106
Turay, Foday, 281
Turks & Caicos Islands, 127, 237
Turner, Elliott, 185

TUV (TOV), 298
Tyler, Martin, 148

U
UEFA Champions League, 33
Ukrainczyk, Juliusz, 108
Umeå, 228
Under-17 Championship
    1993, 284
    2003, 285
Unger, Chris, 229
Unión Española, 109
United Nations (UN)
    non-self-governing territories
        identified by, 132
    sovereign states accepted by, 119
United Passions (film), 331
United States
    dependencies of, 132
    growth of soccer in, 185
    illegality of dual citizenship in, 182
    and Korea, 137
    reaction against dual or
        multinational citizenship in,
        181
    televised games in, 353
    xenophobia in, 43
United States Men's National Soccer
    Team (USMNT), 184
    active recruitment of dual nationals
        for, 185
    dual national players, 179–94
    early World Cups for, 184
    future for, 192–4
    transnationals' reasons for playing
        for, 190–1
    World Cups of 1990s, 185–6
    World Cup team 2014, 187–90
United States national teams, 132,
    138
    recruitment of Latinos for, 190–1
    recruitment of youth players for,
        189
United States Virgin Islands, 132
United States Women's National
    Team, vi
universities (Europe and United
    States), 3
USFA, 184
USSF, 184, 187, 189

V
Vasco da Gama (club), 109, 164, 296,
    298, 304
Viamundi, 108
violence
    Blow Up (Lyle Ashton Harris), 37,
        38
    in diving images, 24–5
    head-butts by Zidane, 32, 33, 45
    in Napoli stadium, 255
    at 2010 World Cup Finals, 147
    in 2006 World Cup Finals, 141
virtue ethics, 343
virtues of players/teams/nations, 344
visual culture
    division of, 27
    footballers' echo of, in diving, 15
    sport as part of, 17 (see also (diving))
visual material
    and borders between disparate
        cultural fields, 15
    illegitimate echo of, 16
    and reactions to diving (see (diving))
    transitory and anonymous images, 20
Visual Studies, 15
Vomero stadium, 257

W
Wahl, Grant, 238
Walker, Karen, 233, 234

Wallis and Futuna, 123
Wambach, Abby, vi
Warner, Jack, 127
Water Slaughter (Polish match), 341
Ways of Seeing (John Berger), 24
wealth distribution, 315
Webb, Jeffrey, 126
Wegerle, Roy, 185
West Africa
  colonial football in, 270, 271
  European football scouts in, 278
  football and politics in, 285
  introduction of football to, 267
  school sports and physical education
    in, 271
West German National Team, 340, vi
West Germany, social, cultural, and
    political trends during 1960s and
    1970s, 212–16
Williams, Danny, 187, 188, 191
Williams, M., 181
Wilson, Jonathan, 113
Wimbledon (The Crazy Gang), 25
Winckelmann, Johann Joachim, 18
Winterstein, David, 49
Women's European Cup (1983), 233
women's football, 227–39
  club ownership and practices, 228
  in England (*see* (British women's
    football))
  in Europe, 347
  FIFA's 1970 survey on, 228
  future of, 236–9
  glory for, 343
  Goldblatt on, 352
  lack of glory for, 351
  in 1970s, 231
Women's Football Association (WFA)
    Cup, 228, 231–3
Women's Premier League National
    title (1993-4), 233
Women's Super Leaguer, 236

Women's World Championship, 237
Women's World Cup
  1971, 352
  1991, 228, 237
  1999, 237
  2007, 237
  2011, 144
World Cup, 138, 267, 319, 320, 327,
    330, 340
  1930, 167, 169, 182, 184
  1934, 63, 78, 184, 250
  1938, 121, 170, 250
  1950, 78, 105, 184
  1954, 216, 300, 340, 348
  1958, 101, 103, 122
  1962, 80, 103
  1966, 101, 104, 139, 206, 231
  1970, 104, 206
  1972, 216
  1974, 104, 206, 215, 216, 300
  1978, 104
  1982, 83–5
  1986, 110
  1990, 185, 284
  1994, 78, 85, 112, 185, 284
  1998, 32, 89, 123, 185, 341
  2002, 33, 186
  2006, 19, 31, 33, 114, 207
  2010, 73, 86, 137–51, 139–42,
    187, 285
  2014, 90, 187, 327, 341, vi
World Cup portfolio (FIFA), 47
World Player of the Year (FIFA), 33
World Soccer magazine, 31
World War II era
  corruption in, 57
  football during, 63
  legacy of, in Italy, 259
  and post-World War II
    internationalization in, 105
Wusum Stars, 281
Wynalda, Eric, 186

Y

Yashin, Lev, 101, 103, 104
Yeboah, Anthony, 284
Yedlin, DeAndre, 192
Young, Donna, 233
Young Fans, 308
Young Fellows, 165, 169
Young Flamengo Fans, 306
Young Flu, 305
Young Power, 304
youth identity, 306

Z

Zagallo, Mário, 207
Zamora, 77
Zarra, 78, 79
Zeller, Manfred, 112

Zenit Leningrad, 111
Zidane, a 21st Century Portrait
    project, 408–11
"Zidane's Melancholy" (Jean-Philippe
    Toussaint), 33
Zidane, Zinedine (Zizou), 31–52, 350
    commodification/fetishization of,
        35–9
    head-butts by, 32, 33, 42, 45, 340
    and immigration, 42–5
    as postcolonial hero, 45–9
    prominence as footballer, 33
    Zidane, a 21st Century Portrait
        project, 39–42
Žižek, Slavoj, 316, 324, 327, 328,
    333
Zimmerman, Preston, 188
Zinedine Zidane (Martin Schoeller), 34

The manufacturer's authorised representative in the EU is Springer
Nature Customer Service Centre GmbH, Europaplatz 3, 69115 Heidelberg,
Germany. If you have any concerns regarding our products, please
contact ProductSafety@springernature.com

Printed and bound by CPI Group (UK) Ltd, Croydon, CR0 4YY
23/04/2026
02095598-0003